iPod & iTunes HACKS™

Other resources from O'Reilly

Related titles

iPod Fan Book

iPod and iTunes: The Missing Manual

Mac OS X Power Hound, Panther Edition

Mac OS X: The Missing Manual, Panther Edition

Hacks Series Home

hacks.oreilly.com is a community site for developers and power users of all stripes. Readers learn from each other as they share their favorite tips and tools for Mac OS X, Linux, Google, Windows XP, and more.

---

oreilly.com

oreilly.com is more than a complete catalog of O'Reilly books. You'll also find links to news, events, articles, weblogs, sample chapters, and code examples.

O'REILLY NETWORK

oreillynet.com is the essential portal for developers interested in open and emerging technologies, including new platforms, programming languages, and operating systems.

Conferences

O'Reilly brings diverse innovators together to nurture the ideas that spark revolutionary industries. We specialize in documenting the latest tools and systems, translating the innovator's knowledge into useful skills for those in the trenches. Visit *conferences.oreilly.com* for our upcoming events.

O'REILLY NETWORK Safari Bookshelf

Safari Bookshelf (*safari.oreilly.com*) is the premier online reference library for programmers and IT professionals. Conduct searches across more than 1,000 books. Subscribers can zero in on answers to time-critical questions in a matter of seconds. Read the books on your Bookshelf from cover to cover or simply flip to the page you need. Try it today with a free trial.

iPod & iTunes HACKS™

Hadley Stern

O'REILLY®

Beijing · Cambridge · Farnham · Köln · Paris · Sebastopol · Taipei · Tokyo

iPod and iTunes Hacks™
by Hadley Stern

Copyright © 2005 O'Reilly Media, Inc. All rights reserved.
Printed in the United States of America.

Published by O'Reilly Media, Inc., 1005 Gravenstein Highway North,
Sebastopol, CA 95472.

O'Reilly books may be purchased for educational, business, or sales promotional use. Online editions are also available for most titles (*safari.oreilly.com*). For more information, contact our corporate/institutional sales department: (800) 998-9938 or *corporate@oreilly.com*.

Editors:	Brian Sawyer Rael Dornfest	**Production Editor:**	Jamie Peppard
		Cover Designer:	Emma Colby
Series Editor:	Rael Dornfest	**Interior Designer:**	David Futato
Executive Editor:	Dale Dougherty		

Printing History:

October 2004:	First Edition.

 This book uses RepKover,™ a durable and flexible lay-flat binding.

ISBN: 0-596-00778-7
[C]

To Meiera

Contents

Credits

About the Author

Hadley Stern is a designer, writer, and photographer residing in Boston, MA. Hadley was born in London, England, relocated at age 4 to Singapore, then to Canada at age 10, and finally to America at age 22, where he met his lovely wife, Meiera.

Hadley studied creative writing and western civilization and culture at Concordia University in Montreal, Canada, before studying graphic design at the Rhode Island School of Design (RISD).

Since graduating from RISD, Hadley has worked as a professional designer at Malcolm Grear Designers, Rykodisc Records, and Razorfish and is currently an Interactive Creative Director at Fidelity Investments. He has worked on corporate-identity projects, CD packages, web sites, Flash banner advertising, and a wide variety of print collateral. His personal site is *http://www.hadleystern.com*.

Hadley has written for WebMonkey, *American Photo* magazine, iPodLounge. com, and O'Reilly Media, and is the Publisher and Editor-in-Chief of AppleMatters (*http://www.applematters.com*). AppleMatters is a serious yet irreverent look at all things Apple. Covering opinions, news, and interviews, AppleMatters has done tremendously well since its launch over a year ago.

Contributors

The following people contributed their hacks, writing, and inspiration to this book:

- Doug Adams is the webmaster of "Doug's AppleScripts for iTunes" (*http://www.malcolmadams.com/itunes*), a web site that offers free Apple-Scripts for iTunes and resources for people who write them. The site was started in late 2001 and originally offered AppleScripts for SoundJam MP, the wicked cool MP3 player for Macintosh computers that was acquired by Apple and that eventually evolved into iTunes. Doug has been working with AppleScript since its debut during the days of System 7, but he has been programming anything that moves since buying a mail order Commodore 64 in 1983. In addition to the iTunes AppleScripts site, he maintains the "AppleScripts for Tex-Edit Plus Archives" (*http://www.malcolmadams.com/te/*). Doug lives in Providence, Rhode Island with his wife, Natalie, and daughter, Ellen. When he's not AppleScripting (which, believe it or not, is most of the time) Doug is a freelance audio producer and commercial voiceover announcer.

- Joshua Benjamin is an aspiring Mac developer with several years spent in systems administration. He's currently studying Human/Computer Interaction within Computer Science and Psychology at the University of Illinois, Urbana-Champaign. Josh keeps information on his software and research at *http://www.jbenjamin.org*

- David F. Bills is a technology architect and multimedia professional residing in New York, NY. He is a musician, computer enthusiast, and runs SmartPlaylists.com among other websites.

- Alan Donovan is a researcher in the field of programming languages and program analysis. He holds degrees from the University of Cambridge and MIT, in whose Computer Science and Artificial Intelligence Laboratory he currently works. He has been programming for over 20 years and has worked on industrial projects involving multimedia, networking, embedded systems, interpreters and compilers. Alan currently divides his time between Boston and New York.

- Rael Dornfest is CTO of O'Reilly Media, focusing on emerging technologies just this side of viability and some beyond the pale. He assesses, experiments, programs, fiddles, fidgets, and writes for O'Reilly in various capacities. Rael is Series Editor of the O'Reilly Hacks series (*http://hacks.oreilly.com*) and has edited, contributed to, and coauthored various O'Reilly books, including *Mac OS X Panther Hacks*, *Mac OS X Hacks*, *Google Hacks*, *Google: The Missing Manual*, *Essential Blogging*, and *Peer to Peer: Harnessing the Power of Disruptive Technologies*. He is also Program Chair for the O'Reilly Emerging Technology Conference. In his copious free time, Rael develops bits and bobs of freeware, particularly the Blosxom weblog application (*http://www.blosxom.com*), is Editor in Chief of MobileWhack (*http://www.mobilewhack.com*), and (more often than not) maintains his Raelity Bytes weblog (*http://www.raelity.org*).

- Razvan Dragomirescu is the cofounder and Chief Technology Officer for SIMEDA GmbH, a leading provider of wireless technology. His time is split between researching new wireless technologies and administrative work (which he really hates :-). Razvan started tinkering with computers at the age of 7, with the help of his dad and a ZX Spectrum computer. He can be reached at *razvan.dragomirescu@simeda.com*.

- Allen Evans is an undergraduate student studying German at the University of Vermont. He enjoys traveling and has lived abroad in Germany. He is an avid skier, cyclist, wakeboarder, and technology enthusiast.

- brian d foy has been an instructor for Stonehenge Consulting Services since 1998, a Perl user since he was a Physics graduate student, and a diehard Mac user since he first owned a computer. He founded the first Perl users group, the New York Perl Mongers, as well as the Perl advocacy nonprofit Perl Mongers, Inc., which helped form over 200 Perl user groups across the globe. He maintains the perlfaq portions of the core Perl documentation, several modules on CPAN, and some standalone scripts. He's the publisher of *The Perl Review*, a magazine devoted to Perl, and a frequent speaker at conferences including The Perl Conference, Perl University, MarcusEvans BioInformatics '02, and YAPC. His writings on Perl appear in the O'Reilly Network, *The Perl Journal*, *Dr. Dobbs Journal*, *The Perl Review*, on *use.perl.org*, and in several Perl Usenet groups.

- Fred Harmon holds BS degree in Avionics Engineering and works for major aerospace company. He is also an avid motorcyclist and is active in several motorcycle touring communities.

- Greg Koenig is an industrial designer who lives in Portland, Oregon.

- Raffi Krikorian is an unapologetic TiVo lover and a digital plumber. If you look hard enough, you can usually find him putting together a hack for some random stray idea that got him sidetracked from his last project. He is currently a graduate student at the MIT Media Lab, where he is both studying systems of *organic scale* and constructing very small IP-nodes that self-organize into larger systems. He freely admits, however, that his serious television addiction is probably getting between him and his goal to finally graduate MIT for the second time. When he's not studying or watching TV, you can find him wandering about or trying something new. And finally, in whatever time is left, he tends to his wasted bits on his blog at *http://www.bitwaste.com/wasted-bits/*.

- Bernard Leach founded ipodlinux in early 2003 to provide an alternate platform for application development on the iPod. Based on a slimmed-down version of the Linux kernel, ipodlinux provides a Unix-like application environment with full support to the audio, display, and storage capabilities of the iPod. Originally from Australia, Bernard now lives and works in Europe.

- John Maushammer began hacking recreationally on an Apple II+ and has since reverse engineered the Sega VMU game system and the Dakota disposable digital camera. Professionally, he designs hardware and software for embedded computers that have traveled to the ends of the earth and into space. His hobbies include photography, bicycling, and hang gliding. His website is *http:www.maushammer.com*

- Jesse Melchior is a 29-year-old amateur special effects artist, writer, and filmmaker. He runs his own business, a digital video and effects company called REELMAGIK, along with his friend, John Tatarelli, and his brother, David Melchior, from his home in Parkside, Pennsylvania. Jesse has been involved in special effects work since he was a young boy. With a natural talent for drawing and painting, his progression took him to the next level, sculpting and make-up FX, and then filmmaking. To date, he has been involved in several short films, two commercials for well-known financial institutions, and a number of local video projects. His other talents include miniatures, optical effects, pyrotechnics, FX animation, and prop building. He is completely self-taught and has had no training in any field.

- David Miller is a programmer by trade, and he prefers tinkering with documents + nodes + attributes + styles rather than with queries + result sets. His site (*http://www.fivevoltlogic.com*) is five years in the making, and should be usable within the next three.

- Chu Moy is a software engineer. He received an undergraduate degree in electrical engineering from Yale University and runs HeadWize (*http://www.headwize.com*), a headphone resource site.

- Gregory Ng is a lover of all things Apple and, most importantly, his iPod. As an advertising art director and proud daddy, he still manages to find time to write for AppleMatters (*http://www.applematters.com*), where he is a contributing editor. His love for music and fame previously led him to be an Elvis impersonator (Chelvis, The Chinese Elvis) and the DJ of a now defunct radio show, "Fresh Cuts from the Audiobarn." His website is *http://www.GregoryNg.com*.

- Jason Rohrer is the lead developer for several open source projects, including MUTE, konspire2b, minorGems, silk, and tangle. He is also a writer, artist, and musician, as well as an activist for personal freedom. He lives voluntarily poor and job-free, dividing his time between parenting and personal projects. He can be found at *http://jasonrohrer.n3.net*

- Chris Roose is a documentary radio producer, jazz/soul/funk DJ, and music store slave living in Brooklyn, New York. His first encounter with a Unix-like operating system was Linux Slackware 1.0 in 1993. It was Mac OS X, however, that inspired him to explore the full potential of Unix. He can be reached at *croose_21@yahoo.com*.

- C. K. Sample, III maintains the weblog "3650 and a 12-inch" (*http://3650anda12inch.blogspot.com*) that discusses the use of a 12" Powerbook G4 and a Nokia 3650. He is a doctoral candidate in English at Fordham University, focusing on twentieth century American and British literature, as well as 20th-century world literature, biblical studies, and critical theory. C. K. (Clinton Kennedy; no relation) works in Fordham's Department of Instructional Technology and Academic Computing as the Lab Coordinator for Marymount College and the Fordham Graduate Center in Tarrytown, New York. His first "computer" was an Atari 400, and his first Mac was a PowerBook 5300CS. Originally from Jackson, Mississippi, C. K. currently lives in Bronxville, New York with his fiancée, Kristin Landgrebe, and his pet Eclectus parrot, Misha, who is two years old.

- Ted Stevko (*http://www.plasticnoodle.com*) has been an illustrator, a programmer, a cartoonist, a network administrator, a Java programmer, and a web designer...usually all at once. He started using Macs in 1989, helping to run a two-computer network for his journalism class while drawing cartoons and writing articles. Currently, Ted builds high-availability web-service applications in Java during the day, and at night he works on comics while listening to the BBC, NPR, and old 1950s radio dramas on his iPod.

- Chris Seibold has been a computer enthusiast since 1990. He has worked as a political cartoonist, radio show producer, and Manufacturing engineer. He is currently a freelance writer in Knoxville, Tennessee.

- Meiera Holz Stern is a writer who lives in Newton, MA, with her family.

- Adriaan Tijsseling is best known as the creator of ecto and Kung-Tunes. He is originally an academic (with a Masters in Artificial Intelligence and a PhD in Cognitive Science), but nowadays works as Senior Technology Manager and Software Consultant for Joichi Ito's private company. This just means he is juggling a variety of tasks that are all Internet-related and involve quite a bit of coding. He blogs regularly at *http://kung-foo.tv* and currently lives in Japan with his wife, Yukari, and daughter, Kee.

- Phillip Torrone is Associate Editor of *Popular Science Magazine*, feature columnist for engadget (*http://www.engadget.com*) and author of numerous books on mobile devices and design. Phillip's work and projects can be viewed at *http://www.flashenabled.com*.

- Owen Watson is 21 years old and recently finished a BSc (Hons) in Computing for Industry at Northumbria University, Newcastle, UK. He is incredibly passionate about technology, especially all things Apple. You can drop him a line at *owenrw@nildram.co.uk*.

Acknowledgments

First and foremost, I would like to thank my family, nuclear and extended. This book could not have been written without the support of my wonderful wife, Meiera. Thanks too to our sons Miles and Alec; thanks to Alec for keeping me company with the late-night writing and thanks to Miles for keeping me company in the early morning. Our many friends also provided support, keeping me (somewhat) sane during busy writing sessions. Thanks in particular to Gregory Ng, for being my partner in crime for all things music and Apple, and for being a great friend.

Thanks to all the contributors of this book, from all corners of the world (literally), contributed their knowledge, passion, and words. Without them, this book could not have been written.

Thanks to Judd Gledhill, Russell Hart, Henry Horenstein, Dennis Lloyd, Michael McClung, Errick Nunnally, and Michael Silverman, Esq., for providing assistance at various points in this project.

Derrick Story did me a great favor, introducing me to the O'Reilly family by inviting me to contribute to *Digital Photography Hacks*.

I would like to thank Rael Dornfest for being receptive to the idea for the book. Throughout the process, he has been patient, giving of advice, and very generous with his time. I feel truly honored to have worked with you, Rael.

Thanks to Molly Wood for her contributions at the genesis of the project, Rachel Wheeler for her editing throughout the project, to Brian Sawyer for his crucial help in finishing up the book, and. C. K. Sample III for his help with the technical edit.

Finally, I'd like to thank Apple for inventing the iPod and inspiring us all with a wonderful combination of technical prowess and stunning design.

Preface

The iPod is only a few years young and yet it is not an exaggeration to call it a phenomenon. In every corner of the world, through every demographic slice, people are rediscovering their love of music and enjoying their collections in ways that weren't previously possible. What makes the iPod such an unmitigated success is its fluid integration of design, technology, and music. It is a product only Apple could have created.

When a product becomes a part of your life, you naturally want to get the most out of it. That is what this book is about. It doesn't cover the basics of how to use your iPod (you already know that). Rather, it lets you tweak your iPod to the *n*th degree, giving you even more pleasure.

But the iPod is only half the story. iTunes is a powerful piece of software. With it, you can rip your music to digital files, organize your collection, buy music from the iTunes Music Store, and transfer everything to your iPod. As your digital music collection grows, you'll probably notice that the obsessive behavior typically reserved for organizing your CD collection (Is The Band under *B*, or *T*? What about 2 Live Crew?) is transferred to the music on your computer. This book reveals a number of ways to extend, organize, tweak, twiddle, and expand iTunes.

The passion for music is universal throughout cultures and history. So too, apparently, is the passion for the iPod and iTunes (well, at least universal for *this moment* in history); contributors for this book come from the United States, Canada, Romania, England, Germany, and Japan. This book celebrates all things iPod and iTunes, allowing you to get even more out of your music. So, set up a nice playlist, sit back, and enjoy.

Why iPod & iTunes Hacks?

The term *hacking* has a bad reputation in the press, where it is typically used to refer to someone who breaks into systems or wreaks havoc with computers as a weapon. Among people who write code, though, the term *hack* refers to a "quick-and-dirty" solution to a problem, or a clever way to get something done. And the term *hacker* is taken very much as a compliment, referring to someone as being *creative*, having the technical chops to get things done. The Hacks series is an attempt to reclaim the word, document the good ways people are hacking, and pass the hacker ethic of creative participation on to the uninitiated. Seeing how others approach systems and problems is often the quickest way to learn about a new technology.

Once you become an iPod and iTunes user, you may suddenly find yourself spending an inordinately large amount of time importing music into iTunes and listening to your iPod. If you're a hacker (in the sense described in the previous paragraph), you might also find yourself wondering, how can I do this better, or differently? *iPod and iTunes Hacks* covers the tools and tricks you need to do just that.

How to Use This Book

You can read this book from cover to cover if you like, but for the most part, each hack stands on its own, so feel free to browse and jump to the different sections that interest you most. If there's a prerequisite you need to know about, a cross-reference guides you to the right hack. So, feel free to browse, flipping around to whatever sections interest you most.

How This Book Is Organized

The book is divided into several chapters, organized by subject:

Chapter 1, *iPod Hardware*
>   This chapter covers the iPod itself, from cleaning it to installing it in your car permanently. If you can do it to the iPod, it's in this chapter.

Chapter 2, *Non-iPod Hardware*
>   As powerful as the iPod is, it can't possibly do everything. This chapter covers how to make third-party devices interact with your iTunes music collection.

Chapter 3, *iPod Software*
>   The iPod is a computer that runs on software. This software can be manipulated, tweaked, twiddled, and otherwise hacked to turn the iPod into far more than just a music player.

Chapter 4, *iTunes*

From hacking the iTunes interface to getting down and dirty with ID3 tags, this chapter helps you take your digital music to the next level.

Chapter 5, *AppleScript for iTunes*

AppleScript is the most powerful tool for extending iTunes and integrating it with other aspects of your computing environment. This chapter teaches you the basics of AppleScripting for iTunes and covers a number of great scripts for iTunes.

Chapter 6, *Beyond iTunes*

There are some things (believe it or not!) that iTunes can't do. This chapter covers tools and methods for doing things with your digital music that just aren't possible within iTunes.

Conventions Used in This Book

The following is a list of the typographical conventions used in this book:

Italics

Used to indicate URLs, filenames, filename extensions, and directory/folder names. For example, a path in the filesystem appears as */Developer/Applications*.

Constant width

Used to show code examples, the contents of files, and console output, as well as the names of variables, commands, and other code excerpts.

Constant width bold

Used to highlight portions of code, typically new additions to old code.

Constant width italic

Used in code examples and tables to show sample text to be replaced with your own values.

Color

The second color is used to indicate a cross-reference within the text.

You should pay special attention to notes set apart from the text with the following icons:

This is a tip, suggestion, or general note. It contains useful supplementary information about the topic at hand.

This is a warning or note of caution, often indicating that your money or your privacy might be at risk.

The thermometer icons found next to each hack indicate the relative complexity of the hack:

 beginner   moderate   expert

Whenever possible, the hacks in this book are not *platform-specific*, which means you can use them on both Mac and Windows machines. However, some things are possible on only one or the other platform, and this book even provides some tools for getting Linux users in on the action. The following icons are included at the end of each hack title to show which of these platforms (or some combination of the three) that particular hack supports:

Ⓜ   Macintosh

Ⓦ   Windows

Ⓛ   Linux

Using Code Examples

This book is here to help you get your job done. In general, you may use the code in this book in your programs and documentation. You do not need to contact us for permission unless you're reproducing a significant portion of the code. For example, writing a program that uses several chunks of code from this book does not require permission. Selling or distributing a CD-ROM of examples from O'Reilly books *does* require permission. Answering a question by citing this book and quoting example code does not require permission. Incorporating a significant amount of example code from this book into your product's documentation *does* require permission.

We appreciate, but do not require, attribution. An attribution usually includes the title, author, publisher, and ISBN. For example: "*iPod & iTunes Hacks* by Hadley Stern. Copyright 2005 O'Reilly Media, Inc., 0-596-00778-7."

If you feel your use of code examples falls outside fair use or the permission given above, feel free to contact us at *permissions@oreilly.com*.

How to Contact Us

We have tested and verified the information in this book to the best of our ability, but you may find that features have changed (or even that we have made mistakes!). As a reader of this book, you can help us to improve future editions by sending us your feedback. Please let us know about any errors, inaccuracies, bugs, misleading or confusing statements, and typos that you find anywhere in this book.

Please also let us know what we can do to make this book more useful to you. We take your comments seriously and will try to incorporate reasonable suggestions into future editions. You can write to us at:

O'Reilly Media, Inc.
1005 Gravenstein Highway North
Sebastopol, CA 95472
(800) 998-9938 (in the U.S. or Canada)
(707) 829-0515 (international/local)
(707) 829-0104 (fax)

To ask technical questions or to comment on the book, send email to:

bookquestions@oreilly.com

The web site for *iPod & iTunes Hacks* lists examples, errata, and plans for future editions. You can find this page at:

http://www.oreilly.com/catalog/ipodtuneshks/

For more information about this book and others, see the O'Reilly web site:

http://www.oreilly.com

Got a Hack?

To explore Hacks books online or to contribute a hack for future titles, visit:

http://hacks.oreilly.com

iPod Hardware
Hacks 1–22

Most of us still remember the first time we saw our brand-new iPod. Unfolding the box is an origami experience that results in the final vision of a gleaming white and metal iPod—a new iPod that is clean and perfect, but not for long. The first hack in this chapter helps you get your iPod looking as good as new again [Hack #1].

But the iPod is much more than an aesthetic masterpiece; it is also a technological one. Within that small space is a hard drive, microprocessor, battery, amplifier, RAM, and much more. All these bits and pieces can be used for much more than a mind-blowing music player. This chapter helps you get the most out of your iPod and, in some cases, take it beyond its originally purpose. How about turning your iPod into a wireless jukebox [Hack #20] or integrating it with your car's remote control system [Hack #12]? Start reading!

But before you do, you should be aware of some conventions. Back in the early days of the iPod, there was just one iPod. Things aren't so simple anymore. Various hacks in this chapter are specific to a particular iPod. Here is the breakdown of all the iPods:

Generation 1 iPod
> This was the first iPod, which Apple released in October 2001. It is the original iPod form factor with a regular FireWire jack and a physical scroll wheel.

Generation 2 iPod
> This version featured a larger, 10 GB hard drive. Otherwise, physically, it is the same as a generation 1 iPod.

Generation 3 iPod
> This design featured a touch-sensitive scroll wheel, a jack that could accept cables for both USB and FireWire cables, and some firmware changes.

iPod mini

> The mini is the littlest iPod with the smallest hard drive (4 GB). It features a scroll wheel with integrated buttons.

Generation 4 iPod

> As of this writing, this is the latest and greatest iPod from Apple. It has a simple white and metal look, but it uses the integrated scroll wheel featured in the mini.

HACK #1   Good as New: Clean Your iPod ⓜⓦⓛ

Clean up your dirty iPod using the tips and tricks in this hack.

Remember those first moments when you unwrapped your new iPod? So clean, so shiny...until you put it in your pocket. The iPod's metal back loves to be scratched, and its plastic front is not much better. Don't get out the bleach and silver polish, though. Your iPod needs the cleaning products and tools appropriate to its outstanding design.

Getting Clean

The best product for cleaning dirt, fingerprints, and small scratches off your iPod is a product called Plexus Plastic Cleaner. Originally designed to polish the windshields of F-16 fighter jets and other aircraft, Plexus does an amazing job of cleaning up any polymer surfaces, so you can use it on everything from CDs and DVDs to your car (which probably has a polymer-based clear coat on top of its paint). The company that makes Plexus sells it only by the case online (*http://www.plexusplasticcleaner.com*), but if you Google "Plexus Plastic Cleaner" you'll find a number of outfits selling it online at a price of about $10 for a big can that will last you years.

A cleaner is only half the battle; you also need something with which to apply it. For that, get a set of microfiber towels. Of course, microfiber everything (T-shirts, towels, mops) is all the rage these days, so you shouldn't have any trouble finding them. I use these towels for almost everything, from waxing my car to cleaning my laptop's LCD display to dusting around the house. The ones I like best come from an outfit in Tacoma, WA, called Griots Garage (*http://www.griotsgarage.com/index.jsp*). Their three-pack of microfiber towels goes for $16, which is expensive, but the ones they sell last forever and clean up to be like new if you put them in the washing machine. (Don't use fabric softener! It will ruin them.)

To clean your iPod, simply spray a small amount of the Plexus onto the towel (*not* directly onto the surface you're trying to clean). Use a toothpick to shove the towel down into the small crevices and lines and get dirt out.

Once your iPod is nice and clean, it's time to deal with all those scratches you've accumulated.

Getting Rid of Scratches

When we talk about getting rid of scratches, we typically use terms such as *polish them out* or *fill them in*. These terms aren't quite accurate, because the definition of polishing is that you are *removing material*. When you make a surface nice and shiny with a polish, you're essentially sanding down the microscopic bumps that reflect light unevenly. When you polish out a scratch, you're removing the surrounding material so that it is even with where the bottom of that scratch was. This might sound sort of frightening, but don't worry. Unless you have a gouge (i.e., a *really* deep scratch), we are only talking about removing a few microns of material here. I am telling you this because it's important to realize exactly what's going on when you're in the process of rubbing out that huge wedding ring scratch that goes right across the front of your iPod's LCD display.

There are a number of kits on the market that do a good job of removing scratches. The kits available from iCleaner (*http://www.ipodcleaner.com*) are good, but you probably already have the most effective iPod plastic polish in your garage or utility closet: Brasso. This old-school, $3-a-can metal polish does a pretty amazing job of safely removing iPod plastic scratches, because it contains a mild abrasive. Twist the microfiber towel so it forms a tight, smooth surface over the pad of your index finger, and put a small amount of Brasso on it. Press hard when you rub, and go back and forth, not in circles.

Back and forth and not in circles, you ask? But Mr. Miyagi told Daniel in *The Karate Kid* that one waxes and polishes in a circular motion! That's just how things are done!

Well, the problem with waxing or polishing in a circular motion is that it produces swirl marks that you can see from a mile away. When you polishing anything, you leave tiny scratches, and if those scratches are circular, light will catch them from every angle and they will be quite visible. If you polish in straight lines, though, those scratches will be visible only when light catches them in 1 of the 360 degrees of the viewing angle, so they will hardly be noticed. This also works on your car (wax/polish front to back for surfaces parallel to the ground, up and down for surfaces perpendicular to the ground).

You'd better be a little patient, because this job takes a good, long time to accomplish on your iPod, but the results are well worth it. Unlike the Plexus, I wouldn't use Brasso to polish out scratches in other plastics. I have heard about bad results from people who were so amazed that it worked on their iPods that they went out and ruined their cell phone screens, because the composition of the plastic was different.

The Ugly Truth About Pretty Chrome

The back panel on your iPod is made of an aluminum part that has been electroplated in chrome. When it's new out of the box, the surface is very pretty, but it scratches very, very easily. The ugly truth is that there's nothing you can do about those scratches once they are there, because you can't polish out scratches in chrome. Chrome is a plating process, and the shiny silver material you see is just a few microns thick, so any scratch you see probably goes all the way through the chrome layer and down to the bare aluminum. To polish out the scratch, you'd need to polish off the whole layer of chrome, and you probably don't want to do that.

Unless your iPod is subjected to the environment the same way the chrome bumper on a truck is, your best bet to keep it shiny is just to use Plexus or another plastic cleaner along with the microfiber cloth, as this will remove any surface contamination that would dull the appearance of your iPod. Most of the chrome polishes you see on the market are intended for automotive applications where chrome is subjected to all sorts of crud (flying bugs, exhaust gasses, dirt, rain, etc.), and these products remove that fouling from the metal to make it shiny again.

With this hack, now know how to keep your iPod in good aesthetic order. Don't overclean your iPod, though; once a month should keep its appearances up nicely.

—*Greg Koenig*

HACK #2   Exercise with Your iPod ⓜⓦ●

Whatever your favorite way to sweat, you've got options with your iPod. Your iPod can become your constant exercise companion.

Exercising without music is unthinkable for some people. It might help psych you up to work your body through those boring miles on the treadmill or the endless reps and sets while weightlifting. Or it might transport you into a meditative state where, in the music's groove, such things as long-distance running, skiing, or even practicing yoga seem to get easier. Given the happy marriage between music and exercise, it's a wonder that Apple has produced such an inadequate case to help us work out with our iPods.

The case supplied with iPods these days isn't very useful. In fact, it can be best described by the things it *doesn't* do. It doesn't stop the iPod from running out of gas 20 minutes (the time limit of the iPod's built-in RAM) into a good run. It isn't waterproof, mud-proof, or drop-proof. In short, it doesn't let you jump around like a hooligan without fearing for your iPod's safety. Luckily, other manufacturers have stepped in to pick up the slack.

A slew of products is out on the market now that claim to make exercising with your iPod a safe and enjoyable experience for both you and your sleek little tune dispenser. Some are better than others, but depending on the type of exercise you like to do, there is a product that can protect your iPod and/ or enhance your overall workout. If you're sick of walking around clutching dearly to your iPod, this hack gives you lots of alternatives.

On the Road

The product that seems to give avid runners, bikers, and other cross-country exercise enthusiasts the most for their buck is Speck Products's iSport (*http://www.speckproducts.com/isport/index.html*; $44.95). It has been carefully designed to meet the rugged requirements of long-distance runners, as well as the casual exerciser. Furthermore, it feels secure whether you're a New York City bike courier or you're running the Boston Marathon, because it sits snugly in a belt around your waist.

Unlike an armband, the belt adds no more weight to one side of your body than the other, and it keeps your arms wire-free—a good thing as you're whizzing down a busy street. The iSport is also equipped with a mesh cloth back where it touches your body, so that your iPod is encased in plastic, but you are not. Thus, you can sweat in it without creating an anaerobic pool for stinky bacteria to flourish in. Basically, it's a well-planned, high-tech fanny pack with a built-in flashing safety light that increases your visibility and zippered pouches that allow for easy storage of credit cards, money, and ID. There's even a separate pouch for keys, so their jingling doesn't get in the way of your listening pleasure.

 Another great thing about this case is that it fits *all* iPod models, so if you're like some who let their old iPods languish on the shelf while they parade their new minis around town, it's *okay*. Whether you're loyal to your first iPod or always in search of the latest model, they all fit in the iSport.

When you are running or biking, you need to be able to hear a little of the outside world, so spending a lot of money on truly expensive headphones that block out all ambient noise **[Hack #4]** is not a good idea. What is helpful is to have headphones that stick securely in or on your ears.

The headphones that come with the iPod don't do that for everybody. A good bet for this type of exercise is Koss's KSC-50s (*http://www.headphone.com/ layout.php?topicID=3&subTopicID=26&productID=0020130050*; $19.95), because they clip securely to your ears. While it might take a few tries to get used to clipping these headphones to your ears, they're worth the effort; there simply isn't a better-sounding headphone under $20. They also fit under most bike helmets (but always be careful while biking with headphones on!).

At the Gym

If you like the idea of carrying the iPod on your waist but don't need bells and whistles, or if you don't want to look like you're wearing a fanny pack, Macally's Podcase (*http://www.macally.com/new/new_cbipodw.html*; $19.99) is for you. Its lightweight, simple shape keeps the iPod securely in place around your waist, like a holster, while you do your thing at the gym. It comes in chic grey or black.

Or perhaps you prefer not to wear your iPod around your waist. Tunebelt (*http://www.macally.com/new/new_cbipoda.html*; $19.95) makes a light-weight armband that stays securely around your upper arm while you move to the groove. It also lets you view the LCD right side up and gives you easy access to the touch wheel and buttons—a bonus at the gym between sets. What's more, should you walk out at night wearing this iPod armband, it's got a reflective strip that will make you more visible to passing cars.

While you're at the gym, you can get a little extra motivation, on the cheap, from your iPod. MP3 Gym (*http://www.mp3gym.com/index.html*; $19.95) provides an audio personal trainer that prods you through a workout. After all, once you've got your iPod armor, you might as well arm your iPod with its own trainer genie. There are 60 different exercise routines to choose from on the MP3 Gym CD, and each of them is illustrated in PDF format. Download them to your iPod, and during your workouts you'll learn proper body mechanics for each exercise. At the same time, the personal trainer and sup-porting music inspire you to do your best with peppy phrases and exercise tips. Whether you find this uplifting or just annoying is a matter of personal preference. But if you need an extra kick in the derriere to sculpt your body, it could be just the thing for you. To check it out before you plunk down the money, go to the web site to see and hear examples of what's on the CD.

Another good bet at the gym is the Teski Roadie (*https://www.teski.com/ shopping/search_display.asp?searchstr=ipod&x=67&y=10*; available with a color pack combo for $29.95), designed to give you full access to your third-generation iPod's controls during physical activity. With a clear plastic cover and a back that changes seamlessly from a belt clip to an armband, it provides a lightweight and simple solution for toting your iPod at the gym. It also comes with three faceplates in three fashionable "colors": black, clear, and sport orange.

In the Water

If you like your sports in or near water, you're in luck. There are some good watertight cases out there. Which one you choose will depend on what you need it for—in short, how deep in the water you go. If you want to skirt the water's edge, confident that if you fall in once or twice your iPod will stay dry, a water-resistant case is fine. However, if you swim laps in the ocean every day or tend to frequently capsize your canoe in deep water, you clearly need to waterproof your iPod.

Water-resistant cases. The best water-resistant cases are the Lilipod (*http://www.lilipods.com/lilipods.html*; $39.99) and the oPod (*http://www.otterbox.com/product.cfm?product=168&code=NA*; $49.95). Both of these advertise themselves as suitable for dips in a bit of water, but they fail to guarantee a completely waterproof experience.

The Lilipod has a compact, 2-mm thick, hard plastic case that is well padded on the inside, and it offers multiple attachment options to ensure your iPod safe passage through all sorts of places that it will find new and exciting. For example, if you're climbing a cliff in the rain and want to make extra sure you don't drop your iPod, it has a tenacious clip on the back that fastens to many types of clothing or belts. To make your iPod doubly secure, you can wear it over your shoulders on the Sterling Rope® lanyard.

You can also don the rope if you're not wearing anything the clip can attach to, as in the case of skinny-dipping, but bear in mind that the case is only water-resistant!

The Lilipod also lives up to its lily pad allusion; if you drop it in the water, it floats nicely to the surface.

Perhaps the only down side to using the Lilipod is that, as with some other types of amphibious cases on the market, you cannot adjust the playlist while the iPod is in its case. On the plus side, it has a built-in ISC-engineered watertight stereo connector that allows you to plug in any set of headphones, while making sure that no part of your iPod is exposed to water.

If you want to tinker with the playlist while your iPod is encased, the oPod is the case for you. Users of third-generation iPods can tap the buttons through the clear membrane to access music selections, volume control, and more. The protective case allows easy access to the remote port and headphone jack. All connections remain water-resistant and keep out sand and dirt. Another nice thing about the oPod is that you can accessorize it with, for example, an armband (*http://www.otterbox.com/product.cfm?product=168&code=NA*; $14.95).

Waterproof cases. If you need more protection than water-resistant cases offer, don't despair; you can swim, snorkel, jet ski, and more with your iPod in a see-through vinyl case that, together with waterproof headphones, guarantees an earful of tunes up to 15 feet under water. Put your iPod in the Aquapac Connected Electronics Case (*http://www.waterproofcases.net/555.html*; $49.99) and slip the wire through the TC clip to lock it down. The case is foam-padded for extra protection; it also floats. It offers three ways to secure your iPod to your body: an adjustable waist belt, a carry cord, and a belt clip.-

Headphones. If you want a complete waterproof set, get waterproof headphones to go with your Lilipod, oPod, or Aquapac. Find a decent pair at Waterproof Cases.net (*http://www.waterproofcases.net/headphones.html*; $24.99).

All-Terrain iPod

We've covered a lot of ground, and water, in this hack, but for those who don't care where they go as long as they get rugged exercise, the most durable case out there might be the previously mentioned oPod. It's a smaller version of the Otterboxes that have been used by the military to keep things bomb-proof. Rest assured, no matter where you go to play or exercise, your iPod can come too.

—Meiera Holz Stern

HACK #3 Store Digital Photos on Your iPod ⓜⓦ◐

A couple nifty products from Belkin allow you to store your digital snaps right on your iPod.

An iPod comes with an immense amount of hard drive space, while your digital camera's memory cards fill up too quickly. This digital divide can be traversed successfully with a little help from Belkin.

Belkin makes two products that allow you to transfer your digital images from your digital camera to your iPod: the Media Reader (*http://catalog. belkin.com/IWCatProductPage.process?Merchant_Id=&Section_Id=201526 &pcount=&Product_Id=158350*; $109.99) and the Digital Camera Link (*http://catalog.belkin.com/IWCatProductPage.process?Merchant_Id=& Product_Id=173207*; $89.99). With the help of either of these products, you can literally store thousands of images (depending on the size of your iPod and your digital camera's resolution) on your iPod.

The Belkin Media Reader

To use the Media Reader, remove your camera's memory card and insert it into the appropriate slot on the side of the Media Reader.

> The Belkin Media Reader supports: CompactFlash (types 1 and 2), SmartMedia, Secure Digital (SD), Memory Stick, and MultiMediaCard.

Now, connect the Belkin Media Reader to your iPod. The Reader works with generation 3 (G3) and later iPods with the newer thin-type FireWire connection. If you have a generation 1 or 2 (G1/G2) iPod with a regular FireWire connector or an iPod mini, you cannot use the Media Reader.

Once you plug in the iPod, a screen shows up with your memory card's information. In the case of Figure 1-1, the Media Reader tells us the media type, the number of photos, and the amount of memory used on the card. You control the Media Reader from your iPod; to import the images to the iPod, just select Import on your iPod.

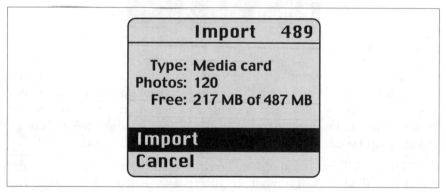

Figure 1-1. The Media Reader Import screen

Once the import has begun, a status screen shows up, as shown in Figure 1-2. Depending on the number and size of your images, you could be in for a bit of a long wait. You can't pick and choose which images you want to import, so if time is not on your side, edit your images in your digital camera before transferring them.

You can view roll information on the iPod, too. Media Reader's Roll Info metaphor is similar to the one iPhoto uses; each import creates a new "roll." You can delete rolls directly from the iPod, as shown in Figure 1-3.

Figure 1-2. The Media Reader Importing screen

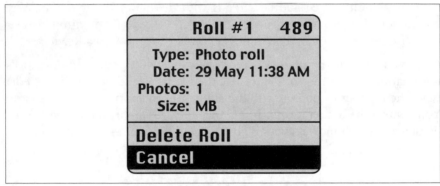

Figure 1-3. The Media Reader Roll Info screen

Once the transfer is complete, plug your iPod into your computer. If you haven't set up the iPod to work in Disk mode, open up iTunes, select your iPod in the Source window, and open up iPod preferences by clicking on the iPod icon in the lower-right corner of the iTunes window. Select "Enable disk use," and your iPod will mount as a device on your computer.

Your images will be in a topmost directory (called *DCIM*) on your iPod. When your iPod is in Disk mode, it behaves exactly like a hard drive. You can copy your digital photos from your iPod to your own computer and then discard them from your iPod.

The Belkin Digital Camera Link

The Belkin Digital Camera Link removes one step from the Media Reader procedure by connecting the digital camera directly to your iPod. Instead of removing your camera's memory card, inserting it in the Media Reader, and connecting the Reader to your iPod, you connect the Digital Camera Link to your digital camera and then to your iPod. There is no interface on your iPod; instead, you tap a button on the Digital Camera Link to get the transfer going. The main advantage of this process is that there is no card to remove. You just take the USB cable from your digital camera and, instead of plugging it into your computer, plug it into the Digital Camera Link. The FireWire cord from the Digital Camera Link then plugs into your iPod.

The Digital Camera Link works with any mass-storage DCF-format and PTP-compliant camera (which includes most digital cameras). Visit Belkin's site (*http://www.belkin.com/ipod/cameralink/*) to find out whether your camera is compatible.

The Digital Camera Link has a three-stage LED light that communicates what the device is doing. While importing, the LED flashes green; when it's done, it goes solid green. A double flashing red light tells you that your camera is not compatible with the Digital Camera Link; a single flashing red light tells you that your iPod is full (a solid red light let's you know your battery is low). If you opt to verify the data transfer, a flashing yellow light indicates that this process is under way. Like the Media Reader, the Digital Camera Link stores the images on your iPod's hard drive.

Neither choice is necessarily better. The Media Reader is more versatile, because even if your camera isn't supported, chances are that the media the camera uses is. However, the Digital Camera Link is a great, direct solution for transferring images. Either way, storing your digital photos on your iPod is a great hack that makes owning an iPod even sweeter.

HACK #4 Upgrade Your Ears 🅜🅦🄻

Take your iPod listening experience to the next level by upgrading your headphones.

Apple spared no expense when it came to designing and manufacturing the iPod. The outside is stunning and the user interface flawless. You probably remember the first time you opened up the package and gasped at the beauty of it all. Then you put the included Apple earbuds in your ears. For many of us they are too uncomfortable to use, but assuming your ears are the large size that seems to be required, you've probably noticed that the sound quality is, well, not good. The sound is tinny and the bass lackluster. Don't believe me? Just try out any of the headphones or earphones mentioned in this hack. For the technical-minded, make sure to take a look at Headphone.com's excellent headphone frequency–charting tool (*http://www.headphone.com/layout.php?topicID=10*), where you can compare and contrast a slew of headphones, including the ones that came with your iPod.

Over-Ear Headphones

In-ear headphones are a relatively recent craze, and the truth is that while old-school headphones might look bulky and cumbersome in comparison, no in-your-ear solution can imitate the audio experience of a good set of over-ear headphones. The ultimate headphone experience for the traveling iPod user is the Bose QuietComfort 2 Noise Canceling Headphones (*http:// www.bose.com*; $299.00). Now, you might be thinking, "$300 for a pair of headphones?!" True, it's a lot of money. But the iPod set you back a pretty penny, didn't it? And you probably bought it because it blows away the competition in terms of design, features, and functionality. Well, if you've invested that much in the device that plays your music, investing a little (okay, a lot) more in the device that helps you hear your music should be worth it too.

The Bose headphones use an acoustic noise-canceling technology to help protect your ears, and your music, from outside noise. The technology works by electronically identifying and reducing the unwanted noise around you. They work by generating counter-noise to the white noise around you, effectively canceling out the sound waves received by your eardrums.

This means if you are in an airplane, you will hear a lot less of the engines and a lot more of your music. However, I've found that the Bose headphones aren't great for cutting out the noise from chatty coworkers; if that's what you're after, in-your-ear earphones might be a better option.

The sound quality of the Bose headphones is fantastic, and if you are looking for a quality headphone experience to complement your iPod, you can't go wrong with these.

In-Ear Headphones

In-ear headphones take your music as close to your eardrums as possible. The result is twofold: audio quality that is clear and, because the earphones go right in your ear, the blocking out of any incidental environmental noise.

Apple, recognizing the popularity of this kind of headphones, sells its own version. They are pretty good, but nothing compared to the ones this hack covers.

The Shure E Series. If you want to really upgrade your ears, check out the Shure E Series of sound-isolating earphones (*http://www.shure.com/ earphones/index.asp*; $99–$499). Shure earphones were originally developed for musicians who need to hear their performances while onstage. Yes, those earphones you see musicians using onstage can be yours! The Shure earphones work by using soft foam or plastic flexible sleeves to isolate out any background sound.

The Shure earphones contain small, high-energy microspeakers that deliver high-quality sound right into your ear. Compared to the earbuds that come with the iPod, Shure's earphones provide a quantum leap in listening quality. Not only do they render audio much better, they also block out all the background noise. This is particularly helpful if you use the subway or bus to commute. You will actually find yourself listening to music at a lower volume than you do with your iPod earbuds. The Shure earphones are so good at blocking out incidental environmental sound that you won't need to blast your tunes.

The Shure E Series comes in three models as described in Table 1-1.

Table 1-1. The Shure E Series line of earphones

	E2C ($99)	E3C ($179)	E5C ($499)
Speaker technology	A single high-energy driver in a comet-shaped enclosure that optimizes the acoustics environment	A single low-mass/high-energy driver with a balanced armature technology for more efficient output	Two dedicated low-mass/high-energy microspeakers and an inline crossover that optimally blends the high and low frequencies provided by each driver
Sound quality	Rich, full-frequency sound	Rich, full sound with an extended high-frequency response	Fully extended frequency for a clear high-end sound, smooth mid-frequencies, and deep, rich bass
Weight	1 oz	.9 oz	1.1 oz
Features	Comes with three sizes of both foam and flex sleeves to personalize your fit	The most compact design	Comes with a memory-fit cable that shapes around your ear for a tighter fit

An in-ear earphone for your ears only. Shure earphones come with different foam and silicone sleeves that you can interchange until you find the best fit for your ear. But what if you want a fit made especially for your ear? The next step is to get custom-molded earphones. Ultimate Ears (*http://www.ultimateears.com*) have made a well-deserved name for themselves by combining high-quality earphones with a seamless process for getting them in your ear. They also look pretty spiffy with the iPod, as you can see in Figure 1-4.

Ultimate Ears takes impressions made by an audiologist and creates a custom pair of earphones. This means that the earphones are made for your ears and

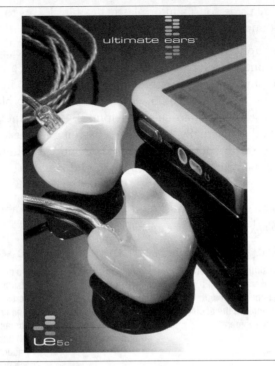

Figure 1-4. The Ultimate Ears earphones

your ears only! Apart from the benefit of not having to share them with any-one else, this also means you will experience unparalleled comfort. You can wear the Ultimate Ears earphones all day and not experience the feelings of soreness and fatigue that you sometimes get with other earphones.

The first step is to get impressions made. Pull out your local Yellow Pages and look up audiologists or hearing aid centers. When you call, let them know that you only want impressions of your ear made. You might hear a little pause at the end of the line; most companies are full-service and are not used to just making impressions for their customers. Explain that you are getting custom musician earphones made, and they should understand. Expect to pay anywhere from $10–$50 for the impressions.

If you've ever had to get an impression of your mouth made at the dentist, getting ear impressions made is very similar. Don't worry; no needles are involved! Ultimate Ears has a document you should download and print from their web site. It gives the audiologist specific instructions pertaining to how the impressions should be made.

The audiologist will first insert a small plastic stopper into each ear to pre-vent the silicone from going all the way to your eardrum. Next, a nice, cool, putty-like silicone substance is inserted in your ears. You'll have to sit for a couple minutes while the silicone hardens, keeping your mouth open the whole time. The audiologist will then remove your impressions from your ears and put them in a box for you. Mail them off to the address Ultimate Ears provides.

Ultimate Ears will build your earphones from these impressions after they receive them. Turnaround from the time they receive your impressions to the time you receive your custom earphones is about a week. At $550–$900 a set, these earphones aren't cheap, but if your music is important to you, they're well worth the expense. You will receive your earphones in a beautiful metallic box with your name custom-printed on it. The best part is when you put an Ultimate Ear earphone in your ear for the first time: it's like putting on a well-worn and comfortable shoe. The earphone feels like it is made just for your ear—wait, it is! Apart from feeling great going in your ears, the earphones also feel great after hours of use. The sound quality is truly stunning, and due to the perfect fit it feels like the music is just in your head.

Final Thoughts

Whether you decide to go with the Bose headphones, Apple's in-ear, Shure's excellent E Series earphones, or custom-made earphones by Ultimate Ears, your music will thank you. You will hear bass you didn't know existed and highlights that are higher than ever.

HACK #5 Broadcast Your iPod to FM Radio Ⓜ︎Ⓦ︎●

Share your iPod's tunes over the airwaves with a variety of FM transmitters.

If you've got an iPod and you've got a car, then you've got a problem. Sooner or later, you're going to want to drive while listening to your masterfully mixed playlists. Though there is no physical or technical barrier to jamming the cool white earphones into your auditory canals while your right foot works the accelerator, such behavior is not the best idea and is, in fact, illegal in some jurisdictions. So are you forever stuck with the commercial-addled commute? The answer is no; by adding the right equipment to your iPod, you can stream your music straight to the FM dial of your car stereo.

The equipment you'll need is known generically as an *FM transmitter*. These devices will broadcast anything streaming out of your iPod to an FM radio, allowing your car, or any other nearby FM radio, to play the sweet sounds emanating from your iPod.

This hack shows how, with minimal effort, to stream your tunes onto the FM dial. All you'll need is an iPod, an FM transmitter, and a willingness to stick an aftermarket item into various iPod ports. For an example of a specific implementation (using Griffin Technology's iTrip transmitter), be sure to check out "Turn Your iPod Mini into a Radio Station" [Hack #13].

Choosing the FM Transmitter

The technology used in FM transmitters is fairly rudimentary, so don't look for a product description that's riddled with technobabble; they're all going to work on the same principle, and they are all going to be limited by the same FCC regulations. This isn't to say that all iPod-compatible FM transmitters are interchangeable; in fact, there are a wide variety of form factors, features, and electronic refinements to consider.

One of the first things you'll want to consider is where you're likely to use your FM transmitter. If you're going to use the transmitter exclusively in your car, you'll probably want a different model than if you desire the ability to stream your tunes to any nearby FM radio.

Some popular models include:

DLO Transpod by Digital Lifestyle Outfitters (http://www.netalog.com; $69.99-$99.99)

- Compatible with iPods featuring 30-pin connectors (generations 3 and 4)
- Models available for older iPods at lower cost
- Powered by automobile cigarette lighter
- Full FM spectrum available
- Recharges iPod when in use
- Attaches directly to the iPod

FM_Transmitter by Pacific Rim (http://www.pacrimtechnologies.com; $29.99)

- Compatible with generation 3 and 4 iPods and the iPod mini
- Powered by automobile cigarette lighter
- Attaches via cable to stereo mini-jack
- Full FM spectrum available

iTrip by Griffin Technology (http://www.griffintechnology.com/products/itrip/; $35.00)

- Compatible with all iPods and the iPod mini
- Powered by the iPod (Griffin Technology claims no significant loss of battery life)
- Allows selection from more than 100 FM frequencies
- Attaches directly to the iPod

TuneCast II Mobile FM Transmitter by Belkin (http://www.belkin.com; $49.99)

- Compatible with any device that has the appropriate headphone jack (3.5 mm, also known as stereo mini-jack)
- Uses two AAA batteries
- Allows selection from four frequencies
- Attaches via cable
- See Figure 1-5

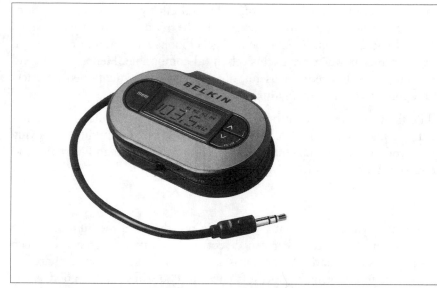

Figure 1-5. The Belkin TuneCast II Mobile FM Transmitter

Podfreq by Sonnet (http://www.podfreq.com; $99.95)

- Compatible with all iPods
- Powered by the iPod
- Features FireWire and mini USB 2.0 ports
- Allows selection from full FM spectrum
- Attaches directly to the iPod
- Provides full dock functionality

irock! 400FM Beamit (http://www.myirock.com; $29.99)

- Compatible with all iPods
- Attaches via cable to mini-jack
- Uses two AAA batteries or included cigarette lighter adapter
- Allows selection from four frequencies

Nearly any FM transmitter will work, as long as it accepts input from a stereo mini-jack. The features and prices of generic FM transmitters will vary.

More Shopping Decisions

This is the most difficult part of the entire process. With the myriad of options available, which one should you choose?

Many of the devices are specifically designed to go with the iPod and try to stay faithful to the iPod's styling. If aesthetics are important to you, take a careful look at the products by Griffin, Digital Lifestyle Outfitters, and Sonnet. These feature tight integration with the iPod and try to match its smooth look. The tight integration and good looks come at a price, though, because these products are exclusively iPod-compatible. Hence, if you find streaming to an FM receiver useful, note that the aforementioned products aren't going to work with anything but an iPod.

While the technology might be fairly standard, all FM broadcasters are not created equal. If possible, test the transmitter you're thinking of buying before you buy it; just remember to bring along your iPod, an FM radio, and a couple AAA batteries when you're shopping.

Some Caveats

Audiophiles will tell you that FM radio is not the ideal medium for audio transmission. The careful ear can detect a substantial difference between CD-quality sound and FM broadcasts. That said, under perfect circumstances, the music being broadcast from your iPod will sound as good as any FM station. If you're satisfied with the sound quality of the FM dial, you'll be as satisfied with the tunes streamed from your iPod.

The power of these devices is limited by federal law, so don't expect your transmitter to work three blocks away. The general obstruction-free range is 10 to 30 feet, and anything that is between the iPod and the FM receiver (particularly if it's metal) is going to degrade the signal quality.

The range restriction might not sound like a big deal if you're going to be using the FM transmitter in your car; after all, your iPod is going to be next to the radio, right? Unfortunately, the situation isn't quite that simple. Certain cars feature a metallic film in their windshields, effectively shielding the outside antenna from the signal emanating inside your car. If your automobile has this feature, chuck the FM transmitter idea and look for an AUX input.

Getting the Best Results

If your FM transmitter supports the entire FM spectrum, and if the middle of the dial isn't populated by *flamethrower* stations, set your transmitter as close to dead center (100.5 MHz) of the spectrum as possible. This will maximize sound quality by giving the largest range of stereo separation (though the improvement was imperceptible to my ears).

Choose a frequency that is unused by any nearby radio station. If you try to compete with your local 100,000-watt station, you'll undoubtedly suffer from a condition called *bleed-through*. Bleed-through might sound like an extremely unpleasant medical condition, but you won't be physically harmed; you'll merely hear your iPod's broadcast and the broadcast of the local station at the same time. A simple way to pick a station is to leave the FM broadcaster on while tuning the receiver. When all you hear is static—no faint music or obnoxious used-car ads—you've found a clear section of the FM spectrum. Tune your FM transmitter to this formerly empty frequency and enjoy.

—Chris Seibold

HACK #6   Build Your Own FM Broadcaster ⓜⓦⓛ

Increase the range of your FM transmitter and broadcast audio around your home.

If you read "Broadcast Your iPod to FM Radio" [Hack #5], you might have noted that the FM transmitters discussed seemed to work like very weak FM stations. Unsurprisingly, that is precisely the function of the mentioned FM transmitters. Their power, and thus range, is limited by FCC regulations. This hack details how to amplify the signal from an FM transmitter to cover a larger area.

Here's what you'll need to complete this hack:

- An iPod
- An FM transmitter
- Various electronic components (listed later in this hack)
- A soldering iron
- Fearless voiding of the FM transmitter's warranty

Building the FM Transmitter Amplifier

Strictly speaking, you don't have to build anything, because there is a wide variety of available kits and prebuilt devices that will save you the trouble. One example is the FM100B Super Pro FM Stereo Radio Station Kit (*http://www.ramseyelectronics.com*; $269.95). This solution will provide much better quality than the following design, but it has a few drawbacks. The first is that it costs $269.95, and the second is that it is much more interesting (and cheaper) to build something like this from scratch.

Before I get to the specifics of this hack, let me note that if you're living in the United States (or one of several other countries), this hack is illegal. That means you shouldn't do it—rather, think of this hack as a Gedanken experiment. After all, no one has attempted Schrödinger's cat. If you live outside the United States, check with your local authorities before starting to make sure you're not violating local regulations. If you're the sovereign of a small nation, by all means proceed with reckless abandon.

The circuit we'll build is a basic design chosen specifically for simplicity and car/home compatibility. Think of it as a learning experience; once you've built this circuit, you'll have the confidence to tackle more intricate designs and be able to tailor the performance of your FM amplifier to your needs. To get started, you'll need the fairly specific parts outlined in the following list.

This list contains RadioShack part numbers and prices for convenience only. Any decent electronics shop should have the parts you need.

- Transistor 2n4401 (part #276-2058; list price $0.96).
- 220-kΩ resistor (part #276-2058; list price $0.99).
- 10-kΩ resistor (part #271-1126; list price $0.99).
- .001μ F capacitor (part #272-126; list price $1.29).
- 100μ H RF choke (part #273-102; list price $1.29).
- 30 inches of solid copper wire (alternatively, you could cannibalize a telescoping antenna from an unused radio, as long as the length is correct).
- Breadboard (part #276-169; list price $22.99). This is not strictly needed (you could just solder everything together), but a breadboard makes the construction process much easier.
- 10-kΩ potentiometer (part #271-215; list price $3.29).
- 12V/500mA AC to DC power converter (part #273-1773; list price $15.99). Get the friendly folks at the electronics shop to mark the positive and ground connections for you; you'll save time and money by avoiding the need for a multimeter.

Preparing the FM transmitter. Time to void the warranty. Crack open whatever transmitter you've chosen for sacrifice (for this project, choose a battery-powered or iPod-powered FM transmitter) and locate the antenna. In the Belkin TuneCast, the antenna is the blue wire inside the mini-jack cable.

For instructions on locating the iTrip's antenna, see "Turn Your iPod Mini into a Radio Station" [Hack #13]. There is no standardized location for the antenna, so I can't say exactly where you will find it on other FM transmitters. You're looking for a length of wire without any obvious function (i.e., it's not connecting the batteries or the headphone jack). If you're having trouble finding the antenna, look carefully at the green circuit board; often, there is a small white ANT label where the antenna meets the printed circuit board, giving away the location.

Once you're sure you've found the antenna, devise a way to expose a length of said antenna outside of the FM transmitter (one inch should be plenty) without destroying the connection to the internal circuitry. Reassemble the unit with the newly accessible antenna wire still proudly outside of the unit. Some FM transmitters use bare wire, while others use insulated wire. If your antenna falls into the insulated category, take this opportunity to remove the insulation from the exposed part of the wire. Congratulations; you've completed the modification the FM transmitter.

Building the circuit. This is the fun or challenging part, depending on your perspective. While the schematic shown in Figure 1-6 might look complicated at first glance, it is much easier to build than a cursory inspection reveals.

Here are a few tips before starting: don't power up the circuit before you're done, don't touch the circuit after you've inserted the plug in the wall receptacle (safety first), and don't be afraid to ask for help. People who know how to construct circuits are generally proud of their knowledge and are usually happy to help. Once you're assured the circuit performs correctly, you can remove all the excess material to make the device as small as possible (done carefully, the entire amplifier circuit could fit on a quarter).

If you bought a breadboard, building the circuit is pretty easy. If not, you can still get through it, but things will be a bit trickier. The instructions that follow are for building the circuit without the breadboard, but they are also applicable when using the breadboard.

A note on connecting the wires: this circuit won't be permanent until you apply solder to all the junctions, but try to make the connections as secure as possible for testing purposes (or use a breadboard).

The potentiometer is a good place to begin. If you examine the potentiometer closely, you'll note that it has three holes to receive wires (the holes are called *lugs*). Get three pieces of equal-length insulated wire (three inches is plenty) and strip off most of the insulation, leaving a one-inch strip of insulation in the middle of each wire.

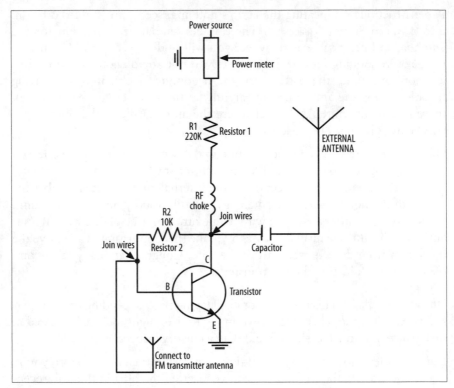

Figure 1-6. The circuit schematic

Connect one wire per lug and trim any excess exposed wire next to the lug. At this point, turn your attention to the wire connected to the middle lug. Attach one end of the 220-kΩ resistor to the wire and trim any excess wire/lead (the leads are the wires coming out of the components). Grab the RF choke and attach it via a wire to the unadorned side of the resistor.

Attach another section of wire to the unused end of the RF choke. Attach similar wires to the leads of the remaining resistor, the capacitor, and all three leads of the transistor. Hold the transistor with the flat side toward you and note the far-left lead (this is called the *collector*). Wire this lead to one wire of the 10-kΩ resistor, and similarly to the RF choke and capacitor (I did this by twisting the bare ends of the four wires together with a wire nut). Take the middle lead (called the *base*) of the transistor and wire said lead to the unused wire of the 10-kΩ resistor.

The project is nearly complete. At this point, we want to add a ground wire (it is probably wise to choose a different color to avoid later confusion). Choose a length of wire long enough to traverse the entire circuit, and strip about an inch of insulation off of each end. Wire one end of the ground wire to the remaining transistor lead (known as the *emitter*). Wire the opposite end of the ground wire to one of the remaining unused wires attached to the potentiometer (do *not* trim excess). Connect the capacitor's remaining unused wire to whatever you've decided to use as your new antenna.

All the circuit lacks now is power and an input. First, add the input. Take the section of wire you exposed on your FM transmitter earlier and connect it somewhere between the base lead (middle lead) of the transistor and the 10-kΩ resistor.

To power the circuit, you'll need the 12V DC power adapter. Leave it unplugged for the moment. If you're using the RadioShack model mentioned earlier, you'll see two small holes. Hopefully, you followed the earlier advice and had the electronics shop folks mark the positive and ground sides; if not, you'll have to use a multimeter to deduce the orientation.

Insert the ground wire into the neutral (ground) side of the plug, and insert the last free wire on the potentiometer into the positive side of the plug (you may want to fold the ends of the wire for a more secure fit). Trim off any excess exposed wire, check to be sure all the connections are secure, and inspect the circuit carefully to ensure that there are no connections that aren't in the diagram. Once you're confident everything is ready, plug the DC converter into the wall and (the moment of truth) fire up your iPod and FM transmitter.

> At some point, you're going to want to solder the circuit together. The connections made by twisting wires together are fine for testing, but for daily use, you need a more permanent solution. You shouldn't find soldering your masterpiece too difficult, but if you do, a nice primer is available at *http://www. epemag.wimborne.co.uk/solderfaq.htm*. There is one common mistake you need to keep in mind: the potentiometer can be destroyed by overheating with the soldering iron, so take special care when soldering that particular component.

Using Your New Amplifier

The hard work is done, and now the fun begins. Before you start using your newly birthed amplifier in earnest, keep the following in mind: the circuit will certainly interfere with, and possibly override, any broadcast stations that share the same frequency. That means that if your neighbor is listening to NPR and you tune your transmitter to NPR's frequency (90.9 MHz, for example), said neighbor is going to be listening to your iPod instead of NPR's careful reporting. Minimize neighbor frustration by picking a dead spot on the FM dial (that is, a channel where you hear only static). Purposefully drowning out the annoying radio station your neighbor is listening to by broadcasting silence on the same frequency **[Hack #13]** is possible, but not recommended.

Once you've selected the frequency, power everything up and grab an FM radio. Tune it to your carefully chosen frequency and take a walk. You're basically checking reception; ideally, what you want is full coverage on your bit of turf and zero coverage elsewhere. That is unlikely to happen, but you can fine-tune the result by adjusting the potentiometer. If the coverage is sub-par, rotate the knob on the potentiometer to decrease resistance, thus increasing the covered area. If the coverage extends beyond the limits of your personal fiefdom, rotate the knob in the opposite direction to decrease the range of your personal FM station. Experimentation yields the best results while providing the most entertainment.

Hacking the Hack

The usefulness of your new amplified transmitter is limited only by your imagination. If you used a transmitter that attaches via the iPod mini-jack only, you can use your new transmitter with any device that the mini-jack plug fits. That means you can stream the music off your desktop Mac to all the radios throughout your house (try that with Airport Express!), broadcast from your portable CD player, use a camcorder as a microphone and broadcast your own monologue, and so on. The applications are limitless.

Also note that the circuit was designed with portability in mind. To use the device in your car, snip the end off a cigarette-lighter adapter and attach the power (usually a red wire) to the potentiometer and the ground wire (usually black) to the ground wire of your amplified transmitter. Your mini-station is now fully mobile.

—*Chris Seibold*

HACK #7   Turn Your iPod into a Portable Stereo ⓂⓌⓁ

Tired of listening through headphones? Turn your iPod into a boom box.

The iPod is a great portable audio device. We all know that. But sometimes you want to listen to music without (gasp!) headphones. With a simple cable, you can hook up your iPod to a boom box or stereo. And, with the addition of a couple products, your iPod can *become* the boom box. Imagine, a boom box with full access to your entire digital library and the small size and portability of the iPod.

Connecting Your iPod to Your Stereo

The easiest way to connect your iPod to an external speaker is by buying a headphone-jack-to-RCA audio cable from an electronics store such as RadioShack. Plug the cable into your iPod headphone jack (or your iPod dock if you have one) and then plug the RCA audio jacks into your stereo receiver. Now, all the music you have on your iPod can be played on your home stereo. The sound quality is surprisingly good. You can also plug your iPod into your boom box this way.

A True iPod Portable Solution

The previous solution is great if you want to use your iPod with your home stereo. But what if you want to listen to your iPod on your deck or take a little iPod stereo with you on vacation so you can jam to some tunes in your hotel room? The best tool for the job is Altec Lansing's inMotion portable audio system (*http://www.alteclansing.com/store.asp*; $149.95), an ultraportable powered speaker system made especially for the iPod. Connecting your iPod to the inMotion unit is as easy as placing your generation 2 or later iPod or iPod Mini into your iPod's dock. The inMotion includes the following features:

- A highly efficient digital amplifier (Class D)
- High-performance, custom-designed neodymium Micro Drivers that delivers crystal-clear sound
- Extra-long battery life that delivers up to 24 hours of continuous playback with four AA batteries
- A lightweight design (15 ounces) that folds to be 8 inches wide, 5.4 inches deep, and 1.2 inches thick
- A convenient auxiliary input jack for connection to other audio devices, including laptops, generation 1 iPods, and other MP3 players (3.5-mm stereo cable included)
- Elegant, integrated power and volume controls
- A headphone jack for private listening

If you have a generation 1 iPod, you can't use the dock. However, Altec Lansing includes a cable for attaching your iPod through the headphone jack.

Visually, the iPod integrates nicely with inMotion, as shown in Figure 1-7. But the real fun begins once you press Play. There is a surprising amount of bass, and the highlights sound great too. The inMotion folds down to a compact slab that you can slip into the included bag for traveling. If you want to take the inMotion to the next level, hook up the naviPod remote (discussed in the following section) to your iPod while it is docked. Now you have a portable audio system that you can control from across the room!

Figure 1-7. The inMotion—a compact unit that gives off some serious sound

Other manufacturers, recognizing the iPod's popularity, are introducing versions of their own products for the iPod. One excellent product is the iPal by Tivoli (*http://www. tivoliaudio.com/pPALIPOD.htm*; $129.99). Tivoli is well known for packing audiophile-like sound into a small package, and the iPal is no exception. It comes in white and chrome to match your iPod. Connect the iPod via an auxiliary jack.

I've seen inMotions at the beach (be careful of the sand!), in the gym, and on bedside tables. Now you don't need to carry around that cumbersome portable CD player that plays only one CD (how quaint is that!) at a time. With this hack, your iPod can rock the house wherever it goes.

Hacking the Hack

If you are using an iPod dock, a nice addition to your setup is a remote control. Check out TEN Technology's naviPod (*http://www.tentechnology.com/ products/products_navipod_gen2.php*; $49.95). Due to differences in the design of the generation 1 and later iPods, the naviPod comes in two versions.

Both versions are comprised of three parts. First, there is a small infrared (IR) unit that plugs into the top of your iPod. The second component is the actual remote which you can use to control the iPod from across the room. Functions include pause, rewind, fast-forward, and volume up/down. The remote's capability is similar to that of a TV remote. In fact, if you have a universal remote for your TV, DVD player, etc., you can use it with the navi-

Pod. The third piece is a metal stand that clicks into the side of the IR unit and holds up your iPod.

HACK #8 Use Two iPods to DJ ⓜⓦⓛ

Got a party coming up? Leave that stack of vinyl at home and take two iPods with you to mix it up digital-music style.

It's inevitable that when a new music format becomes popular, people will want to DJ with it. It happened with vinyl, it happened with CDs—well, okay, it didn't quite happen with eight-tracks or cassettes. But what about digital formats such as MP3 or AAC? It is possible to DJ with your iPod, and although the iPod presents some barriers to creating a professional-sounding DJ show, you can still achieve good results. There are two main ways to DJ with your iPod: the first way consists of connecting two iPods to a mixing board, and the other is achieved when you connect two iPods to your computer.

Two iPods and a Mixing Board

To DJ using two iPods and a mixing board, you will need the following items:

- Two iPods
- Two headphone-jack-to-RCA cables
- A mixing board
- An amplifier
- Speakers

This setup mimics the traditional basic DJ setup of two turntables connected to a mixing board. We are substituting iPods for turntables, but unfortunately, this is not just a simple matter of swapping one for another. There are a few issues we need to address first.

Connectivity and amplification. For this setup, we will utilize the headphone jack on the iPod. This allows us to cut a computer out of the equation, providing a more portable setup. Simply connect your two iPods to your mixing board using headphone to RCA cables. There is, however, a problem with using the headphone jack: the lack of adequate amplification. Sure, the iPod offers enough power to jack up the volume on your headphones, but when you're trying to blast the ears off your audience with speakers, it's simply not enough. If you connect your iPod directly to your mixing board through the headphone jack, you'll find that the sound quality degrades tremendously right around the halfway volume setting on your iPod. You will be able to increase the volume significantly from that point, but the quality of sound will be unacceptable.

You could run your iPods through your receiver for amplification first and then out to the mixing board, but this presents a problem when it comes to transporting equipment. If you plan on setting up a permanent system to DJ, this might be a viable option. But if you're like me, you'll find the idea of lugging around a receiver in addition to your mixing board and speakers undesirable. To fix this problem, I have run each of my iPods through the PowerWave USB Audio Interface and Desktop Amplifier, from Griffin Technology (*http://www.griffintechnology.com/products/powerwave/*; $99.99), and then connected the amplifiers to the mixing board. This provides a huge boost in fidelity, especially at high volume.

> Mixing boards span the gamut in sophistication, quality, and price. If you are just looking to fool around with mixing two iPods together, you can get a basic mixer at RadioShack for around $75. If you are a more seasoned DJ, you probably already have a mixing board so you don't need to upgrade your current mixing board to use iPods with it—just get hold of some headphone-jack-to-RCA cables.

Pitch control and beat matching. One of the fundamentals of seamless mixing is the ability to beat match. *Beat matching* is the term given to speeding up or slowing down one song to match the beats of the next song. This technique is executed by adjusting the pitch of the audio, thus speeding up or slowing down the music. Unfortunately, the iPod currently does not allow you to do this. So how in the world can you DJ, then? Well, you won't sound like Fatboy Slim, but you can still string together songs by using the cross-fader on your mixing board. The lack of pitch control only means that you have to carefully choose the order of your songs.

Song choice is key to a good DJ set. Without the ability to beat match, it is important to be able to choose songs that sound good together, especially at the endings and beginnings. By reducing the volume of song 1 while increasing the volume of song 2, you can create a smoother transition between tracks. I have found that songs with talking at the beginning of the song are good to transition to. This is common in hip-hop and rap songs. That way, you hear talking on song 2 over the music of song 1. In addition, you can sometimes use spoken-word or other multimedia clips, such as excerpts from TV broadcasts or movie quotes, as bookends to a song with music.

Scratching. Another barrier to a professional iPod DJ show is the inability to *scratch*. This technique was created by DJs working with vinyl records, but with the new CDJ units, DJs have been able to mimic the effect with CDs. Unfortunately, this is not currently possible with the iPod. It's a shame, too, because the scroll wheel would be a perfect interface for it. You will find some instances on the Internet where people have suggested creating a *faux scratch* effect with their iPods. Tapping the center button and gently jogging the music back a fraction of a second achieves this. However, all my tests of this technique produced an unsatisfactory sound, similar to a skipping CD. I recommend *not* doing it, because it might confuse the audience into thinking you ripped your music incorrectly.

The two iPod/mixing board setup is convenient to transport and simple to set up, but lackluster when it comes to overall quality of sound. It's an inexpensive way to entertain your party guests, but if you're looking for an authentic DJ-show sound, you'll need to add a computer into the mix.

Two iPods and a Computer

The other option when DJ-ing with two iPods is to connect both iPods to a computer. This configuration has many advantages. First and foremost, DJs can create a more professional-quality show by using mixing programs such as Traktor DJ Studio Pro (*http://www.nativeinstruments.de/index.php? traktor2_us*; $229). Traktor DJ Studio Pro allows DJs to use all the techniques they normally would with turntables: they can simulate scratching, adjust pitch, loop samples, beat match, and fade. And they can do all this without dragging around milk crates full of records!

In addition, having a computer setup allow DJs to connect to the Internet or private FTP servers while performing. This enables access to a wide range of music and samples, far beyond what you can hold on your two iPods.

Here's what you'll need for this setup:

- 2 iPods
- A laptop
- 2 FireWire ports or a FireWire hub
- An audio-out port
- Traktor DJ Studio (or a similar mixing program)
- An amplifier
- Speakers

By connecting both iPods to your computer, you can create great mixes quickly and easily. Traktor DJ Studio is fully compatible with iTunes, so all the songs in your iTunes library are accessible on the fly, as are the songs loaded on your iPods. Between two full iPods and the hard drive on your laptop, you could have 30,000 songs at your fingertips. With that amount of material, you should be able to find enough songs to play in your set! And with Traktor DJ Studio, you can beat match, loop samples, and scratch flawlessly. This is a must for DJs who want to use digital audio files for their sets.

When you first open Traktor DJ Studio, a setup window appears. Set your preferences for importing iTunes playlists in the Browser tab, as shown in Figure 1-8.

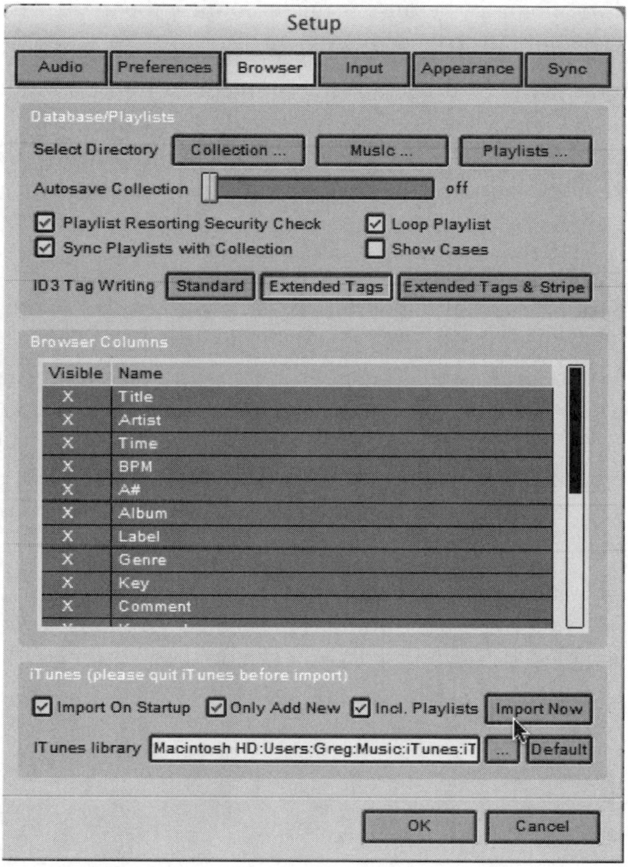

Figure 1-8. Traktor DJ Studio's Preferences window

When you've completed your setup, your iTunes playlists appear in the Browser window. I have named the playlist for this demonstration "New Mix," as shown in Figure 1-9.

While a track is playing, you can "scratch" by simply clicking and dragging. To create a more "turntable" feel and scratch the track with finer resolution, hold the Shift key while clicking and dragging, as shown in Figure 1-10.

Cross-fading between two songs is easy. Simply click and drag the cross-fader slider to transition the first song to the second, as shown in Figure 1-11.

Figure 1-9. Your available iTunes playlists

Figure 1-10. Scratching, digital style

Sometimes, it is necessary to adjust the tempo of one song to match the tempo of another. This can be accomplished by using the tempo level adjuster, as shown in Figure 1-12. Drag the slider up, and the speed of the song slows down. Drag it down, and the speed increases.

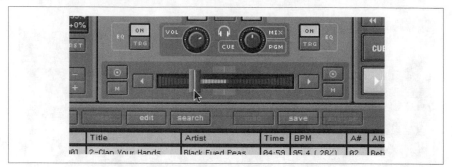

Figure 1-11. Cross-fading between two tracks

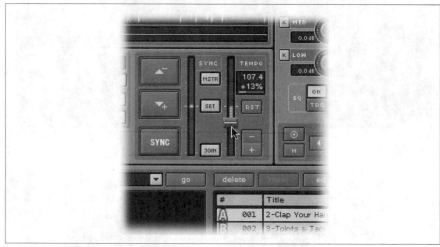

Figure 1-12. Adjusting the tempo

Looping samples from a song is another common technique used by DJs, and Traktor DJ Studio makes it easy (see Figure 1-13). For example, clicking on the 8 button and then clicking on the SET/IN button tells the program to set a loop eight beats long from the beginning of the playhead. The loop is marked by green lines and boxes that read *S* and *E*. Click Play, and this sample loops continuously.

These features are the tip of the iceberg. Traktor DJ Studio allows the most seasoned DJs to do virtually everything they can do with conventional equipment.

Whether you are using the traditional two-iPod/mixing board setup or the two-iPod/computer setup, you can achieve great results. These setups have become invaluable to some DJs. The iPod is not just a great consumer product anymore; with its huge song capacity, small size, and excellent sound quality, the iPod is now perfect for the seasoned professional too.

—Gregory Ng

Figure 1-13. Looping a sample

Turn Your iPod into a Universal Remote Control ⓂⓌⓔ

Use a Pocket PC to record the "sounds" an infrared remote makes, transfer them to your iPod, and start changing channels with your new universal remote control.

We're going to take an iPod and turn it into a universal infrared (IR) remote control, which can be used to control all your home electronic equipment, or just about anything that uses a remote control. For example, in my home, my iPod controls my TV, DVD player, Direct TV, Ultimate TV PVR, Media Center PC, Xbox, XM Satellite Radio, Roomba, and a few other random things, such as a robot. Figure 1-14 shows a variety of remotes your iPod can replace.

To do this, we are going to "record" the "sounds" an infrared remote makes on a PC and then put them on an iPod as songs. Adding a special sound-to-IR converter then turns those sounds back to IR and allows you to use your iPod as a remote control. As an added bonus, it works from up to 100 feet away. It's a slick all-in-one unit, and you'll never go back to using multiple remotes again.

Here's what you'll need for this hack:

- An iPod (doesn't matter which one)
- A Mac or PC with sound recording software
- A Pocket PC (any Pocket PC 2002/2003 should work)
- Griffin's Total Remote software and IR device
  (*http://www.griffintechnology.com/griffinmobile/totalremote/*; $24.99)

Figure 1-14. One iPod to control a collection of remotes

Getting the IR Signal

The most important element is the sound-to-IR converter from Griffin, shown in Figure 1-15. This device (and software) was meant to extend the range of Pocket PCs and add consumer IR capabilities. You are first going to use the Pocket PC software to input the IR signals from your remotes, convert these signals to sound files, and then use your iPod to play those sounds through the sound-to-IR converter to control your devices.

Figure 1-15. Griffin's IR device

First, install the Total Remote software on your Pocket PC. Follow the instructions and start entering all the remotes you'll ultimately want to use on your iPod. To keep this example simple, we're going to begin by turning the TV on and off.

On the Pocket PC, choose Start → Programs → Total Remote. Then, choose Edit → Start One-Shot Sampling, as shown in Figure 1-16. Pick the power button on the interface.

Figure 1-16. Sampling your remote

As shown in Figure 1-17, Total Remote prompts you to hold the remote (in our example, the TV remote) up to the IR port on the Pocket PC. This records the IR signal.

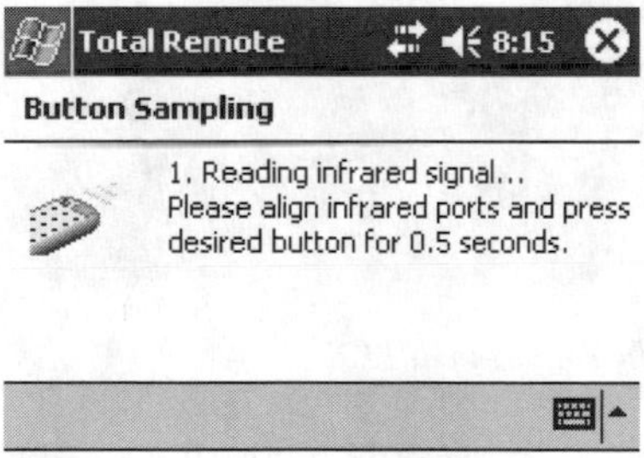

Figure 1-17. Total Remote, prompting you to align your remote

Once you've captured the IR signal, you can test it by using the IR device included with Total Remote. After you verify that it works, it's time to get that IR signal off the Pocket PC and onto a computer as a sound file.

Recording the Signal

Remove the Total Remote IR device from the Pocket PC headphone jack and run a line-out cable from the Pocket PC to the microphone or line-in port. You can get a 3.5 mm stereo audio cable such as this from RadioShack or any computer store. Many computers come with one to run sound out to speakers; that'll work too.

On your desktop computer (for our example, a PC, as shown in Figure 1-18), use a sound-editing program that can edit sounds and remove channels (left and right). This example uses SoundForge (*http://mediasoftware.sonypictures.com/Products/*; $399.00).

Figure 1-18. Recording the sounds on a PC

In your recording application, set the recording format to the following (this is really important):

    44 Hz, 16bit Stereo. PCM

We're ultimately going to save the signal as a WAV (Windows sound file).

Press Record in the sound-recording application. Then, on the Pocket PC (with the line out from the headphone jack to the line in on the desktop computer), press the button to which you assigned the Power signal.

Stop the recording and press Play. If you recorded the signal properly, you'll hear some weird beeps and pulses. That's what the IR signal "sounds" like. In SoundForge, you can actually see the pulses and signal on a WAV graphic, as shown in Figure 1-19.

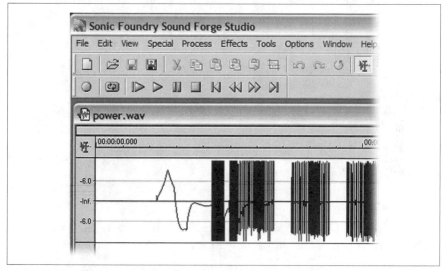

Figure 1-19. The pulses and signals in SoundForge

Next, highlight the right channel and mute it. If you skip this step, the sound won't process through the IR device properly.

Now, save the sound recording as a 44 Hz, 16 bit Stereo, PCM WAV file. We called ours *power.wav*.

Putting the Signal on the iPod

Pop your iPod in the cradle. In iTunes, make a new playlist (I called mine TV) and then add the WAV file to the playlist, as shown in Figure 1-20.

The file transfers to the iPod, and we're ready to test our new remote.

Figure 1-20. iTunes playlist with remote sound

Ready, Aim, Fire

Remove the iPod from the cradle and put the Total Remote IR device in the iPod's headphone jack, as shown in Figure 1-21.

Figure 1-21. iPod with Total Remote IR device

Go to the playlist and point the iPod at the TV, as shown in Figure 1-22.

Figure 1-22. iTunes playlist with remote sound

Click Play. If you've done everything right, your TV should turn on and off each time you play this sound. Go back and input all your other devices. Congratulations! You can now control your TV—or anything else, for that matter—with your iPod.

—Phillip Torrone

HACK #10 Integrate Your iPod with Your Motorcycle

The iPod is perfect for road trips on your motorcycle (or scooter). You just have to make your iPod play nice with the open road.

Installing the iPod for motorcycle use can be done fairly easily with a little time and effort. Two primary considerations are whether you are integrating the iPod into an existing intercom/audio system and whether the iPod will be run off its own battery or will need to be powered off the bike.

> It goes without saying that safety comes first when riding. Listening to music while riding adds another layer of distraction. I recommend listening to your music through headphones built in to your helmet, rather than blasting it through external speakers. Either way, exercise discretion when listening while riding, and check your state laws.

If you are integrating the iPod into an existing audio system, it is very likely that this audio system will have its own internal amplifier that will take over the volume functions. If your motorcycle does not have an existing inter-com or audio system for you to add the iPod to, you will need to consider adding an additional amplifier, as the iPod's volume will not be enough for you to hear your music clearly through your helmet speakers. There are several small audio amps on the market that can do the job. The one I like best is sold both in kit form and as an assembled amp and can be purchased online from Hobbytron.com (*http://www.hobbytron.net/CK122.html*; $14.00 or $29.95 fully assembled).

Two basic problems present themselves for installing an iPod on a motorcy-cle. The first is what to do with the wires, and the second is how to be able to use the remote. Typically, you will want to mount the iPod on some foam in an out-of-the-way location where it is protected from rain, such as in a fairing pocket or a non-magnetic tank bag. As a side note, never put an iPod in a magnetic tank bag, because that will damage the hard drive.

Repositioning the Remote

One way to help alleviate the wiring mess is to break the audio lines out of the remote cable, so that your headset or audio connector does not have to be plugged into the end of the remote control. This allows you to route the remote to a position on the handlebars where it is convenient to use, yet you don't have the additional audio output cable plugged into the end of it. It requires that you carefully slice open the sheath on the remote cable and extract and splice into the three small audio wires. These wires are color-coded red, white, and black.

> However, their color-coding does not match the convention of normal audio wires. Normally, the red wire is the right channel positive, the white wire is the left channel positive, and the black wire is the return path or ground (shield).

On the iPod remote, the red wire is the ground or shield, the white is the right channel positive, and the black wire is the left channel positive.

Once you've extracted the three audio wires, you can then solder them into your motorcycle's audio cable. Alternatively, you can attach a female mini-stereo jack to these wires so you can plug and unplug the connection—how-ever, for use on a motorcycle I like to use soldered joints wherever I can to eliminate connection problems from vibration. Frequently, jacks and con-nectors are sources of failures, and solder joints covered in a heat-shrink wrapper will be the most reliable long-term connections.

You need to consider exactly where you want to splice into the remote cord. This position will vary depending on your particular application. Choose a spot that helps to facilitate installation and minimizes wire lengths.

 Another benefit of carrying the iPod when you travel by motorcycle is that there are several third-party applications that let you download phone and contact information into it from a PDA or address book. This info can be handy to have on the road with you, and it makes the iPod useful for more than just tunes.

Hacking the Remote

Another interesting modification you can make is to hack into the actual remote circuit card itself and run parallel switches to control the remote functions. My particular motorcycle had some unused CB switches on the handlebars for a CB I never installed, so it made sense for me to make use of them. They are much larger and easier to operate while riding than the iPod remote's controls, so I wanted to take advantage of them.

I first removed the plastic case from the remote by carefully prying it apart. Once I got the circuit card free, I could access the points on the circuit card where I needed to piggyback my wires. Be warned that this card is extremely small, and the contact points even smaller. You will need an extremely small soldering tip and small wires to be able to attach onto the existing switch connections. You will also need to use a magnifying glass to inspect your solder joints and to make sure you didn't splash any solder onto nearby contacts. Both the volume and skip functions on the remote board have an up and a down contact and a common contact. Three wires control volume up and down, three more control skip up and down, and two wires are needed for play/pause.

Once the wires are attached, you will need to tie them all together and attach them to the circuit card to provide strain relief for your delicate solder joints. Use a bit of hot melt glue to stick the wires in place. Once all the wires are in place, simply hook them up to the switches that you want to control the various functions. With the plastic cover off the remote, the circuit card was small enough that it could be mounted inside the housing for the unused CB switches on my motorcycle, so I just routed the wires and soldered them to the new switches. Your scenario might be different.

Powering the iPod

If you want to power the iPod off the motorcycle's electrical system, there are several good cigarette-type power adapters on the market that you can use to connect your iPod to a vehicle's 12-volt electrical system. There are some considerations for using these, though, as they can introduce noise into the audio system if you have other audio devices running off the bike's power or if the iPod is connected to an onboard intercom system that is powered from the motorcycle. The problem stems from ground loops forming between the audio circuits in the iPod and the audio circuits in the intercom amplifier. Solve the problem by installing a ground loop isolator, which is simply a transformer that prevents DC current from flowing back through the audio connections. RadioShack sells these (part #270-054), and they are simply installed in line (series) on the audio output wires from the iPod. This eliminates any ground loops and gets rid of any alternator whine or buzz that results from the use of a power adapter.

Final Thoughts

Once you have the iPod installed, it is truly a joy to have on a motorcycle, especially if you take long trips. You can build your playlist at home, and then when you ride just start the iPod and never have to mess with it again. It is one of the nicer audio solutions for motorcycles, due to its resistance to vibration and trouble-free operation. And since you are not constantly trying to change channels to find a good song or fiddle with the controls, it allows you to keep your eyes and concentration focused on the road, where they belong. I have now ridden over 40,000 miles with the iPod installed and have had no problems with it ever skipping or locking up.

—*Fred Harmon*

HACK #11 Install Your iPod in Your Car, Permanently ⓜⓦⓛ

Upgrade your car's console to house the iPod and integrate the iPod with your car's audio and electrical systems.

Sure, you can easily listen to your iPod in your car **[Hack #5]**. However, if you want to take your hacking skills to the next level, this hack gives you the knowledge you need to give your iPod the props it deserves by integrating it into your car's interior. Once you've completed this hack, your iPod will have a permanent place in your car, integrated with the car's electrical systems. Take a look at Figure 1-23 and get pumped up!

This hack involves some dangerous chemicals and materials. Make sure you observe extreme caution and care when handling them.

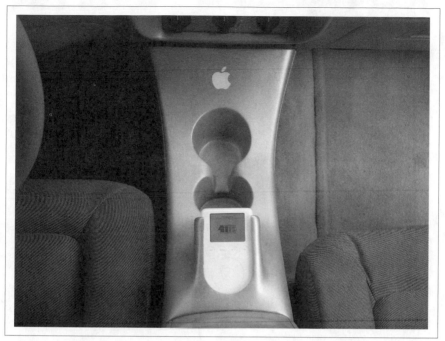

Figure 1-23. An iPod integrated into the car's console

Gathering the Supplies

Here's a list of the materials you will need and where you can purchase them. Materials should cost you $400–$500:

CompUSA or the Apple Store

- Monster iCable for iPod (with stereo mini-jack to RCA jacks)
- Belkin car charger

Alcone Theatrical Supply (http://www.alconeco.com/frame_popular.html)

- Klean Klay (at least 10–12 1-lb bars)
- Ultracal 30 plaster (25 pounds)
- Loose-weave burlap (2–3 yards)

Burman Industries (http://www.burmanfoam.com)

- Sculpting tools
- One-gallon mixing tub or one-gallon bucket
- X-acto knife
- Dental acrylic (polymer and monomer)
- Large bristle brushes

- Plastic eyedroppers
- Rubber mold bands

Smooth-On (http://www.smooth-on.com/default.htm)

- Universal mold release spray
- Smoothcast 305 two-part plastic (one-gallon kit)
- Oomoo 25 two-part silicone (one-gallon kit)
- URE-FIL plastic filler (one pound)

Fiber Optic Products (http://www.fiberopticproducts.com)

- Bright white 3-mm LED
- 4 feet of 1-mm unjacketed fiber-optic cable

Local hardware store

- Large piece of particle board (slightly larger than your console)
- Masking tape
- Blue painters tape
- Black weather-stripping (if your car uses it on your existing console)
- Flat black spray paint
- Soldering gun
- Roll of solder
- Screwdriver
- Black electrical tape
- Dremel tool with various sanding and cutting bits
- Sandpaper (various grits)
- Electric drill
- Silicone caulk and caulk gun
- Four 1"×12" boards, about 3 feet long each (will be cut later)
- 2" screws
- Rubber gloves
- Dust masks
- 1-mm drill bit

Grocery store

- Vaseline
- Rolling pin
- Plastic mixing spoons
- Popsicle sticks

- Wax paper cups
- Rubber spatula
- plastic wrap

Pep Boys Automotive (or a similar auto supply store)

- Automotive plasticoat spray paint to match your interior
- Dual-outlet cigarette-lighter adapter
- Dual LEDs with cigarette-lighter plug

Fabric store

- 1/8" foam rubber pad (gray)

Other

- Apple sticker (if you plan to add a backlit logo). Apple gives you a couple free stickers when you buy a computer; if you threw them out or already used them elsewhere, check out eBay (*http://www.ebay.com*) or Redlightrunner (*http://www.redlightrunner.com*).

Creating the Design

The first step in this process is a simple one. Look for the spot in your car that will best house your iPod, and then come up with a design.

 Take into consideration that you will have a few wires to run, so make sure there will be room somewhere underneath.

I chose my center console, shown in Figure 1-24, simply because it was a large area with unused space and could be removed rather easily.

You can sketch out your concept, or simply dive right in with clay and start sculpting until you have the shape you want. I prefer to sketch first, but that's not necessary. Begin roughing out your design in clay. Concentrate on the position of the iPod, and what will be most comfortable for you when operating it.

Once you have your basic shape in clay, you need to create a place for the iPod to sit (or lie), where it will connect to the charger. For this, you will need your actual iPod or iPod mini. Wrap your iPod with plastic wrap, completely covering it, and then tape it shut. Wrap tape around it a few more times, until you have about a 1/16" thickness. You need to do this to ensure that your iPod can slide freely in and out of whatever space you create for it in your final piece. Once you have cut out an area for the iPod to fit into, slide the iPod into the space, pushing gently to make an indentation in the clay.

Figure 1-24. My center console before I started the project

Make sure the walls around your iPod are fairly snug, but not so tight that it can't be pulled out, as shown in Figure 1-25. Once you are satisfied, you can pull the iPod out of the clay, taking care not to destroy the enclosure you created.

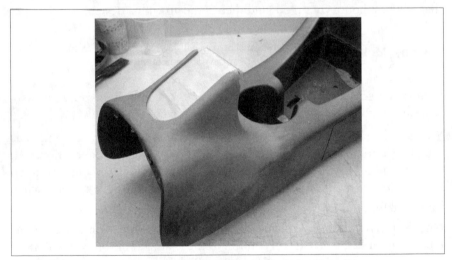

Figure 1-25. Fitting the new enclosure for the second-generation iPod

 The iPod is encased in plastic wrap and masking tape to ensure its protection, while at the same time creating a slightly larger space for easier insertion and removal of the iPod in the final casting.

Continue to fine-tune your sculpture, smoothing out and shaping the clay to fit your design. To ensure that your iPod fits in your final piece, slide the iPod into your enclosure every so often while you continue to sculpt. When you are satisfied with your creation, place your console on a large, flat board, making sure there is at least 5" from the edge of the console to the edge of the board on all sides. Rest the console on something flat to raise it up about half an inch from the board. You will need to build a wall completely surrounding it, and block off any sections that allow access underneath your sculpture to hold the silicone needed to take the mold of your sculpture.

Next, take a lump of clay and, using a rolling pin, roll out a large piece, keeping it about 1/4" thick. Cut this into strips, trimming off the ends. Repeat this until you have about 12 strips. Place the strips around the bottom of your console, pressing them firmly to lock the clay in place. The weight of the silicone will press against the clay, and any silicone that is able to leak around the clay and under your console will make it very hard to de-mold. Once all the sections on your console are blocked off with clay, cut your boards and place them around your console, leaving at least 1" around the perimeter of your console. The height of the boards must be at least 1" above the highest point of your sculpture or console. Lock the boards in place using the 2" screws, then take your silicone caulk and seal all the gaps and edges along the outside of your wall. Allow it to dry for 30 minutes.

Taking a Mold

You are now ready to take a mold of your creation. Using the mold release, spray your console and sculpture, making sure to cover every square inch. Now spray the insides of your walls and the board on which your console is sitting. Mix up the silicone using a one part A–to–one part B ratio. Don't worry if you don't make enough the first time; silicone will stick to itself, and you can always add another layer to fill up the mold if you need to. Pour in the silicone at the lowest point of your sculpture and let it rise on its own. This will help to fill in the small crevices and push out any trapped air. When the silicone is covering your sculpture by at least 1", you can stop and let it cure. The cure time for the Oomoo 25 silicone is 75 minutes, but cure times vary, so check the directions that came with yours if you did not purchase this type.

Now, you must build a two-part plaster support shell to hold the shape of your silicone mold. Begin by removing the screws holding the boards together. Pull gently but firmly to release the boards from the silicone. Coat the silicone with a thin layer of Vaseline, continuing down to the board on which your sculpture is lying. Now, take your burlap and cut it into strips. Make about 25 12"×5" strips, 12 8"×5" strips, and 6 6"×3" strips. Fill your bucket with approximately four cups of lukewarm water, and begin adding your plaster. Add a little at a time, sifting it with your hands.

When you begin getting small white areas, or *islands*, you have added just about enough plaster. Add a little more, and then mix it up. You should have a pancake batter-like consistency. To make the first half of your shell, take one of the larger burlap strips and dip it into the plaster, fully submerging it. Pull it out and wring off some of the excess plaster. Now, fold it in half lengthwise and lay it on top of your silicone mold directly in the center, dividing the mold in half lengthwise, as shown in Figure 1-26.

Figure 1-26. The silicone mold with one half of its plaster support shell

Continue laying the strips down, going from one side of the mold to the other, until you have built a wall about 1" high. Then, begin laying more strips without folding them, until the left side of your mold is completely covered in about 2" of burlap strips. Let the plaster set up and dry. It will become very warm when it sets, so be careful not to touch it.

Once the plaster cools, begin brushing a thick coat of Vaseline all over the inside edge of your plaster shell, as shown in Figure 1-27. This prevents the next coat of plaster from sticking to the first, making the two halves easier to separate.

Now, repeat the burlap layering process, this time covering the right side to make the second half. Let the plaster set up and dry.

When the second half is cool to the touch, you can separate the two halves. Use a screwdriver to pry apart the plaster until it becomes loose enough to remove by hand. Be careful not to pull too hard and crack the shell. Set the two halves aside for now, as shown in Figure 1-28.

Figure 1-27. Brushing a layer of Vaseline on the first half of the plaster shell

Figure 1-28. The plaster shell after it has been separated from the silicone mold

Removing the Mold

It is time to de-mold your sculpture. With the plaster shell removed, work your fingers carefully under the edges of the silicone until it comes loose from the bottom board. If necessary, use an X-acto knife to cut the silicone free from the board. Pick up the entire silicone mold and flip it upside down. Now you must peel the strips of clay from the silicone until you have access to your original console. Again, work your fingers around the edges of the silicone, prying it gently from your console. It should release very easily. Carefully pull the console from the silicone. You now have a perfect negative of your piece!

Cleaning out the mold is almost always necessary. You can simply take the mold outside and spray it down with a garden hose, but use a gentle setting, because a hard stream could damage the silicone. When the mold is completely dry, you need to place it back into its plaster shell. Place the silicone mold into one half of the plaster shell, making sure it is the correct half. Bring the other plaster half together with the first, closing it around the silicone. Strap the halves together with two large rubber mold bands. Your mold should look like Figure 1-29.

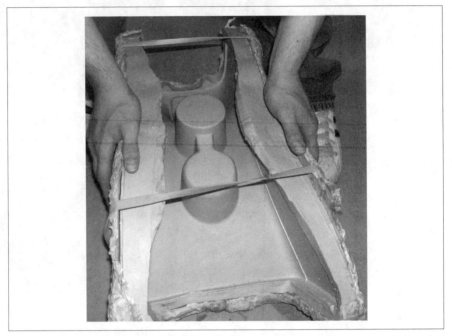

Figure 1-29. The silicone mold after it has been encased in its plaster support shell and bound with rubber mold bands

Spray the inside of the mold thoroughly with the universal mold release. Repeat to ensure proper coverage.

Coating with Plastic

Now, it's time to pour in your first coat of plastic. The amount of plastic to mix depends on the size of your mold. The console I made took approximately 1 1/2 cups of plastic to cover the entire surface area with a thin layer.

Mix the plastic according to the directions, using equal parts of the A and B chemicals. Mix thoroughly and pour it in the mold. Pick up your mold and tilt it slowly from side to side, turning it around as you do to cover the entire surface area of the mold. Dump the excess into your mixing container, wait about 30 seconds, then pour it back in, repeating the process until the plastic begins to set up.

Wait about 30 minutes for the plastic to cure. Mix up about two more batches of plastic, repeating the last process and waiting 30 minutes between each coat. When the third coat is cured, mix up another batch of plastic, this time adding a filler to thicken it up, as shown in Figure 1-30. The filler helps to lighten the weight while adding density to the final casting.

Figure 1-30. A layer of thickened plastic being added to the mold

Pour a cup of part A into your mixing container. Add a few spoonfuls of the URE-FIL filler, until the mixture becomes pasty. Add a cup of part B, and mix thoroughly. Pour it into your mold, turning and tilting it to fill in all the gaps and crevices until the mixture begins to harden. Wait 30 minutes.

Repeat this process two more times, waiting 30 minutes between each layer. You can add as many layers as you want, depending on the thickness you desire. After the last coat is cured, you can remove the piece from the silicone mold. Remove it gently, because silicone can tear if stretched too far. Your console should resemble Figure 1-31.

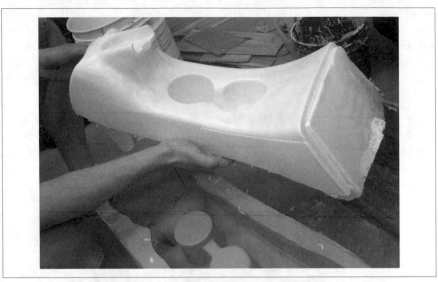

Figure 1-31. The final casting after being removed from the mold

Sanding, Painting, and Cleaning Up

You must now trim and clean the edges of your piece, using a Dremel tool and sandpaper, as shown in Figure 1-32. A clean edge is important for a matching fit back into your car.

Figure 1-32. Using a Dremel tool to trim and sand the excess plastic from the edges of the casting

After the edges are clean, sand the piece until you achieve a smooth surface. Start with a coarse sandpaper, 80–100 grit, and work your way up to 300–400 grit. If you are planning to backlight a logo in your piece, you will need to sand down the area on the inside of your piece where your logo will be placed. This will allow the light to shine through. Be careful not to sand down too far! Use the Dremel tool to cut out a space for the dock connector to fit into where it will connect with your iPod, as shown in Figure 1-33.

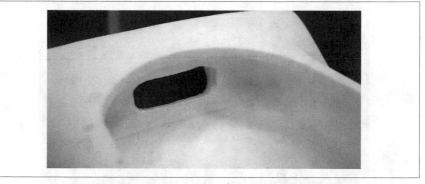

Figure 1-33. Cutting an opening just large enough for your dock connector to fit into

Place the iPod where it will sit or lie, push the dock connector through the hole you made, and connect it to your iPod. Mix some dental acrylic and cover the back side of the connector to hold it in place. When it is hard, remove the iPod and mix up another small amount of the dental acrylic, using slightly more of the monomer for a thinned-down mix. Use an eyedropper to fill in the gap around the connector, as shown in Figure 1-34.

Let it harden, and then sand as needed. On either side of the connector, drill two small holes the size of the fiber-optic cable you will insert for lighting up that space, as shown in Figure 1-35.

Wipe down the piece with a damp cloth to remove excess dust. Before you start painting, you need to tape off the areas you don't want to be painted. I chose to paint the enclosure where the iPod lies a glossy off-white. Tape up the connector if you choose to paint this area. After putting a few coats on that section and letting them dry completely, I taped off that whole section and applied the Apple logo sticker (to be removed later) so I could begin painting the rest of the console a light silver-gray to match my interior. Light-colored metallic car paint is slightly translucent, unless applied in numerous, heavy coats. I chose to use a darker metallic charcoal gray as a base color, and then paint over that with the lighter color. This also helped to block any light from coming through the area around the outside of the backlit Apple logo that I added.

After you've applied a few coats of paint, let it dry for about two hours, and then remove the tape and the Apple sticker. Cut a section of the foam rubber

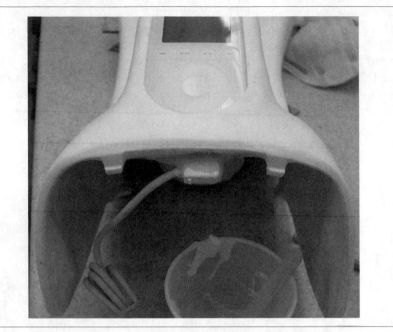

Figure 1-34. Using dental acrylic to seal the dock connector in place

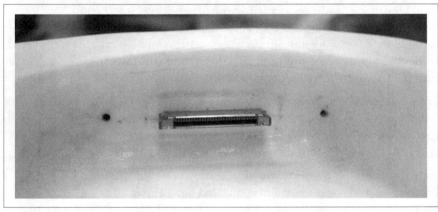

Figure 1-35. Access holes for fiber-optic cable insertion

padding to fit the surface of the enclosure, so the iPod has a soft base to slide in and out on. Use spray adhesive to attach it. You can now add the lighting.

Cut off one of the cigarette-lighter adapter's blue LEDs, and solder on a bright white LED in its place. The white LED is for the Apple logo, while the remaining blue one will be used to light the interior of the iPod's enclosure. Make a separate enclosure for the white LED out of a spray paint can lid, to block any light from escaping through the sides of the console and at the same time direct it toward the Apple logo. Drill a hole in the center of the lid, and then use dental acrylic to hold it in place behind the logo. Insert the light into the hole in the center and tape it up. Then, take the fiber-optic cable and cut two pieces about two feet long. Push them into the small holes drilled next to the dock connector, and glue them in place. Turn them into the blue LED and tape them to it.

Hooking up the Electronics and Installing the Console

The final step in this process is to hook up all your electronics and install the console. Take all of your materials, the console, and any tools you will need into the car with you. First, you need to connect your dual-outlet cigarette-lighter adapter, which can be purchased from your local auto supply store. This can be done a few different ways, but the easiest way for me was to just disconnect the wires from the existing dashboard lighter outlet and reconnect them to the outlet I'd purchased. Since I don't smoke and I don't use a cell phone, I really didn't have any use for that outlet. Besides, many cars have an extra one on the passenger-side panel, down by the floor. If you find that you do need your outlet, you can purchase a separate lighter with a wiring kit to run off of the existing outlet. Connect the dual lighter adapter to the new outlet. You can now connect the car charger to one of them and your LED lighting to the other.

Connecting the iPod to your car stereo might pose a problem for some. Not all car stereos accept auxiliary input from an external source. Unfortunately, there is no way around this. You simply must have the correct type of stereo. Quite a few stereos now feature front-mounted RCA inputs, but you may have to purchase a separate adapter, as I did. If so, you'll need an IP-Bus interconnector with left and right RCA inputs. The IP-Bus connects to the rear of the stereo and features two RCA jacks that protrude from the unit, allowing an external audio source (such as a CD changer or an iPod) to be connected. I chose to use the iCable, which is basically a stereo mini-jack that converts to dual RCA jacks. I plugged the stereo mini-jack into the Belkin car charger and ran the two RCAs to the adapter on the car stereo. The iPod is now connected directly to your car stereo (some car stereos require manually changing the menu to accept an auxiliary input). After double-checking that everything is connected and functioning properly, attach the console and put the interior back together.

The Final Installation

Now that your new console is connected and functioning, enjoy it, but be very careful when driving! As beautiful as this installation might look (see Figures 1-36 and 1-37, don't give your iPod more attention than the road

—*Jesse Melchior*

Figure 1-36. The final results

HACK #12   Integrate the iPod Remote with Your Car ◍◍◍

Sure, the new BMW/Apple integrated iPod/car solution is cool—if you have a BMW. If you don't, you can still integrate your iPod into your car's electronic system in no time.

When I'm driving, I want easy access to a wide variety of music that doesn't take up a lot of space. The iPod is an almost perfect solution, and third-party vendors offer a wide range of accessories that make integrating an iPod into your vehicle easy.

Still, controlling the iPod while driving can be awkward and distracting. My car, like many others, has steering wheel buttons that can be used to control the factory-installed radio and CD player. With this hack, you will be able to use these buttons to control your iPod from your steering wheel. How? By hacking the iPod remote.

Anatomy of an iPod Remote

It's always fun to take things apart, so let's start with that. I have a generation 2 (G2) iPod, which means that it has a standard FireWire connector instead of a dock, and it uses a different connector for the remote than the latest iPods do. The shiny exterior that looks like metal really is metal—

Figure 1-37. The iPod at night

don't try to bend it! Remove the white plastic portion (the clip and back of the remote) by using a small screwdriver to pry it out of the case, as in Figure 1-38. The best place to do this is on the same side as the hold switch, just past the green dot, by the *b* in the phrase "assembled in China." The PC board (including the headphone jack) will remain in the metal case.

There are two pins in the metal case that hold the PC board. These don't bend and make removing the PC board somewhat difficult.

Although the connector at the end of the G2 iPod's remote differs from that of the G3 or G4 iPod, both cables carry six wires: three analog signals are fed directly to the headphone jack, and three go to a small microcontroller and handle the remote-control functions. To reduce noise, the analog and digi-

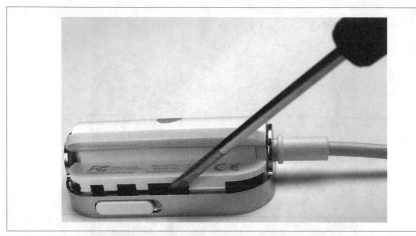

Figure 1-38. Opening the remote (be gentle!)

tal grounds are kept separate in the remote. The extra pin on the later iPod's connector is not connected to any wires in the cable. See Figure 1-39 for a peek at the button side and chip side of the opened remote.

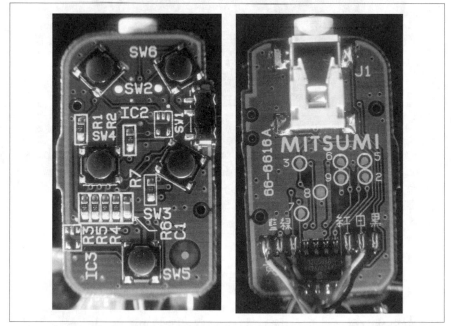

Figure 1-39. The button (left) and chip (right) sides of the remote

The heart of the remote is a general-purpose Microchip 12C508A microcontroller. This is a simple self-contained computer designed to execute only one simple program. This tiny chip has eight pins: two are for power (3.0–5.5 volts) and six are general-purpose input/output (I/O). Most microprocessors require a reset signal and a clock, but this chip generates those internally so as not to waste precious pins. Programs may occupy up to 512 words of memory and use 25 bytes of RAM. Two other unpopulated five-pin integrated circuits (ICs) are on the button side of the circuit board, but it's not clear what their purpose is.

Using a multimeter, we can trace all the signals from the connector back to the processor. Microchip's web site (*http://www.microchip.com*; search for "12C508A") has the datasheet for the microcontroller that tells us which pins are used for power and ground. The last pin goes through a 1kΩ resistor (R7) to reach pin 7 of the IC, a general-purpose I/O pin. Table 1-2 shows the wire colors and signals for G2 and G3/G4 iPods.

Table 1-2. Wire colors and signals for G2 and G3 iPods

Wire color	G2 iPod	G3/G4 iPod	Signal
Black	Tip	Tip	Audio, left
White	Ring (next to tip)	Ring	Audio, right
Red	Ring 2 (third ring from end)	Ring 2	Audio ground
Green	Sleeve (fourth ring from end)	Pin 1	Data to iPod
Blue	Inner ring	Pin 4	Power to remote, +3.3V
Yellow	Outermost ring	Pin 3	Digital ground
		Pin 2	Serial port transmit signal from the iPod to the remote
		Sleeve	No connect/unknown

Since only one pin is used to tell the iPod which pin is pressed, the data must be transmitted serially—that is, the message is sent one bit at a time at a preset speed, and with a known pattern so that it can be decoded. It's similar to Morse Code, and if the data was sent slowly enough, you would be able to see it turn a light on and off. But, since this data is sent much faster than a person could interpret, you must use an oscilloscope to make a plot of the voltage on the pin.

Pressing a button causes the remote to send a stream of data similar to that illustrated in Figure 1-40, but varying slightly depending on which button is pressed.

Although the G2 and G3/G4 iPods' remotes share the same circuit boards, the processors are programmed differently, and the G3/G4 remote uses a slightly different protocol to talk to the iPod.

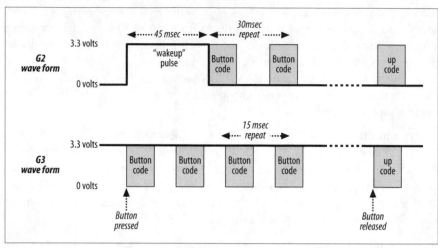

Figure 1-40. Remote wave forms

The iPod uses a voltage of 3.3 volts to represent a logical 1, while 0 volts is used to represent a logical 0. A standard RS-232 serial port uses −12 volts for 1 and +12 volts for 0, so don't try connecting an RS-232 port to an iPod without some special circuitry to change the voltage levels!

Second-Generation Button Codes

The G2 iPod's remote most likely uses specialized hardware to detect the initial 45-millisecond pulse and wake the processor out of a low-power sleep. It then listens for the specific button codes to determine which button is being pressed. Each G2 code depicted in Figure 1-41 is a three-byte serial message, sent one bit at a time every 104 milliseconds (9,600 bits per second, or *baud*).

To help the iPod identify the message reliably, a start bit (0) is issued before each byte, and two stop bits (1) follow. Some systems use a simple error-checking code known as a *parity bit* before the stop bits, but the iPod does not. In standard serial-port terminology, this is referred to as *8N2*, because each byte has 8 data bits, no parity is used, and there are two stop bits. Each byte is transmitted with the least-significant bit first. Figure 1-41 shows the results.

Most serial ports remain at the 1 state when idle. The G3 iPod's remote follows this convention, but the G2 iPod does not: the 1 state is used only for the wake-up pulse and for a few clock cycles before the start of each message burst. Most serial ports would see the 1 to 0 transition at the end of

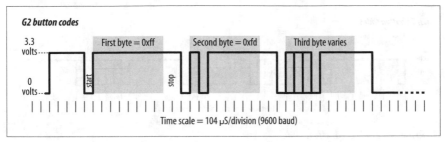

Figure 1-41. G2 button codes

each burst as either a malformed byte (detected because it won't have a 1 where the stop bit is expected) or a special signal called a *break*.

Third- and Fourth-Generation Button Codes

The G3/G4 iPod's remote uses a slightly different protocol than the G2 iPod. The wakeup pulse has been eliminated, and the G3/G4 hardware has a lower-power serial port that can be left on while the processor sleeps. The baud rate has been upped to 19,200 baud, while the message format now uses just one stop bit (8N1). The code repetition rate has also been doubled to 66 times per second, which should allow more precise control. However, the most interesting changes are in the new seven-byte code:

- The first two bytes, 0xFF and 0x55, were probably chosen because they are interesting patterns: 0xFF has the lowest possible frequency signal (a 9-bit high pulse), while 0x55 has the highest frequency (alternating 1s and 0s). A sophisticated receiver could use these pulses to measure and adapt to the transmitter's rate, allowing both components to use lower-cost, lower-precision frequency references.

- Instead of a numeric code indicating which button has been pushed, the buttons are bit-mapped. This means that the remote can now indicate that more than one button has been pressed by setting more than one bit. The presence of a 0x00 before the sixth byte suggests that a total of 16 buttons may be accommodated by this protocol.

- The messages are protected from errors by a checksum. The last byte varies so that the sum of bytes 3–7 will form an even multiple of 0x100.

Figure 1-42 shows the button codes for the generation 3 and 4 iPods.

Table 1-3 lists the three-byte and seven-byte button release codes for the G2 and G3/G4 remotes.

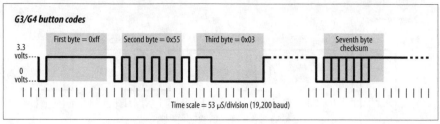

Figure 1-42. G3/G4 button codes

Table 1-3. Button release codes for G2 and G3/G4 iPods

Button	G2 three-byte code	G3/G4 seven-byte code
PLAY/PAUSE	0xFF 0xFD 0xF1	0xFF 0x55 0x03 0x02 0x00 0x01 0xFA
VOL+	0xFF 0xFD 0xF2	0xFF 0x55 0x03 0x02 0x00 0x02 0xF9
VOL-	0xFF 0xFD 0xF3	0xFF 0x55 0x03 0x02 0x00 0x04 0xF7
SKIP>>	0xFF 0xFD 0xF4	0xFF 0x55 0x03 0x02 0x00 0x08 0xF3
<<SKIP	0xFF 0xFD 0xF5	0xFF 0x55 0x03 0x02 0x00 0x10 0xEB
Button release	0xFF 0xFD 0xF0	0xFF 0x55 0x03 0x02 0x00 0x00 0xFB

Bit-Banging Versus Serial Port

If you read the datasheet for the Microchip microcontroller carefully, you'll notice that it does not have a serial port. Yet, we've seen that the output mostly looks like a standard serial output, and the iPod (which has a built-in serial port) recognizes that signal.

The trick lies in the microcontroller's blazing speed: it can execute 1,000,000 instructions per second. To generate serial output at 9,600 bits per second, the code must be carefully written so that it takes exactly 104 instructions to generate each new bit. The program to do this is relatively simple, and in fact it spends most of its time idly waiting for the exact moment to release the new bit.

The technique is called *bit-banging*, because the output bit is manipulated (*banged*) under direct software control. Since many low-end processors are sufficiently fast enough to do this, it's often cheaper for a simple device to implement a serial port in software rather than hardware. The down side to this technique is that while the processor is carefully controlling its output, it's too busy to do anything else. In the iPod's case, there is plenty of time to check for button presses during the relatively long pauses between code bursts.

Implementation

My car, like many modern cars, uses a single wire (called the *bus*) to communicate serially between many of its different systems. This approach saves wiring, which in turn lowers weight, lowers cost, and increases reliability. There is no dominant standard yet, but many manufacturers use the same general protocol over a range of their models. My steering wheel contains a small microcontroller similar in concept to the one in the iPod's remote: both monitor buttons and output codes to a serial bus. Controlling the iPod from the steering wheel is a simple matter of listening for the steering wheel's output (while ignoring other messages on the bus) and translating that into a format that the iPod can understand.

After searching on the Web, I found specifications for my car's bus on OpenBMW.org (*http://www.openbmw.org*). Most BMWs built since about 1996 use a bus called the I-Bus. It is a single white wire marked with a red and yellow stripe, and it's accessible from a number of places in the car. For experimenting, it's often easiest to find this in the trunk (where a CD changer would connect), but this hack's final installation will tap into the harness that connects the radio.

Electrically, this bus can be considered a simple serial port operating at 9,600 baud, with eight data bits, even parity, and one stop bit (8E1). A logical 0 is represented with 0 volts, and a logical 1 is nominally represented with 12 volts (a simple resistor divider chain can reduce this to a voltage safe for our microcontroller translator).

While the general format of the packets sent over the bus is more complicated, the data we need to look for from the steering wheel is relatively simple. Pushing or releasing a button on the steering wheel generates one of the messages shown in Table 1-4.

Table 1-4. Messages sent by various button presses

Action	Message (hex)
Pressing TRK+	50 04 68 3B 01 06
Releasing TRK+	50 04 68 3B 21 26
Pressing TRK-	50 04 68 3B 08 0F
Releasing TRK-	50 04 68 3B 28 2F

Since the radio already responds to the volume-control buttons, we can ignore them.

There is a little more to it than that, though, because a good program will listen to all the messages on the bus so that it can keep in sync with the start of each message. Otherwise, if one of the codes above just happened to appear in the middle of a longer, totally unrelated message, the iPod might erroneously react.

I decided to use a different microcontroller for my project than Apple did for their remote. For a simple project like this, there isn't much difference between microcontrollers; for me, it came down to availability of programming tools, personal preference, and what I had on hand. Most major manufacturers will provide example code that either controls a built-in serial port or emulates one by bit-banging; this can serve as a good basis on which to build the real code.

The chip I used, an Atmel ATtiny12-8PI, is comparable in specifications to the Microchip controller used in the remote. If we stop listening to the car's bus while sending a command to the iPod, we might miss an important message (such as "buckle up"), so we need to simultaneously transmit and receive. Unfortunately, this chip doesn't have a built-in hardware serial port, and it's difficult to do these two things simultaneously with bit-banging. Using two of these relatively cheap ($2) processors is a compromise solution that makes programming it much simpler.

A 7805 voltage regulator converts the car's 12-volt power down to the 5 volts that can safely be used by the processors, while two capacitors help reduce noise that could cause malfunctions. Two resistor dividers translate higher voltages down to lower ones: one knocks the 0–12V I-Bus down to 0–5V for the first processor, while the second brings the 0–5V output of the second processor down to 0–3.3V. The first processor just listens for the messages of interest on the I-Bus. It then recreates the state of the steering wheel buttons on the "track-" and "track+" wires: +5 volts indicates that the button is pressed, 0 volts means it's not. The second processor monitors these and outputs the proper codes to the iPod. Since the timing of these two inputs isn't critical, this works well with bit-banging. This give us the final remote schematic, shown in Figure 1-43.

As a finishing touch, the second processor will sense when the iPod is connected (using the +3.3V power line that would normally power the remote) and use this to issue a series of phantom volume-up keypresses until maximum volume is reached. This way, the sound will be at a consistent level, so that the radio's knob is the only thing that affects the actual volume.

The Future

The third- and fourth-generation iPods (including the mini) have a more robust remote connector with one or two additional pins that appear to currently be unused. My best guess is that these mystery pins, with the proper firmware upgrade, will provide some sort of textual "currently playing song" output. This could be incorporated into a fancier remote control with a small screen of its own, or it could be used to provide titles to a car stereo's display.

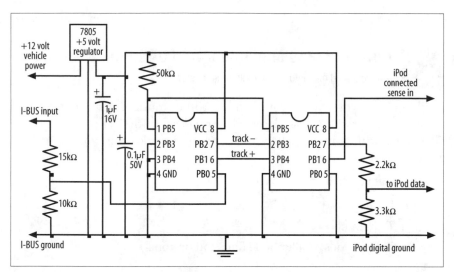

Figure 1-43. The hacked remote schematic

Resources for Hacking Your Remote

I document the original hack on my web page (*http://www.maushammer.com/ systems/ipod-remote/ipod-remote.html*). You can download the program I used to control the iPod from this web page.

BMW uses a bus called the I-Bus to control noncritical devices, including the radio. More information is available at *http://www.openbmw.org*.

Other car manufacturers and radio manufacturers use other buses. Here are some of the major ones:

- Alpine Ai-Net/MBUS: *http://kiora.ath.cx/alpine/*
- Sony UniLink: *http://www.cus.org.uk/~cleggy/*
- JVC J-Link: *http://www.jvc-victor.co.jp/english/tech/jlip/index.htm*

You can find the datasheet for the microcontroller used in the iPod by searching for "12C508A" at *http://www.microchip.com*.

You'll find the datasheet for Atmel's AVR ATtiny12-8PI microcontroller at *http://www.atmel.com/products/avr/*.

The 7805 voltage regulator is a common part made by many manufacturers. National Semiconductor has a datasheet at *http://www.national.com/pf/LM/ LM78M05.htm*.

Dension (*http://www.densionusa.com*) sells an I-Bus-to-iPod adaptor that pretty closely matches the functionality of this hack.

—John Maushammer

HACK #13 Turn Your iPod Mini into a Radio Station ●◗●

Turn your iPod mini into a mini radio broadcaster.

With an iPod, you have in your hands a ton of music. Ever wanted to be a DJ at a radio station? Just add an FM broadcaster (the iTrip mini) to your iPod and, with a little hackery, you can be broadcasting your own little local-area radio station.

Here's what you'll need for this hack:

- An iPod mini
- An iTrip mini
- Additional iPods, iTalks, and iTrips (all optional)

Getting Started

To become your own pirate broadcast station, you'll first need to increase the range and signal of your iTrip mini. It's not obvious, but there is an antenna built inside the iTrip mini. All you need to do is remove the top sticker-like protective covering that hides the antenna and then, using tweezers or your fingernails, pull out the antenna. I've found that this produces a 20% to 30% increase of range, on average. Be warned, though, that this likely voids the warranty.

The iTrip mini allows you to install and broadcast to all the stations on the dial. Make sure you've installed all the stations, because when you're on the go you might need to be able to switch to other options. Remember, the iTrip is an FM broadcasting device, intended to broadcast 10 to 30 feet to an FM radio.

Next, choose your broadcast. It can be any song or a spoken-word MP3; don't worry, I have a few suggestions. A lot depends on the situation you're in.

Pirate Broadcasts

I usually keep a couple tracks of silence or calming music ready to go. Ever get stuck at a stop light for 10 minutes with the dude in the next car blasting a song you hate on the radio? With the super-easy iPod interface, you can quickly get to the station he's on and send over whatever you want. Gentle ocean waves or birdsong usually works well.

While many of the suggestions in this hack are for pure fun, please make sure to check with your state laws regarding radio frequency use.

Another great use of this hack is at a street party. Place your iPod mini on your lawn, and broadcast to any boom box within 10–30 feet. Suddenly, your neighborhood is alive with music, all from your iPod mini. Inside your house, walk from room to room with your iPod mini and antenna and, as long as your boom boxes or stereos in each room are on and set to the correct frequency, music will follow you around the house. For more on music throughout your house, check out "Stream Music with AirPort Express" [Hack #26].

If you've ever gone to the gym, or stared into one from the outside, you may have noticed that the TVs are muted and set to broadcast on specific FM frequencies. Folks then tune in their radio headsets to whatever stations they like to listen to as they exercise. Now, we're not suggesting you go around and broadcast over CNN or anything, but we think broadcasting "Aliens have landed today; the President and UN will be making an announcement immediately" could be quite fun.

There are other times where you simply need to broadcast back. Let's say you're at the park, enjoying a nice quiet day with your family, and then someone comes along blasting the radio. We've found broadcasting a silent track tends to work nicely; sure, you need to be within 30 to 40 feet of the offender, but no one will even suspect that you're usurping their FM broadcast.

Advanced Broadcasting Techniques

If you use the iTalk (Griffin's voice recorder accessory) with a G2, G3, or G4 iPod, you can record your pirate broadcast on the fly. Simply pop in the iTrip and start broadcasting. Pretending to be an omnipotent being and asking folks to build a waterproof car and drive across the English Channel carrying two of every gadget usually gets some interesting reactions.

—*Phillip Torrone*

Use Your iPod as a Dictaphone ◍◍◍

With a couple handy additions from Belkin, you can turn your iPod into a Dictaphone.

In this age of voice-recognition technology, the almighty Dictaphone is still, well, almighty. Dictating to a computer will still render your eloquent speech garbled, even though great strides have been made in voice recognition. When the iPod first came out, many people thought that because it looked like a Dictaphone, it must be one. Sure enough, when a newer version of the iPod's firmware came out, irreverent hackers like you and me noticed that there was a voice-recording ability (albeit only six seconds) embedded deep in the iPod's firmware. This discovery was a hint of great things to come. With this hack, your iPod can become a Dictaphone extraordinaire.

Belkin makes two recording products for the iPod. The first is called the Voice Recorder for iPod (*http://catalog.belkin.com/IWCatProductPage.process? Merchant_Id=&Section_Id=201526&pcount=&Product_Id=158384*; $59.99). It is a self-contained unit; just plug it into your iPod, and start talking into the built-in microphone. The second product, the Universal Microphone Adapter (*http://catalog.belkin.com/IWCatProductPage.process?Merchant_ Id=& Product_Id=169368*; $39.99), has no built-in microphone. Instead, you plug a microphone into it.

Another key difference between the two is the quality of the recorded audio. The Voice Recorder saves mono WAV files, making it appropriate for (as its name portends) voice recording. The Universal Microphone Adapter saves 16-bit audio at 8 kHz, which, while not exactly studio quality, is much better than mono audio.

> The two Belkin voice recorder products will record hundreds of hours of audio. If you are a reporter working your own beat, you can use your iPod to record interviews, store digital photos **[Hack #3]**, *and* listen to music in between.

If you plan on using the iPod to record your epiphanies or soliloquies, the Voice Recorder is probably your best bet. If you want to record interviews or meetings, the omnidirectional built-in microphone on the Voice Recorder will certainly suffice. However, using a microphone plugged into the Universal Microphone Adapter will yield clearer results, particularly in circumstances where the room is large.

Here are the specs for the Voice Recorder for iPod:

- iPod creates audio files in mono (true) WAV format
- Records personal memos, notes, and interviews easily, on the go, with high-quality, omnidirectional microphone
- Features 16-mm speaker for quick playback
- Attaches securely to your iPod through remote/headphone connector
- Indicates recording status of Voice Recorder with LED indicator

And here are the specs for the Universal Microphone Adapter:

- Designed for use with non–battery-powered microphones
- Fits any audio microphone with a 3.5-mm plug
- Features 3.5-mm audio out jack for headphones or speakers
- Adjusts microphone sensitivity easily with three-level gain switch
- Includes real-time recording level LED indicator
- Records 16-bit audio at 8 kHz

Both devices interface with the iPod in a similar fashion. They both work only with generation 3 and later iPods with the dock connector; neither of them works with the iPod mini. The user interface on the iPod is identical for both products.

For the purposes of this hack, let's get the Voice Recorder working. There is no software to install; just plug the adapter into the headphone and remote ports of your iPod. As soon as you plug it in, the interface on your iPod will change to look like Figure 1-44. To begin recording, select Record. A timer will load on your iPod's screen. Once the timer begins, simply speak! While the range of the Voice Recorder is good, you need to be relatively close to the microphone. If you are at a loss for words, you can select Pause at any time. Once you are done recording, select Save.

Figure 1-44. The default Voice Recorder interface

Your audio file will be saved in mono (true) WAV format. One extra feature that the Voice Recorder has is a built-in speaker, so you can listen to what you've recorded. In fact, you can use it to listen to your music, too!

The Belkin products' ease of use extends to transferring the recordings to your computer. In fact, no transferring is required; just open up iTunes, and a playlist appears with all of your recordings. Press Play to listen. If you want to edit your recordings, your best bet is to upgrade to QuickTime Pro, which is available for Macintosh or Windows (*http://www.apple.com/quicktime/ upgrade*; $29.99). If 30 bucks is too steep, check out Audacity (*http:// audacity.sourceforge.net/*; free).

HACK #15 Replace Your Generation 1 or 2 iPod's Battery ⓂⓌⓁ

Breathe some new life into your generation 1 or 2 iPod by replacing its battery.

Much hoopla has been raised about the life, or lack thereof, of the iPod's battery. And while many users of the first 5 GB iPod model are still using the battery with no problem whatsoever, the fact is that batteries do eventually run out of juice. You won't wake up one day to find your battery dead; rather, expect a long, slow descent that involves shorter and shorter battery life between recharges. Eventually, you're going to have to replace the battery.

> This hack shows how to replace the battery for a G1 or G2 iPod. If you have a G3 iPod, see "Replace Your Generation 3 iPod's Battery" **[Hack #16]**. If you have an iPod mini, see "Replace Your iPod Mini's Battery" **[Hack #17]**.

Replacing the battery yourself is a pretty easy task, but if you're the kind of person who frets about dings or if you have no mechanical ability whatsoever, your best bet is to send your iPod to Apple or a quality third-party shop to get the battery replaced. Apple's iPod Battery Replacement Program (*http://www.apple.com/support/ipod/service/battery.html*) will cost you $99.00, plus $6.95 for shipping. Apple will take a week or two to put a new battery in your iPod and return it to you. If you're adventurous, or too impatient to go two weeks without your magical music box, then read on.

Before you get started, you'll need to acquire a new battery for your iPod and one of the following tools:

- A thin, flathead screwdriver; I use a 2.5-mm flat blade made by Wiha of Germany (*http://www.wihatools.com*)
- The PDA Smart plastic disassembly tools
- A guitar pick (the hard plastic kind, not the newer rubberized kind)

Far and away, the best tool for the job is the one supplied by PDA Smart, because it's plastic and won't scratch or mar the original case. Since I'm of the school that a ding here and there adds character to an item, I just use a screwdriver. A guitar pick is easy to get hold of and will get the job done, but it's a pain to work with.

Disclaimer

Apple did not design the iPods to be disassembled. Once they are snapped (or, in the case of the iPod mini, glued) together, Apple essentially considers them to be a disposable item, and warranty/repair work consists of swapping the broken iPod for a new one. For the iPod hacker, this means two things:

- Opening an iPod without causing at least minimal cosmetic damage is very difficult. Before you embark on a journey into your iPod, you need to accept the fact that you're probably going to mar the case. You might get lucky, but chances are, it's going to get dinged up.
- If you break your iPod, you're going to pay for it. Apple charges a flat repair fee of $250 (even for the iPod mini), and there is no source for individual parts. This hack provides very detailed instructions expressly to help you avoid any possible pitfalls with regard to damaging your iPod, but there is always a chance that the patient won't make it through surgery.

The iPod batteries are all standard off-the-shelf units, so it doesn't matter where you buy them. PDASmart.com (*http://www.pdasmart.com*) and ipodbattery.com (*http://www.ipodbattery.com*) are both good sources. PDASmart.com provides both detailed instructions and the plastic disassembly tools noted previously.

Opening the Case

Turn off the iPod and place the hold button on (so orange is showing).

Insert the edge of your tool of choice vertically between the plastic and the metal, next to the FireWire port (as indicated in Figure 1-45, which shows a G1 iPod top). Insert the tool as far as you can, and then slide it up and around the sharp metal upper-left corner of the iPod until it's about 10 mm from the edge. At this point, pry up and release the first of the five clips (on the left side) holding the two case halves together.

Once you've released the first clip, continue to slide the blade down the side of the iPod and the remaining four clips will come apart fairly easily. Check out Figure 1-46 (a G1 iPod) for a view of the clips. With one side of the iPod case released, you can now lift the plastic case half away from the metal portion. With it will come all the electronic components, in one unit. Congratulations; your iPod is now open!

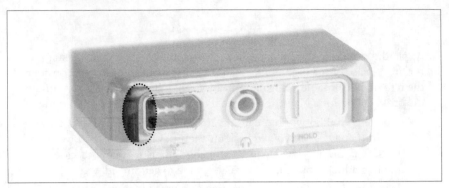

Figure 1-45. Insert the disassembly tool of choice between the plastic and metal just to the right of the FireWire connector

Figure 1-46. The five clips that hold the two case halves together

Removing the Battery

G1 and G2 iPods have the battery attached directly to the hard drive by two strips of rubber featuring some sort of evil adhesive. This stuff sticks! Use your screwdriver or other thin, flat implement of choice to loosen the battery from the hard drive. Try to keep the rubber strips attached to the hard drive and not to the battery.

When it's free of the sticky death grip, disconnect the battery and throw it away.

Installing the New Battery

The new battery will install only one way because of the length of the connecting wires, so plug it in and lay it down on the hard drive. Line it up so one edge isn't hanging off and press it firmly so the adhesive grips it.

Putting It Back Together

Once this is done, you can just snap the metal half of the case back on. Charge up your new battery, and your iPod will have juice again!

—Greg Koenig

HACK #16   Replace Your Generation 3 iPod's Battery ①①①

It's not quite as easy as changing batteries on a Walkman, but you can change your generation 3 iPod's batteries yourself.

The procedure is slightly more complicated with a G3 iPod than it is for a G1 or G2 iPod, but it's still perfectly manageable.

> For more about why you might want to replace your iPod's battery yourself and what your other options are, see "Replace Your Generation 1 or 2 iPod's Battery" **[Hack #15]**. If you think you want to try the operation yourself, be sure to also read the disclaimer at the beginning of that hack.

Here's what you'll need for this hack:

- A thin, flathead screwdriver; I use a 2.5-mm flat blade made by Wiha of Germany (*http://www.wihatools.com*)-
- The PDA Smart plastic disassembly tools
- A guitar pick (the hard plastic kind, not the newer rubberized kind)
- Needle-nose pliers
- A new iPod battery

Far and away, the best tool for the job is the one supplied by PDA Smart, because it's plastic and won't scratch or mar the original case. Since I'm of the school that a ding here and there adds character to an item, I just use a screwdriver. A guitar pick is easy to get hold of and will get the job done, but it's a pain to work with.

The iPod batteries are all standard off-the-shelf units, so it doesn't matter where you buy them. PDASmart.com (*http://www.pdasmart.com*) and ipodbattery.com (*http://www.ipodbattery.com*) are both good sources. PDASmart. com also provides the plastic disassembly tools noted previously.

Opening the iPod

The G3 metal case backs are much tighter than the G1 and G2 iPods' case backs and contain some limited electronic components (the audio port hardware is soldered onto the metal case back). Thus, the metal case half is tethered to the main component board by a very delicate ribbon cable that you should not disconnect; the cable is extremely delicate!

Turn off the iPod and place the hold button on (so orange is showing).

Start on the left side of the iPod. This is very important, because there's another ribbon cable on the right side that you can easily damage when you insert your prying tool between the case halves. I've found that the best place to insert the tool is right next to the Back button (perhaps known as the Rewind button for those of you joining the iPod from analog land) on the iPod's front.

Once you've inserted the tool, pry it up and unclip the middle of the five clips on the left side that are holding the two case halves together. Once that one is unclipped, the other four will come undone rather easily. With the left side free, the two case halves will also come apart easily.

Be careful with the tethered connection between the two halves! Do not stress that ribbon cable too much. I disconnected it to make photography easier, but laying the metal half on a book or just holding it while you perform the rest of the procedure is much safer.

Removing the Hard Drive

With the metal case half unclipped, lay the iPod on a flat surface so the LCD display is facing down and the metal half is to your left. The large metal object you're looking at is the PCMCIA-based hard disk. It is surrounded by a blue Delrin (a high-tech rubber material) shock isolator and is sitting on another blue Delrin shock isolation pad. That second isolation pad has a ribbon cable on it that connects the hard drive with the main board.

Carefully reach under the bottom blue Delrin pad and disconnect the low profile connector for the hard drive. The drive and Delrin pad will still be connected. Figure 1-47 shows a G3 iPod with the main board detached from the main enclosure half.

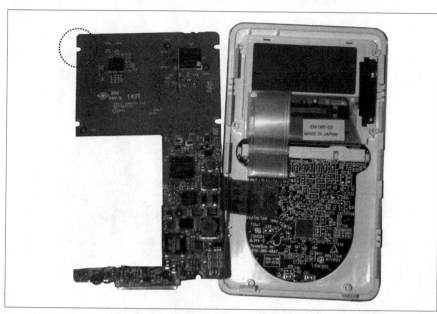

Figure 1-47. Using a screwdriver to lift up the LCD display by inserting it at the indicated notch

Installing the New Battery

The battery is the black plastic rectangular object in the upper-right corner of your iPod. It is not glued in or attached in any way other than by the battery cable. Disconnect this with the needle-nose pliers, and slip the connector cables under the corner of the main board.

Put the fresh battery in place, work the connectors around the main board cable, and plug them in.

Installing the Hard Drive

With the drive out, as shown in Figure 1-48, you can now easily see the shock isolation pad mentioned earlier; it's the big blue thing hanging off the hard drive. The easiest way to get the drive back in is to unplug this pad from the drive itself so you can reconnect the extremely low-profile PCMCIA connector on the main board. Just grab the copper connector on the drive and gently pull it off. Being a PCMCIA connector, it is fairly robust; don't be afraid to tug a bit.

> The low-profile hard drive connector (in the upper-right corner of Figure 1-48, surrounded by black insulating plastic film) and the connector (in the lower-right corner) should not be disconnected.

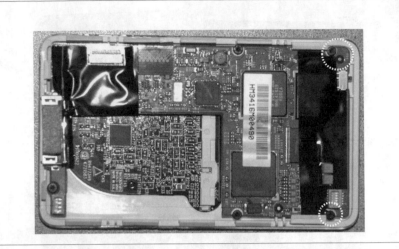

Figure 1-48. The shock isolation pad, hanging from the removed hard drive

Once the drive and isolation pad are apart, connect the ribbon cable on the isolation pad back onto the main board. If you flip the pad over, you will see an extremely low-profile, black, 40-pin connector (yup, I counted!) that will snap into its mate in the lower-right corner of the main board. Snap these two connectors back together. It can be a bit tricky, so just take your time and pay careful attention to the feel; it should positively snap into place. Press it down to ensure a good connection; you don't want to snap the case halves back together only to discover that you didn't connect the drive properly. It's a delicate job, but the low-profile connector is fairly robust, so don't worry about damaging the pins as you blindly slide the two connectors together trying to get them to mate.

With the ribbon cable reconnected and the isolation pad installed, slide the hard drive back onto the copper pin connectors. The iPod does not utilize all of the PCMCIA interface pins, and the connector lines up with a block on the lower right.

Putting It Back Together

Line up the case halves and make sure the battery cable is not going to get pinched between them. Snap them together, and you're done.

—*Greg Koenig*

Replace Your iPod Mini's Battery 🌑🌑🌑

HACK #17

Has your iPod mini run out of gas? You can replace the battery yourself.

If it seems ridiculous to you to send your iPod mini back to Apple (or a qualified third-party shop) just to have a new battery installed, you might want to have a go at doing it yourself. The procedure is similar to that for changing a G1 or G2 iPod's battery **[Hack #15]**. It might sound daunting, but with the right tools and the instructions in this hack, you'll be able to accomplish the task in no time at all.

 Before you get started, be sure to check out the disclaimer in "Replace Your Generation 1 or 2 iPod's Battery" **[Hack #15]**.

Here's what you'll need if you decide to undertake this battery-changing mission:

- A thin, flathead screwdriver; I strongly recommend the Wiha brand (*http://www.wihatools.com*)
- A #000 Phillips screwdriver (Wiha strongly recommended)
- A hair dryer
- Needle-nose pliers (the smaller, the better)
- A new battery

Removing the Plastic End Caps

Turn off your iPod mini and place the hold button on (so orange is showing).

The white plastic end caps on the iPod mini are held in place with an adhesive substance that will give up some of its stick when heated, so use your hair dryer to gently warm up the end caps to make the job much easier. By *gently*, I mean you shouldn't turn the dryer onto High and blast away; start on a low power setting and move the dryer back and forth. You want to avoid changing the iPod's temperature too quickly to avoid even the slightest chance of thermal shock.

Working on one end at a time, once the plastic bits are warm/hot to the touch, use the thin-bladed screwdriver to gently pry up the end caps. Start by inserting the blade at the middle of the enclosure and work your way around. Take your time and be careful not to slip. The top cap is held on with nothing more than the adhesive, but the bottom cap has two plastic tabs on either side. They are relatively strong, but be careful when prying on the edges. The bottom cap also has some tiny plastic standoffs that will probably break off when you remove the cap. I broke off most of them when I disassembled my minis, but it doesn't seem to have had any ill effect.

Once the caps are off, try not to handle them too much, and place them somewhere clean so the adhesive doesn't get mucked up and lose its effectiveness.

Opening the iPod Mini

The top of the Mini has two Phillips #000 screws that hold the main electronics board in place, as shown in Figure 1-49. Remove these with, you guessed it, a #000 Phillips screwdriver. I like to stick such tiny screws to a piece of Scotch tape to ensure I won't lose them.

Figure 1-49. Top of the iPod mini with the plastic cap removed

The bottom of the mini has a custom-designed clip that fits into four slots machined out of the aluminum case. Insert the tip of the #000 screwdriver into each of the four holes in turn and disengage the clip while pulling it up, as in Figure 1-50. If you're having trouble, use the flathead screwdriver to exert upward pressure with one hand while disengaging the clip with the other. As with everything in these instructions, don't use too much force!

Finally, there is a pin connector at the bottom of the mini that connects the button assembly to the main board. You will see it on the mini's lefthand side when you remove the bottom clip. Use the needle-nose pliers to unplug this ribbon connector.

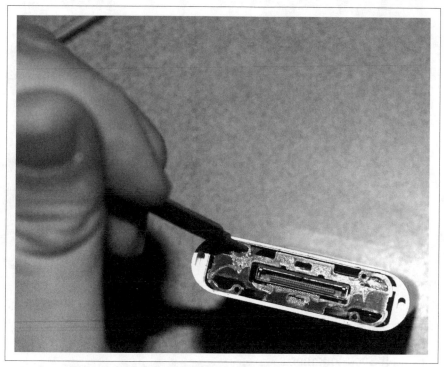

Figure 1-50. Unclipping the lower retainer spring

Removing the Battery

Are you positive you disconnected the ribbon cable at the end of the previous step? Good. Now, gently press on the dock connector and the mini's main electronics board, LCD display, hard drive, and battery will all slide out in one integrated unit, as shown in Figure 1-51.

Installing the New Battery

With the main components out, turn them over and place the LCD display on a clean, flat, soft surface (such as a couple of paper towels). You'll see the battery. Apple connects the battery to the main board with a double-sided adhesive neoprene block that you need to pull in half when you take off the old battery. Use the needle-nose pliers to disconnect the battery, and then pull it off.

Plug the fresh battery into the connector (it will plug in only one way) and place it on the main board in the same orientation as the old battery. You'll have torn the neoprene block in half when you removed the old battery, but it really doesn't make much difference; there is still enough of the block left

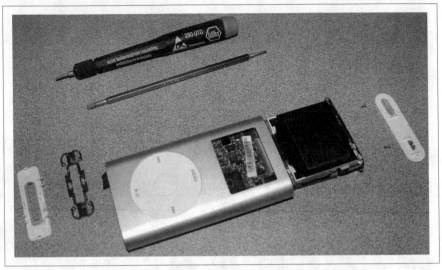

Figure 1-51. The mini fully taken apart

to hold up the new battery, and Apple glues them in place only to make mass-assembly easier.

Putting It Back Together

With the fresh battery in place, slide the main electronics back into the aluminum shell. You'll notice two rails inside the aluminum; you want the green main board to be *under* these rails. You'll meet some resistance about halfway through, so carefully insert one of the screwdrivers up through the bottom of the case and press down on the center of the main board. Be gentle, and never force anything. If you continue to meet resistance, pull the main board out and start over again.

Once the main board is in, make sure to reconnect the ribbon connector for the button assembly. Nothing would suck as badly as getting everything back together only to find out you forgot to make this connection. Install the bottom clip by placing the top two clips into their respective tabs and then pulling the bottom two tabs into place with your #000 screwdriver. Snap on the bottom cap.

On the top, make sure to line up the tiny Hold switch (the actual switch on the main board) with the actuator (the plastic/metal switch on the top cap). Once you've done this, just stick the top cap back on and press it down until it's smooth. Your iPod mini should be working like a champ again!

—*Greg Koenig*

HACK #18 Build Your Own iPod External Charger 🖙🖙🅛

Sometimes an electrical outlet is not available. This hack contains all the information you'll need to build your own battery-based iPod External Charger.

The iPod External Charger allows iPod users to run their iPods off (and charge their iPods' internal batteries with) eight standard and easily replaceable AA batteries. One of the best aspects of the charger is that it's really cheap to build!

Table 1-5 lists the parts you need. RadioShack parts can be found at your local RadioShack or at *http://www.radioshack.com*.

Table 1-5. The parts you will need

Part	What the part does	How many you need	Part #	Cost
RadioShack AA battery holder	Holds four AA batteries	Two	RadioShack Part #270-383	$1.59 each
RadioShack fully insulated 9V connectors	Attaches the battery holders	Two	RadioShack Part #270-325	$1.99 each
RadioShack heat-shrink tubing	Shrinks when heated to seal connections	One packet	RadioShack Part #278-1627	$2.39 each
FireWire Cable	Gets the power from the batteries to the iPod	Only half of cable is used	Any computer supply store	About $10

In addition to the parts in Table 1-5, you will need some electrical tape and a case. The case must be one that will be safe even if the batteries used in it should become warm or even hot. The iPod External Charger was originally designed for the G1 and G2 nondocking iPods. Because of this, a workaround is needed to make the charger compatible with all G3 and later docking iPods. One compact and reasonably inexpensive way to make the charger compatible with newer docking models is to use the PocketDock, by SendStation. This product is essentially a FireWire-to-dock adapter and costs $18.

You'll also need the following items to put the charger together:

- A knife capable of cutting wire, stripping wire insulation, and cutting cables
- Scissors, a soldering iron, and solder (although the project can be done without a soldering iron and solder)
- A hair dryer

Before we get to building, here are a couple things to keep in mind:

- Always cut a larger section of the heat-shrink tubing than it looks like you'll need. This leaves you with enough tubing to go over the top and below the bottom of the connection after the tube has shrunk. Never give the heat-shrink tubing too much heat from the hair dryer, as it can overshrink and damage what could be crucial connections.

- If you choose not to solder your connections, I recommend that you make sure your connections are good and that they won't disconnect with the wear-and-tear your charger may be put through (especially when you remove your charger from its case to change the batteries).

Building the Charger

Cut around your FireWire cable's plastic/rubber insulation, and then cut through the outer layer of metal shielding. Make your incision about halfway along the cable, leaving enough cable on one end to reach from your charger to your iPod, as shown in Figure 1-52.

Figure 1-52. Dissecting the cable

There will be six wires total within the FireWire cable: four data wires and two power wires. Identify the data and power wires within the FireWire cable. There are four data wires in total, but they can be easily spotted as they are wrapped in two sets of two by yet more metal shielding. The data wires need to be isolated, cut, and insulated. Do this by stripping the metal shielding off all the data wires, cutting through the data wires, and then insulating the naked data wire ends that you exposed when you cut them. Insulate each of these wires using electrical tape, then heat-shrink tubing. Now identify the two remaining wires inside the FireWire cable. These remaining wires are your power wires; they carry the electrical current through the FireWire cable. If you're using the cable I specified earlier, the wires will be white and black. Strip the insulation from these power wires.

You'll be attaching the power wires to different parts of the RadioShack battery snap connectors, so strip both wires on both of the connectors now. Next, you'll make the connections. Twist together the red wire from battery snap connector A and the black wire from battery snap connector B, and then solder them together (I label one A and one B to avoid confusion, but as long as you keep track of which is which it doesn't matter which you call A and which you call B). Insulate this connection using electrical tape, then heat-shrink tubing.

Connect the FireWire cable to the battery snap connectors. Do this by connecting the only loose black wire from the (now attached) battery snap connectors to the black wire coming from your FireWire cable. Insulate this connection using electrical tape, then heat-shrink tubing. You've just connected the negative (electrically speaking) side of things.

Now, it's time to connect the positive side of things. Twist, solder, and insulate the positive wires by connecting the positive battery snap connector wire to the positive FireWire wire. You'll be connecting the only loose red wire (from the snap connectors) to the only loose white wire (from the FireWire cable). Your battery-charger-to-be should look like Figure 1-53.

Figure 1-53. The positive and negative connections

Use a larger-diameter piece of heat-shrink tubing to cover over all your connections, to keep them secure and in place. Wrap electrical tape around the base of this larger piece of heat-shrink tubing to keep it in place at the end of the FireWire cable.

Add batteries to your two battery holders (four AA batteries in each). Connect a battery snap connector to each of the battery holders.

> The snap connectors are designed to connect only one way, so you can't flip the positive and negative currents of the batteries to the connectors.

I recommend using standard AA batteries and replacing all eight of them at the same time. I do not recommend using rechargeable batteries in the iPod External Charger, because they might not have consistent charges or might be too powerful; even though they say they supply the same 1.5V as standard AA batteries, some don't. Figure 1-54 shows the completed External Charger.

Figure 1-54. The finished piece

Now, you can charge your iPod on the road, in the sky, on the sea, or anywhere. You won't need any sort of power adapters for travel in other countries, because standard AA batteries are available almost everywhere!

—*Allen Evans*

HACK #19   Change the Colors of Your Generation 3 iPod's LCD Screen ⓂⓌⓁ

With a sheet of acetate and a few simple tools, you can convert your iPod's LED lights to any color you want.

Personally, I like my pants to match my shirt, and on the generation 3 (G3) series iPods, the fact that the LED buttons and LCD display light up like a police car pulling me over is a bit annoying. No worries, though; with a sheet of acetate paper from the local art supply store and a couple of tools, I can get my G3 iPod ready for duty on a submarine at battle stations!

Here's what you'll need for this hack:

- A case-cracking tool [Hack #16]
- A Torx T6 screwdriver (see *http://www.wihatools.com*)

- Red acetate film, cut to $1.9'' \times 1.5''$
- A pair of tweezers (optional)

Acetate film is available at art supply and plastics stores. I think red is the only color that really looks good, but feel free to take your iPod into the store and cover the LCD display with whatever colors you fancy testing.

> Refer to "Replace Your Generation 3 iPod's Battery" **[Hack #16]** for detailed instructions on how to get the iPod apart. Also, heed the warnings in "Replace Your Generation 1 or 2 iPod's Battery" **[Hack #15]** and consider just how badly you really want to change your LCD's colors. There *is* risk involved here.

Removing the Hard Drive and Battery

Follow the instructions in "Replace Your Generation 3 iPod's Battery" **[Hack #16]** to open your iPod and remove the hard drive and battery.

You do not need to disconnect the audio connection jack (soldered into the metal case half) from the main board. The connection is extremely delicate, and you're best off leaving it intact and being careful not to stress the ribbon cable too much.

Releasing the Main Board

The main board of the iPod is held in the case by six T6 torx fasteners: remove them. Use the tip of the T6 screwdriver to gently pry up the main board. Keeping it connected to the LCD/button daughterboard, rotate it to the left and lay it down on top of the metal case half. Use a towel or something similar to protect it from the sharp edges of the metal case.

Flipping the LCD and Installing the Acetate

The LCD display is held tight against the clear window by the main board when it's fastened into place. Since the main board is out of the way, the LCD is now loose, and you can carefully flip it upside down, keeping it connected to the daughterboard.

Once this is done, carefully lay the acetate into place over the clear plastic case window. You could, in theory, use an adhesive substance to keep it in place, but the risk of air bubbles and kinks in the acetate is not worth it. There is a neoprine seal on the LCD unit that will hold the acetate in place just fine.

It goes without saying that you need to be careful about fingerprints. If you get your iPod back together and find a messy fingerprint on the acetate, the inside of the case window, or the LCD display, you're going to be pretty miffed. Your best bet is to use tweezers to place the acetate into the case, being careful not to touch any of the display components with your fingers. Should you get a fingerprint on anything, use Plexus or another plastic cleaner to get it off.

Flip the LCD display back into place, and place the main board on top of it.

Refastening the Main Board

The main board fits snugly between the six standoffs that the Torx fasteners screw into, so it is easy to get into place. When you reinstall the Torx fasteners, do not over tighten them! Snug pressure is all that's required.

Refer to "Replace Your Generation 3 iPod's Battery" **[Hack #16]** for instructions on putting your iPod back together, and you're done!

—Greg Koenig

HACK   Turn Your iPod into a Wireless Jukebox ⓜⓦ◐
#20
Stream music from your iPod to your local area network using Rendezvous and a Pocket PC.

Taking your music to a party has always been a problem. You had to select a few CDs that you could carry, pack them, take them to the party, play them, and then make sure you recovered them and took them safely home. Portable music players partially solved the problem: you no longer had to select the CDs, because you could just take your entire music collection with you. But you still had the problem of connecting your player to the music system. It's the same with bringing your music collection to your workplace: few allow you to connect an iPod to your computer.

One option is to turn your iPod into a portable boom box **[Hack #7]**. You can hook your iPod up to a stereo with a headphone jack to RCA audio cable, or you can pick up a set of Altec Lansing's inMotion portable speakers (*http://www.alteclansing.com/store.asp*; $149.95). But wouldn't it be nice to be able to do all this wirelessly, without even having to take your iPod out of your bag?

Pocketster (*http://www.simeda.com/pocketster.html*; free) is an application that allows your Pocket PC to be discovered by other Pocket PCs in the area or by any computer running a Rendezvous network. You can also discover other Pocketster users anywhere on your wireless LAN. Pocketster includes a web server (which you can use to publish information) and a music preview utility that allows you to stream music files from nearby Pocketster users.

Pocketster Pro (*http://www.simeda.com/pocketster.html*; $ 14.95; limited trial version available), the advanced version of Pocketster, takes the idea a step further and adds an iPod module. The module enables you to publish your iPod playlists and have anyone in the area listen to previews or download tracks wirelessly from those playlists.

> This procedure allows you to broadcast and/or share the music on your iPod. You must check the legislation that applies to you and decide accordingly whether this is legal. While some uses might be legal (e.g., bringing your music to a party and playing it from a computer), others (e.g., sharing your music with others on your network) might not be.

The iPod module can be used by Pocketster Pro users with a PDA with a host USB port. The first (and probably the most popular) Pocket PC PDA to contain a host USB port is the Toshiba e800 (*http://www.toshibadirect.com/td/b2c/pdet. to?poid=263419&seg=HHO&sel=1&rcid=-26367&ccid=1291021*; $599.00), used in the following tests. You can also add a host USB port to any Pocket PC with a CompactFlash Type II slot, using an adapter from Ratoc Systems (*http:// www.ratocsystems.com/english/products/subpages/cfu1u.html*; $139.99).

In the case of the Toshiba e800, you need the USB host cable as well as the USB/FireWire cable, which you can get from the Apple store.

Installing Software

The first thing you need to do is install the Mass Storage drivers for Pocket PC 2003, available from Ratoc (*http://www.ratocsystems.com/english/ support/driver/cfu1_2003.html*). You do not need the entire bundle, just the Mass Storage drivers. Download the *CFU1_PPC2003.EXE* file, double-click it to extract the files, then go into the *PPC2003 CFU1 Driver\ MassStorageDriver* folder and copy the *usbmsc.PPC2003_ARMV4.CAB* file to your Pocket PC. Open it with File Explorer to install the drivers. Soft-reset your device after the installation completes.

Connecting iPod to PDA

Now, you're ready to connect your iPod to your PDA. Plug the host USB cable into your Toshiba (or plug your Ratoc adapter into your Compact-Flash slot).

Connect the USB/FireWire splitter cable to your iPod, as shown in Figure 1-55.

Then, connect the USB end of the iPod cable to the PDA's USB host cable, as shown in Figure 1-56.

Figure 1-55. Connecting the USB/FireWire splitter cable to your iPod

If everything went well (and both your iPod and your Pocket PC are turned on), you should see the display of your iPod change to the screen shown in Figure 1-57.

Now that you've got the iPod and the Toshiba e800 connected, you can check that your devices are properly connected using File Explorer on your PDA. There should be a new folder under My Device called *Hard Disk*, as shown in Figure 1-58.

If you open that folder you will see the file structure on your iPod, which should be similar to the one shown in Figure 1-59.

Starting the Application

You are now ready to start the application. Go to Start → Programs and click on the Pocketster icon.

The first thing you want to do is name your wireless jukebox, as shown in Figure 1-60. I called mine Razvan's Jukebox. The name defaults to your owner ID, so you can leave it as that if you don't feel like changing it.

Press the Start Discovery button and then the Publish button. This will enable the web server within Pocketster Pro and start advertising it to nearby devices. You should see the name of your jukebox appear in the "Discovered

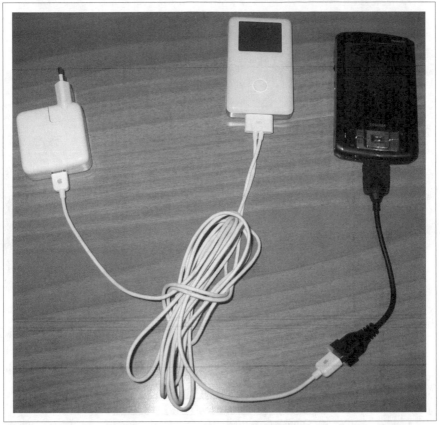

Figure 1-56. Connecting the USB end of the cable to the PDA

services" area in a few seconds (yes, it discovers itself). If anyone else is running Pocketster in the area, you will discover them too, as shown in Figure 1-61.

We will now start the iPod module to configure your jukebox and make it interact with the music files on your iPod. Open the Options menu and select iPod Setup. The iPod Setup screen is really simple; it just prompts you for a subdirectory in which to store the HTML files that it generates based on the playlists on your iPod, as shown in Figure 1-62. I suggest leaving it as *ipod*, but you can change it if you don't like the default.

Press the Generate HTML button to start the interaction with your iPod. Note that this is a lengthy process (it can take up to five minutes for it to parse your entire music database and create the HTML files for each playlist). It is important that you do not disconnect your iPod or turn off the

Figure 1-57. Your altered iPod screen, once the connection is made

Figure 1-58. The My Device window

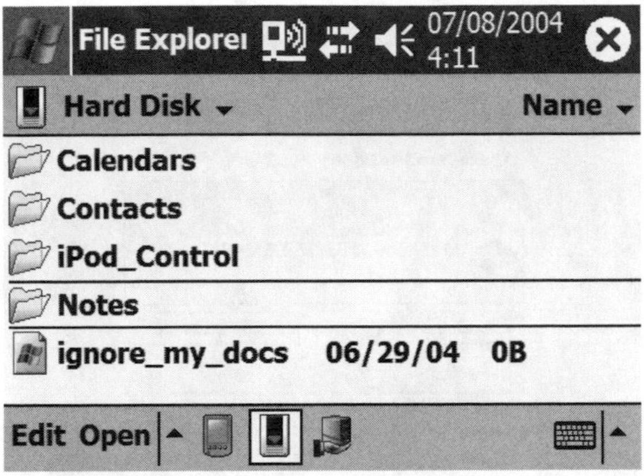

Figure 1-59. The iPod's disk structure on your PDA

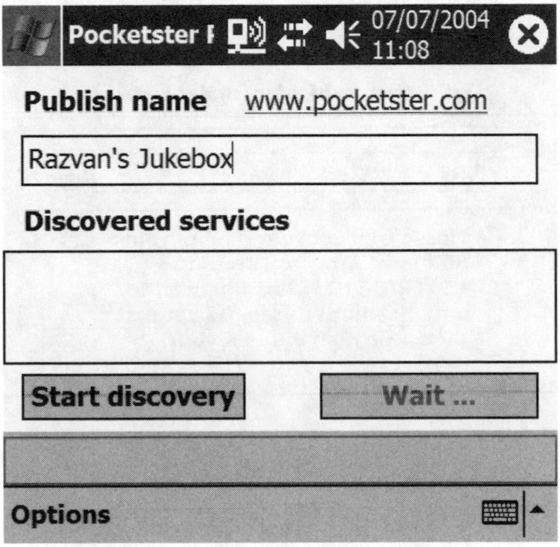

Figure 1-60. Naming your jukebox

PDA or the iPod during this operation. Wait for the screen to return to the main Pocketster Pro screen before doing anything else.

Once the iPod setup is complete, you will be returned to the main application screen. You can click on your jukebox's name in the "Discovered services" area to preview the content on your web server (now including the music from your iPod).

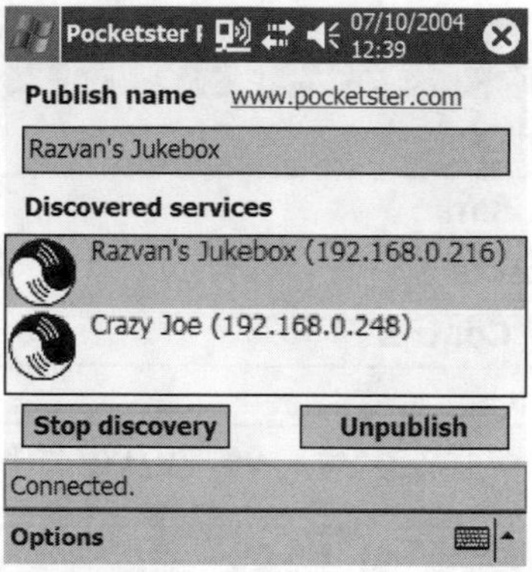

Figure 1-61. *Taking a peek at other shared devices*

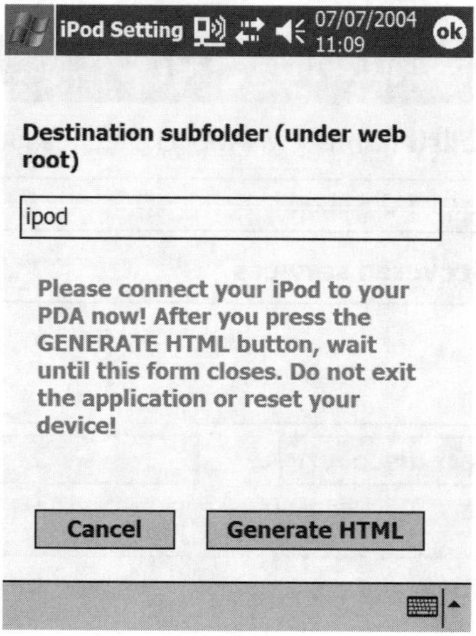

Figure 1-62. *Setting up the iPod*

You will see a list of your current playlists. The one on top bears the same name as your iPod and contains *all* your music. If you have a lot of music on your iPod, loading that list can take a long time, so either load a smaller playlist or be patient.

Clicking on a playlist takes you to a detailed list of all the songs in the list, as shown in Figure 1-63.

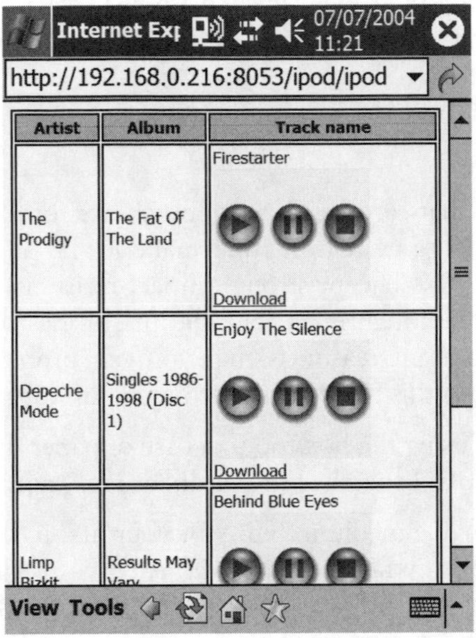

Figure 1-63. Your iPod's playlist

The green Play/Pause/Stop buttons allow you to preview each song or stream it to your computer/PDA. You can also download the files by clicking the Download link next to each song name.

—*Razvan Dragomirescu*

HACK #21 Craft an iPod Case from Cardboard ❶❷❸

Make your own custom iPod case out of cardboard for next to nothing.

You've eyed them in the Apple Store, online, and in various other computer stores. Yet none of the commercially available iPod cases that you have seen manages to substitute individuality for the coolness of the raw iPod in the necessary ratio to warrant its purchase. You want something to protect your cool, sleek iPod, but you also want something that maintains the coolness factor and makes your iPod definitively *yours*.

Aside from marring the surface of the iPod itself with an engraved quotation (and thereby limiting the resell value of your iPod when Apple comes out with that new 200 GB Video iPod that you have been dreaming of upgrading to) and encasing it in one of the available see-through cases, the only option left within easy reach is to design and make your own iPod case. This hack walks the do-it-yourselfers through the necessary steps to make your own iPod case out of cardboard.

Why Cardboard?

The short answer is, "Why not cardboard?"

The longer reply is that cardboard is a good choice for a do-it-yourself iPod case for many of the same reasons that make it one of the most common forms of packaging. It's cheap, strong, impact-resistant, easily replaceable, and bendable, and although it can be rigid, it still has some give. But perhaps the most important reason is that you can probably find a suitable piece of cardboard for this project lying around your house or place of work.

For this hack, I am using the box top to a case of paper that I snatched from work (note to my boss: I snatched the cardboard *top*, not the case of paper).

Cardboard is a forgiving medium to use for your first iPod case; if you screw up, it won't cost you anything to start over! After you've gone through these instructions with cardboard, you can try designing your own case out of other materials.

Some of you are probably thinking, "I want to try better, more stylish materials." For you cardboard haters out there, I just want to point out that designers such as Frank Gehry actually build furniture out of cardboard. Google "cardboard chair," and you'll find some of Gehry's designs alongside design-school assignments that require students to design chairs out of cardboard. As the price tags associated with Gehry's designs will testify, cardboard might be inexpensive, but—when nicely styled—*it ain't cheap!*

Besides time, patience, and a steady hand, here's a short list of things you will need or that you might find useful for this hack:

Dimensional Drawings for Carrying Case Developers (PDF)
Available from Apple's Developer Connection (*http://developer.apple. com/hardware/ipod/index.html*). This document is a little dated, since it provides all the measurements (in millimeters) for the 10, 15, and 30 GB iPods, with no mention of the iPod mini, the 20 GB iPod, or the 40 GB iPod. The rough dimensions for all these models are available on Apple's spec page for the iPod (*http://www.apple.com/ipod/specs.html*).

If you use "Dimensional Drawings for Carrying Case Developers" for your measurements, you can easily convert millimeters to inches via Google by typing X millimeters to inches in the Google search box, replacing X with the number you wish to convert.

Corrugated cardboard
I recommend 1/8" thick.

A sharp knife
Scissors won't cut it; they'll squeeze and bend the cardboard, marring the surface. I use a box cutter, but an X-acto knife or other suitable tool for making precision cuts in cardboard will work.

A pencil
For taking notes and marking the cardboard for cutting.

Some sort of straight edge with a ruler
A T-square would be ideal, but two good-quality rulers with nice flat ends can be used together as a makeshift T-square. The straight edge will be used both for drawing lines and for directing your cuts.

Metal paperclips
For holding things together.

Glue (optional)
I recommend Elmer's Wood Glue for this project, although any glue capable of holding cardboard together is workable. If you want to make your iPod case a glue-free foldable masterpiece, you can always include tabs and inserts in your design.

Sandpaper (optional)
For smoothing any rough cuts in the cardboard. It can be useful for cleaning out the small circles you cut for the iPod's controls.

A compass (optional)
For drawing the circles for the iPod's controls. If you don't have a compass, you can simply draw boxes around these areas and then use the boxes as guidelines for drawing the circles freehand. Either way, when it comes time to cutting the circles, you will be working more or less freehand.

If you have a computer and a printer handy, you can easily design the layout for your cardboard iPod case in Quark, Illustrator, Photoshop, or any other program with a ruler that is capable of accurately drawing measured lines. Then you can print out this template on a regular piece of paper, glue that paper to your cardboard, and start cutting away.

Designing the Case

We're going to start by flattening out the iPod's three-dimensional cover into a two-dimensional drawing, much in the way that a world map represents a flattened globe. We first need to get the overall size of the piece of cardboard we need—for these purposes, the measurements provided on Apple's iPod spec page (*http://www.apple.com/ipod/specs.html*) will suffice, but if available, I prefer the slightly more precise measurements from "Dimensional Drawings for Carrying Case Developers" in parentheses for comparative purposes:

- iPod mini: 3.6"×2.0"×0.5"
- 10–20 GB iPod: 4.1" (103.49 mm/4.07") × 2.4" (61.80 mm/2.43") × 0.62" (15.7 mm/0.62")
- 30–40 GB iPod: 4.1" (103.49 mm/4.07") × 2.4" (61.80 mm/2.43") × 0.73" (18.7 mm/0.74")
- Cardboard thickness: 0.125" (3.18 mm)

When flattening out the iPod/iPod mini, start out with a rectangular section of cardboard that will be folded around the iPod. There will be three sides where overlapping and gluing occur: the top, the bottom, and one side of the iPod. So, to determine the height of the rectangle, add the height of the iPod to twice the thickness of our iPod and factor in the thickness of the cardboard twice (for the two horizontal seams where the cardboard folds). The cardboard rectangle's height will be 4.85" for the iPod mini, 5.59" for the 10–20 GB iPod, and 5.81" for the 30–40 GB iPod.

To determine the width of the rectangle, add twice the width of your iPod to three times the depth of your iPod (two sides, plus an extra overlapping flap that will be glued onto one of the side flaps) and factor in the thickness of the cardboard four times (for the four vertical seams where the cardboard folds). The cardboard rectangle's width will be 6" for the iPod mini, 7.22" for the 10–20 GB iPod, and 7.52" for the 30–40 GB iPod.

When marking your cardboard, make sure you draw lightly with your pencil on the side you want to be the outside of the case. All drawings will be made on the side where we will cut. After cutting, you can lightly erase any remaining marks. All cuts into the cardboard should be made on the outside of the case, because slight tearing on the underside of the cardboard can occur if your knife isn't sharp enough. Although such minor blemishes can be overlooked if they are on the inside of your case, they may be a reason to start over if they are on the outside.

Start by marking off the appropriate rectangular section of cardboard for your iPod model:

- 4.85" × 6" for the iPod mini
- 5.59" × 7.22" for the 10–20 GB iPod
- 5.81" × 7.52" for the 30–40 GB iPod

This rectangle is the main piece of cardboard that you will cut and fold to fit your iPod.

> When marking off this bit of cardboard, you are immediately faced with a choice involving the corrugated lines of the cardboard. If you run these corrugated lines horizontally parallel along the length of the cardboard, then all vertical scoring cuts in the design can be used to produce a ribbed effect along the vertical folds in the case. Running these lines vertically parallel along the height of the cardboard has the reverse effect, producing a ribbed effect across all horizontal cuts. If you want all cuts to have some sort of ribbed effect, mark this rectangular section diagonally against the grain of the cardboard's corrugation. See Figure 1-66, later in this hack, for an example.

Now, for each of the four sides of your rectangle, use your ruler to measure in exactly the thickness of your iPod. Place a light mark at this point near each end of the side you are working on, and then draw a straight line between these points. Do this for each side of the rectangle. The result is a frame around a new inner rectangle. Now, from each of the lines you just drew, measure in the .125" width of your cardboard, and draw another set of lines. If you measure the distance between the innermost of your horizontal lines, the result should be the height of your iPod, or very close to it. If this is not the case, then something was incorrectly measured and you will need to adjust some of the lines.

Next, from the innermost vertical lines, measure in the width of the face of your iPod and draw new vertical lines at that point. Then from these new lines, measure in the .125" width of your cardboard, and draw another set of lines. If you measure the distance between these two innermost vertical lines, the result should be the thickness of your iPod, or very close to it. If this is not the case, then something was incorrectly measured and you will need to adjust some of the lines.

After you have marked off this rectangular section and made sure all the internal measurements line up, use your straight edge and your knife to cut the outside border of the rectangle, removing it from your larger piece of cardboard. Using the measurements provided in "Dimensional Drawings for Carrying Case Developers" or your own measurements, go ahead and mark the rectangle for your iPod's screen and the different circles for the controls within the larger rectangular on the left of your current design. This is the most tedious aspect of this project.

A good idea when measuring these controls is to think in rectangles and boxes. The screen is a box, drawn easily enough. Think of the large circular pad that you use to control your iPod as a box with a circle in it. Think of the four small controls between the control pad and the screen first as one long, thin rectangle and then separately as little boxes within that rectangle. Draw lines from the corners of your boxes to locate their centers. If you are using a compass, you can then draw the circles rather easily. If you do not have a compass, try it freehand or consider drawing several boxes at different angles around the same axis to provide a better guide for your circle.

On the flaps located above and below both the front and back panels of your iPod case, simply mark rectangles to accommodate the docking port and the headphones. For the purposes of this case, we are not going to leave a place open for the lock switch, because the top is where we will insert and remove our iPod from the case. The result of all this measuring and marking should look similar to Figure 1-64, a Photoshop sketch of the basic template that I worked up for my 15 GB iPod, complete with rulers in inches. The light grey lines separating major sections will be folding areas.

Cutting, Folding, and Assembling

After marking up your cardboard satisfactorily, it's time to start bending, cutting, and piecing together your iPod case.

The first thing I did was mark the areas where I would be bending the cardboard by slightly darkening those areas. You basically have two options here. One is to use something blunt, such as the back part of the blade on a pair of scissors or a flat edge of your straight tedge, to flatten the corrugated cardboard along the seam where you want to fold it, in effect crimping the cardboard at the folds. This method will make your case a bit more durable.

The second option (which I elected to use) is more difficult, but also more stylish. Corrugated cardboard is made of two thin pieces of paper sandwiched around another piece that is folded in waves. Carefully making sure to cut through the outermost layer of paper only, I traced each vertical and horizontal grayed-out section, one by one. After cutting the top layer, I gently and carefully pulled it free, revealing the ribbed effect of the cardboard. I then fully removed the small sections surrounding the middle squares at the top and bottom of my template. Finally, I carefully folded the piece along the

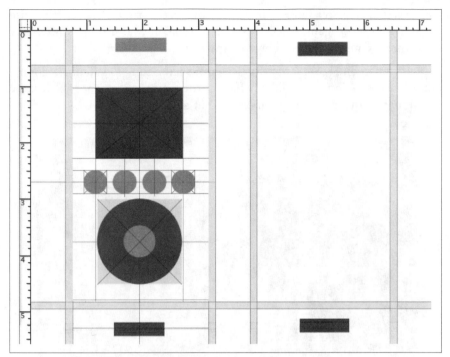

Figure 1-64. Sketch of the basic template

different seams, using my straight edge to help bend along the lines and shaping the piece around my iPod, making slight adjustments where necessary.

> If you do not like either of these methods, consider using some thread and a needle to sew along the seams, pulling the thread tight to collapse the cardboard into a crimped seam.

When you wrap the piece of cardboard around your iPod, you will have numerous extraneous flaps. Some will overlap and be glued together, whereas others will end up being cut off, depending upon your preference.

The next step is to cut out all the areas needed to control your iPod. I waited until after bending for this part to ensure that there wouldn't be any accidental bending along the middle of the screen or the touchpad area. I recommend first cutting an X through all the circles and rectangles that must be removed, and then slowly and carefully cutting around the perimeter of these shapes.

If you go too fast, or your knife is dull, the bottom layer of paper that makes up the sheet of cardboard may bunch and tear irregularly. If you notice this starting to happen, simply stop, take a breath, and slow down. Nothing is ruined yet. After you have removed all the necessary bits, wrap the case around your iPod again to see how it fits. Make any adjustments necessary to accommodate your iPod's controls and ports.

As you can see in Figure 1-65, I've accomplished a functional, albeit sloppy, cut to my case. Notice the ribbed effect at the seams and the horribly erratic attempt at cutting circles in cardboard. That's stylish!

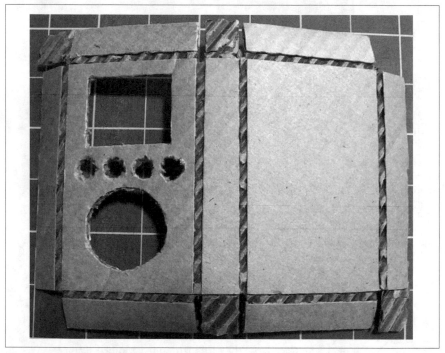

Figure 1-65. My case before assembly

Now, for assembly, you have to decide what to do with the bottom and top flaps and how you are going to make the top open and close for iPod insertion and removal. See Figure 1-66 for my solution to the first problem.

Rather than cut a rectangle the exact size and position of the port on the bottom of the iPod, I instead removed a middle rectangle from the bottom flap (the one coming from the front of the case) and left a corresponding flap on the top that covers the port when it's not in use. You could simply glue the remaining flaps to each other to close up the bottom, but I took the extra step of making two cuts into each of them, about two-thirds in, and interleaving them. Just a slight spot of glue works nicely on each of the mini-flaps, and due to the porous nature of cardboard, simply holding the pieces together for a few seconds allows enough seepage to keep the pieces together.

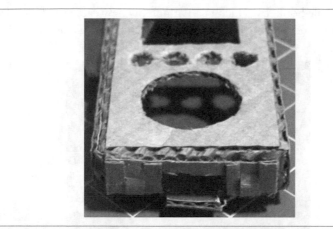

Figure 1-66. The bottom flap of my iPod case

After all the bottom bits are glued, fold the two side flaps inside the bottom of the case (or cut them off). Fold the flaps over each other and glue them together. Before doing so on mine, I went ahead and removed the top piece of paper from the bottom of these two flaps (the one that folded down from the face of the case). If you do this, you will need to hold this seam together for a bit longer while it dries. I used my calipers to hold them together, but a paperclip will suffice in a pinch.

For the top of the case (see Figure 1-67), I simply cut the necessary holes for the headphone jack and didn't worry about any interlocking sections or tabs. In order to keep this part of the case open for inserting and removing the iPod, I took advantage of the corrugated cardboard again, running two paperclips that I bent specifically for this purpose inside the two flaps. They will securely hold the flaps closed when the iPod is held within, while remaining easy to bend and remove when I want to reopen the case.

Figure 1-67. Ugly but effective use of bent paperclips to hold together the top of the case

As an added touch, I took some copper gardening wire that I had lying around the house and ran it through the corrugation of the back of the case to create a bendable hook, by which I can attach my new cardboard iPod case to my belt. Figure 1-68 shows the completed project, hanging from my belt.

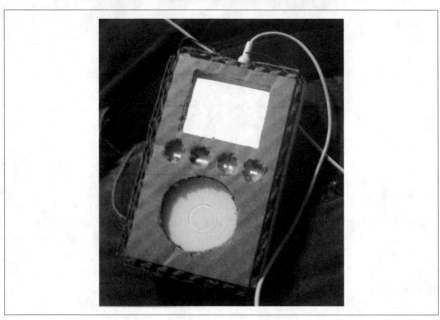

Figure 1-68. My finished cardboard iPod case

Hacking the Hack

I chose cardboard because it is freely available and because if I drop my iPod when it is in my cardboard case, the cardboard will offer protection from scratching and some absorption of the impact with a bit of pushback bounce (unlike materials such as metal or a hard wood, which lack the sponginess of cardboard). If you are a woodshop hobbyist and would like to go the wood route, consider using a softer wood such as balsa that you whittle to the right shape and size, and then covering it with a thin veneer of some harder wood to protect against scratches.

If you stick with the cardboard design, consider ways to make the case water-resistant with different paints or sprays. If you get your cardboard from a liquor store, consider designing your case so that the logo of your favorite drink adorns the back of the iPod. I'm considering taking some soda cans and trying to glue some flattened aluminum to my cardboard case to make it match my AL PowerBook. If cardboard, box cutters, and glue aren't your cup of tea, but fabric and sewing machines are, consider using these measurements to design yourself a quilted and padded iPod case out of your favorite fabric. What ever you choose to do, have fun and be creative!

—*C. K. Sample III*

Repurpose a Dead iPod ⓜⓦⓛ

If you should find yourself the unfortunate owner of an utterly dead iPod that is out of warranty and beyond resurrection as that music player you once loved so much, there is still a variety of things you can do with it.

You're past the denial stage where you sat rocking back and forth in the corner of your room for hours, cold and alone, clutching it close to your chest, repeatedly holding down special key combinations, hoping that suddenly your iPod would turn back on. You took it to a friend skilled in the art of soldering. He opened up your iPod, gently reconnected all the aged connections, and perhaps even replaced the FireWire port on your first-generation iPod, all to no avail. You tried new batteries and even an odd voodoo ritual that you discovered online. Nothing has worked. You've finally come to grips with the dreadful reality of it all: your iPod is dead.

Although everything has seemed hopeless during your futile attempts to resurrect your iPod, don't throw it away in frustration. There are several different things you can do with it, and this hack will discuss several of the possibilities.

Using Your Dead iPod to Get a New iPod

You're already in serious withdrawal from the days and days of personalized music you are used to having streamed to your ears by your little white friend. You need to replace your iPod. Here are three ideas for ways to recoup some of the money you invested in your dead iPod, either to help in the purchase of your next iPod or simply to pad your wallet:

Repeat after me: eBay (http://www.ebay.com) is the seller's friend.   If you have a broken iPod, chances are, there is a technician obsessed with buying things on eBay who is willing to spend some money on your iPod just to see if he can resurrect it. A quick search on eBay for "broken iPod" will turn up lots of results. As I write this, there are 43 minutes left on an auction featuring a dead 20 GB iPod with 17 bids on it that is currently going for $83. That's almost a third of the way to an iPod mini!

Mantra #2: people pay more for iPod parts than for an entire iPod.   If you decided to build your own iPod from scratch, you would quickly discover that buying all the necessary parts would cost you more than buying it complete from Apple. Why? Because Apple is a big corporation with the resources to buy in serious bulk, which helps drive down the prices on the materials. You are just you with a dead iPod. However, there are probably lots of other people in similar situations to yours who still think they can fix their broken iPods with that magic part. Pop open your iPod and carefully remove any parts that aren't broken. Sell the screen. Sell the hard drive. Sell the earbuds. Sell every bit you can. Make sure you say that you cannot guarantee that any of these items will actually work. It won't matter. Someone will buy them.

A final tip: international sales might bring a higher payday. When you're auctioning off all these items, make sure that you offer to sell and ship them internationally. iPods are more expensive outside the U.S. (and sometimes harder to come by), so if you are selling parts that might help repair some poor Brit's ailing iPod, he will be likely to pay more than possible U.S. customers. Also, point out to them that the high taxes for importing a fully functional iPod won't apply to the parts you are selling. Make sure your auction states that the buyer pays for the actual shipping cost, because international shipping is pricey.

If you don't want to pay eBay's fees, you could try to barter or sell your dead iPod or its parts on craigslist (*http://www.craigslist.org*). If, on the other hand, you are a wealthy person who has five or more iPods lying about and you don't want to bother with eBay or craigslist, there are other things you can do with your dead iPod.

Using Your Dead iPod for a Different Purpose

Here's a short, no-frills list of other things you can do with your dead iPod:

- If it's just the battery that is dead, use it as a portable hard drive.
- Use your dead iPod as a stylish paperweight, bookend (assuming you've got two), or doorstop.
- Open your iPod [Hack #15], [Hack #16], [Hack #17]. Gut the iPod, seal the case with a watertight adhesive such as the silicone used in fish tanks, and fill it with water and sea monkeys. Watch 'em grow!
- Gut the iPod and seal the case with a watertight adhesive. Leave the space where the screen was out and open. Drill small holes in the back of the iPod for drainage. Fill your deceased iPod with soil and the seeds of your favorite small flower or grass. Water and watch 'em grow! Voilá—your own stylish Manhattan-apartment sized garden!
- Use the dead iPod to test the moral fiber of your friends, neighbors, and coworkers. Leave it lying around and watch to see if anyone takes it!
- Use it as a people-repellant: sure, it might be broken, but nobody else has to know. Put those earphones in and walk around town ignoring people as you please, pretending that you are in your own little portable music world, impervious to their intrusive "Can I interest you in taking a brief survey?" type of questions. This is also a good way to listen in on unsuspecting suspects when you start up your own private detective agency.

- Find a really small portable color TV. Remove all of its insides. Gut the iPod. Squeeze the TV's innards into the gutted iPod's case. Cause a media storm with your announcement that you've found the fabled video iPod!

Think of your dead iPod as a crafts project waiting to happen. Be creative, and have fun! The important thing is to make sure that you aren't focusing on your recent loss. Life goes on.

—C. K. Sample III

Non-iPod Hardware
Hacks 23–31

In Chapter 1, we looked at the variety of ways the iPod can be used above and beyond its original design. But, believe it or not, there are some things even the iPod can't do. Sometimes, you have to find a third-party device to help you enhance the enjoyment of your music collection. This chapter looks at various non-iPod hardware options. You might already have some of these third-party devices lying around (say, an old Pentium box or an old Mac). Others are projects you can build yourself.

HACK #23 **Control iTunes from Your Palm** M W C

You can access your playlists, pause and play music, and much more, all from your Palm Pilot or other web-enabled handheld device.

If you have AirPort Express set up in your home Stream Music with AirPort Express **[Hack #26]**, you have probably noticed one catch in the whole wireless-music deal: in order to change songs, you have to schlep to wherever your host iTunes machine is. Not very convenient, is it? This hack will turn your wireless, handheld, web-capable device into an iTunes remote, allowing you to control iTunes from anywhere in the house.

Software

So, how is this magic possible? webRemote (*http://www.deadendsw.com/ Products/webRemote.html*; $10; limited trial version available), a piece of software that you install on the machine that runs iTunes, is a server package that acts as an intermediary between your web-enabled device and iTunes. It allows you to control iTunes from any web browser and, for the purposes of this hack, from a wireless PDA.

To check it out for free, simply download and install the software. The unregistered version works for only one hour at a time and limits you to using only two skins (more on these later).

The settings of webRemote are all accessible from the Preferences menu shown in Figure 2-1.

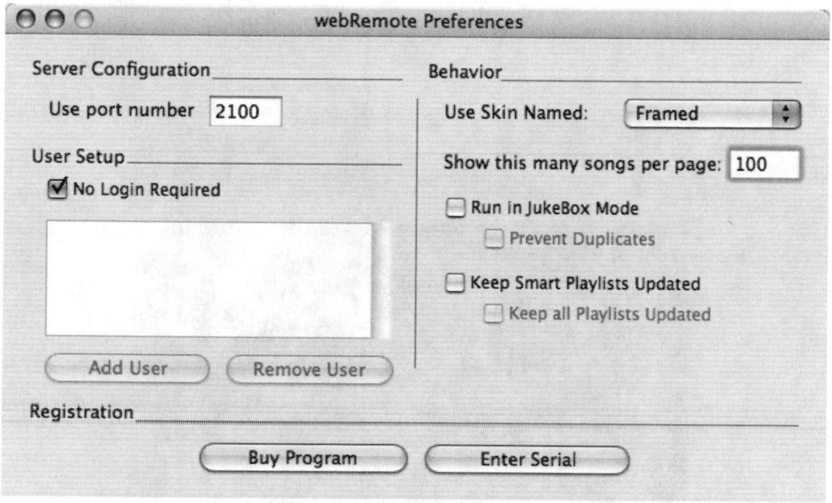

Figure 2-1. webRemote's Preferences panel

webRemote uses port number 2100 by default. There is no need to change this, unless you are using that port for another application. If you want to make sure no one in the general public can control your iTunes remotely, you should set up users. Otherwise, just leave No Login Required selected. Getting webRemote going is surprisingly easy; all you have to do is launch it!

Hardware

This hack requires a web-enabled handheld device. If you have a cell phone that will connect to the Internet, you're all set. For this hack, I used a Palm Tungsten C (*http://www.palmone.com/us/products/handhelds/tungsten-c/*; $399.00) with a built-in wireless card. The advantage of this is that it is super-fast.

To access your iTunes library on the Palm, install webRemote on the machine whose library you want to access. Then, using your web-browser of choice on your web-enabled device, enter the IP address of your machine in the Address bar, adding :2100 (or whatever port number you have designated) to the end of the address.

If you're unsure of your Mac's IP address, go to your Apple menu, select About This Mac, click the More Info... button, and select Network from the column on the left. Your IP address should appear in the bottom right field. Alternately, go to System Preferences → Network, select your interface (AirPort, Ethernet, etc.), and choose the TCP/IP tab. Your machine's IP address is listed.

webRemote comes with a few default skins you can use for its web interface, depending on the size of your device. Check out the default skin on the Palm Tungsten C in Figure 2-2.

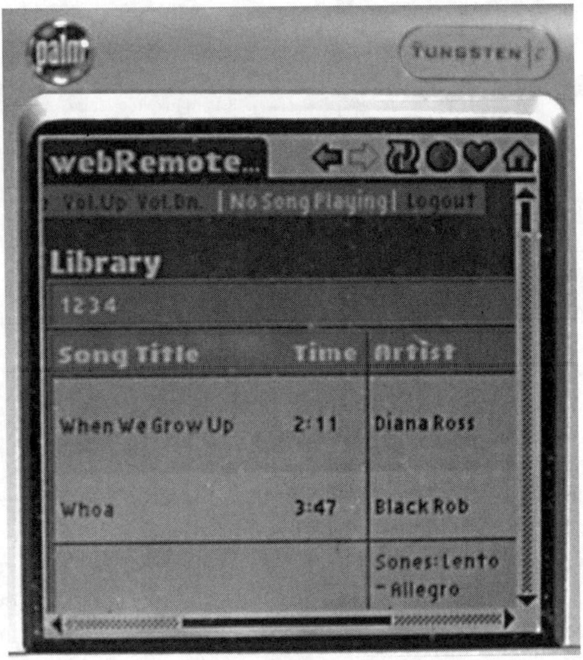

Figure 2-2. Controlling iTunes remotely, all from a Palm

Hacking the Hack

Many a complaint has been lodged about the lack of a remote control for Airport Express and other network players, but with this hack, you can create your own. Just set up your computer to work with your network player of choice [Hack #25]. Then, connect to your iTunes library using your Palm. Booyah! You have a remote control for iTunes, just like that.

Control iTunes from Your Mobile Phone Ⓜ Ⓥ Ⓛ

#24 Use your Bluetooth mobile phone as a remote to control iTunes from across the room.

This hack turns your Bluetooth cell phone or Palm into a remote control for iTunes. Apart from the wow factor when your friends come over for a party, there is a convenience factor too. Want to pause iTunes from your phone? You can. Want to skip to the next track or select a slow-dance playlist to spice things up a little? You can do that too.

Hardware

For this hack, you need a Bluetooth phone or PDA. If you have any of the following devices, you're in luck:

Sony Ericsson phone
> T630, T628
> 600, Z608
> T610, T616, T618
> T68m, T68i
> R520m
> T39m, T39mc
> P800 (R1D firmware)
> P900

Siemens phone
> SX1

Nokia phone
> 3650
> N-Gage

Palm OS handheld
> palmOne Tungsten T, T2, T3
> Sony Clié UX50

On the computer side, all you need to get things going is a Mac with Bluetooth and OS X 10.2 or later. PowerBook G4s come with Bluetooth preinstalled. Bluetooth options are available for an iBook, PowerBook, or Power Mac if you purchase your computer from Apple's online store and add built-in-Bluetooth to your order. If you already own a Mac sans Bluetooth, D-Link makes an after-market USB adapter (*http://www.dlink.com/products/?pid=34*; $45). The adapter plugs into an available USB port (you can even use an extra port on your keyboard on the Power Mac G4 and iMac).

Bluetooth

For this hack, your computer and phone must play nicely via Bluetooth. To get things going, set your cell phone's Bluetooth mode to "discoverable." Now, switch to your Mac and take a peek at your menu bar. Right next to the volume indicator is the Bluetooth icon, as shown in Figure 2-3. If the Bluetooth icon isn't in your menu bar, go to System Preferences → Bluetooth → Devices → Set Up New Device.

Figure 2-3. The Bluetooth icon

Click the Bluetooth icon and select Bluetooth Setup Assistant. The assistant will walk you through the steps necessary to get your computer and phone working together. The assistant will first look for your phone. If it doesn't find your phone, chances are that you haven't set up your phone to be discoverable. Check your phone's manual for instructions if you are not sure how to do this. Once the assistant finds your phone, it will show you a six-number code that you need to enter on your phone. This is for your protection; otherwise, whenever your phone was in the range of a Bluetooth device, it could be used for potentially nefarious purposes.

Software

In addition to having Mac OS X 10.2 or later and iTunes ready to go, you'll need to get your hands on Salling Software's Salling Clicker (*http://homepage.mac.com/jonassalling/Shareware/Clicker/*; $19.95; limited trial version available). There are two parts to the installation process: software for your phone and software for your Mac. However, some phones do not require the software to be uploaded. If you have a phone that does require software to be installed, go ahead and do that first by double-clicking on the appropriate package, as shown in Figure 2-4.

Once your phone has been set up, it's time to install Salling Clicker on your Mac. Make sure System Preferences and AppleScript Editor are not open; otherwise, the install cannot run.

Once install is complete, a Salling Clicker button is added to System Preferences → Other and a new Salling Clicker Menu item shows up in your menu bar. Click the Select Phone button in the Salling Clicker Preferences window. Most of us are lucky to have even one Bluetooth device. If, however, you have a Bluetooth phone *and* a PDA, Salling Clicker will prompt you to select the device you want to use.

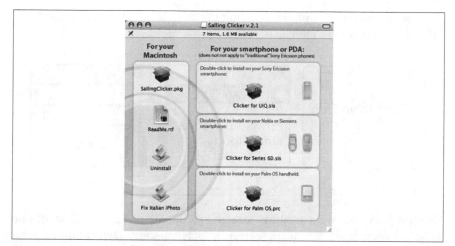

Figure 2-4. The Salling Clicker install window

After you select your phone, it appears at the top of the Preferences window, next to the Connect to Phone button. Click to connect. Now, your phone and Salling Clicker are simpatico, and things should look like Figure 2-5. It's time to play!

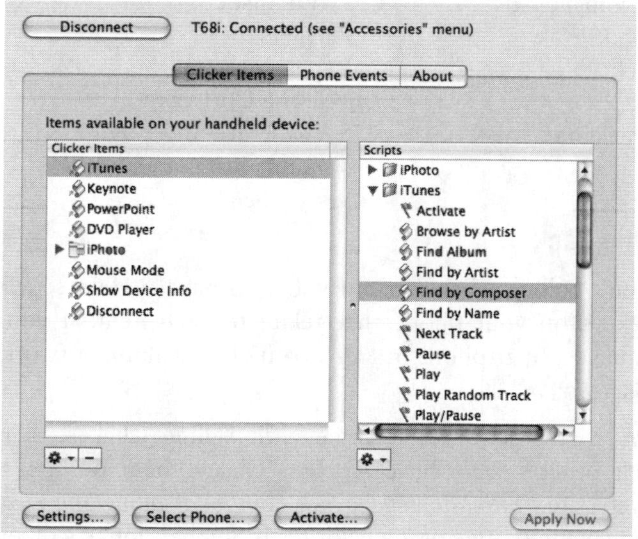

Figure 2-5. Salling Clicker, letting you know your phone is connected

Salling Clicker will inform you where to find its main menu on your phone. In the case of my phone, an Erricsson T68i, it's located under the phone's

Accessories menu. The phone's Salling Clicker menu (shown in Figure 2-6) reflects the items found in Clicker Items.

Figure 2-6. Salling Clicker on an Ericsson phone

For this hack, we want to jump straight to the iTunes item. Select it, and your phone will show you the currently playing song. Depending on your phone's hardware configuration, you use the phone's various controls to control iTunes. Here are the items you can control on your phone:

Browse by Artist	Find Album
Find by Artist	Find by Composer
Find by Name	Next Track
Pause	Play
Play Random Track	Play/Pause
Playlist Shuffle	Playlists
Rate Track	Repeat
Rewind	Volume Up/Down
Speak Track and Artist	Speak Track and Playlist
Stop	Visuals On/Off

Hacking the Hack

Your phone's Salling Clicker menu will also have a Help screen that displays the keys on your phone that relate to each item. If you are lucky enough to have a smartphone or PDA, your iTunes album artwork will show up on the screen.

In addition to the scripts that come with Salling Clicker, there are also scripts that other people have written. Check them out on the Salling Clicker web site (*http://homepage.mac.com/jonassalling/Shareware/Clicker/scripts20/index.html*). One of my favorites is Stephen Jonke's Queuing Agent (*http://homepage.mac.com/sjonke/clicker/*; free). It allows you to place songs in a queue right from your phone.

Don't just rely on other people's scripts, though. With all the knowledge you'll gain in "Tame iTunes with AppleScript" [Hack #72], you can whip up some scripts yourself!

HACK #25 Stream Music Around Your House ⓜⓦⓛ

With a little third-party software and hardware, you can stream your music around your house.

The great thing about your iTunes digital music collection is that it lets you store your music all in one place and access it quickly and easily. This is all hunky-dory, until you realize you sometimes want to listen to music while you're away from your computer—say, in your bedroom or den. Instead of going out and buying a bunch more computers, you can pick up a network music player and, with a little network hackery, you can enjoy your music in different rooms all over your house.

Hardware

There are a number of manufacturers out there who have jumped on this bandwagon, and they all approach the problem a little differently. The Slim Devices Squeezebox (*http://www.slimdevices.com*; $199) is a self-contained unit that you plug into your stereo receiver. The device has built-in 802.11b wireless, a built-in fluorescent display, and digital and analog RCA outputs. The SlimServer software required by this player (*http://www.slimp3.com/su_ downloads.html*; free) runs on various flavors of Windows, Mac OS X, and Linux. You can even download the Perl source code if you want!

Elgato takes a different approach with their EyeHome digital media player (*http://www.elgato.com/index.php?file=products_eyehome*; $249). Unlike the Squeezbox, the EyeHome has no display. Instead, you plug the EyeHome into your television and control the interface using the included remote control. The advantage of this is that a television affords much more space for the user interface. The disadvantage is that you need a television to use the EyeHome. The Mac-only EyeHome is a wired Ethernet device. If you want a wireless version, you need to purchase a wireless Ethernet adapter or hook it into a wireless Ethernet bridge. EyeHome is not just for your music; you can use it to access your entire iPhoto library, play QuickTime movies, and even browse the Web.

Macsense's HomePod (*http://www.macsense.com/product/homepod/*; $249) is another great little device that is interesting because it is entirely self-contained. The unit has a built-in display, wireless Internet, and speakers. You can take this device anywhere around your house and listen to your entire iTunes collection. If you want, you can also plug it into your stereo via the RCA jacks, or coaxial and digital outputs. You might think a product made by a company called Macsense would be for Macs only, but the HomePod works with either PCs or Macs.

Network

Regardless of the player you choose, you will still have to prepare your home network in the same way. All you need is a hardware router to manage transferring the data from your computer to the player. If you currently have a broadband connection, a router is a great way to share that connection with other computers in your house.

There are dozens of routers on the market; Apple's AirPort is one example, but Mac users should note that you don't have to go with Apple's product. Routers (including wireless routers) are based on standard Internet protocols, so which one you choose is totally up to you. If you are not lucky enough to have a broadband connection, don't worry. It isn't required for this hack, because the devices work (except when using features that require the Internet) inside your home network.

Software

Once you have your router set up, it's time to install the software for your player. All the players mentioned in this hack rely on software installed on the machine that contains your music. The software is essentially server software, turning your machine into a server not for the Web, but for the player itself.

 In the case of SlimServer, you can use the software to listen to your music collection over the Internet [Hack #95]!

Once you've installed the software on your machine, you can plug in your player and you should be good to go in a matter of minutes. Each player has a slightly different way of configuring itself to your network, but once the setup is done the player is simply a node on your network.

Plug RCA jacks from the player to your stereo, and suddenly you have a digital stereo. The Slim Squeezebox sports a backlit tube display that is a little retro but easy to use. EyeHome's player, as mentioned earlier, requires a television, because it has no built-in display. Macsense's HomePod is the most versatile of all, because it has built-in speakers and wireless Internet capabilities. In effect, it's a portable radio (it also has a built-in FM/AM radio) that streams your music collection. Granted, the speakers aren't high quality, but the ability to carry your iTunes music around anywhere in range of your wireless network is mondo cool.

Stream Music with AirPort Express ⚫⚫◐

Using Apple's AirPort Express to free your music's collection from your computer and play your music on any stereo.

The more you get into your iPod and iTunes, the more your computer will become the center of your musical universe. All those ripped CDs and iTunes Music Store purchases add up. At some point, you will scratch your head and think, "Hmm, how can I get all that music to play on my stereo without burning a CD?"

"Stream Music Around Your House" [Hack #25] is one option. Apple's AirPort Express (*http://www.apple.com/airportexpress/*; $129.00) is another.

AirPort Express is a small, self-contained unit that you plug into your wall. Its size betrays its power. Using AirPort Express, you can stream music from your computer to anywhere within your house (within 150 feet), share a USB printer, and extend your Apple AirPort network. For iTunes users, Air-Port Express liberates your music from your computer, allowing you to play it anywhere in your house.

Apple calls AirPort Express's music streaming capability AirTunes (*http://www.apple.com/airportexpress/airtunes.html*). To use it, all you need is a Mac running Mac OS 10.3 and an AirPort or AirPort Extreme Card. On the Windows side, you need Windows 2000 or XP and a Wi-Fi–certified IEEE 802.11b or 802.11g wireless card.

Connect your powered speakers or stereo to AirPort Express's audio port. You can use either an optical digital or analog audio cable. These do not come with AirPort Express; you'll need to purchased the AirPort Express Stereo Connection Kit ($39.00).

Plug your AirPort Express into an electrical outlet. There is no On switch; the base station turns on automatically once it's plugged in. The status light glows yellow until you've completed setup.

AirPort Express includes an install CD with an AirPort Express Assistant and the latest version of iTunes (in case you don't have it already). The software runs you through all your options, detects your AirPort Express automatically, and installs software on your computer to get things going. You will also have the opportunity to name your AirPort Express unit.

Once you've installed the software, your AirPort Express's status light turns to green, indicating everything is good to go. To start streaming music, open iTunes. Your AirPort Express will show up in the lower-right corner. Just select the name you chose for your AirPort Express (I named mine *Living Room* in this example) from the pull-down menu, as shown in Figure 2-7.

Figure 2-7. Music to your living room, just like that

Now that you've set up your AirPort Express, let the fun begin! Got a barbecue? Simply take your AirPort Express and plug it in outside. Hook it to your boom box or Tivoli Audio's iPal (*http://www.tivoliaudio.com/pPALIPOD.htm*; $129.99), and your barbecue will be rocking with your iTunes.

> You can place multiple AirPort Express units throughout your house; however, you can stream to only one unit at a time.

One limitation of AirPort Express is the lack of a remote control. Ostensibly, your computer is the remote control. However, using "Control iTunes from Your Palm" **[Hack #23]** or "Control iTunes from Your Mobile Phone" **[Hack #24]**, you can easily overcome this limitation.

HACK #27 Buy or Build a Headphone Amplifier ●●●

If the tunes from your iPod seem to lack punch or drama, the solution might be to add a headphone amplifier. You can buy one or build your own.

A question often raised in audio forums is whether the iPod benefits from boosting its output with an external headphone amplifier. When Apple redesigned the iPod back in 2002, among the upgrades was a new 30-mW-per-channel headphone amplifier circuit that is still the standard today. 30 mW is a hefty figure compared to that of other energy-conscious portable audio players (a paltry 5–10 mW per channel), and many iPod owners have appreciated the extra power for driving their favorite power-hungry headphones.

> High-end audio guru John Atkinson (reviewing the iPod with Sony MDR-7506 headphones) gushed about the iPod's sound quality, calling it "excellent, cost-effective audio engineering from an unexpected source" (*Stereophile*, October 2003).

However, the 30-mW-per-channel specification does not tell the whole story. iPods sold in Europe, for example, have output limiters that can prevent headphones from reaching maximum volume. Even on iPods without limiters, many headphones will never see 30 mW. The 30-mW spec is applicable only to 32-ohm loads, the nominal impedance of the stock iPod earbuds. When driving 100-ohm headphones (such as the in-ear Etymotic ER4S or Shure E5c), the maximum output is less than 10 mW per channel. With 300-ohm headphones (such as Sennheiser's audiophile-revered HD600), the amp's output drops to a mere 3 mW. Certainly, the HD600 will produce sound with 3 mW of power, but there is little reserve power or headroom to accommodate music with wide dynamic range and powerful transients, or the iPod's bass boost. Under these conditions, the internal headphone amp can be overloaded, resulting in distorted sound. This distortion can be just a vague, subtle feeling that something's not right with the sound.

Because Apple (as well as other portable-player OEMs) continues to design with low power consumption, cost effectiveness, and miniaturization as major goals, a dedicated external headphone amp can perform better than the iPod's internal amp and offer extra features, and it will extend the battery life of the iPod itself. Since iPods are meant to be mobile devices, it makes sense to choose a lightweight, battery-powered headphone amp, which is the main focus of this hack.

At the time of this writing, headphone amps are still specialty items. Most models must be purchased online, without the opportunity to compare brands firsthand (unless you're willing to order multiple amps on a trial basis). The next section will present some tips for buying amps.

If you're handy with a soldering iron, or if you have an interest in learning do-it-yourself (DIY) electronics, another option is to build a portable amp. The cost of parts for a basic battery-powered headphone amp is as little as $30. The advantage of building an amp is that it can be customized with unusual features (such as multiple headphone jacks or a mono switch) or a sound processor or equalizer not available in commercial units. DIY electronics is a rewarding hobby, but beginners should be prepared to spend time troubleshooting circuits. This hack contains the plans for a simple yet high-performance pocket headphone amp. Since its original publication on HeadWize, it has become one of the most popular electronics projects around the world (or so I'm told).

Buying a Headphone Amplifier

First and foremost, an iPod fan must determine whether there is a real need for a headphone amp, either to drive currently owned headphones or for a future purchase. The iPod's internal amp should be evaluated with a target group of coveted headphones, preferably with nominal impedances from 16 to 300 ohms—the range covering the majority of consumer headphones on the market today. The music should be a mix of favorite tracks and tracks containing wide dynamic range (sections that are quiet and loud) and lots of bass.

During playback, listen at a comfortable volume level, such that the quieter sections are audible, but not so high as to cause hearing damage during the louder sections. Try boosting the bass on the iPod's equalizer. The most obvious signs that the iPod's internal amp is stressing out with a particular set of headphones are distortion, buzzing, and/or crackling noises. More subtle indications include lightweight (lacking in bass) or lifeless (compressed) sound quality. Confirm that the problem is with the iPod's internal amp (and not the headphones) by connecting it to a high-quality headphone amp (either in a home audio system or at an audio retail store) and listening with the same headphones.

Cost and portability. In any in-depth discussion of mating a headphone amp with an iPod, two concerns repeatedly arise: the cost of an amp can approach that of the iPod itself, thereby increasing the overall cost of ownership, and connecting a separate amp compromises the portability and sleek design of the iPod. For those who want to get the best sound from their portables, these obstacles can be overcome.

Portable headphone amps range in price from as low as $20 to over $200 and come in a variety of form factors. Figure 2-8 shows a selection of amps, modeled with the Sennheiser HD600 and Shure E5c headphones, respectively.

Price alone does not determine overall utility or quality. Even a bargain amp might be superior to the iPod's internal amp, but the real question is whether there is enough of a performance gain to make it worth buying. A headphone amp should be regarded as a long-range, versatile investment. Besides being paired with an iPod, it can add or augment a headphone output for other gear, such as a portable CD player, a PC sound card, or a home audio system. In fact, there are portable amps with built-in digital-to-analog converters (DACs) that can function as auxiliary sound cards. Consumers should be careful, though, to distinguish portable DACs that do not incorporate true headphone amps.

Just as inexpensive amps are available, it is possible to choose a battery-powered headphone amp that minimizes any impact on the iPod's portability.

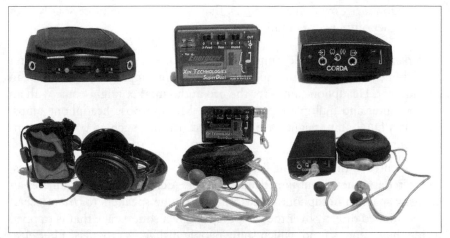

Figure 2-8. From left to right: HeadRoom's BitHead (USB DAC/amp combo) and GigaBag, Xin Technologies's SuperDual, and Meier Audio's Porta Corda II with belt clip and impedance adapter

Some amps are as small and unobtrusive as the inline volume controls on some models of headphones. The average portable amp is about the size of a deck of playing cards. An iPod and amp pressed together could still fit comfortably inside a shirt pocket or a roomy iPod carrying case. There are also bags specifically designed to house both an iPod and an amp (and even large headphones).

Specifications. I do not recommend buying an amp on specifications alone. One reason is that few amp makers have published complete sets of specifications that make comparisons between models meaningful. For example, Apple's spec sheet for the iPod omits any distortion measurements and lists a frequency response without meaningful corner points. The second reason is that specs don't always tell the whole story. On occasion, an amp that does not measure as well as the iPod's internal amp might still sound better.

Here are some broad guidelines for evaluating specs:

- An amp that specs at more than 30 mW per channel (into 32-ohms) will probably sound louder (reach higher volume levels) than the iPod's own amp.

- Breaking down the 30-mW spec into volts and amps, a headphone amp must be able to deliver more than 1 volt and .03 amps into 32-ohm headphones to outperform the iPod's internal amp.

- High-impedance headphones will play louder and more confidently from an amp that has a higher output voltage capability. Low-impedance headphones (lower than 32 ohms, that is) may rumble more solidly with a higher output current rating.

Features. Popular portable amp features include a crossfeed filter, extra headphone jacks, an output impedance selector, a clipping indicator, and an AC adapter. Headphone amps for the pro audio market might come with an audio limiter and multiple inputs/outputs. Multipurpose headphone amps, such as a DAC amp, might have specialized features such as USB and optical inputs.

Two features in the preceding list are unique to headphone amps: the crossfeed filter and the output impedance selector. A crossfeed filter simulates an acoustic space in headphones. Because headphone speakers (or *transducers*) are positioned directly over the ears, they create a soundstage that is trapped inside the listener's head, which some people dislike. A crossfeed filter electronically repositions the transducers so that the soundstage is pulled forward. There are many crossfeed circuit designs, and they do not sound alike, so buyers interested in this feature may wish to audition more than one brand of headphone amp. Electronics hobbyists can build their own filters. The HeadWize library has plans for several crossfeed designs.

Crossfeed filters are meant to operate on stereo signals (unless otherwise stated in the product description). They are a subcategory of a class of circuits called *virtualizers*. A surround virtualizer can simulate the positioning of 5.1 or more speakers inside stereo headphones. At the time of this writing, surround virtualizers (such as Dolby Headphone and SRS TruSurroundXT Headphone) have begun appearing in home audio gear and portable DVD players. As the costs of these technologies drop, they may begin to appear in portable headphone amps as well.

The output of a headphone amplifier has its own impedance, which is typically much less than the impedance of the headphones it's driving. Sometimes, headphones sound better with an amp that has a higher output impedance. An output impedance selector allows the user to increase the output impedance of the amp through a switch.

Building Your Own Pocket Headphone Amplifier

This portable headphone amp design was first published online on HeadWize (*http://www.headwize.com*) back in 1998. Figure 2-9 shows it in a standard electronics projects case, but many hobbyists have installed it in fancier cases, such as candy mint tins (e.g., Altoids and Penguin Mints) and woodcrafted boxes.

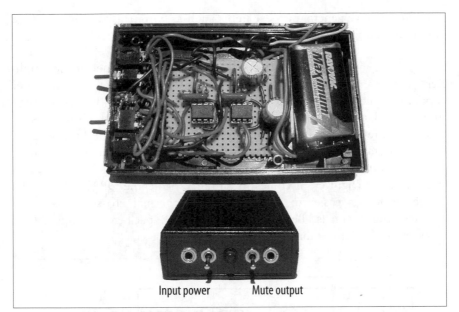

Figure 2-9. Your very own iPod headphone amplifier

The amp can be connected to the iPod's headphone output. The only volume adjustment is a *level* switch, because the iPod has its own volume control. The power supply is a single 9V battery that is split into a dual 4.5V supply with a virtual ground.

 The instructions for building the amp have been whittled down to the necessities here. The full plans (including details on adding a real volume control, more power supply options, and other updates) are available at *http://www.headwize.com*.

All of the parts are available from online parts suppliers such as Digi-Key (*http://www.digikey.com*), Mouser Electronics (*http://www.mouser.com*), and RadioShack (*http://www.radioshack.com*). RadioShack has many retail locations, but lately these stores have been reducing their electronics parts inventories, so you might have better luck online.

This project is easy enough for a beginning electronics hobbyist who has constructed one or two previous projects and knows how to use a soldering iron. For complete beginners, I recommend visiting local public libraries and bookstores for instructional materials about this fun and exciting hobby. The total cost for this project should be no more than $20–$25, assuming you already have general-purpose items such as wire (I used solid 22-gauge copper hookup wire).

The circuit. Figure 2-10 shows the schematic for one channel of the amplifier. The main active component is the OPA134 operational amplifier (opamp), which was selected for its excellent specs—FET inputs for high input impedance and low offset current, 8-MHz bandwidth, 20-uV/S slew rate, ultra-low noise and distortion, and so on. It can run on as little as 2.5V (very important in a portable design) and includes built-in current limiting (the maximum current output is 40 mA). The OPA134 costs less than $3.00 per unit from Digi-Key. It comes in a dual version, the OPA2134, but the single version is easier to wire and avoids thermal crosstalk distortion between the channels. Be sure to get the DIP package opamps; SOIC opamps are miniatures that are difficult to handle.

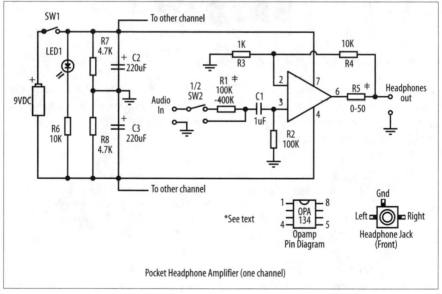

Figure 2-10. The iPod amp schematic

The OPA134 is wired as a noninverting amp with a gain of 11. At this gain, the output impedance of the amplifier is less than 0.2 ohms throughout the audio range. The high-pass filter C1-R2 at the input blocks DC current and has a bass corner frequency of about 1.5 Hz.

If there is residual hiss when the amp is driving low-impedance headphones such as the Grados (32 ohms), two possible solutions are to either lower the gain of the amp or add a load resistor to the output. To lower the gain to 5, set R4 to 3.9K ohms (or any value between 3.6K and 4.3K ohms). If the hiss is still there, try adding a load resistor, R5. Because the voltage drop across R5 reduces the maximum output of the amplifier, I recommend trying a low value, such as 30 ohms first.

The input for the amp is taken from the iPod's own headphone output. While the amp relies on the iPod's volume control for general settings, the level switch (SW2) is a quick way to mute the volume. With R1 = 100K ohms, the level switch drops the input voltage by 50% (6 dB). At R1 = 470K ohms (the value I used), the switch attenuates the input by 15 dB.

The power supply. The power supply circuit converts the 9V battery into a 4.5V dual supply with a *virtual* ground (R7, R8, C1, C2). To boost the amp's output voltage capability, two 9V batteries can be put in series for 18VDC (or 9VDC) if the capacitors are rated at 25V or higher.

Although the OPA134 could run from a single supply, it and other opamps are optimized for dual supplies, and a dual supply is required for direct-coupling the output. The virtual ground (0V point) actually sits at 4.5V but works because opamps only care about relative power supply voltages. At idle, the opamp output relative to ground is still 0V (plus or minus a millivolt or two of offset) without capacitor coupling. However, if the headphone amp will also double as a preamp, add a capacitor to the opamp output to block DC, if the input stage of the power amplifier is also direct-coupled.

Assembly. All resistors are watt metal film types. Capacitor C1 should be a metal film type, and all capacitors should be rated 25V or higher. If a small 1-mF capacitor for C1 (such as the 1-mF metal-film box capacitor from BC Components—Digi-Key part #3019PH-ND) is not available, a 0.1-mF capacitor can substitute, but the bass corner frequency will go up 15 Hz.

I assembled the pocket amp on a printed circuit protoboard (a Vector Circbord from Mouser Electronics; part #574-3677-6). This Circbord pattern includes bus strips, which can carry the power supply. Non–solder-plated boards are an acceptable substitute, but the exposed copper will oxidize in time. With a utility knife I cut a small square (about 2" × 1.75") of the protoboard to fit the case (mark a section on the board, score it several times with the utility knife and a straight edge, and then break off the section). The integrated circuits (ICs) are socketed with gold-plated machined-contact sockets, which work with low insertion force.

If the amplifier is housed in a plastic enclosure, the level switch must be grounded; otherwise, the amplifier will hum when the switch is touched. To ground the switch, strip about 1.5" of insulation from a 5" length of 22-gauge solid wire, tin the exposed end if necessary, and tightly wrap the exposed end around the groove at the rear of the metal mounting flange of the switch, twisting the end to form a secure, closed loop. Trim the other end of the wire to a suitable length and solder it to the circuit ground.

The plastic case measures 2.75" × 4.6" × 1" and has a 9V battery compartment (Digi-Key and Mouser sell similar cases in a variety of colors). It comes with both opaque and red plastic front panels. I chose the red plastic panel because the opaque panel was too thick to mount the headphone jacks. The headphone jacks are enclosed units for 1/8" stereo plugs. RadioShack sells a version of these jacks, but I ordered higher-quality units that have spring-loaded contacts from Mouser Electronics (part #161-3502).

Figure 2-9 shows the layout of the switches, jacks, and the power LED on the front panel. The placements are a little tight, but I think it turned out well. By the way, the LED is a 2-mA (max) low current type. It is biased at less than 1 mA to conserve battery power and still produces a very bright light. The LED was placed in an LED holder before being mounted on the front panel. My amplifier does not have a belt clip, but add-on belt clips are available at RadioShack.

—*Chu Moy*

HACK #28   Access Your iTunes Music Library Through TiVo

Listen to your iTunes music collection via your TiVo with the Home Media Option.

The TiVo Home Media Option (HMO) is included free in the TiVo subscription for the Standalone Series 2 TiVo (*http://www.tivo.com/4.9asp*). The HMO brings a whole slew of features, including the ability to schedule recordings over the Web, play MP3s through your television and attached stereo system, display digital photos on your TV, and even stream television shows between Series 2 TiVos.

Unfortunately, there is no Home Media Option support for Series 1 TiVos or DirecTiVos (a TiVo/DirecTV combination) at the time of this writing.

The latest TiVos that are being sold may already have the HMO installed. It's easy to tell—if you have a "Music and Photos" menu item on the front TiVo menu, then you're set.

Signing up for the Home Media Option is pretty simple. First, get your networked Series 2 TiVo onto your home broadband connection. Any high-speed connection will do just fine.

TiVo recommends two adapters: the WUSB11 Version 2.6 (a WiFi 802.11b adapter) from Linksys's Instant Wireless Series and the USB100TX USB-to-Ethernet (10/100 BaseT) adapter from their Instant Etherfast Series.

Users have also reported success using non-TiVo USB-to-Ethernet adapters, such as these:

Linksys USB100M   Linksys USB200M
NetGear FA101   NetGear FA120
Belkin F5D5050   3Com 3C460B
Microsoft MN-110   Hawking UF200
Hawking UF100   D-Link DSB-650TX
D-Link DUB-E100   Siemens SS1001
SMC SMC2208

On the WiFi front, Table 2-1 lists non-TiVo-recommended USB-to-802.11b adapters and the TiVo service numbers with which they are most likely to work. You can find your service number with a quick trip to TiVo's New Messages & Setup System Information screen. Look for it a couple of lines down from the top.

Table 2-1. Non–TiVo-recommended USB-to-802.11b adapters and associated TiVo service numbers

Initial digits of TiVo service number	Alternative USB-to-802.11b adapters
110, 130, 140	NetGear MA101 V.A, D-Link DWL-120 V.A
230, 240	D-Link DWL-120 V.D, Linksys WUSB12, Hawking WU250, Microsoft MN-510
Any	NetGear MA101 V.B, D-Link DWL-120 V.E, SMC 2662W V.2, Belkin F5D6050

That said, unless you have one of the unsupported adapters lying about your house, I'd recommend going with one of the recommended ones.

Simply plug the adapter into the back of your Series 2 (running TiVo OS 4.0 or later), and follow the onscreen directions to get it onto the network.

Point your browser to *http://www.tivo.com* and click the HMO link, or go directly to the HMO page (*http://www.tivo.com/4.9.asp*). You will need the email address and password you provided TiVo, Inc. when you first activated your TiVo. Don't worry if you've forgotten your password; you can either have a new password assigned and sent to your email address or set up everything again by providing TiVo, Inc. with your service number. You can find that number on the New Messages & Setup System Information screen.

Once you're signed up and have your TiVo connected to your home network, you will have to wait for your TiVo to connect to the service to activate itself. If you're a little impatient, you might try forcing your TiVo to connect and download the HMO option right away by having it make its Daily Call: go to the New Messages & Setup System Information screen and select Settings → Phone & Network Setup → Connect to the TiVo service now. If you notice the addition of Photos and Music to your TiVo Central menu, then the install worked.

Now that your TiVo is good to go, you need to install software on your Mac or PC. TiVo cannot currently play AAC files, and it can recognize iTunes playlists only on the Mac. Follow the included instructions for turning on MP3 sharing on your Mac or PC, and you'll be able to listen to music on your TiVo in no time.

—Raffi Krikorian

HACK #29   Run iTunes on an Old Mac ⓜⓔⓔ

Give your legacy Mac hardware a nudge into OS X with this XPostFacto hack and bring it into the digital music age.

Wait! Don't throw out that old Power Mac or Umax clone; it just might be up for a little Mac OS X sprucing. Some of those old Macs will actually run Mac OS X, with a little help from an unassuming-looking control panel. Once you've Pantherized your old Mac, it will run iTunes quite nicely. While you won't want to use the machine as a dedicated iTunes machine, it can make a great node on your network. You can throw it in your den and access your iTunes collection anytime, thanks to the Rendezvous sharing built right into iTunes.

I recently gave an old 7500 a G3 upgrade card from Sonnet (*http://www. sonnettech.com*), a quad-port FireWire card, and a dual-port USB card (only $37, combined). Mac OS 9 ran rather snappily and the machine served quite nicely as a USB print server. Then I stumbled across a little something called XPostFacto (*http://eshop.macsales.com/OSXCenter/XPostFacto/*), which is open source and free.

XPostFacto is a little hack that brings Mac OS X, OS X Server, and Darwin to older, unsupported, and forgotten Mac models—those draped in the unfashionable beige of times past.

> Before you think of giving XPostFacto a whirl, consult the compatibility chart at *http://eshop.macsales.com/OSXCenter/ XPostFacto/framework.cfm?page=XPostFacto.html#preparing.* Also, make sure your machine has been recently backed up. You're dealing with an unsupported hack here.

Find the XPostFacto site's comprehensive documentation at *http://eshop. macsales.com/OSXCenter/XPostFacto/framework.cfm?page=XPostFacto.html.*

Here's the procedure in a nutshell:

1. Boot into Mac OS 9.

2. Insert your standard-issue Mac OS X installation CD.

3. Run the XPostFacto application.

4. Point XPostFacto at the install CD and target volume.

5. Click the Install button.

6. Follow the usual installation instructions.

It'll take a while, mind you. Have some coffee, read the *New York Times,* watch a movie, and have a good meal. When you return, if all's gone according to plan, OS X should be humming away on your old throwaway Mac. Install iTunes, and suddenly you have a very cheap Mac stereo!

—*Rael Dornfest*

Build a Cheap MacMP3/AACServer ⓂⓋⒸ

HACK #30

Turn that old Mac gathering dust in the closet into a powerhouse MP3/AAC server.

There is no doubt that the G5 is a fantastic machine—fast as heck, beautiful, and, well, fast as heck. But the G5 form factor has one disadvantage over the G4 and G3 form factors: it is hard to add hard drives. You can purchase an after-market kit (*http://www.wiebetech.com/pricing/WebPricing. htm#G5Jam*) that lets you put up to four hard drives in your G5, but for a cheap MP3 server in your home nothing beats an older G4 or even G3. They are fast enough to run iTunes and OS X, and big enough inside to put in some serious storage drives.

For this hack, I am going to use an old blue and white G3 I have lying around. You can use the same kind of machine or any kind of G4, up to the latest models. In the past, I have installed four drives (which made for a total of five hard drives) in an old beige G3 and used that as an MP3 server for my house. However, Panther won't run without using a third-party utility like Xpostfacto [Hack #23], so a blue and white G3 or G4 is your best bet for this hack.

The first thing you need to do is get hold of some large, cheap hard drives. When the Mac lineup moved over to IDE hard drives from SCSI, suddenly Mac users had access to the same cheap drives that PC users use. This means you can go down to your local Best Buy, Circuit City, or other outlet and buy the hard drives they have on special and be almost certain they will work in your machine. Just to be sure, though, it's best to check the manufacturer's web site; the box often won't say whether it's Mac-compatible, but the web site will. If you look carefully, you can find hard drives for between $0.50 and $1.00 a gigabyte. This means you can get four 200-GB drives for $400–800. Assuming 20 albums per gigabyte, this means you can hold approximately 16,000 albums in AAC format. Now that's a music server!

In addition to the hard drives, you will also need a PCI card controller to control them. There are a number of options available, including Sonnet Tech's line of controllers (*http://www.sonnettech.com*). Once you've got hold of a PCI card, open your Mac and install the PCI card and hard drives. You will need to make sure you have the correct master/slave settings for the hard drives. The PCI card will have two ribbons. One ribbon is capable of running two hard drives. Make sure you seat all the connections firmly, without being too rough; you don't want to break anything!

After installing the hard drives and PCI card, it's time to boot up. The hard drives should show up right on your desktop. If they do, open up Apple's Disk Utility program, which you'll find within Applications/Utilities. Select the Erase tab and erase each drive, one by one. There are a number of options when you erase a hard drive, including partitioning. Since we are going to use these hard drives just to store MP3s/AACs, however, there is no need to partition the drives.

If your drives don't show up, something is wrong either with the master/slave settings on the hard drives or in how the drives and/or PCI card is physically installed. First, shut down your machine; then open it up and make sure all the equipment is tightly seated. If so, close it up, reboot, and see if the drives show up. If they don't, chances are that your master/slave settings aren't correct. Shut down, check these settings, and then reboot. The drives should appear, in which case you can proceed.

Once your hard drives are working, you'll have an incredible digital juke-box at your fingertips! Now it is just a question of transferring your digital music collection onto your new machine. In the past, you might have had to keep music on multiple machines or been unable to keep a copy on your iPod and in iTunes. This will no longer be a concern.

After copying over all your MP3s, fire up iTunes and import all the tunes to your library. Do this either by going to File → Import within iTunes, or by simply dragging the folders of music from your desktop over to the iTunes window. Make sure you have deselected the "Copy files to iTunes Music folder when adding to library" option, as shown in Figure 2-11; otherwise, iTunes will duplicate all your music, which isn't necessary.

Figure 2-11. Adding songs from your new hard drives to iTunes

In the past, you might have kept all your music in your */Home/Music* folder. However, you don't have to keep your music there; that is just the default folder iTunes uses when it rips CDs to MP3s. I keep my music organized by folders for each letter: Talking Heads goes in *T*, U2 goes in *U*, and so on. iTunes really doesn't care how you organize your files. When you import to your library, iTunes will keep everything in order by reading the embedded ID3 tags.

You now have a machine capable of holding an immense amount of music. Using the power built into iTunes, you can stream this music throughout your house to any other Mac or PC that has a network connection and iTunes 4.0 or later. Open your iTunes preferences and check "Share my music," as shown in Figure 2-12.

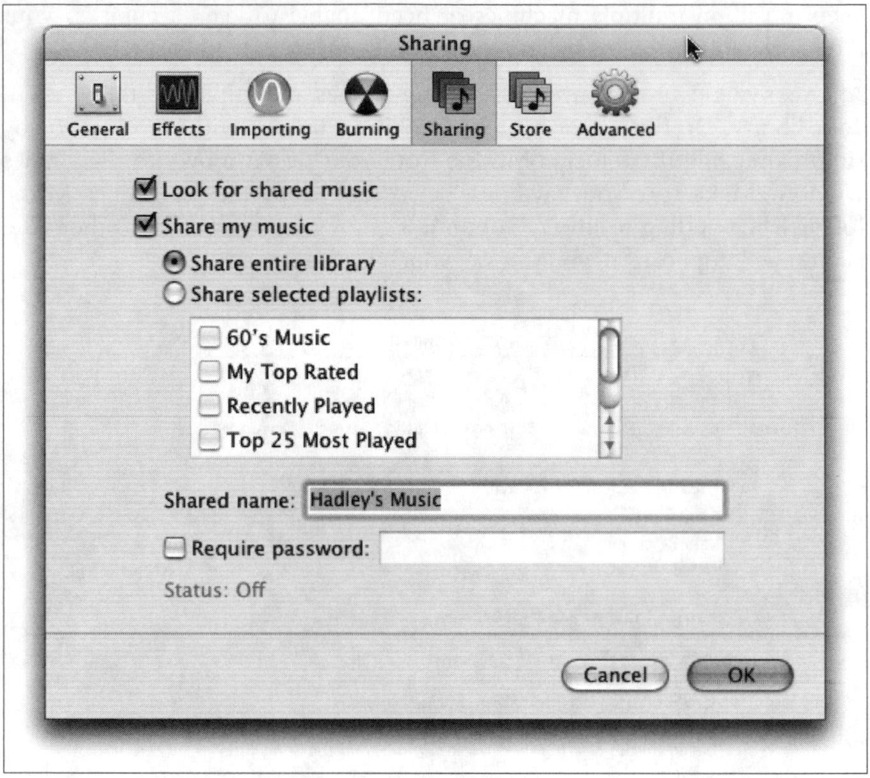

Sharing

General Effects Importing Burning Sharing Store Advanced

☑ Look for shared music
☑ Share my music
   ⦿ Share entire library
   ◯ Share selected playlists:

   ☐ 60's Music
   ☐ My Top Rated
   ☐ Recently Played
   ☐ Top 25 Most Played

Shared name: Hadley's Music

☐ Require password:

Status: Off

Cancel   OK

Figure 2-12. Streaming your music to any PC or Mac in your network

Enter any name you want for your Shared name. You can, if you want, share only specific playlists. This is a great feature if you want to stream children's music to your kid's room but want to pass on that Snoop Dog album. As an extra measure of protection, you can also password-protect your collection. That's it! Your music will now be available throughout your home network.

> If you are using iTunes at work, be aware that anyone within the subnet of your network can now see your music.

Building a digital jukebox is surprisingly easy and affordable. Add in iTunes's ability to stream music using Rendezvous, and your house will be full of music.

Build a Cheap Linux Music Server ⊗ ⊙ ❶

Build a Linux-based music server to store all your digital songs in a stable and affordable package.

"Build a Cheap MacMP3/AACServer" [Hack #30] covered how to create an awesome Mac-based digital music server. But what if you have a spare PC or a Mac that is too old to run OS X? For the old Mac, check out "Run iTunes on an Old Mac" [Hack #29]. Otherwise, your best option is to look at creating a Linux music server for your iTunes music collection.

That's right, with an old machine you have lying around, and the best open source operating system out there, you too can easily build a jammin' music server. To make your jukebox complete, you can route your music to your stereo with AirPort Express and AirTunes.

Hardware

If you need to go out and buy a computer, I recommend a cheap PC. It doesn't need to be the latest and greatest, because Linux can perform very well on modest hardware.

Here are the PC music server specifications:

- A Pentium II or AMD K6-III processor and 128 MB of RAM (so, a system manufactured in around 1999) should be fine. More speed and memory will hurt nothing but your pocket.
- A CD-ROM drive to run the Linux installer CDs.
- A monitor, at least temporarily, for server installation and configuration.
- A network card.
- A large hard disk.

> My friend just bought a fast 120-GB hard drive at Best Buy for $100. By the time you read this, there will no doubt be much larger drives available at that price.

For networking, assume a Linksys, D-Link, or similar router that does automatic DHCP IP assignments. For Linux, Debian is a great choice. Debian takes care of package management; you need only run the update command. How do you acquire this gem? At *http://www.debian.org*, you can choose to order the CDs or download and burn them yourself.

If you have an old Macintosh desktop that can't handle Mac OS X (even with XPostFacto [Hack #23]), you can give Linux for PowerPC a shot. The distribution to get right now is Yellow Dog Linux (*http://www.yellowdoglinux.*

com). You can download or order the CDs from the Yellow Dog folks. Make sure you install the *apt* package with Yellow Dog so you can follow the configuration instructions for Samba or NFS, later in this hack.

Getting Linux to Talk to iTunes

There are many ways to go about setting up an iTunes remote library configuration. I suggest a universal method using Samba, which is best for novices. You could also set up Rendezvous on your music server, but in my opinion, the way iTunes 4 does Rendezvous library sharing is not ideal. By using the Samba file-sharing method, you keep the power to rate your songs as well as change the genre and other (ID3) song information.

Before we get started, there's one more bit to twiddle. By default, the "Copy files to iTunes Music folder when adding to library" option in iTunes is selected. Turn off this option before adding songs from your new hard drives to iTunes, as shown in Figure 2-13.

Figure 2-13. Adding songs from your new hard drives to iTunes

During the Linux installation, make sure you allocate a hefty partition on your hard drive for the music files. For help with Debian GNU/Linux installation, see *http://www.aboutdebian.com* and, of course, Google.

Here are a few tips:

- Once networking is working on your Linux installation, use Terminal in Mac OS X or download Putty for Windows so that you can SSH into your server from your other computer.

- Some knowledge of Unix commands is helpful.

- nano is a good basic text editor.

- Use the df -h command and note the "Mounted on" area where your music should go. I recommend using */Music* for the mount point.

Once you've completed this hack, you'll have an easily expandable place to keep your music. If you add another hard drive to your server, set it up using Google and the Debian manual. Then, repeat these steps to serve another share.

Server-Side File Sharing

If your main machine is a Mac, then on your Linux box you can use either Samba or NFS to share your files (Windows users do not have the NFS option). Though the NFS option is faster, Samba is easier to implement.

Option one: Samba. Samba is your best bet to get off to a quick start. Its performance is not likely to be as fast as NFS's for large file copies between your computer and server, but it is good enough. Security is handled with user-based control, where you set up user accounts and passwords. It uses the same user information as Linux.

To install Samba, simply run sudo apt-get install samba. Now, you must configure the shares. You probably already created a user during the Linux installation, but you can add more users with the command /usr/sbin/adduser (if it's not installed, run apt-get install adduser) and set passwords with the passwd command.

To set up shares, Samba configuration is done in the */etc/samba/smb.conf* file. To improve performance, I recommend adding this line after the [global] section:

```
[global]
read size = 32768
```

To set up your share, put the name of your share in brackets, followed by the share information:

```
[music]
comment = Josh's Music
writable = yes
path = /music
public = yes
valid users = josh, dan
admin users = josh
```

In my example, I have Unix accounts on my Linux system named *josh* and *dan*.

Now, it's time to create the connection to your Samba server. On your server, run /sbin/ifconfig to get its IP address.

If you're using a Mac, go to the Finder and select Go → Connect to Server. Then, enter smb:// followed by the IP address you just found. You can then log in and choose your music share. Add it as a favorite for quick access in the future.

If you're using a PC, go to the Start menu and select Run. Enter *ip_address*\ music, replacing *ip_address* with your server's IP address.

Option 2: NFS. I have found NFS on Debian GNU/Linux to perform significantly faster than Samba, but it comes with some catches. The security isn't user-based, but rather IP-based. I actually use NFS myself, but I suggest Samba to the general population, because it is easier. To install NFS, run apt-get install nfs-common nfs-user-server. To add your share, edit the */etc/exports* file. My exports file is lax and allows anyone connected to my network full access to my music. Here is an example full-access */etc/exports* file:

```
/music 192.168.1.0/255.255.255.0(rw,insecure)
```

You might want to identify your iTunes-running machine specifically for more security. To do this, just enter its IP address. Here is an example restrictive */etc/exports* file:

```
/music 192.168.1.2(rw,insecure)
```

Now, it's time to create the connection to your NFS server. On your server, run /sbin/ifconfig to get its IP address.

If you're on a Mac, go to the Finder and select Go → Connect to Server. Enter nfs://*ip_address*/music (replacing *ip_address* with your server's IP address), and add it as a favorite.

> Having problems reading, deleting, or copying files? I am assuming your server is to be used only by you or trusted people, so you can log into your server and run chmod -R 777 /music. This lets any user read, delete, and add to your music library and guarantees that Samba and NFS can do it as well.

Managing Your Library

If you are using a Mac, you can use either Samba or NFS as your server. For library management, use Doug Adams's iTunes Library Manager AppleScript (*http://www.malcolmadams.com/itunes/itinfo/ituneslibrarymanager.shtml*). It is shareware, free for up to two libraries—one for at home and one for on-the-go!

If you are using Windows, you must use Samba for your server. For library management, you might be in a tough spot, because I do not currently know of an available VBScript to manage iTunes libraries. One option is to use iTunes at home and use Winamp for your laptop's smaller collection of music when you're on the go.

Congratulations! Using off-the-shelf components and free software, you have set up a system to feed your music files to iTunes through file sharing over a network. Rock on!

—*Joshua Benjamin*

CHAPTER THREE

iPod Software
Hacks 32–49

The iPod's software is what makes your iPod tick. It allows you to scroll through playlists with aplomb, rate songs on the fly, and much, much more. This chapter shows how to take your iPod's software to the next level by revealing the many features of the iPod and showing you how to hack the iPod to do things it wasn't necessarily designed to do.

After reading this chapter, you'll be able to use your iPod to get news updates [Hack #33], read your email [Hack #43], dial your phone [Hack #47], and even run Linux right on your iPod [Hack #49]. This chapter also covers what to do when things go wrong with your iPod [Hack #34], revealing the iPod's hidden diagnostic mode, and shows Linux users how to get in on the action [Hack #46].

HACK #32 Run Your iPod in Disk Mode ⓂⓌⓁ
Use your iPod's copious disk space to store and back up data from your computer.

The iPod's hard drive can be used to store much more than your music. If you want to transfer files between two machines, nothing does the trick as quickly as an iPod. This book has been written entirely using the iPod as a hard drive, so when I go from my laptop (while writing on the road) to my desktop, all my files are available. Even if you don't use the iPod's hard drive as an everyday storage device, it makes a handy backup device; and, with the many gigabytes of storage available on today's iPods, you should have space to spare. Using the iPod in Disk mode is pretty simple, and knowing how to do it will help you in many hacks throughout this chapter.

Connect your iPod to your computer. If you haven't twiddled with the preferences already, iTunes should launch automatically; otherwise, launch iTunes. Your iPod will show up in the source window, as shown in Figure 3-1.

Figure 3-1. The iPod in the iTunes Source window

Select your iPod and access the iPod's preferences by clicking the iPod icon, (shown in Figure 3-2) in the lower-right corner of the iTunes window.

Figure 3-2. The iPod's Preferences icon

The iPod's preferences window will now pop up, as shown in Figure 3-3.

Figure 3-3. The iPod's iPod Preferences window

There are a couple ways to turn on the iPod's Disk mode. If the machine you are on is the primary machine where the iPod syncs with iTunes, select "Enable disk use." If the machine isn't your primary machine or if you want to manage your playlists and songs manually (my preferred method, because my music collection is larger than my iPod's capacity), select "Manually manage tracks and playlists." When using the manual setting, "Enable disk use" will become grayed out, *with* the checkbox selected. By default, when "Manually manage tracks and playlists" is selected, Disk mode is turned on.

Your iPod now shows up on your Mac desktop and in the Mac disk menu list, as shown in Figure 3-4. On Windows, your iPod shows up under My Computer. If you want to use your iPod with a Linux desktop, see "Use an iPod with Linux" [Hack #46].

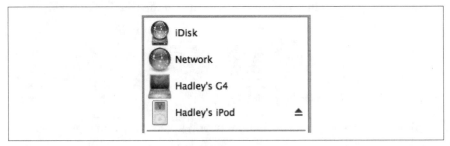

Figure 3-4. The iPod as just another hard drive

Treat your iPod as you would any external hard drive. Thanks to the FireWire or USB 2.0 interface, you can transfer files blisteringly quickly. Note that while your first temptation after mounting your iPod might be to look for your iPod's music files, you won't find them. Take a gander at "Access Hidden Files on Your iPod" [Hack #41] for details on how to see your iPod's *hidden* music files.

HACK #33   Read News and More ⓂⓌ⬤

Use the iPod's built-in Notes feature to turn your iPod into an information machine, carrying news, stock quotes, notes, and other scraps of information around with you.

The iPod is much more than a music device. With some nifty hackery, you can transfer loads of data to your iPod. If you've followed the manual, you've probably already transferred your Palm Contact and Calendar items. With this hack, we will add News, Weather, Movies, Stocks, Horoscopes, Lyrics, Text, and Directions to that list.

If you're on a Mac, Pod2Go (*http://www.kainjow.com/pod2go/*; donateware) is for you. If you're on a Windows box, check out iPodSync (*http://iccnet. 50megs.com/iPodSync/*; $13.95; trial version available), which does many of the items covered in this hack. iPodSync works in a fashion similar to

Pod2Go; we won't discuss it directly in this hack, but the discussion of Pod2Go should give you plenty of info to get started.

When you launch Pod2Go the main window will load up, as shown in Figure 3-5. Here is where you configure Pod2Go with all the information you want to transfer to your iPod. Once you have made your selection, Pod2Go will download the data from the Internet and then transfer the data in note format to your iPod.

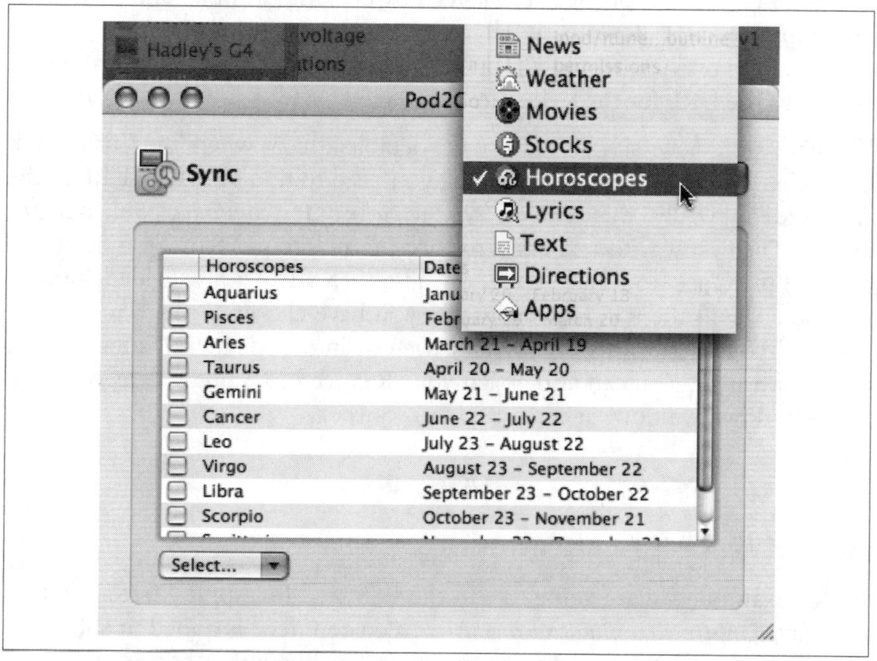

Figure 3-5. The Pod2Go interface

First, let's pick some data to transfer. Pod2Go can transfer News, Weather, Movies, Stocks, Horoscopes, Lyrics, Text, and Directions, as well as sync your Apple Address Book, Calendar, and Safari bookmarks. In this hack, we'll look at one example (News) in depth; you can use it as a springboard for further exploration.

News

To add news updates to your iPod, select News from the drop-down menu (as shown in Figure 3-5), and then click on the plus sign (+). A window will pop up with two tabs, Feeds and Custom. Feeds are preset newsfeeds that you can select. All the feeds are based on the RSS or Atom protocols, which are widely used across the Web. To add a feed, select a category from the pull-down menu, click the newsfeed you want to add (you can ⌘-click to select multiple items), and click Add Selected. Once you've added all the feeds you want to add, hit the Close button. Now, all your feeds will show up in the News window, with checkboxes next to them. If you don't want to have a particular feed sync, just deselect it by clicking on the checkbox. Or, if you find that a feed gets old after a week, just delete it by selecting it and clicking the minus button (–).

At any time, you can preview a newsfeed by clicking the *i* button. By default, Pod2Go does not download full articles; however, you can enable this option in the preview window. You can also see more details about the feed as well as the URL for the feed's site.

If your favorite news site isn't one of the defaults, this is where the Custom tab comes in. Give it a click. The first thing you need to find out is the URL of the RSS feed. Typically, this URL is *http://www.website.com/index.xml*, but not always. The best way to find out is to click on the site's RSS or Atom icon (see Figure 3-6). Once you click on it, an all-text XML page will load in your browser. This is the RSS feed. Now that you have clicked through to the RSS URL, all you need to do is copy and paste it into Pod2Go's "Enter URL of feed" form field. You can also assign your RSS feed to a preset category from the drop-down window, or enter your own category.

Figure 3-6. The RSS icon

In this example, we are going to add the RSS feed for Apple Matters (*http://www.applematters.com/index.xml*). After a custom feed is added, it shows up in your News window, and you can preview it like any other newsfeed, as shown in Figure 3-7. You should definitely do this for custom feeds, just to make sure everything works before you transfer any data to your iPod.

Hacking the Hack

There is much more to Pod2Go than the news. All the other modules work in a similar way to the News module. In Pod2Go's preferences, you can have the application sync to your iPod once the iPod is connected to your computer. Pod2Go also installs a convenient menu where you can do quick syncs of individual items. From this menu, you can also select Note Editor. With the Editor, you can rearrange the order of your notes and even create your own notes. Want to have your resume on hand on your iPod? Just create a new note and copy and paste in your text.

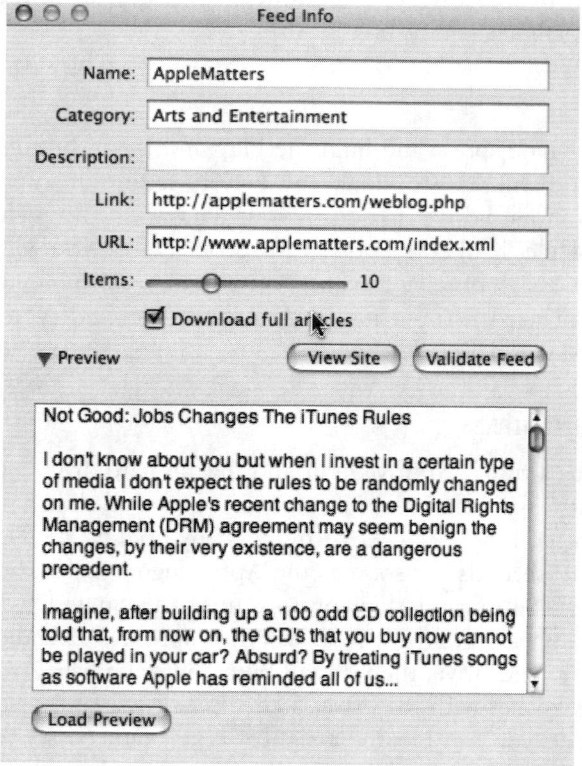

Figure 3-7. *Previewing your RSS feed after adding it to make sure everything works*

HACK #34 Diagnose iPod Problems ⓜⓦⓞ

Sometimes, things go wrong in iPod-land. This hack shows you how to figure out what the problem is.

It can happen to the best of us. You wake up one day, take a quick shower, and head off to work. On the subway, you pull out your iPod and hit play. Nada. Nothing. Your iPod is dead. Before you break into a cold sweat trying to figure out where the closest Apple store is, think back to this hack. While it won't solve every iPod problem, this hack will give you access to the troubleshooting tools Apple's technicians use to fix and diagnose problems.

On Hold?

The first thing you should check when your iPod appears to be dead is the Hold button. Don't be insulted; we've all done it—cursed out the iPod and all things digital until we realize that the Hold button is on. There, now, with that out of the way, let's continue with the next basic tool in your iPod's self-repair arsenal: the reset.

Reset

To reset your iPod, press and hold the Play and Menu buttons for 10 seconds. The iPod will reset to the default factory settings it shipped with, but (as long as your hard drive isn't dead) your data will be fine. The Apple logo will appear while the iPod reboots. Ten seconds later, you will almost definitely breathe a sigh of relief as your iPod comes back to life. If you own an iPod, you will need to reset it occasionally; however, if you are doing it daily, something is definitely wrong.

Scan the Hard Drive

Your iPod has a tiny hard drive in it, and like all hard drives, it can become corrupt or just plain old break. If resetting your iPod didn't fix things, the next test is a hard disk scan. Reset the iPod by holding the Play and Menu buttons for 10 seconds. As soon as the Apple logo appears, hold down the Previous, Next, Select, and Menu buttons until an icon with a disk and magnifying glass appears. A progress bar will now appear. Depending on the size of your iPod's hard drive, the test will take approximately 2–10 minutes. If everything is kosher with the drive, a checkmark will appear over the hard drive icon, and you can breathe a sigh of relief. Otherwise, your iPod will display the dreaded message, "HDD fail." Yes, it is as bad as it sounds. Your hard drive is hosed. You need to call Apple for service.

Diagnostics

If you pass the hard drive test and your iPod is still acting funky or being uncooperative, here is how to access the diagnostic mode to figure out what may be wrong. First reset the iPod. Once the Apple logo appears, press and hold down the Previous, Next, and Select buttons. Let go after a couple of seconds, and you will hear a quick chirp and the diagnostic screen will appear.

To navigate through the various tests, use the Previous button. To run a test, hit the Select button, and to get back to the diagnostic main menu at the end of a test, hit the Play button. Take a look at Table 3-1 for a breakdown of all the tests available. Clarification for a number of the tests was originally researched by iPoding.com (*http://www.ipoding.com*).

If your iPod fails any of the diagnostic tests, something is very wrong with it. Take your iPod into your local Apple store to have a Genius take a look at it, or give Apple a call.

Table 3-1. *iPod diagnostic mode tests*

Test	What it does
A. 5 in 1	Automatically runs tests J through N.
B. Reset	Resets the iPod.
C. Key	Allows you to test if the iPod's buttons are working.
D. Audio	Tests the audio subsystem. A passed test returns "0X00000000 DONE." If you have headphones on, you will hear a beep at the end of the test.
E. Remote	Checks the remote. If no remote is plugged in, or if the remote is not working, the message "RMT FAIL" will appear.
F. FireWire	Checks the built-in FireWire bus. A passed test returns "FW PASS."
G. Sleep	Forces the iPod to go to sleep. It is unclear why this "test" exists! You have to reset the iPod to wake it up again.
H. A 2 D	Tests the power subsystem.
I. OTPO CNT	Tests the scroll wheel. Use the scroll wheel, and turns will be represented by hexadecimal values.
J. LCM	Tests the display. Hit Action to go through three patterns.
K. RTC	It is unclear what this test does, although it appears to test the built-in clock.
L. SDRAM	Tests the RAM.
M. Flash	Tests the ROM.
N. OTPO	Tests the scroll wheel.
O. HDD Scan	Tests the hard drive.
P. Run In	Runs continuous tests on the iPod's chipsets.

Use Your iPod with a Mac and a PC   HACK #35

Listen to music on and transfer music between multiple machines and multiple platforms.

Back in the day, you were either a Windows person or a Mac person. Of course, some of us are still that way, but many of us live in a world where we have to use a Windows box at work and have a Mac at home. Others have just recently discovered (or rediscovered, with OS X) the Macintosh and have decided to purchase one for home use. Either way, can't we all just get along?

Well, when it comes to the iPod, yes—but not necessarily out of the box. Apple snobs now have permission to raise their noses a tad higher: a Windows iPod goes from Windows to Mac with aplomb, but try it the other way around and you have a problem. Why? Because the Macintosh operating system, probably due to its minority status, can read Windows-formatted disks (the iPod is, after all, just a hard drive), while Windows (perhaps due to its majority—read, monopolistic—status) cannot read Macintosh-formatted devices.

When Apple first started selling Windows iPods, they sold a Mac version and a PC version. Apple has since changed that model, so that now you buy the same iPod for either platform. The difference is that when you plug an iPod into a Mac, it is good to go. With a PC, the drive is reformatted to a PC device (see "Use an iPod with Linux" [Hack #46] for more details on how this works).

If you want to use your iPod with both a Mac and a PC, you need to either have a PC-formatted iPod or convert your current Mac iPod into a PC version. This procedure will wipe out any songs or data you have on your iPod, so make sure everything is available in iTunes before proceeding. Download the software updater for Windows from Apple's iPod support site (*http://www.apple.com/ipod/download/*) before following the directions in this hack.

Converting Your iPod

On your Windows machine, carry out the following steps:

1. Open the iPod Software Updater application.
2. Click Restore. An alert box will appear to confirm whether you want to restore the iPod (remember, all your data will be erased!). A progress bar will appear while the iPod is wiped clean.
3. When the factory settings have been restored, unplug the cable from the iPod.
4. When prompted by the iPod, reconnect the cable. After the iPod has booted up, it will display a "Do not disconnect" message. Close the Updater application, and iTunes will automatically open.

> For iPod Software 1.1, when the iPod is in Disk mode, a FireWire logo appears on the screen instead of the "Do not disconnect" message.

5. Give your iPod a name in the iTunes setup window.
6. The "Automatically update my iPod" option is selected by default. Deselect this option if you'd rather update manually, and then click Done. The iTunes main window appears, and, if you selected "Automatically update my iPod," iTunes starts copying over music to your iPod. Wait until the iTunes display says the update is complete.
7. Quit iTunes.
8. Disconnect the iPod from the computer. After a few moments, the Language display appears on the iPod's screen.
9. Select a language.
10. Quit the iPod Software Updater application.

That's it! Your iPod has now been converted to a Windows iPod and updated with the music and playlists from your Windows library. If you want to use your new Windows iPod with your Mac, go ahead and attach it. Your Mac will treat your iPod as it would a Mac iPod, with one small caveat. If you want to create an emergency boot volume [Hack #42], you won't be able to. You can create a Mac emergency boot volume only with a Mac-formatted iPod.

Otherwise, you are free to go back and forth between your Mac and your Windows machine. Be sure to select "Manually manage songs and playlists" in your iPod's preferences on both machines. That way, your iPod won't get updated with the contents of each machine's iTunes library every time you plug it in. Also note that even though you can play the iPod and put music onto it from either machine, you won't be able to transfer your music from the iPod to your computers. For that, you'll need "Access Hidden Files on Your iPod" [Hack #41].

HACK #36   Play Games on Your iPod

Waiting for the bus and tired of just listening to music? You can also play games on that music player of yours.

Some of you might not even know that there are games on your iPod. Navigate to Extras → Games and, assuming you have a generation 3 (G3) iPod, you will find Brick, Music Quiz, Parachute, and Solitaire. If you have a G1 iPod, only the Breakout game is available, and that only as an *Easter egg* (a bit of hidden code on the iPod): access it by navigating to the iPod's About screen and holding down the button in the centre of the jog wheel for about five seconds. Breakout will appear on your screen. Then, use the jog wheel to move the racket and play while you listen to your favorite songs.

Apart from the games Apple includes on your iPod, though, there are a few other options out there to whittle away your time.

Text-Based Games Available for Your iPod

Remember those Choose Your Own Adventure books you used to read as a kid? Well, now a company called XOPlay (*http://www.xoplay.com*) designs choose-your-own-adventure–type books/games for your iPod or iPod mini. Three titles are currently available, for $14.99 each:

The Rise of the Lost
    A fantasy book/game where your character, Sir Jacob Zavier, Knight of the Royal Order in the Kingdom of Valance, travels around fighting the minions of the Darkened Kingdom Of The Lost in a quest to vanquish these enemies from Valance.

Herbert's Big Adventure
    You play Herbert, a lady-chasing guy who is looking for love in all the wrong places.

BUM: Rags to Riches
>XOPlay's newest release, where you start out as Rufus, a bum who searcjes for free meals and shelter but who has entrepreneurial dreams of working his way up the ladder of success.

The games are installed in and accessed via the *Notes* folder of your iPod (G3 or later). At the end of each page, you are presented with clickable hyperlinked choices that take you to the next page in your adventure.

Another place where you can find choose-your-own-adventure–type games for the iPod is iPodSoft's iStory download page (*http://ipodsoft.com/Downloads.aspx*; free), which as of the writing of this hack features 33 free iStories written by end users like yourself. These vary from Harry Potter adventures, to a variation of the Grand Theft Auto games, and on to raunchy virtual cyber-sex sessions. If none of the iStories currently available from iPodSoft are your cup of tea, then why not write your own [Hack #37]?

Non-Text-Based iPod Games

Unfortunately, the only truly non-text-based games available for the iPod are those included with your iPod. Until Apple increases the iPod's capabilities via a firmware update or releases a more open SDK for the iPod, this limitation will most likely remain.

The one currently available exception to the text-only games dilemma uses text alongside audio and is only available in German. If you happen to be fluent in German, *Don't Know iPod*, a game in the spirit of *You Don't Know Jack*, is available for download from the games page of pochoirs.de (*http://www.pochoirs.de/spieletxt.htm*; free). The game features audio clips of an enthusiastic announcer asking questions and providing multiple-choice options for the answer. You then select your answer from the text file via your iPod's Notes, which takes you to another text file that tells you whether you were right or wrong and links to the next audio file question with its clickable list of answers.

Hacking the Hack

Take a look into making your own games for the iPod. Either make your own text-based adventure, or combine text and audio as in *Don't Know iPod* to make a multimedia game. Alternately, you could install Linux on your iPod [Hack #46] and try to code something on that platform.

—*C. K. Sample III*

Write an iPod Adventure Game

Create your own Notes-based adventure game for your iPod, either for your
personal enjoyment or to share with your friends on the World Wide Web.

"Play Games on Your iPod" [Hack #36] introduces the games that are currently
out there for the iPod. Right now, the pickings are slim, so you might want
to take matters into your own hands. This hack shows you how to create
your own iPod adventure game using a nifty piece of software written just
for this purpose. If you are a Mac user and want to create your own games,
all is not lost. Using the methods discussed in "Write Your Own iPod Book"
[Hack #39], you too can create an iPod adventure game.

iStory Creator from iPodSoft

In addition to offering several free iStories [Hack #36] for download from their
web site, iPodSoft also makes freely available iStory Creator (*http://ipodsoft.
com/iCreator.aspx*; free), a tool to help people make their own iPod text-
adventure games. The software is only available for Windows, but if you have
a copy of Virtual PC running on your Macintosh you can run the software in
your emulated PC environment and simply drag the completed folder into the
Notes directory of your iPod to install the game.

If you do not have Virtual PC and are running Mac OS X or Linux, or if you
would simply rather write your masterpiece game/book from scratch, feel
free to skip ahead to "Write Your Own iPod Book" [Hack #39], which provides
a cross-platform do-it-yourself (DIY) option (although reading through this
hack to see how iStory Creator operates will help you get an idea for what
you will be doing in the DIY hack).

> To install iStory Creator, you must have Microsoft's .NET
> Framework on your computer (*http://download.microsoft.com/
> download/a/a/c/aac39226-8825-44ce-90e3-bf8203e74006/dot
> netfx.exe*). After installing the .NET Framework, go ahead and
> download iStory Creator and run its rather straightforward
> installer. If the .NET Framework was not properly installed,
> the iStory Creator installer will stop and ask you to make sure
> you install it.

Upon first launching iStory Creator, after being greeted with the attractive
splash screen shown in Figure 3-8, you will be asked to set some preferences.
Under basic preferences, give yourself a name or nickname. This will be associated with your iStory, so if you intend to write under a pseudonym, use that
name here.

Figure 3-8. iStory Creator's splash screen

Also, you will need to set a root folder where all of your iStories will be saved. I set my root folder inside the *Documents* folder of my Windows XP emulation running in Virtual PC. As you can see in Figure 3-9, the field name reads "iStories Root Folde," and this is indicative of the somewhat clunky interface of the program. But, hey, it's free and highly functional, so let's not complain too much.

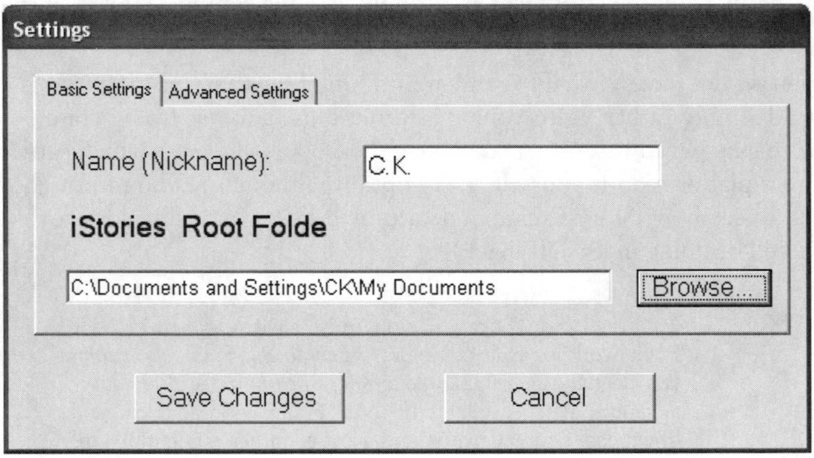

Figure 3-9. Giving yourself a name/nickname and setting a root folder where all your iStories will be saved

After filling in these basic settings, click on the Advanced Settings tab and set the auto backup interval. I recommend setting it to back up the current file every five minutes, as shown in Figure 3-10.

Once you have set the preferences, the main window of iStory Creator will open, as shown in Figure 3-11.

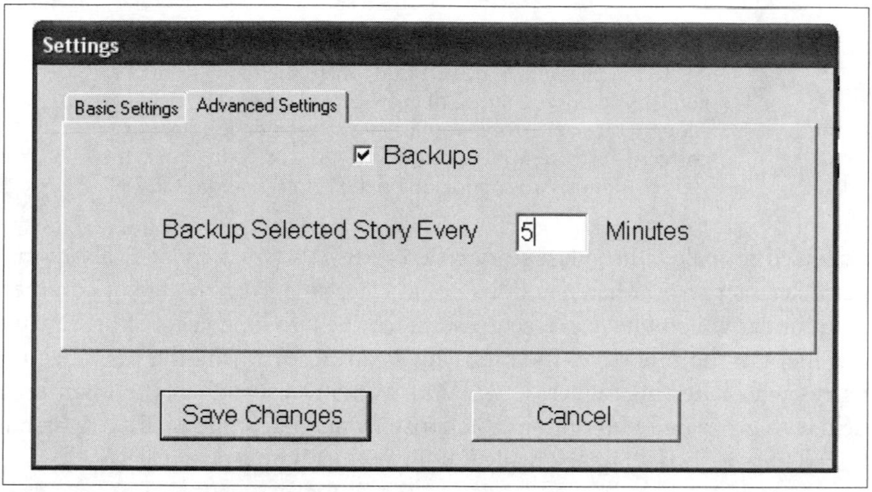

Settings

Basic Settings | Advanced Settings |

☑ Backups

Backup Selected Story Every   5   Minutes

Save Changes   Cancel

Figure 3-10. Don't forget to set up auto-save!

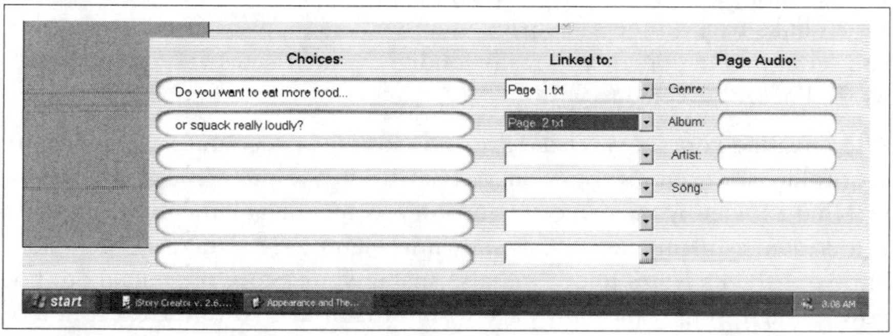

Choices: Linked to: Page Audio:

Do you want to eat more food...   Page 1.txt   ▼   Genre:

or squack really loudly?   Page 2.txt   ▼   Album:

                                                     ▼   Artist:

                                                     ▼   Song:

                                                     ▼

                                                     ▥

start   📘 iStory Creator v. 2.6...   📘 Appearance and The...   3.06 AM

Figure 3-11. iStory Creator's main interface

After you've written the first page of your story, check out the six multiple-choice fields provided below the main window. You can simply write "Next..." and link to the next page if you merely want to continue a linear story. Otherwise, you can fill up as many options as possible, linking each to another page that you will compose. Unfortunately, you cannot create a link to a page that doesn't exist yet, so click the New Page button a couple of times to populate your file column. Simply type in the options your reader can choose from, and then, from the drop-down menu next to it, select one of the files to be the connecting link for that selection.

> You can also add audio to certain pages, but these links are created by helping your iPod find where the file is located in your music library, rather than by a hard link to its location. Along with your iStory, you'll have to provide the necessary correctly tagged MP3s; make sure to correctly enter the Genre, Album, Artist, and Song fields for each audio file.

I decided to make a little test story called "Misha's Great Escape" about my pet Eclectus parrot, Misha, and his desire to escape from the life of confinement under which I have persecuted him for the two long years of his torturous life. On the title page, I wrote "This is a test for Misha the pet Eclectus parrot who hates his owner, C. K., and wants to escape" in the main text field. I then created two options to choose from: "Eat some seed...," which I linked to page 1, or "Squack really loudly," which I linked to page 2.

On page 1, I wrote "If you sit around eating food all day, you'll never escape" and provided two more choices: "Do you want to eat more food," which links back to the same page in an endless loop for as many times as you select it, and "or squawk really loudly?," which takes you on to page 2, which I never bothered to write.

After creating your story, click Save and close the program. Navigate to the root folder for your iStories that you set up in the preferences. There you will find a folder by the name of your story, containing all the different pages you created as plain-text files, as shown in Figure 3-12. Dragging this folder into your iPod's *Notes* folder will also install your iStory on your iPod. For now, though, simply pick any page within that folder (with the exception of the iStory Creator file for your story) and open it within Notepad.

```
aTitle - Notepad
File  Edit  Format  View  Help
Mishasgreatescape written by C.K. and created with the iStory Creator
This is a test for Misha the pet Eclectus parrot, who hates his owner, C.K. and wants to escape
1. <a href="Page 1.txt">Eat some seed...</a>
2. <a href="Page 2.txt">Squack really loudly....</a>
```

Figure 3-12. A page created by iStory Creator opened in Notepad

When you open the file, you will find that it closely resembles the source code of a basic web page (see Figure 3-13). That's because the linking that iStory Creator automates for you is based on a very basic bit of HTML, which the iPod's Note Reader understands. This is good news for those of you wanting to do away with iStory Creator and hardcode your own adventure [Hack #39].

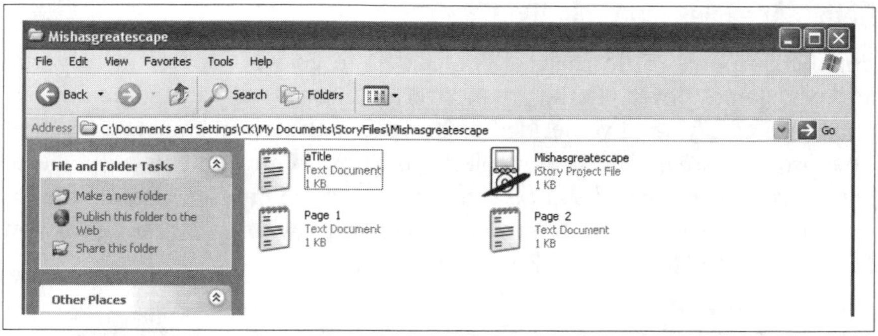

Figure 3-13. The folder containing all the files associated with my iStory

The Hardest Part

The hardest part of this hack is making your adventure a good piece of writing that proves easy to read, easy to understand, and entertaining. You might have hated English in high school and college, but any spelling or grammatical errors that you make in your story are going to interfere with your readers getting into the game.

Also, think about characters and plot. What makes a good character? What makes for an interesting plot? If you want some ideas, watch lots of movies, play lots of games, and read lots of books. And don't forget to watch the people around you and the drama of everyday life.

Hacking the Hack

After you have your story together, consider sharing it. Zip it up and post it to your web site or your blog, or email it to your friends. Make it the next great chain letter to troll around the Internet for the next 10 years. Submit it as an iStory through iPodSoft, or start up your own iPod game company like XOPlay (*http://www.xoplay.com*).

—*C. K. Sample III*

HACK #38 Convert Text Files into iPod Books ⓂⓌ

Convert the many readily available text files on the Web into readable iPod notes.

Since there aren't a ton of books out there to read on your iPod, if you want more choice you will have to get down and dirty and convert some text files yourself. Finding source material isn't hard; check out Project Gutenberg (*http://www.gutenberg.net*) for thousands of free books.

Getting the Files onto Your iPod

For the purposes of this hack, I've decided to go with one of my favorite authors, James Joyce. Rather than overload my iPod with something as grandiose as *Ulysses*, I've decided to download the much shorter collection of short stories, *Dubliners* (available from Project Gutenberg at *http://www.gutenberg.net/etext01/dblnr11.txt*), as shown in Figure 3-14. Feel free to choose another text to walk through these steps with me, although if you haven't read *Dubliners*, I highly recommend it.

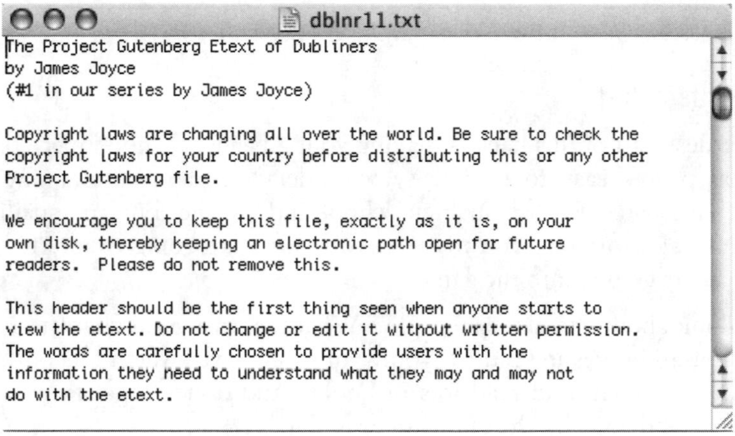

dblnr11.txt

The Project Gutenberg Etext of Dubliners
by James Joyce
(#1 in our series by James Joyce)

Copyright laws are changing all over the world. Be sure to check the
copyright laws for your country before distributing this or any other
Project Gutenberg file.

We encourage you to keep this file, exactly as it is, on your
own disk, thereby keeping an electronic path open for future
readers. Please do not remove this.

This header should be the first thing seen when anyone starts to
view the etext. Do not change or edit it without written permission.
The words are carefully chosen to provide users with the
information they need to understand what they may and may not
do with the etext.

Figure 3-14. Project Gutenberg etext of Dubliners, by James Joyce

After saving this file to my local drive, I need a way to convert it into something that the iPod can handle. The iPod can read any plain-text file put in its *Notes* folder, as long as the file isn't greater than 4 KB in size. Any text in the file over the 4-KB limit will be cut. As *dblnr11.txt* weighs in at 388 KB, a full 97 times the allotted size, we need to split up the file.

If you're using Windows, you will have to do this manually within a bare-bones text editor such as Notepad. Cut and paste successive segments of the original document into new files, naming all of the files in a numeric order and placing them inside one folder, which you will copy into your iPod's *Notes* folder. If you're on a Mac, you could do the same thing in TextEdit, but there are two programs that can help you get around the monotony of this task: Text2iPod X (*http://homepage.mac.com/applelover/text2ipodx/text2ipodx.html*; free) and iPoDoc (*http://burtcom.com/lex/#Anchor-iPoDoc-49575*; free).

Text2iPod X converts your text file into a Contact file that you can place inside the *Contacts* folder on your iPod. The benefit of this method is that the Contacts feature works on older iPods that do not support the Notes feature of newer iPods. The down side is that while the file can be larger than the 4-KB limit of the Notes files, it will still tend to get cut at around 32 KB. This was the case when I tried to load up the converted *Dubliners* via the Contacts menu on my iPod. Nevertheless, if you have an older iPod, cutting the text into a dozen 32-KB text files (which you then run through Text2iPod X) is a workable solution.

Your other option, iPoDoc, is a very effective little Applescript droplet that splits up your files into 4-KB chunks. Simply make sure that your iPod is loaded on your Mac and drag the *dblnr11.txt* file onto iPoDoc. The script will launch and quickly run. If your iPod isn't attached, the script will end, displaying a dialog saying that the iPod was not found. Otherwise, it will quickly split up your file into multiple 4-KB files, linked to each another and placed by tens into subfolders; the subfolders will be organized within a folder by the name of *dblnr11.txt* inside the *Notes* folder on your iPod. See Figure 3-15 to get an idea of how iPoDoc splits up files.

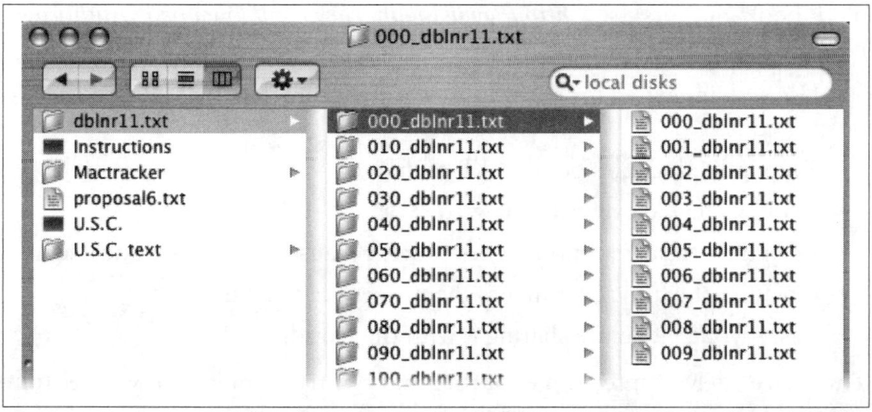

Figure 3-15. The folder hierarchy for dblnr11.txt after it has been run through iPoDoc

The left column contains all the files and folders inside the Notes directory on my iPod. Inside the main *dblnr11.txt* folder, there are 11 subfolders, depicted in the middle column. In the right column, we have the 10 4-KB text files that make up the first section of the book. On the iPod, simply navigate to the first file, *000_dblnr11.txt*, and select it to begin reading from the beginning. At the end of the file—and this will be wherever the 4-KB limit was reached, even if it's in the middle of a word—iPoDoc will have inserted a NEXT PAGE link to the next file in the sequence. Click on that link and it will open up *001_dblnr11.txt*, which in turn will end with a link to *002_dblnr11.txt*.

To go back a page or navigate to a previous section, you will have to hit the Menu button on the iPod and navigate to the name of the page to which you want to turn, just like you do when selecting another song. Take note of the way the numbering works for ordering within the iPod, because it will be useful if you decide to make your own iPod book [Hack #39].

—C. K. Sample III

HACK #39 Write Your Own iPod Book ⓜⓦⓛ

If you think you'd like to write your own iPod book, this hack provides you with the necessary guidelines for file length, formatting, and linking.

Apple has provided a nice set of instructions for how to take full advantage of your G3 or later iPod's Note Reader: the *iPod Note Reader User Guide*, available from Apple's Developer Connection page for the iPod as a free, 76-KB PDF file (*http://developer.apple.com/hardware/ipod/index.html*).

iPodLibrary.com also provides the following useful instructions for aspiring iPod book authors (see *http://www.ipodlibrary.com/downloads/Authoring_ podBooks.pdf*):

- Use a plain text editor to avoid unwanted characters that a word processor adds.
- Keep individual files below 4 KB each.
- Avoid using file extensions (e.g., *.txt* or *.rtf*).
- Keep the title and section names short, because long titles truncated.
- Organize the files according to the proper file structure.
- Test it yourself before sharing it with the world.

This hack delves into some of the nitty-gritty details, so you're fully equipped for your literary undertaking.

Organizing Your Files

If you decide to write an iPod book, there are a few ground rules regarding length that you must bear in mind. Each page of your book will be a separate note, and each note must not exceed 4 KB (your iPod will truncate the file when it reaches that limit).

Another important consideration for would-be iPod book publishers is that the Note Reader supports only up to 1,000 notes. As with the 4-KB limit, Note Reader displays the last bit up to that virtual fence and ignores the rest. If you have an encyclopedic novel in the works that spans several thousand pages, you might want to consider releasing it in serial form, several chapters at a time, so that your book doesn't exceed the capacity of your readers'

Notes folders. Also, according to Apple, the Notes files are cached in chunks of up to 64 KB at a time, so keeping your work under 64 KB makes for snappier reading. If that 64-KB cache limit is exceeded, page turning might incur a slight delay, because older notes must be removed from the cache as the new notes are read in.

When planning your file structure, bear in mind that the iPod will order your sections and chapters alphabetically. You'll need to name your files carefully to ensure that they show up and run in the correct order; starting each file with a number (*001, 002, 011, 012*, etc.) is a good idea. For an example naming scheme, check out the *Dubliners* file structure in "Convert Text Files into iPod Books" [Hack #38].

Formatting Your Files

The good news for you formatting freaks, despairing at the thought that you must distribute your book in plain old drab text, is that the iPod's Note Reader supports a few basic HTML formatting tags. Unfortunately, this only means that you can force paragraph breaks by wrapping them in `<p>` and `</p>` tags or by using `<br>` tags for spacing through manual line breaks. You can also use the `<title>` tag to name the files, but remember that they are ordered according to their names. Thus, `<title>000_Start Here</title>` would be a good title for the first page of your book.

Underlining by Dummy Linking

Since links are underlined when displayed on the iPod, you can underline sections of text by creating dummy link tags around the text to be underlined. You can either link to an actual dummy file located in the root folder of your book that says something like "Oops! This wasn't a real link. I hope you remember what page you were on!", or you can simply include a slash to redirect the reader up one level. For example, to display:

My favorite book is <u>Ulysses</u> by James Joyce.

You could write:

My favorite book is `<a href="/">Ulysses</a>` by James Joyce.

Unfortunately, you cannot simply leave the link empty, because doing so disables the underlining.

This is indeed a cheat, and a potentially annoying one at that. You probably won't want to do this when your document does indeed contain hyperlinks, because mixing the two—underlines as underlines and underlines as links— is sure to have your readers scratching their heads.

Linking Your Files

One of the most powerful HTML-like features of the iPod's Notes files is the ability to use links in them. They can be relative (starting in the same folder as the current note) or absolute (starting in the itself). Links can be made to different files within your book's hierarchy, to different folders within the Notes folder, to a *.link* file (a file ending in *.link* that contains a single link and acts as an immediate redirect to another file), or to a *.linx* file (a file ending in *.linx* that contains a list of links).

When a *.linx* file is selected on your iPod, it opens as if it were a folder and the links are all displayed as files in the folder. For this reason, *.linx* files can be a good way of creating a large index or table of contents page for your entire book.

Links cannot link to the *Notes* folder itself or to files outside the *Notes* folder. The following is an absolute link taken from the bottom of the first page of the *dblnr11.txt* file we processed with iPoDoc in "Convert Text Files into iPod Books" [Hack #38]:

```
<a href="/dblnr11.txt/000_dblnr11.txt/000_dblnr11.txt">NEXT PAGE</a>
```

If this link were to a file in the same folder as the note containing the link, we could use a relative link instead:

```
<A HREF="000_DBLNR11.TXT">NEXTPAGE</a>
```

As you can see, I shifted to all caps for the second example, to illustrate additionally that the Note Reader is fully case-insensitive when it comes to both the HTML tags and the filenames used in links.

Although iPoDoc creates a link forward to the next virtual page, you might want to include another link back to the previous page somewhere in each of your pages in order to ensure easier browsing for your readers.

Hacking the Hack

No matter what you do, play around with all the features, be creative, and have fun making your book. If you produce something that you think others will enjoy, submit it to iPodLibrary.com or release it yourself. There are various things you can do that I haven't discussed here by using a little XML to set preferences for your Notes files.

Also, there's a whole section in the *iPod Note Reader User Guide* that discussies creating links to specific songs on the iPod, so that you can integrate music into your story or article. If you like to code, iPoDoc is available free for your hacking as long as you keep it free, so open it up in your text editor of choice and start hacking away at it to make it into the ideal printing press for your iPod publishing house!

—*C. K. Sample III*

Change Your Battery Icon 〽️Ⓦ⚪

#40

Convert your iPod's battery icon into a much more useful voltage indicator.

Your iPod's battery indicator is represented by a visual icon of a battery. Sure, it's pretty, but it isn't necessarily the most intuitive way to tell how much life is left in your charge. This hack replaces your battery icon with numbers, as shown in Figure 3-16. The numbers represent how much voltage is left in your battery. Granted, it is not so ideal as a countdown timer, but it does gives you a better indication of how much juice you have left before you'll have to take out your earbuds and (gasp!) listen to the world around you.

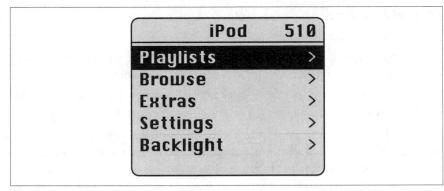

Figure 3-16. An iPod with the voltage indicator

On the Mac

Mac users can use the Terminal to turn on show voltage:

```
touch /Volumes/your_iPod's_name/iPod_Control/Device/_show_voltage
```

or turn off show voltage:

```
rm /Volumes/your_iPod's_name/iPod_Control/Device/_show_voltage
```

On Windows

Windows users can use DOS to turn on show voltage:

1. At the root of your *C:* drive, create a new text file called *_show_voltage*.
2. Go to Start → Run and type cmd.
3. Type your iPod drive letter (e.g., j:)

4. Type cd iPodControl_Device.

5. Type copy c:_show_voltage.

To turn off show voltage:

1. Go to Start → Run and type cmd.

2. Type your iPod drive letter (e.g., j:)

3. Type cd iPodControl_Device.

4. Type del _show_voltage.

Alternatively, you can use Windows to turn on show voltage:

1. Make sure your iPod is connected.

2. Double-click My Computer.

3. Select Tools → Folder Options. Go to the View tab, and make sure Show Hidden Files and Folders is checked.

4. Double-click your iPod's drive icon.

5. Double-click the *iPod_control* folder.

6. Double-click the *Device* folder.

7. In an empty spot in the device window, right-click with your mouse and select New → Text Document from the pull-down menu.

8. A new text document will appear, titled *New Text Document.txt*. Rename the file *_show_voltage* (don't enter an extension).

To turn off show voltage using Windows, follow the previous instructions to view hidden files and folders on your iPod. Navigate to \iPod\Device and delete the *_show_voltage* document.

HACK #41   Access Hidden Files on Your iPod

Apple keeps the music files on your iPod hidden, but with a little hackery, all your music will be revealed, allowing you to copy the files (legally, of course) from one machine to another.

If you have ever activated your iPod's Disk mode [Hack #32] and taken a peek at the disk in either the Macintosh Finder or the Windows File Manager, you might have found something missing—your music, that is. Sure, it shows up in iTunes, but where is it on your iPod? Hidden, that's where. In order to put some muscle behind the label that is slapped on every iPod (in multiple languages)—"don't steal music"—Apple hides the iPod's tracks in disk view.

Sneaky. But not quite as sneaky as us iPod/iTunes hackers. Of course, we are not doing this to steal music! We are doing this because we want to be able to copy our music from our iPods to our other machines, so we can listen to it in iTunes on those days when we accidentally leave our iPods at home, at the office, or at a friend's.

Since the music files are invisible, all we need to do is make them visible. Computers actually use invisible files quite a bit to store, for example, system-related information that you should never see or open. However, both Mac OS and Windows make it easy to view and search invisible items.

On a Mac

Launch the Terminal.application and type:

```
find /Volumes/[iPod'sNAME]/iPod_Control/Music -print | awk '¬
  { gsub(/ /, "\\ "); print }'
```

Substitute the name of your iPod for [iPod'sNAME]. Any spaces should be replaced with underscores (_). This will print a list of all the songs inside the *Music* folder with \ in place of spaces. Then, simply copy the location to the song you want and type open followed by that location to begin playing that song. You can then use a standard copy command such as cp to copy any file you select to its new location. This is tedious though. To copy your entire iPod's entire *Music* folder to your local computer, simply open the Terminal and write:

```
%ditto /Volumes/[iPod'sNAME]/iPod_Control/Music/ ~/Music/iPodTunes/
```

Again, substitute your iPod's name for [iPod'sNAME], using an underscore for any spaces in the name. This will copy the entire contents of your iPod's *Music* folder into a new folder inside your home directory's *Music* folder called *iPodTunes*.

On Windows

On the Windows side, you can also easily access your iPod's hidden files. First, right-click your iPod. Then, select Tools → Folder Options. This takes you to Control Panel → Folder Options. Select the View tab, as shown in Figure 3-17.

Under "Hidden files and folders," change "Do not show hidden files and folders" to "Show hidden files and folders." Click Apply to All Folders, and now all the invisible files on your iPod will be visible, as shown in Figure 3-18.

To get to your music files, navigate to *iPod_Control\Music*. There you will find a series of folders starting with a letter and ending with a number. Congratulations! You are now looking at your iPod database, where all your

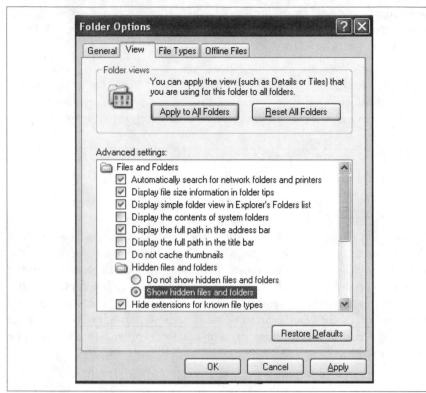

Figure 3-17. Showing your hidden files

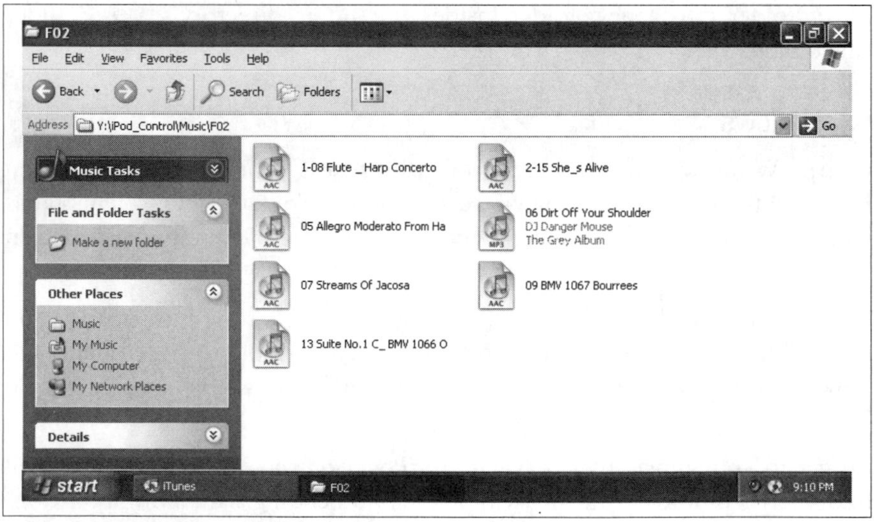

Figure 3-18. The iPod's music files exposed

music files are kept. As with any other file, you can now copy your music to anywhere on your computer.

You might also have come across several shareware or freeware utilities that allow you to automagically select songs on your iPod. They work by viewing the invisible files on your iPod and giving you an interface for copying the files. Because of the popularity of bringing this function to life, there are a plethora of options, especially on the Mac side.

One of the best applications for the Mac is PodWorks (*http://www.scifihifi. com/podworks/*; $8; limited trial version available). Using PodWorks, you can not only copy songs from your iPod to another computer, but you can also copy them directly to iTunes. Once you've downloaded the application and opened it up, you'll be greeted by the main interface shown in Figure 3-19.

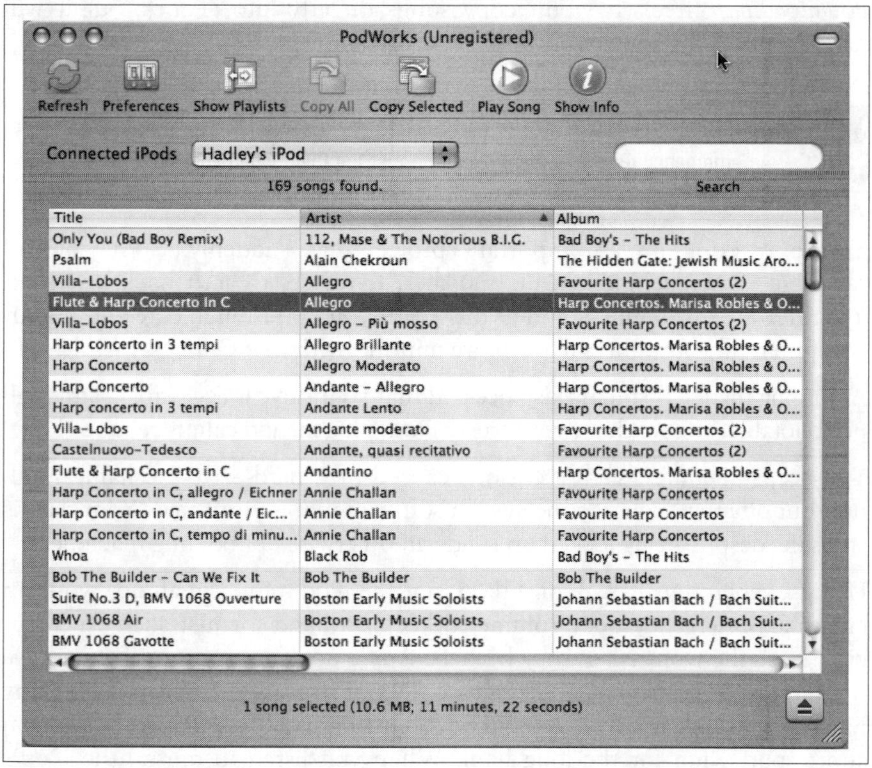

Figure 3-19. The PodWorks interface

The trial version has a 30-day time limit and a 250-song limit, will let you copy only one song at a time, and won't let you copy playlists. Once you open up the application and give it a try, you'll probably decide the $8 it'll cost you to buy it is well worth it.

To copy your songs from your iPod to iTunes, simply select all the songs and go to Pod → Send All Songs to iTunes. If you think you might have some duplicate songs on your iPod and in iTunes, make sure to go to Preferences → iTunes Export and select Actively Prevent Duplicates. It will slow down the copying process, but at least you'll end up with no duplicates.

Once the songs have finished copying, select the iPod's playlists in Pod-Works and select Pod → Recreate Selected Playlists in iTunes. PodWorks will now copy over your iPod playlists to iTunes. Easy, eh?

PodWorks is one of many options for Mac users; for other options, check out iPodLounge's download section (*http://www.ipodlounge.com/ downloads_macosx.php*).

Windows users can use PodUtil 2.0 (*http://www.kennettnet.co.uk/software/ download.php*; free). It won't copy songs directly into iTunes, but it will allow you to copy songs from your iPod to your PC.

HACK #42 Build an Emergency iPod Boot Volume Ⓜ Ⓝ Ⓞ

An emergency iPod boot volume can be just the thing when your hard drive goes south.

You're working on an important project and suddenly, poof!, out of nowhere your machine just up and dies. It refuses to start back up again. Your deadline is looming, and at this point you don't much care about your computer; all you want is a few more minutes with that *Omnigraffle* file.

Assuming the file is still in existence and that your drive is accessible, although not bootable, you reach for your trusty iPod, plug in, and calmly reboot.

You see, sometimes, such a crash is caused by a hard-drive mechanical failure, but often enough, it's the system software that is corrupted. Your data is still safe, despite being locked up inside an otherwise nonbooting machine.

Using a generation 1, 2, 3, or 4 iPod (not the iPod mini, I'm afraid), you can create an emergency boot volume to keep on hand for just such emergencies. I use the word *emergency* because Apple does not recommend you use the iPod as a permanent boot volume. Doing so wears out your iPod's tiny hard drive quickly, because the iPod's hard drive is designed to be used in short spurts, not for the long haul. When you listen to music, the iPod's hard drive spins only to fill up the iPod's built-in RAM cache. It then quickly spins down and parks the hard drive's heads until they're needed again.

 When used continuously, heat can build up inside the iPod case and literally fuse the hard drive platters together.

You can install any version of the Apple operating system on your iPod, as long as your particular machine can boot it. So, if you have a G5 Mac, don't bother installing OS 9 on your iPod (unless you want to access Classic within Panther). And if you have a beige G3 Mac, Panther will be useless to you unless you use XPostFacto **[Hack #29]**. Instead, you'll need a previous version of Mac OS X.

With that decided, it's time to install OS X.

Plug in your iPod. Installing Panther or OS 9 on your iPod is just the same as for any other hard drive. This isn't true for Jaguar (OS X 10.2), though; to install Jaguar, you'll need to get a copy of Carbon Copy Cloner (*http://www. bombich.com/software/ccc.html*; donateware) and clone an already-installed version of Jaguar, then transfer it to the iPod.

You'll need to be able to access your iPod as a FireWire drive. If your iPod doesn't mount and show up on the Desktop, you haven't enabled FireWire disk usage for it. To do so, open iTunes, make sure you have the iPod selected, and click the iPod Preferences icon in the lower-right corner of the window (leftmost in Figure 3-20). In the iPod Preferences window, select "Enable disc use." Your iPod should now mount on your Desktop as expected.

Figure 3-20. Clicking the iPod button to reach the iPod Preferences pane

Before getting to the installation itself, make sure your iPod has at least 2 GB available (Control- or right-click your iPod on the Desktop and select Get Info). If it's too full, hop into iTunes and delete any songs on your iPod you've grown a little weary of.

You are now ready to install Panther. Insert Panther Install Disc 1. Once the CD mounts on your Desktop, open it and click the Install icon. The CD takes over, shutting down the computer, restarting it, and launching the Installer application. Follow the installation directions until you are asked to select a target drive on which to install OS X.

Because every little megabyte on your iPod is precious, let's do a Custom Install. Unless you are a polyglot, there shouldn't be any reason to have the 10+ languages that are included with Panther. You'll save a lot of disk space if you deselect all the language options you don't need; after all, this is an emergency boot volume, not a system that you'll be running for any other purpose. That done, you are ready to install. Do as your Mac tells you to until the installation is complete.

You do not need to erase your iPod to install Panther. Indeed, you shouldn't! In fact, initializing your iPod through the installation process or through Apple's Disc Utility can cause problems.

If you want this boot partition to be a robust troubleshooting tool, you should consider installing Disk Warrior (*http://www.alsoft.com/ DiskWarrior*), Norton Utilities (*http://www.symantec.com/nu/nu_mac*), and, for good measure, an antivirus tool such as Norton Antivirus (*http://www. symantec.com/nav/nav_mac/ index.html*) or Virex (bundled with every .Mac account and available from *http: //www.networkassociates.com/us/products/ mcafee/antivirus/desktop/virex.htm*).

Now that you have Panther on your iPod, you can use it to boot up that ailing machine. Plug in your iPod and hold down the Option key while booting your Mac. After a few seconds, you'll see a list of all available startup volumes on your Mac and attached FireWire devices—most importantly, your iPod. For some reason, your iPod's name won't show up; look for a little FireWire icon instead. Select it, and you're good to go!

If your original machine's hard drive is usable but the system is corrupted, you can now either troubleshoot using your disk utilities or just grab or work with those vital project files you were after. Heck, you could do your presentation right from your iPod-powered Mac if necessary (assuming you have the right application available to you). Just remember not to spend any more time using the iPod as a boot volume than you absolutely need to.

The iPod makes for a terrific fallback in case anything goes wrong. And it plays music, to boot!

Get Your Email on Your iPod ⓜⓦ◐

Sync your iPod with your email client, so you can read emails on the move.

With the latest version of the software that runs on the iPod, Apple has built in the Notes function [Hack #33]. We are going to use it to get your email onto your iPod.

As with getting news onto the iPod, you'll need to sync your iPod with a computer, because the iPod is not currently a networkable device. Using email on your iPod is not like having a Blackberry or Internet-enabled Palm; you won't be able to delete mail or answer it, but you will be able to read it. This can come in handy if you have a long commute—sync your email in the morning, and read it while listening to tunes. Once you get to work, you can delete or answer messages you've already read on your computer.

There are several programs for checking email on your iPod, and in this area, Windows users are actually ahead of the game for once! That's because using K-Pod (*http://k-deep.com/k-pod.htm*; donateware), you don't have to have an email client installed on your machine in order to sync your inbox with your iPod; K-Pod connects directly to your email server. On the Macintosh side, PodMail (*http://www.podmail.org*; freeware) will also let you read your email. As with K-Pod, you can transfer IMAP and POP accounts; however, for POP accounts you will need to use Mac OS X's Mail application as your email client. In addition, PodMail will let you check your .Mac email account directly.

On Windows

Let's get started with K-Pod. Once you start it up, you will be greeted by K-Pod's main interface window, shown in Figure 3-21.

Figure 3-21. K-Pod's main interface window

Select the IMAP or POP protocol by clicking the appropriate radio button. If you aren't sure which protocol your Internet service provider (ISP) uses, give them a call. Most email providers use the POP-3 protocol. Here is the information K-Pod needs to get your email:

Your username
    Typically, your email address.

Your email password
    K-Pod allows authentication against your email server. Passwords are sent encrypted.

Your email server name
> This is typically *mail.yourisp.com/net*. If your ISP is Comcast, the server address is probably *mail.comcast.net*.

Your iPod drive letter
> Enter the drive letter Windows has assigned to your iPod. If you haven't activated the iPod's Disc mode, go to your iPod's preferences in iTunes and select "Enable disc use."

Now you're ready to sync! Hit the Sync button, and let K-Pod do its work. The program will connect to your ISP and download all the messages available on your email server to the Notes section of your iPod. K-Pod will not delete your messages from your email server, so there is no need to worry about your emails not showing up the next time you download them to your computer. Due to a limitation in the iPod's Notes protocol, you will be able to read only the first 4 KB of each email on your iPod. All is not lost, however, because 4 KB of text is approximately 600 words.

On the Mac

PodMail provides Mac users a few more options than K-Pod for Windows, including the ability to sync multiple email addresses at the same time and to limit the number of emails downloaded. You can enter any number of .Mac, POP, or IMAP email accounts by clicking on the plus icon in the lower-left corner of PodMail's main interface window, as shown in Figure 3-22.

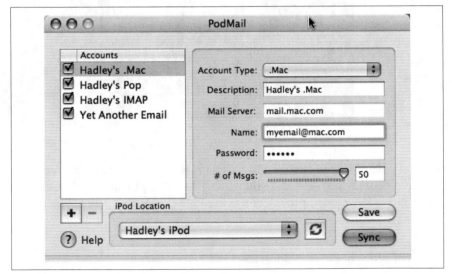

Figure 3-22. PodMail's main interface window

As with K-Pod, you will need to enter your mail server name, email address, and password. Click Save after you've entered all your data, and then click Sync to transfer your messages to your iPod.

Using either K-Pod or PodMail you can read your email anytime, anywhere on your iPod.

HACK #44 Publish a Web Page from Your iPod

Plug your iPod into your Mac and create a web page from your iPod's image library in a snap.

"Store Digital Photos on Your iPod" [Hack #3] shows how easy it is to use your iPod as a storage device for your digital images. This hack takes your iPod's integration with your digital camera a step further, allowing you to easily create a web page to display the images you have transferred to your iPod. This is great for both professional photographers and amateurs alike. If you are a pro, you can transfer your shots to your iPod as you shoot throughout the day. When you get back to your studio, just plug your iPod into your Mac and, following the directions in this hack, you can produce a quick and easy web page for your clients to review your photos. Amateurs can use this to quickly share photos of a family outing.

To get the job done, we are going to rely on Image Capture. Image Capture is included with Mac OS X and can be found in the *Applications* folder. This nifty little app is sort of like iPhoto's stripped-down sibling—albeit with a ton of hidden power.

To get started, upload some photographs [Hack #3].

 If you want to test this hack but don't own either of the Belkin products discussed in "Run Your iPod in Disk Mode" [Hack #32], you can simply create an *Images* folder on your iPod and copy some digital snaps into it.

Connect your iPod to your Mac and launch Image Capture. Image Capture will automatically recognize your iPod as a capturable device, as shown in Figure 3-23.

The first pull-down menu in the dialog box that pops up allows you to select the location where you want your images copied. If you want the images to upload via FTP to your own web site, go ahead and select your *Documents* folder. You can also select your Mac's *Sites* folder and, thanks to the power of OS X's web sharing, serve up your new web page right from your Mac.

Under Image Capture's Automatic Task menu, go ahead and select Build Webpage. Press the Download Some button to pick and choose which

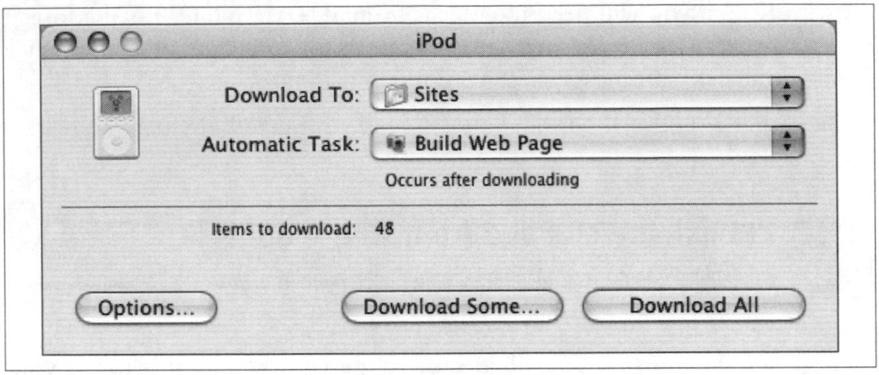

Figure 3-23. Image Capture, recognizing your iPod immediately

images you want to include, or press Download All. In what seems like a second, Image Capture will download your images from your iPod (see Figure 3-24), resize them into a thumbnail and full-size view, and spit out the HTML to build the page, as shown in Figure 3-25. Clicking on a thumbnail loads a full-size image. Now that's service!

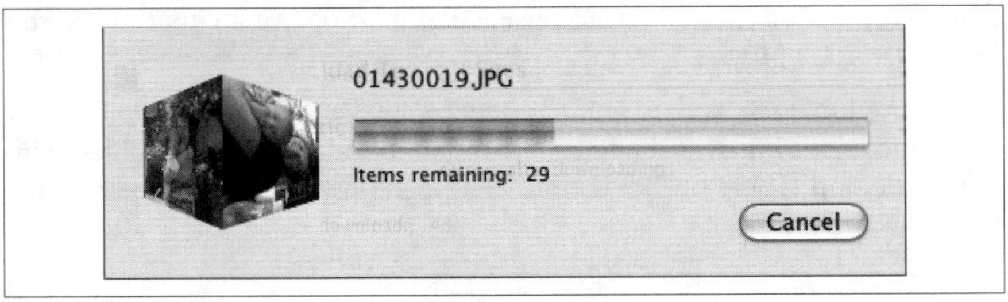

Figure 3-24. Image Capture importing

To share your web page using OS X's built-in web server, go to System Preferences → Sharing and select the Services tab. Select Personal Web Sharing to turn your computer into a web server, with the *Sites* folder where Image Capture just created the HTML page as the principal shared folder. The Sharing panel will also tell you your computer's IP address. If you are using a router, you will need to open up port 80 to your computer.

HACK #45   Feed Streaming Audio to Your iPod   ⓜ①①

Capture an Internet audio stream to an MP3 file, save the file to your hard drive, and automatically upload those files to your iPod when it connects to your computer.

Before the Internet, the wonders of nonlocal radio were out of reach of most people; the fabulous BBC World Service broadcasts only on shortwave

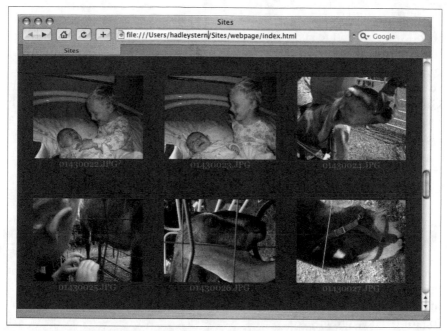

Figure 3-25. A web page created from an iPod

radio, or occasionally late-night radio. These days, eight BBC channels and World Service are streamed over the Internet 24 hours a day. You can hear not only World Service daily, but also old *Dr. Who* and *Goon Show* episodes that were nearly impossible to obtain in the U.S.

On the other hand, being next to a computer to listen isn't always practical. Sometimes, you need to get out just to get some sunshine. Wouldn't it be nice to have your favorite streams recorded and uploaded automatically to your iPod?

This hack shows how, with a few simple steps, you can put together a few programs to time-shift that BBC broadcast, or any streaming audio, onto your iPod. Here is what you'll need:

- Rogue Amoeba's (*http://www.rogueamoeba.com*) Audio Hijack ($16) or Audio Hijack Pro ($30) or Wiretap (*http://www.ambrosiasw.com/utilities/freebies/*; free)

- An iPod (natch)

- LittleAppFactory's iPodScripter (*http://www.thelittleappfactory.com/download/iPodScripter.dmg*) or Zapptek's iPod Launcher (*http://www.zapptek.com/ipod- launcher/*)

- Apple's Script Editor

Getting the Audio

If you want to capture audio from an audio stream, the easiest way to do so is to get Rogue Amoeba's Audio Hijack or Audio Hijack Pro or WireTap. All of these programs are built to record any audio your computer plays, including streams of many different types, such as RealAudio, Windows Media Player, QuickTime, and MP3 streams. Depending on your needs and budget, each has its advantages. Audio Hijack, as of Version 2, can record a stream from a URL and is a little cheaper, but it can encode streams only as AIFF files. Audio Hijack Pro can record to MP3 directly and can use VST audio plug-ins to modify the stream, even multiple sources at the same time. Pro does cost a little more. Also, Pro must have a file to load from the program you want to record. For example, if you want to record a Real Audio stream, you have to have a file that's associated with RealPlayer that will open that stream. This does make it a tad more complex to get it up and running.

Audio Hijack. To record, Audio Hijack requires a URL, file, or AppleScript and the name of the program that the URL will open. Launch Audio Hijack and select File → New Preset, then File → Edit Preset. You'll arrive at a dialog for the new preset.

The Preset Settings window contains four tabs: Target, Timer, Recording, and Effects. In this hack, you need concern yourself with only the first three.

On the Target tab (Figure 3-26), you can name your preset, set the application for Audio Hijack to record, and set the URL that the application (or file or AppleScript) needs to open. Find a link to the stream itself—the link which, when clicked, starts streaming the stream. Right- or Control-click the link, copy its URL, and paste it into the Open URL/File/AppleScript text area.

Next, you need to select which application the audio will be coming from. If you're not sure which program the link will launch, just click it and see what pops up. It's most likely one of the big four: RealPlayer, Windows Media Player, iTunes, or Quicktime. But it could be nearly anything, even the browser itself. Whatever program is in the foreground and appears to be playing the stream after you click that link is the one to select from the Application field on the Target tab.

The Timer tab (Figure 3-27) is where you specify the date and time at which to record this stream. You also have the options to mute the program while recording and quit the program once you're done with it.

To record a BBC stream from 6:00 p.m. to 6:30 p.m. local time, Monday through Friday, select each of the day checkboxes for Monday through Friday. Then, set a start time, using 24-hour time (add 12 to every hour after noon). I recommend you set the clock to start a little before and end a little

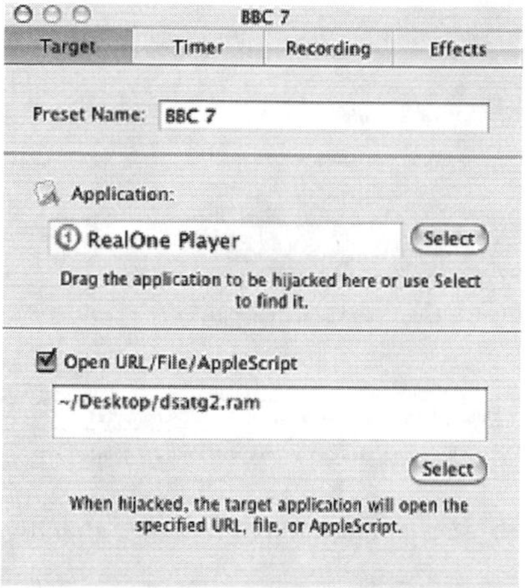

Figure 3-26. Audio Hijack's Target tab

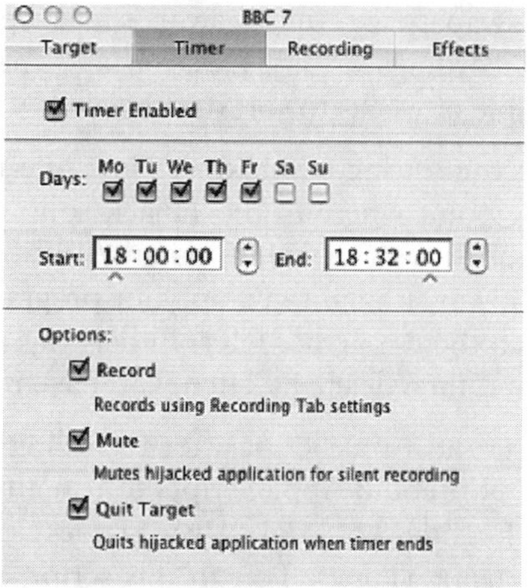

Figure 3-27. Setting a date and time to start recording

after the time that you want, to allow for slight differences in clocks at your house and the BBC studios. Select Record as well; otherwise, this timer will kick off your stream but won't record it. Finally, select Mute if you're not interested in hearing the stream while it's recording, and select Quit Target if you want the application to shut off after it's done.

The Recording tab (Figure 3-28) provides options for where to save the recording and how large to make the files.

Save the recorded files to whatever location you wish, but note that location; you'll need it in a minute. I recommend picking someplace to record

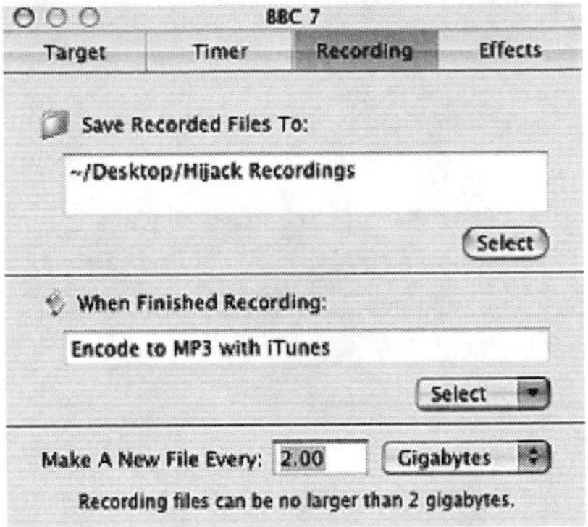

Figure 3-28. *Specifying the size and location of recorded streams*

your files that is either obvious, such as a folder on your Desktop, or not on your main hard drive at all. It's easy to forget that you have Audio Hijack recording files on your computer. Mac OS X uses empty disk space on its main hard drive as swap space; filling swap space up can kill your hard drive. I put all my recordings on my Desktop and then go through them about once every couple of weeks to sort out the chaff.

As for file size, keep the setting at Make A New File Every at 2 GB. This value lets you set the point where Audio Hijack splits the recording into a new file. Audio Hijack saves the stream as an AIFF file, which gets quite large. If you leave it lower, it might cut up your program into multiple files and then have to stitch them together later. Either way, convert the AIFF file as soon as possible, and then delete it. Then, you have room for more audio.

You can optionally run an AppleScript after recording a file. Audio Hijack comes with a couple of prebuilt AppleScripts to run after recording. One of these AppleScripts, Encode To MP3 With iTunes, converts your newly recorded file to MP3 using iTunes. To run this script, double-click a preset and select Recording in the inspector window that pops up. In the section marked When Finished Recording, select the drop-down menu to find this built-in AppleScript and others.

> Before you run Encode To MP3 With iTunes, you'll want to set your iTunes conversion preferences (iTunes → Preferences → Importing → Setting) to Good Quality, High Quality, Higher Quality, or a custom set of values. Otherwise, iTunes will convert your file using its current settings, whatever they are at the time.

Audio Hijack Pro. Audio Hijack Pro's preset settings (Window → Show Presets) look quite different from the regular version, as shown in Figure 3-29. All the options are in one dialog window, but the options themselves are nevertheless similar.

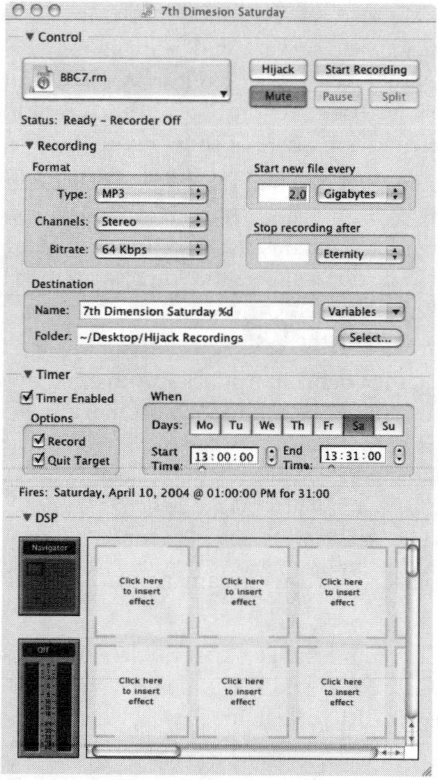

Figure 3-29. All settings consolidated into one Preset dialog box

Almost everything said of Audio Hijack still applies, with two major exceptions. First, Audio Hijack Pro automatically records MP3 files, so you won't need to convert the files afterward.

Second, to open, Audio Hijack Pro needs a file from the program you want to record, not just a URL. To record from Safari, just click and drag the link to the Desktop. For applications like RealPlayer and Windows Media Player, the easiest way to get a file is to right-click on the link to your favorite audio stream, select Download Linked File As..., and save it to the Desktop with a memorable name. This *kickoff file* loads the stream into the right application, as long as that application is associated with that file type. Be sure to save these files in a location where they won't be accidentally removed; if they disappear, your stream won't get recorded.

The Case of the Ever-Changing Stream URL

Some web sites that stream change their URLs daily or use JavaScripts to load the stream. You might think that these streams cannot be recorded; they can, although they might take a little effort. The key is to figure out *how* the link you're clicking tells the server which show to stream. By looking at a couple of URLs for a particular show, you can figure out how the URL changes and then play around with the URL to find out which URL will get you what you want. Most radio shows use either the date or the show number to archive the file, so the URL often uses the date or show number.

Web sites that use JavaScript to build this kind of URL can be a little tougher to crack, but doing so is by no means impossible. JavaScripts are embedded inside the web page that contains the link. If you look at the source of the HTML page, the JavaScript will be either directly in the HTML page or in a file that the HTML page loads. Once you have the script, you can then find out how the site is building the URL you want.

Either way, you can then build an AppleScript to open a program with a particular show and use Audio Hijack to kick off that AppleScript. If you want to record, say, NPR's *Wait Wait... Don't Tell Me*, which uses a date to archive its programs, opening today's URL might look something like this:

```
set today to (do shell script "date +%Y%m%d")
tell application "RealOne Player"
        GetURL "http://www.npr.org/dmg/dmg.php?mediaURL=/waitwait/"
               & today & "_waitwait&mediaType=RM "
end tell
```

The do shell script command gets today's date in the form *YYYYMMDD* (e.g., 20040522 for May 22, 2004) and tacks it onto the URL for the show. This AppleScript opens the URL in RealOne Player, which in turn downloads a file and runs it.

Getting the Files into Your iPod

Unfortunately, there are no off-the-shelf products to shuffle audio files right from your Desktop to your iPod. However, quite a few products synchronize playlists created in iTunes. If you're looking for programs to synchronize all your music between your iPod and your Mac, try iTunes.iPod from crispSofties (*http://www.crispsofties.com*), iPodRip from LittleApplication-Factory (*http://www.thelittleappfactory.com/software/ipodrip.php*), or iPodit from Zaptekk (*http://www.zapptek.com/ipod-it*). iPodIt also synchronizes iCal, Address Book, Mail, Stickies, and even Entourage if you want. iPod-Rip is tuned for individualized manual syncing and specifically allows for importing and exporting files. iTunes.iPod synchronizes a little differently but has the added benefit of syncing AAC and Audible tracks as well.

Using any of these apps requires placing the audio in an iTunes playlist, which means you have to load them into iTunes. It is possible to do this automatically. The Audio Hijack post-recording script menu also lets you add the files to iTunes, but the script menu allows you to run only one script after you record a stream; if you use the post-recording script menu to put files into iTunes, you can't also convert your Audio Hijack files to MP3. To do so, you have to either deal with AIFF files (which take up a lot of space unnecessarily) or convert these AIFF files by hand. Neither of these options is exactly what I'm after.

When I connect my iPod, I want to have a script start up, read what's in my Audio Hijack recording folder, add anything that's in that folder to my iPod, put all of my files into a separate folder for discarding later, and remove anything on my iPod that I've listened to already or that is out of date.

If you're looking for a good resource for iTunes- and iPod-specific AppleScripts, Doug's AppleScripts for iTunes (*http://www.malcolmadams.com/itunes/index.php*) has an Apple-Script to move tracks from one iPod to another, another to copy your clipboard to the iPod contacts, and one that copies news to your iPod (NetNewsWire Subscription to iPod Contacts v1.0), to name but a few.

The Code

I really have two problems: I need a script that does what I want it to do and something needs to see the iPod is attached to my computer and run the script.

Choosing which language can be pretty important, especially when you're trying to connect multiple programs. Most of Apple's programs can work with shell scripting or Perl, and I prefer their speed and flexibility to other scripting languages. But Apple has built AppleScript into iTunes, the program I want, so it's a little easier to work with AppleScript for this task.

Here's the AppleScript I use to copy my files to my iPod:

```
property thePlaylist : "TestPlaylist"
property theiPod : "Professor Processor"
property theRecordingFolder : "Powerbook ¬
    G4:Users:stevko:Desktop:hijack"
property theStorageFolder : "Powerbook ¬
    G4:Users:stevko:Desktop:hijack:storage"
property tempPlaylist : "TempPlaylist"
property timeToKeepFilesInDays : 7

set fileList to (list folder theRecordingFolder)
```

```
tell application "iTunes"

    set onList to {}
    try
        set pod to source theiPod
    on error
        display dialog ¬
            "Could not find iPod " & theiPod buttons {"Cancel"}
    end try
    try
        set podPl to user playlist thePlaylist of pod
    on error
        display dialog ¬
            "Could not find playlist " & thePlaylist & " on iPod " &
theiPod buttons {"Cancel"}
    end try

    if fileList is not {} then

        -- create temp playlist
        try
            set tempPl to (make new user playlist)
            set name of tempPl to tempPlaylist
        on error
            display dialog ¬
                "Could not create playlist with name " ¬
                    & tempPlaylist buttons {"Cancel"}
        end try

        -- add files to temp playlist

        repeat with q from 1 to (count of fileList)
            set thisFile to item q of fileList
            if thisFile is not ".DS_Store" then
                try
                    set pth to theRecordingFolder & ":" & thisFile
                    add file pth to tempPl
                on error
                    -- ignore; if we can't get one,
                    -- we might be able to get more
                end try
            end if
        end repeat


        -- find if any of the names of the temp playlist items
        -- are the same as the ones on the iPod playlist

        set deleteList to {}
        repeat with r from 1 to (count of tracks in tempPl)
            set temptrack to track r of tempPl

            repeat with s from 1 to (count of tracks in podPl)
```

```
            set podtrack to track s of podPl
            if name of podtrack is name of temptrack then
                set n to name of temptrack
                set deleteList to deleteList & n
                exit repeat
            end if
        end repeat
    end repeat

    repeat with y in deleteList
        try
            delete track y in tempPl
        on error
            -- again, ignore; it's nice to delete extras,
            -- but not necessary
        end try
    end repeat


    -- remove any from iPod that are more than a week old,
    -- or that have already been heard.
    -- THIS DOES DELETE FILES OFF OF YOUR IPOD WITHOUT A WARNING!!

    -- (That's one of the points of this Applescript)

    set delList2 to {}
    repeat with p from 1 to (count of tracks in podPl)
        set ptt to track p of podPl
        if (played count of ptt is greater than 0) or ¬
            (played date of ptt is ((current date) ¬
                - (timeToKeepFilesInDays * days))) then
            set pptn to name of ptt
            set delList2 to delList2 & name of ptt
        end if
    end repeat
    repeat with y in delList2
        try
            delete track y in podPl
        on error
            -- again, ignore
        end try
    end repeat


    -- copy everything that's on playlist to the iPod
    -- optionally, this will also convert the files
    -- at the same time; uncomment the line below to do so.
    repeat with m from 1 to (count of tracks in tempPl)
        set mt to track m of tempPl
        -- convert mt
        duplicate mt to podPl
    end repeat


    -- remove temp playlist
```

```
        set delList3 to every track in tempPl
        repeat with t in delList3
            delete track (name of t) in library playlist 1 ¬
                in source "Library"
        end repeat
        delete tempPl

    else
        display dialog ¬
            "Could not find any files in folder " ¬
                & theRecordingFolder buttons {"Cancel"}
    end if
end tell

-- this moves the files from the recording folder to a storage folder
-- if you use delete instead of move, you can trash the files instead.
tell application "Finder"
    repeat with t in fileList
        try
            move file t in folder theRecordingFolder to
theStorageFolder
        on error
            display dialog ¬
                "Could not move file" & name of t & " from " ¬
                    & theRecordingFolder & " to " ¬
                    & theStorageFolder buttons {"Cancel"}
        end try
    end repeat
end tell
```

This AppleScript has five major functions. The first is to find the iPod and
the playlist on the iPod that we're going to use. If we can't find these, it
errors out automatically. After all, there's no point in uploading to an iPod's
playlist if you can't get to the iPod or the playlist.

Second, it creates a temporary playlist of all of the items inside our Audio
Hijack recording folder and then sees if any of these new files are already on
the iPod (no point in reloading files that are already there). The temporary
playlist is necessary because we need to compare apples and apples, not
apples and oranges—in this case, files and tracks. The files inside of the
Hijack folder are just that, *files*, while the files on our iPod register only as
tracks in iTunes. The name of a file is its filename, and the name of a track is
the ID3 tag name; and those often don't match. The easiest way to compare
the two sets of files is to make them the same type, and doing this through
iTunes is a tad easier, especially since we want to build a playlist with these
files anyway.

After determining which files aren't to be found on the iPod, the script then
moves on to determine which files are on the iPod and need to be removed.
The criteria for files to be removed includes items that have been played

through once or files that are more than *n* days old. In this case, *n* is the property timeToKeepFilesInDays; set it to suit your fancy. Once a file meets either of those criteria, the file is trashed; in theory, we don't want it anymore. The script also trashes these files because getting files off of an iPod is another hack altogether, and I want to stick to the topic.

After removing the unneeded iPod files, the script copies the files on the temporary playlist to the iPod. The temporary playlist should contain only the subset of files that were in the folder and were not already on the iPod when the script started. So, you should get a nice batch of new files on your machine and get rid of the old ones at the same time so that you don't fill up the iPod with old tracks.

Finally, the script performs a little cleanup. First, it gets rid of the tracks we added temporarily, by deleting them from the Library. When you add tracks, they automatically go into the library. Since you don't want them added permanently, kill them off. The script then kills off the temporary playlist, just to make things nice again. Finally, it moves the files from the recording folder to a storage folder in case it's needed later.

So, now you have an AppleScript that copies what you want to the iPod. To finish, we need something to kick off the AppleScript when the iPod connects. As mentioned, there are several applications that do just that. I like iPodScripter the best, because it's only a System Preferences panel installation. iPod Launcher, on the other hand, is a background application and preference panel that checks every specified number of minutes for the iPod. Both work equally well, and either will do.

Download either app and install it. The interfaces for the programs are similar: iPodScripter displays a list for applications and a second list for scripts (as shown in Figure 3-30), while iPod Launcher displays just one list for both. Just drag and drop the script on the appropriate list. The script runs whenever you dock your iPod.

Now that you're all set up, it's time to find some interesting shows, record them, and connect your iPod for a quick transfer. Enjoy the unlikely mix of sunshine and British broadcasting!

—*Ted Stevko*

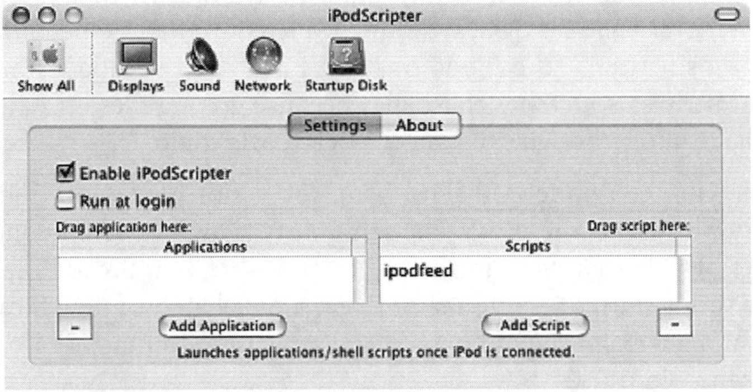

Figure 3-30. The iPodScripter user interface

HACK #46   Use an iPod with Linux   ⊗ ⊗ ●

You don't need a Windows PC or Mac to use an iPod. If you are a Linux user,
you too can join the iPod revolution.

This hack shows how to use an iPod with Linux. It's aimed at Linux pur-
ists—that is, people who don't want to have to use a Mac or Windows–
based PC, nor Wine nor Windows software—to get going. (I fall into this
category, not because of any religious convictions, but merely because Linux
is all I have. For updates, visit *http://pag.csail.mit.edu/~adonovan/hacks/ipod.*
html)

> This hack assumes that you have reasonable level of Linux
> competence. You should be comfortable with downloading,
> compiling, and installing software, as well as general system
> administration tasks.

Here's what you'll need if you want to use an iPod with your Linux box:

A Mac or Windows iPod (obviously)

The iPod is basically just a FireWire hard disk, with its own operating
software stored in one partition. The two variants of the iPod are formatted with different filesystems: HFS+ in the case of the Mac, and
FAT32 in the case of Windows. Indeed, this is the only difference.

Ideally, you want to start with a Windows iPod. Linux has extremely
limited support for the Apple HFS+ filesystem, and thus it is necessary to
convert HFS+ iPods to FAT32, erasing the disk in the process. The iPod
firmware is identical, though, so you must save this before you begin.

To do the conversion, don't mess around with Wine, or with Winnie-
Pod Updater, the Apple-sanctioned tool for HFS-to-FAT32 conversion.

The GNU instructions for how to convert are sufficient and require only `fdisk`, `dd`, and `mkfs.vfat`, which are standard Unix tools.

> The latest breed of iPod appears to come in a single flavor called "for Windows and Mac." They are actually HFS-formatted, but come with software for Windows that invisibly does the conversion the first time they are used. So these are really just Mac iPods. If you have access to a PC with MS Windows, you can use that to do the conversion to FAT32. (Thanks to Zach Hobbs for this information.)

A Linux system with a recent, FireWire-capable kernel (2.4.12 or later—now might be a good time to upgrade to RedHat 9.0 or similar)

Note that the version of RedHat Package Manager (RPM) that comes with RedHat 9.0 (Shrike) has an annoying bug: sometimes it will crash, and on subsequent executions, it will hang, waiting for a `mutex` (in the `futex` syscall, as can be observed using `strace`). If this happens, simply remove the */var/lib/rpm/__dbxxx* temporary files from the RPM database and try again.

A working FireWire interface

I use an Orange Micro PCMCIA card (*http://www.orangemicro.com/firewire.html*; $59.00) for a laptop. It still seems that the kernel support for FireWire is a little flaky, so try to avoid issuing and/or interrupting commands unnecessarily, or removing the interface while the drivers are doing something.

The `GtkPod` package

GtkPod (*http://gtkpod.sourceforge.net*; free) is a graphical tool for transferring files to and from the iPod. It is the Linux equivalent of the iTunes software used for this purpose on the Mac.

I used the gtkpod 0.50 RPM, available free from *http://www.rpmfind.net*. This package requires the `id3lib` package.

You must use a tool such as GtkPod; you cannot simply copy files onto the iPod's hard disk, because the iPod's database must be updated for it to see the new tracks. Furthermore, the first time you use GtkPod, you must select File → Create Directories to set up the database on the iPod.

The `grip` package

grip is a free, graphical tool for ripping CDs and encoding them as MP3s.

Note that when ripping CDs to files, the actual filenames are not important to the iPod. However, because its music database is populated from the ID3 tags embedded within the MP3 files, it *is* important that these are accurate.

This means that you should encode MP3 files from an album all together, or else you will lose the album track-numbering information. It also means that you can use convenient filenames (such as *track07.mp3*) instead of naming the files with the actual track names (e.g., *07. Voodoo Chile [Slight Return].mp3*); the shell metacharacters present in the latter make them a pain to work with.

Setting Up Your Linux Desktop

Assuming you're using a PCMCIA FireWire card, once the card is inserted, the cardmgr daemon should take care of loading the ieee1394 and ohci1394 modules. If you have a PCI card, these should be loaded by system startup (/etc/rc.local).

When you attach the iPod to the FireWire interface, the sbp2 module is loaded automatically. (If it's not, load it with modprobe.) You should see messages appear in dmesg indicating that the device is recognized. Additionally, /proc/bus/ieee1394/devices contains information on each device, including the string [Apple Computer, Inc.] for the iPod:

```
ieee1394: Host added: Node[00:1023]  GUID[00d0f5cd4008049d]  [Linux OHCI-
1394]
ieee1394: Device added: Node[00:1023]  GUID[000a2700020e545e]  [Apple
Computer, Inc.]
ieee1394: Node 00:1023 changed to 01:1023
SCSI subsystem driver Revision: 1.00
ieee1394: sbp2: Logged into SBP-2 device
ieee1394: sbp2: Node[00:1023]: Max speed [S400] - Max payload [2048]
scsi0 : IEEE-1394 SBP-2 protocol driver (host: ohci1394)
$Rev: 707 $ James Goodwin SBP-2 module load options:
- Max speed supported: S400
- Max sectors per I/O supported: 255
- Max outstanding commands supported: 64
- Max outstanding commands per lun supported: 1
- Serialized I/O (debug): no
- Exclusive login: yes
  Vendor: Apple      Model: iPod            Rev: 1.40
  Type:   Direct-Access                     ANSI SCSI revision: 02
Attached scsi removable disk sda at scsi0, channel 0, id 0, lun 0
SCSI device sda: 58595040 512-byte hdwr sectors (30001 MB)
sda: test WP failed, assume Write Enabled
  sda: sda1 sda2
```

The iPod appears as a fake SCSI device (typically /dev/sda if you have no other SCSI devices) and can be accessed using the regular Unix tools for block devices. However, if you are using a Mac iPod, fdisk will not recognize the partition map, and you will get a message resembling "Device contains neither a valid DOS partition table, nor Sun, SGI or OSF disklabel." In this case, it is time to follow the GNU instructions (for conversion).

At this point, the Linux IEEE1394 drivers (ieee1394, ohci1394) should have recognized the hardware:

```
% cat /proc/bus/ieee1394/devices
Node[00:1023]  GUID[001106000000649a]:
  Vendor ID: `Linux OHCI-1394' [0x004063]
  Capabilities: 0x0083c0
  Bus Options:
    IRMC(1) CMC(1) ISC(1) BMC(0) PMC(0) GEN(0)
    LSPD(2) MAX_REC(2048) CYC_CLK_ACC(0)
  Host Node Status:
    Host Driver      : ohci1394
    Nodes connected : 2
    Nodes active    : 2
    SelfIDs received: 2
    Irm ID          : [00:1023]
    BusMgr ID       : [00:1023]
    In Bus Reset    : no
    Root            : no
    Cycle Master    : no
    IRM             : yes
    Bus Manager     : yes
Node[01:1023]  GUID[000a2700020ec65a]:
  Vendor ID: `Apple Computer, Inc.' [0x000a27]
  Capabilities: 0x0083c0
  Bus Options:
    IRMC(0) CMC(0) ISC(0) BMC(0) PMC(0) GEN(0)
    LSPD(2) MAX_REC(2048) CYC_CLK_ACC(255)
  Unit Directory 0:
    Vendor/Model ID: Apple Computer, Inc. [000a27] / iPod [000000]
    Software Specifier ID: 00609e
    Software Version: 010483
    Driver: SBP2 Driver
    Length (in quads): 8

% cat /proc/scsi/scsi
Attached devices:
Host: scsi0 Channel: 00 Id: 00 Lun: 00
  Vendor: Apple    Model: iPod          Rev: 1.40
  Type:   Direct-Access                 ANSI SCSI revision: 02
```

Performing the HFS-to-FAT32 conversion involves the following steps:

1. Save the first 32 MB of the second partition, which contains the iPod firmware image. Keep this file safe somewhere on your PC:

   ```
   % dd if=/dev/sda2 of=backup_firmware
   ```

2. Splat zeros all over the partition map so that all disk data is effectively erased. We unload and reload the sbp2 driver to update its world-view:

   ```
   % dd if=/dev/zero of=/dev/sda bs=1M count=10
   % rmmod sbp2 && insmod sbp2
   ```

3. Create two partitions. The first should be large enough to hold the 32-MB file you saved earlier; the second will hold the remaining 30 GB of the disk. Tag the two partitions as Empty and FAT32, respectively:

```
% fdisk /dev/sda
n    [make new partition]
p    [primary]
1    [first partition]
     [just press enter -- default first sector is 1]
5S   [5 sectors -- big enough to hold 32MB]

n    [make new partition]
p    [primary]
2    [second partition]
     [just press enter -- default first sector is 6]
     [just press enter -- default size uses all remaining space]

t    [modify type]
1    [first partition]
0    [first partition has no filesystem; ignore warning]

t    [modify type]
2    [second partition]
b    [second partition is FAT32]

p    [show partition map]

    Device Boot    Start      End    Blocks   Id  System
/dev/sda1              1        5     40131    0   Empty
/dev/sda2              6     3647  29254365    b   Win95 FAT32

w    [commit changes to disk]
```

4. Copy the firmware back to the first (small) partition:

```
dd if=backup_firmware of=/dev/sda1
```

5. Make a FAT32 filesystem on the second (large) partition:

```
mkfs.vfat -F 32 -n "My iPod" /dev/sda2
```

If all goes well, resetting the iPod (by holding down the Menu and Play buttons for 10 seconds) will cause it to reboot to the familiar menus. If not, go through the instructions again. Remember, the iPod is just a hard disk, so as long as you have the original firmware backed up correctly and safely on your PC, you can reformat it as many times as you like. (It worked for me the first time.) Be wary about installing different firmware from the one it came with, however.

At this point, you should be able to mount the disk in the usual way. Once this works, setup is complete and you are through to the normal usage instructions described in the following section.

Normal Usage

The Linux drivers for the iPod are still a little flakey; sometimes, the sbp2 driver gets stuck indefinitely in its initializing state and cannot be removed, and at other times the machine hangs.

To minimize the risk of such errors, I strongly advise you to follow a disciplined procedure for docking and undocking the iPod. Here's the order of events I usually employ:

1. Insert the IEEE1394 PCMCIA card into my laptop. Check that this succeeded by running lsmod and looking for ieee1394 and ohci1394.
2. Attach the iPod. This time the sbp2 driver should appear. If it does not, try detaching and reattaching it.
3. Mount the iPod as a disk, copy files across, and then unmount it again.
4. rmmod the sbp2 driver.
5. Detach the iPod.
6. Remove the IEEE1394 card.

Note that these steps are perfectly symmetrical. This seems to achieve greater reliability than performing them in an arbitrary order.

I use two scripts, *dock-ipod* and *undock-ipod*, whenever I attach or detach the iPod to or from the interface card. Here's *dock-ipod*:

```
#!/bin/sh

modprobe sbp2
mount /dev/sda2 /mnt/ipod/
```

And *undock-ipod*:

```
#!/bin/sh

umount /mnt/ipod
rmmod sbp2
```

They must both be run as root:

```
% su - root -c ./dock-ipod
```

or:

```
% sudo ./dock-ipod (if the user is a sudoer)
```

or:

```
% su - root
Password:
root$ ./dock-ipod
```

Downloaded MP3 Files and ID3 Tags

The iPod does not care about the filenames of MP3 files; all its database information is supplied by ID3 tags within the MP3 files. Therefore, these must be present for transferred files even to appear on the iPod.

You might want to add MP3 files that did not come from a CD (e.g., those downloaded from Napster, Kazaa, etc.) to your iPod. The ID3 tags in such files are often inappropriate; for example, because they feature the original artist/album name from the CD they came from, instead of the logical group to which they will belong on your iPod (e.g., *Misc/80s Synth Pop*). If you do nothing about this, you will find each song appearing in its own artist/album category, with no useful grouping. You'll also need to tag manually when CDDB lookup fails (e.g., for *non-industry* CDs) or for MP3 files that were hand-encoded from WAV.

To change the tags, you'll need a tool such as ID3ed (*http://www.dakotacom.net/~donut/programs/id3ed.html*; free). This tool is pretty straightforward, and it comes with a helpful man page. The synopsis says:

```
id3ed [-s songname] [-n artist] [-a album] [-y year]
[-c comment] [-k tracknum] [-g genre] [-q] [-SNAYCKG]
[-l] [-L] [-r] [-i] [-v] files...
```

Obviously, you don't need to include all of those options. Here's an example:

```
% id3ed -s "Red House" -n "Jimi Hendrix" \
-a "Are You Experienced?" -k 3 redhouse.mp3
```

Alternatively, you can use a graphical tool such as xid3 (*www.nebel.gmxhome.de/xid3/*; free), which has a Tcl/Tk-based front end for ID3-tag editing that makes it a lot easier to use for this information. The most important ID3 tags for the iPod are Artist, Album, Title, and Track Index (and Genre, if you actually bother to use that).

With minimal effort, your iPod will play nicely with Linux. No, you won't be able to buy songs from the iTunes Music Store, but you'll still have most of the functionality Macintosh and Windows users have.

—Alan Donovan

HACK #47   Dial a Phone with Your iPod   ⓂⓌⓞ

You can use your iPod to dial a touch-tone phone.

In the '70s, there was a boy who could whistle a 2,600-cycle tone. He discovered that if he whistled this note into a phone, he could make long-distance calls for free. Someone else discovered that a toy whistle included with Cap'n Crunch cereal boxes also produced a 2,600-cycle tone. This tone was the same used by the post–live-operator phone company to access the system that controlled the network. This 2,600-cycle tone unlocked the ability to make free long-distance calls, and *phreaking* (etymology: a mashed remix of *freak* + *phone* + *free*) was born. Phreaking was one of the earliest forms of hacking. Two of the 1,337 early hackers and phreakers from the Homebrew Computer Club in California, infamous for building Blue Boxes, went by the handles Berkeley Blue and Oak Toebark. You are probably more familiar with them as Steve Jobs and Steve Wozniak, the founders of Apple Computer, Inc., the company that now manufactures that little white wonder, the iPod.

So, now we're in the twenty-first century, and many of the tricks of the past no longer work. The system has changed somewhat, with more digital bits in the way that won't be fooled by a Captain Crunch whistle. However, one of the pieces of equipment you *can* use for phone tricks is that sleek musical machine, the iPod. In a completely legal way, you can use your iPod to dial numbers over a compatible touch-tone phone via Dual Tone Multiple Frequency (DTMF) tones.

Table 3-2 shows the combined tones that make up the touch-tone dialing system. The four alphabetic keys are sometimes used internally by the phone system.

Table 3-2. Tones that make up the touch-tone dialing system

DTMF chart	1209 Hz	1226 Hz	1477 Hz	1633 Hz
697 Hz	1	2	3	A
770 Hz	4	5	7	B
852 Hz	7	8	9	C
941 Hz	*	0	#	D

Table 3-3 lists the tones you'll need if you find yourself on an international system that supports Consultative Committee on International Telegraphy and Telephony (CCITT) tones.

Table 3-3. CCITT tones

CCITT	700 Hz	900 Hz	1100 Hz	1300 Hz	1500 Hz	1700 Hz
700 Hz	N/A	1	2	4	7	Code 11
900 Hz	1	N/A	3	5	8	Code 12
1100 Hz	2	3	N/A	6	9	KP
1300 Hz	4	5	6	N/A	0	KP2
1500 Hz	7	8	9	0	N/A	ST
1700 Hz	Code 11	Code 12	KP	KP2	ST	N/A

The best place to find tones is on Google (*http://www.google.com*). You can easily find all the tones necessary for a Red Box, a Green Box, or a Blue Box (devices that reproduce the tones coins trigger when they are deposited in payphones), as well as all the DTMF tones, CCITT tones, and Canadian tones. Alternately, you can generate audio files for the numbers you will be dialing using DailABC.com's Generate DTMF Tones service (*http://www.dialabc.com/sound/generate*).

Once you load all the necessary tones into your iPod, all you have to do is find a public payphone that will accept the tones. If you've created a complete, ready-for-dialing string of numbers using the Generate DTMF Tones service, or if you spent a lot of time in a program such as Audacity or GarageBand arranging the different individual tones in the correct order and converting them to MP3, you can simply turn up the iPod's volume to the max, hold your headphones up to the receiver, and click play to dial the number. If you wanted to break the law, you could try seeing if any of the coin tones work on your local public phone to get you some free calls.

Alternately, a good method for iPod dialing is to have all the relevant DTMF numbers saved to a particular playlist on your iPod, with a few extra seconds at the end of each file, or a separate file that is a few seconds of silence. Then, whenever you encounter a particularly dirty-keyed public phone that you don't want to touch, simply create an on-the-go playlist of the number you want to dial by mixing and matching the corresponding number files in the correct order (make sure you have shuffle turned off in your settings for this). Hold the headphones up to the receiver, and click play.

Theoretically, under the right circumstances, these methods should work. However, the phone system keeps changing and updating, frequencies are slightly different for different areas, and different model payphones react differently to different tones, so the corresponding tones continue to change as well.

—*C. K. Sample III*

HACK Use .NET to Access the iPod's Database ⓃⓌⓁ
#48 Code applications in Visual Studio to access your iPod's database using .NET.

When you install the iPod software for Windows, a file called *ipodservice.exe* is installed. This runs constantly in the background, checking to see if an iPod has been plugged in. If it has, the *.exe* launches iTunes, ready to update all your music. Needless to say, if you don't have this *.exe* running, these useful features will not work.

However, this file is interesting for another reason. Through the wonders of Microsoft's Component Object Model (COM), a fairly substantial application programming interface (API) is exposed for performing numerous operations on the iPod.

As this is presumably the Apple-sanctioned way of accessing the iPod, rather than accessing it simply as a FireWire drive, taking a peek at the API exposed by *ipodservice.exe* should be easy—and it is!

Using the Object Browser in Visual Studio to investigate the API further, it turns out you can do almost anything you want with your iPod, ranging from simple tasks such as these:

- Mounting and unmounting the iPod
- Getting the Windows drive letter
- Getting the iPod's name (for example, "Owen's iPod")

to advanced features such as these:

- Formatting the iPod's hard disk
- Writing to individual sectors on the hard disk
- Writing files to the hard disk

Getting Started with Visual Studio

Although theoretically, you can just use the .NET Framework for this hack, it is much easier to use Visual Studio .NET. Unfortunately, Visual Studio is a fairly expensive piece of software (although Microsoft does offer discounts for students, as well as a free 60-day trial). As an alternative, it should be possible to use the open source SharpDevelop (*http://www.icsharpcode.net/ OpenSource/SD/*; free), though this hasn't been tested.

For the purposes of this hack, we'll assume you're using Visual Studio. To begin, you need to create a new project in Visual Studio:

1. Go to File → New → Project.
2. Under VB Projects, select Console Application.
3. Give your project a name (such as *iPod*), choose where you want to save it, and hit Next.

You will now be presented with a module code window, as shown in Figure 3-31.

The first thing you want to do is add a reference to *ipodservice.exe*, because this contains the API functions:

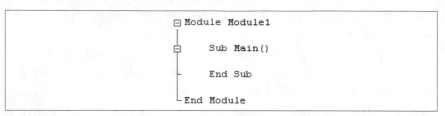

Figure 3-31. *The blank module code window*

1. In the Solution Explorer window, right-click References and click Add Reference.

2. Choose the COM tab.

3. Scroll down until you find iPod Service Type Library in the list, or browse to the location of the file. Select it, and click the OK button.

ipodservice.exe should now be listed in the References hierarchy, as shown in Figure 3-32. If it's not, you've probably done something wrong, so try repeating the previous steps.

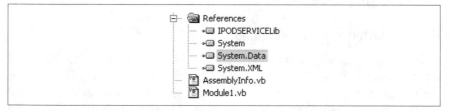

Figure 3-32. *ipodservice.exe should appear in the References hierarchy*

Now that you've got Visual Studio set up, let's start writing some code!

Writing the Code

When you're writing any code to access the iPod, the first thing you need to do is declare and instantiate a reference to `IPODSERVICELib.iPodManagerClass`. This contains a lot of the API calls you'll use when developing for the iPod. In the code window, under the line that reads `Sub Main( )`, type the following line:

```
Dim iPodManager As New IPODSERVICELib.iPodManagerClass( )
```

You have now declared `iPodManager` to be a reference to `iPodManagerClass( )`.

Now might be a good time to build the project to make sure everything is working. Go to Project → Build Solution. The build window at the bottom of the screen should look like Figure 3-33.

In this example, all we're going to do is get the name of the iPod and pop up a window telling you the name.

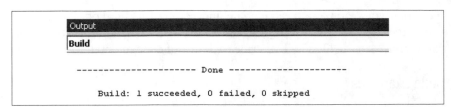

Figure 3-33. Building your project and checking out the results

To do this, we need to declare an integer that will hold the numeric ID of your iPod and a string value to hold the name of your iPod:

```
Dim iPodID As Integer = 0
Dim DeviceName As String = ""
```

Before we can start doing anything with the iPod, we first need to log into it:

```
iPodManager.Login(1)
```

The number in parentheses represents the ID of the application we want to log in as. In this case, we chose 1, because that is the ID of the iPod Updater; however, we could also have chosen the value 4, which is the ID of iTunes. A complete list of the registered applications can be found in the Windows Registry under the following key:

```
HKEY_LOCAL_MACHINE\SOFTWARE\Apple Computer, Inc.\iPod\RegisteredApps
```

Now that we have logged in successfully, we can get the name of the iPod:

```
iPodID = iPodManager.FindFirstiPod(1)
DeviceName = iPodPrefs.DeviceName(1, iPodID)
```

This gets the ID of the first iPod found, then stores its name in the string DeviceName.

Once we have the iPod's name, we can log out and display a message box with the name:

```
iPodManager.Logout(1)
MsgBox("Your iPods Name is :" & DeviceName)
```

It's as simple as that. The majority of the API calls work like the preceding example: first, you log into the iPod using the Login( ) function, and then you simply call the desired API function with the appropriate parameters. For example, the DeviceName( ) API call used in the previous example has as parameters the ID of the application used to log in and the ID of the iPod.

It's worth remembering that before you use any of the Updater API calls (they all begin with U_), you first need to call U_InitUpdater. Otherwise, the Updater API calls will fail and return an error or a blank/null value.

Now that you know the basic idea behind coding for the iPod, it might be useful to look at a couple samples. We'll look at a few basic operations you can perform on the iPod and describe each line of code in detail.

Code Examples

In order to help explain the principles of accessing the iPod, this hack includes some code samples. They should help you get started with writing your own programs.

The first is a relatively simple program that gets the name of the currently attached iPod, and the second is a slightly more complex program that returns the drive letter of the iPod and the hardware version.

Getting the iPod device name. This small sample listing provides the code necessary for retrieving the name of the iPod currently attached to the system. It demonstrates how the iPod should be accessed—logging in, performing the desired actions, and logging out again:

```
'Declare an Integer value to store the ID of the iPod.
Dim iPodID As Integer = 0

'The name of the iPod is returned as a string value, so a
'variable is declared to hold this value and set to be empty.
Dim DeviceName as String = ""

'IPODSERVICELib.iPodManagerClass() is the main class
'that ipodservice.exe exposes. It contains all the functions
'for manipulating the iPod.
'An instance of the class is declared as iPodManager
'to allow access to its functions.
Dim iPodManager As New IPODSERVICELib.iPodManagerClass()

'Log into the iPod using the Login() API call exposed
'by IPODSERVICELib.iPodManagerClass().
iPodManager.Login(1)

'Using the FindFirstiPod() method, get the numeric
'ID of the iPod attached to the system.
iPodID = iPodManager.FindFirstiPod(1)

'Once the ID of the iPod has been determined, it can be used
'to obtain the name of the iPod as it appears in iTunes.
'Use the DeviceName() method, passing as a parameter the ID
'of the iPod. It returns the name as a string value,
'which is stored in the DeviceName variable.
DeviceName = iPodPrefs.DeviceName(1, iPodID)

'Once all the operations have been performed on the iPod,
'call the Logout() method.
```

```
iPodManager.Logout(1)

'Display a pop-up message with the name of the iPod.
MsgBox("Your iPods Name is :" & DeviceName)
```

This is a simple example of how to retrieve information from the iPod. It simply displays a message box with the name of the iPod as it appears in iTunes.

Getting the hardware version and drive letter. A slightly more complicated sample involves retrieving the iPod's hardware version and the drive letter currently assigned to the iPod by Windows.

This sample uses the Updater APIs to gather its information. Though these are no more difficult to use than the regular functions, they require a call to initialize the updater before they can be used, as shown in the following code:

```
'Both the hardware version and the drive letter
'are returned as unsigned 32-bit integers, so the
'variables to store the values need to be declared
'as that type.
Dim HWVersion As System.UInt32
Dim DriveLetter As System.UInt32

'As in the previous sample, the iPod ID is stored
'as an integer, and again to access the API calls
'an instance of IPODSERVICELib.iPodManagerClass()
'needs to be declared.
Dim iPodID As Integer
Dim iPodManager As New IPODSERVICELib.iPodManagerClass()

'Log into the iPod and retrieve the numeric ID
'of the iPod attached to the system.
iPodManager.Login(1)
iPodID = iPodManager.FindFirstiPod(1)

'In order to get information about the hardware
'version and drive letter, the iPod needs to be locked
'to ensure that other applications can't access it.
'To do this, call the LockiPod() method, passing it
'the ID of the iPod you want to lock.
iPodManager.LockiPod(1, iPodID)

'To get information about the iPod's drive letter,
'the iPod needs to be mounted and the HDD accessible.
'To ensure this is the case, call the Mount()
'method, again passing the ID of the iPod you want
'to mount.
iPodManager.Mount(1, iPodID)

'The methods for getting the drive letter and the
'hardware version are part of the Updater API calls.
```

```
'As discussed in the text, before these can be used, the
'U_InitUpdater( ) method MUST be called.
iPodManager.U_InitUpdater( )

'To get the drive letter, call the
'U_GetDriveLetter( ) method, passing as a parameter
'the variable in which to store the drive letter.
iPodManager.U_GetDriveLetter(DriveLetter)

'As with getting the drive letter, to get the hardware
'version, call the U_iPodGetHWVersion( ) method,
'passing as a parameter the variable in which to
'store the hardware version.
iPodManager.U_iPodGetHWVersion(HWVersion)

'Display a pop-up message with the hardware version.
'In order to be displayed, it is converted to a
'string using the ToString( ) method built into the
'.NET Framework.
MsgBox("iPod Hardware Revision" & HWVersion.ToString( ))

'Display another pop-up message, this time with the
'drive letter. As the drive letter is returned as a
'number, it also needs to be converted to a letter.
'First, the returned value is converted to a 16-bit
'integer. This value is then used with the
'Chr( ) function, which converts a number to its
'ASCII equivalent (A-Z is 65-90).
'Once the conversion has been done, the letter is
'displayed in the pop-up message.
MsgBox("iPod Drive Letter : " &
Chr(System.Convert.ToInt16(DriveLetter)))

'All the operations have been performed on the iPod,
'so it needs to be unlocked, unmounted, and logged out,
'ready for access by other applications.
iPodManager.UnlockiPod(1, iPodID)
iPodManager.Unmount(1, iPodID)
iPodManager.Logout(1)
```

Although more complicated than the first example, the basic idea stays the same. All you need to do is call the desired function with the correct parameters and then read the result.

Observations and Issues

A couple of things are interesting to note when playing with the API.

If you do a GetDeviceUniqueID( ), you get back a fairly large string of information. The first bit of this is presumably the manufacturer and model. The next bit seems to be random junk, though it obviously means something (it might be the region code). The last six characters are the FireWire Global Unique Identifier (GUID), which is specific to your iPod. On my iPod, this value is 5CB92D.

One strange thing I've noticed is that you can issue a LockiPod( ) command, but you don't seem to need to issue an UnlockiPod( ) command before you exit the program. It might be that because the same application ID is always used, you don't need to unlock it again. However, if you were to lock with one ID and then try to access the iPod with another, you might have problems.

Also note that one of the methods in IPODSERVICELib.iPodManager is RegisterApp( ), which you can use to successfully register your own application. However, even though an application you register with this method appears in the Registry as a valid application, trying to log into the iPod using its appID returns a "Login Failed" error.

Hacking the Hack

Although it isn't possible to write .NET software that will actually run on the iPod, you can write programs that will do anything with the iPod that Apple's software can do. You can launch iTunes and start a music transfer, get the name of your iPod, get its capacity (10 GB, 20 GB, 40 GB), and more. The possibilities are limited only by what Apple's software allows.

Using methods like those listed in the previous sections, we'll now write an application that gives you detailed information about your iPod, including hardware and software versions, the amount of free space left, and whether it is set up for Windows or Mac.

The following code is a complete VB.NET listing for a small console application that queries the iPod and returns information about it. The example is fully commented and should be reasonably easy to follow, giving you a good grounding for writing your own applications.

```
Module ipod

    ' A 'structure' for holding the information retrieved about the iPod
    ' to allow it to be easily passed between functions.
    Structure iPodStruct
        Dim DeviceID As String
        Dim DriveLetter As String
        Dim Filesystem As String
        Dim DeviceName As String
        Dim DiskSize As Decimal
        Dim DiskFree As Decimal
        Dim FirmwareVersion As String
        Dim FirmwareRevision As String
        Dim OwnerName As String
```

```
            Dim HomeMachineName As String
            Dim APIVersion As Integer
            Dim HardwareVersion As String
    End Structure


    ' This function takes a single parameter of type iPodStruct.
    ' It then writes the information contained within to the
    ' screen in a neat fashion.
    Sub Display(ByVal ipod As iPodStruct)


        ' Temporary variables to hold the value of the DeviceID string
        ' when it is split into its component parts.
        Dim DeviceIDCol1 As String()
        Dim DeviceIDCol2 As String()


        Console.WriteLine("")
        Console.WriteLine(" iPod information utility, using the dotNet
Framework")
        Console.WriteLine(" -----------------------------------------------
----")
        Console.WriteLine("           (Written by Owen Watson, 2004)")
        Console.WriteLine("")
        Console.WriteLine(" iPod 'Owner' Information:")
        Console.WriteLine("  -Owner Name          |    " & ipod.OwnerName)
        Console.WriteLine("  -HomeMachineName     |    " ¬
            & ipod.HomeMachineName)
        Console.WriteLine("")
        Console.WriteLine(" iPod General Information:")
        Console.WriteLine("  -Device Name         |    " & ipod.DeviceName)
        Console.WriteLine("  -Drive Letter        |    " & ipod.DriveLetter)
        Console.WriteLine("  -Format              |    " & ipod.Filesystem)
        Console.WriteLine("  -Disk Size (GB)      |    " ¬
            & ipod.DiskSize / 102400)
        Console.WriteLine("  -Disk Free (GB)      |    " ¬
            & ipod.DiskFree / 102400)
        Console.WriteLine("")
        Console.WriteLine(" iPod Technical Information:")
        Console.WriteLine("  -Firmware Version    |    " ¬
            & ipod.FirmwareVersion)
        Console.WriteLine("  -Firmware Revision   |    " ¬
            & ipod.FirmwareRevision)
        Console.WriteLine("  -Hardware Version    |    " ¬
            & ipod.HardwareVersion)


        ' The DeviceID is made up of one large string, which can be broken
down
        ' into several parts, as shown below (FireWire GUID, Manufacturer,
etc.).
        ' The first split splits on the # character, the second on the &
character.
        DeviceIDCol1 = ipod.DeviceID.Split("#")
        DeviceIDCol2 = DeviceIDCol1(1).Split("&")
```

```
    Console.WriteLine("")
    Console.WriteLine("   -Device ID: ")
    Console.WriteLine("    *Interface Type    |    " & DeviceIDCol1(0))
    Console.WriteLine("    *Firewire GUID?    |    " & DeviceIDCol1(2))
    Console.WriteLine("    *Manufacturer      |    " & DeviceIDCol2(0))
    Console.WriteLine("    *Device Type       |    " & DeviceIDCol2(1))
    Console.WriteLine("    *Device Location   |    " & DeviceIDCol2(2))

    Console.WriteLine("")
    Console.WriteLine("")
    Console.WriteLine(" Notes on the Device ID:")
    Console.WriteLine(" -----------------------")
    Console.WriteLine(" The Interface Type of SBP-2 is a protocol used ¬
        for wrapping SCSI commands")
    Console.WriteLine(" over a Firewire bus.")
    Console.WriteLine(" The location 'LUN' is, I assume, its SCSI ¬
        location ID")
    Console.WriteLine("")

    MsgBox("Finished Retrieving Information!")

End Sub


' Main function. This is called as soon as the application is run.
' In this example, it handles all the processing except writing
' the information to the screen.
Sub Main( )

    ' Declare an iPodStruct to hold the information retrieved from
    ' the iPod.
    Dim ipod As iPodStruct

    ' A temporary variable to hold the iPod's numeric ID.
    Dim iPodID As Integer

    ' A temporary variable, this time to hold the filesystem
    ' type of the iPod.
    Dim iPodFAT As Integer

    ' Two temporary variables, to hold the drive letter and
    ' the hardware version.
    Dim driveletter As System.UInt32
    Dim hardware As System.UInt32

    ' IPODSERVICELib.iPodManagerClass( ) is the main class
    ' that ipodservice.exe exposes. It contains all the
    ' functions for manipulating the iPod.
    ' An instance of the class is declared as iPodManager
    ' to allow access to its functions.
    Dim iPodManager As New IPODSERVICELib.iPodManagerClass

    ' Log into the iPod using the Login( ) API call exposed
    ' by IPODSERVICELib.iPodManagerClass( ).
```

```
iPodManager.Login(1)

' Using the FindFirstiPod( ) method, get the numeric
' ID of the iPod attached to the system.
iPodID = iPodManager.FindFirstiPod(1)

' The methods for getting the drive letter and the
' hardware version are part of the Updater API calls.
' As discussed in the text, before these can be used, the
' U_InitUpdater( ) method MUST be called.
iPodManager.U_InitUpdater( )

' Get the long DeviceID string of the connected iPod.
ipod.DeviceID = iPodManager.GetDeviceUniqueID(1, iPodID)

' The firmware version and revision are both retrieved
' by calling the GetVersionInfo( ) function. This returns
' a value representing the firmware revision. The firmware
' version is returned in a parameter.
ipod.FirmwareRevision = iPodManager.GetVersionInfo(1, iPodID, ¬
    ipod.FirmwareVersion)

' To get the drive letter, call the
' U_GetDriveLetter( ) method, passing as a parameter the
' variable in which to store the drive letter.
' Once the drive letter has been obtained, convert it from a
' numeric value to a character representing the letter assigned.
iPodManager.U_GetDriveLetter(driveletter)
ipod.DriveLetter = Chr(System.Convert.ToInt16(driveletter))

' Like getting the drive letter, to get the hardware
' version, call the U_iPodGetHWVersion( ) method,
' passing as a parameter the variable in which to
' store the hardware version.
' Then convert the hardware version to a string value.
iPodManager.U_iPodGetHWVersion(hardware)
ipod.HardwareVersion = hardware.ToString( )

' The next set of API calls are fairly straightforward;
' they are simply called with the iPod ID and the application to
' impersonate as parameters.
' The value is then returned and stored in the structure for later
' use.
ipod.DeviceName = iPodManager.DeviceName(1, iPodID)
ipod.OwnerName = iPodManager.OwnerName(1, iPodID)
ipod.HomeMachineName = iPodManager.HomeMachineName(1, iPodID)
ipod.DiskSize = iPodManager.GetDiskSize(1, iPodID)
ipod.DiskFree = iPodManager.GetiPodFreeSpace(1, iPodID)

' To get the platform the iPod is used on, a call to IsFormatted( )
' is required. This function returns a value from 0-4 inclusive
```

```
' that represents the formatted state of the iPod, with 1 being
' a Windows iPod and 2 being a Mac iPod.
iPodFAT = iPodManager.IsFormatted(1, iPodID)

Select Case iPodFAT
    Case 0
        ipod.Filesystem = "Unknown"
    Case 1
        ipod.Filesystem = "Windows"
    Case 2
        ipod.Filesystem = "Mac OS"
    Case 3
        ipod.Filesystem = "Windows (No Firmware)"
    Case 4
        ipod.Filesystem = "Mac OS (No Firmware)"
End Select

' Once all the operations have been performed on the iPod,
' call the Logout( ) method.
iPodManager.Logout(1)

' Call the Display( ) function to write the information to the
' screen.
Display(ipod)
    End Sub

End Module
```

—*Owen Watson*

HACK #49 Run Linux on Your iPod 🅜🅦🅛

Turn your iPod into a Linux-running machine and write your own iPod
applications.

Ever since the original iPod was released, users have come up with new and
interesting ways to use their iPods as more than just MP3 players. Apple's
various updates have added to the firmware new features, such as calendars
and contacts **[Hack #33]**, games **[Hack #36]**, HTML-like notes **[Hack #39]**, and now
photo storage capabilities **[Hack #3]**.

Unfortunately, these new features can come only from Apple, so we are
beholden to their timelines and commercial interests.

This is where Linux—or more specifically, uClinux (*http://www.uclinux.org*;
free)—comes to the rescue. uClinux is a special port of the Linux kernel that
supports CPUs without a memory-management unit. Other than that, it's
basically a full-featured Linux kernel, including filesystem support for FAT32
and HFS+, TCP/IP networking, and FireWire, all with a nice Unix API.

By porting Linux to the iPod, we can create a freely available development platform where software can be developed for the iPod independently of the Apple firmware. What's more, basing it on such an open system gives us immediate access to all the resources available on the Linux platform—that is, all those open source packages people use to build great software.

Installation

Installing Linux on your iPod consists of two basic steps: patching the iPod operating system stored on the hard drive, and installing a root filesystem for Linux. Installation is possible from Windows (using a third-party installer), Linux, or Mac OS X.

> You must have root permissions to install Linux on your iPod.

Installation of Linux on your iPod is a nondestructive process and will leave all your existing configurations and music intact on your iPod. The included boot loader will also allow you to choose either the Apple or the Linux software to start at reset, so you can continue to enjoy the full-featured Apple firmware while you experiment with the Linux world.

FireWire/connection setup. To install Linux on your iPod, you first need to have your system configured for your iPod. If you are using Mac OS X, there is probably nothing further to do. However, if you are using Windows or Linux (especially if this is the first time!), you need to ensure that you have either FireWire or USB correctly configured for your iPod. To configure FireWire or USB for your system, consult the documentation provided with your operating system.

Once the operating system is configured, you need to determine how your operating system identifies your iPod. To do this, plug your iPod into your PC and ensure that it switches to Disk mode. Normally, it should do so automatically when the appropriate connection is established by your operating system; however, you can force entry into Disk mode by resetting your iPod (by holding down Menu and Play/Pause for three seconds) and then, when the Apple icon appears, holding down Fast-Forward and Rewind.

Once in Disk mode, you should see the message "Do not disconnect" on your iPod. You should then check your operating system configuration to see how your iPod is configured.

This hack covers installing Linux on the iPod with a Linux-based PC. If you want instructions for a Mac OS X or Windows machine, visit iPodLinux.com (*http:// ipodlinux.sourceforge.net/installation.shtml*).

This hack works better with a Windows-formatted (FAT32) iPod. If your iPod is Mac-formatted (HFS+), it is generally easier to reformat it as FAT32 before you get started. See "Use Your iPod with a Mac and a PC" [Hack #35].

Locating your iPod. To locate your iPod under Linux, check the file */proc/scsi/ scsi* for an entry where the Vendor is Apple and the Model is iPod. For example:

```
# cat /proc/scsi/scsi
Attached devices:
Host: scsi0 Channel: 00 Id: 00 Lun: 00
Vendor: Apple Model: iPod Rev: 1.50
Type: Direct-Access ANSI SCSI revision: 02
```

The scsi0 (Host) portion indicates that the iPod is the first SCSI device on your machine and so will be visible as /dev/sda. If on your system you see scsi1, your iPod will be visible as device /dev/sdb. The following example commands will use sda as the device address for the iPod. Please replace this with the correct device address for your configuration.

Backing up. Since we will update the partition information and replace the hard-drive firmware image, we will first make a backup of this data. Use the following commands to create the two necessary backup files:

```
# dd if=/dev/sda of=ipod_boot_sector_backup count=1
# dd if=/dev/sda1 of=ipod_os_partition_backup
```

The first backup file is simply a copy of the master boot record (MBR), which contains the partition table for the disk. The second backup file is a complete backup of the operating system partition on the iPod and includes the Apple iPod operating system (this file is 40 MB and can be compressed once the installation process is complete). Should you need to restore these backups for any reason, simply use the following commands:

```
# dd if=ipod_boot_sector_backup of=/dev/sda
# dd if=ipod_os_partition_backup of=/dev/sda1
```

Note that if you want to upgrade the Apple firmware, you should first restore the iPod operating system backup.

It is also possible to completely restore your iPod to its factory state by using the Restore program from Apple. This will restore the original operating system and standard partitioning to your iPod. Unfortunately, this means any settings or music will be erased and will have to be copied back to your iPod.

Partitioning. Now that the backups are done, we will add a new partition to the iPod to hold the root filesystem for Linux. This is required on Windows iPods, because Linux cannot use a FAT32 partition for its root filesystem.

The following commands describe a session with fdisk that deletes the existing firmware partition and then creates a new, smaller partition to hold the firmware. The additional space is then used to create a new partition, which we will format for use with Linux.

The output displayed in the following steps is correct for a 20-GB iPod. Some output will be different for different-sized iPods; however, the values entered by the user remain the same.

1. Start fdisk:

   ```
   # fdisk /dev/sda
   The number of cylinders for this disk is set to 2431.
   There is nothing wrong with that, but this is larger than 1024,
   and could in certain setups cause problems with:
           1) software that runs at boot time (e.g., old versions of LILO)
           2) booting and partitioning software from other OSs (e.g., DOS
           FDISK, OS/2 FDISK)

   Command (m for help):
   ```

2. Delete the firmware partition:

   ```
   Command (m for help): d
   Partition number (1-4): 1
   ```

3. Create a new primary partition with a length of 1 cylinder:

   ```
   Command (m for help): n
   Command action
   e extended
   p primary partition (1-4)
   p
   Partition number (1-4): 1
   First cylinder (1-2431, default 1): 1
   Last cylinder or +size or +sizeM or +sizeK (1-5, default 5): 1
   ```

4. Activate the first partition:

   ```
   Command (m for help): a
   Partition number (1-4): 1
   ```

5. Set the partition type to Empty:

```
Command (m for help): t
Partition number (1-4): 1
Hex code (type L to list codes): 0
```

6. Create the third primary partition from the second to fifth cylinders:

```
Command (m for help): n
Command action
e extended
p primary partition (1-4)
p
Partition number (1-4): 3
First cylinder (1-2431, default 1): 2
Last cylinder or +size or +sizeM or +sizeK (1-5, default 5): 5
```

7. Review the changes. Note that this is for a 20-GB iPod; for other iPod versions, the sda2 partition size will vary.

```
Command (m for help): p

Disk /dev/sda: 20.0 GB, 20000268288 bytes
255 heads, 63 sectors/track, 2431 cylinders
Units = cylinders of 16065 * 512 = 8225280 bytes
```

Device	Boot	Start	End	Blocks	Id	System
/dev/sda1	*	1	1	8001	0	Empty
/dev/sda2	*	6	2431	19486845	b	Win95 FAT32
/dev/sda3		2	5	32130	83	Linux

```
Partition table entries are not in disk order
```

8. If everything looks okay, write out the partition table:

```
Command (m for help): w
```

9. fdisk will now exit, and we can create the new filesystem:

```
# mke2fs -j /dev/sda3
```

10. Set the maximal mount count to never:

```
# tune2fs -c 0 /dev/sda3
tune2fs 1.34 (25-Jul-2003)
Setting maximal mount count to -1
```

Kernel installation. To install the kernel, you need the iPod boot loader (*ipod-loader*), a version of the iPod Linux kernel, and the iPod operating system backup created earlier in the backup process.

First, extract the *ipodloader* and iPod Linux kernel archives into a working directory and check for any last-minute release notes. In the following steps, the make_fw tool and *loader.bin* file are from the ipodloader distribution, and the iPod Linux kernel version is uclinux-2.4.24-ipod0.bin.

1. Extract the Apple OS from the backup image:

```
# make_fw -o apple_os.bin -e 0 ipod_os_partition_backup
```

2. Create a new image including the Linux and Apple operating systems:

```
# make_fw -o my_sw.bin -l uclinux-2.4.24-ipod0.bin -i apple_os.bin loader.bin
```

3. Copy the new image (which is about 4–5 MB in size) back to your iPod:

```
# dd if=my_sw.bin of=/dev/sda1
```

4. Copy the kernel modules onto the iPod, noting that the directory */mnt/ipod* must exist and should not be in use. The *lib* directory refers to the directory from the kernel release and contains the *modules* directory:

```
# mount -t ext2 /dev/sda3 /mnt/tmp
# cp -r lib /mnt/tmp
# umount /mnt/tmp
```

Userland installation. The iPod Linux Userland contains the operating system tools and libraries (including the Podzilla and mp3 applications). This archive should be installed on the root partition of your iPod, created during the partitioning step in the previous section.

1. Mount your iPod root partition:

```
# mount -t ext2 /dev/sda3 /mnt/tmp
```

2. Extract the root filesystem:

```
# cd /mnt/tmp
# tar zxf /tmp/ipod_fs_040403.tar.gz
```

3. Update the root filesystem with the latest kernel modules:

```
# tar zxf /tmp/uclinux-2.4.24-ipod0.tar.gz lib
```

4. Unmount your iPod root partition:

```
# umount /mnt/tmp
```

Finishing up. The current release contains a number of usability bugs that can be resolved by executing the following commands:

1. Mount your iPod root partition:

```
# mount -t ext2 /dev/sda3 /mnt/tmp
```

2. Perform fixes for */etc/rc*. Replace */mnt/tmp/etc/rc* with the following:

```
hostname ipod
mount -t proc proc /proc
ln -s /dev/pty/m0 /dev/ptyp0
ln -s /dev/pty/m1 /dev/ptyp1
ln -s /dev/ide/host0/bus0/target0/lun0/disc /dev/hda
ln -s /dev/ide/host0/bus0/target0/lun0/part2 /dev/hda2
ln -s /dev/ide/host0/bus0/target0/lun0/part3 /dev/hda3
ln -s /dev/tts/1 /dev/ttyS1
mknod /dev/ttyp0 c 3 0
mknod /dev/ttyp1 c 3 0
modprobe tsb43aa82
modprobe eth1394
```

```
ifconfig eth0 192.168.222.2 mtu 170
mount -t vfat -o ro /dev/hda2 /mnt
mount -o remount,rw /
hdparm -S 3 /dev/hda
```

3. Perform fixes for */etc/inittab*. Replace */mnt/tmp/etc/inittab* with the following:

```
inet:unknown:/bin/inetd
pz:unknown:/bin/podzilla
```

4. Unmount your iPod root partition:

```
# umount /mnt/tmp
```

5. Eject your iPod. The following command will unload the FireWire driver for your iPod. Once unloaded, your iPod will either reboot automatically or display the "OK to disconnect" message.

```
# modprobe -r sbp2
```

6. If your iPod did not automatically reboot, hold down the Menu and Play/Pause buttons for three seconds to reboot it.

Starting Linux on the iPod

Using the configuration in the previous section, your iPod will automatically start Linux on reboot. You should see the Tux logo, as shown in Figure 3-34, and then the normal Linux boot console messages will scroll by.

Once the operating system is booted, the Podzilla application will start, as shown in Figure 3-35. This work-in-progress interface mimics the Apple interface.

When you are finished with Linux, you can reboot the iPod by holding down the Menu and Play/Pause buttons for three seconds. When the Apple logo appears, hold down the Rewind button to start the Apple firmware.

To completely remove Linux from your iPod, restore the original firmware partition from your backup:

```
# dd if=ipod_firmware_partition_backup of=/dev/sda1
```

Writing Your Own Applications

To develop applications for your iPod running Linux, you'll need to use a special compiler that targets the ARM processor, because this is the instruction set used by the CPU on the iPod. You can download this for either Mac OS X or Linux from iPodLinux.com (*http://ipodlinux.sourceforge.net/ download.shtml*).

This compiler includes a special flag to generate binaries that will run on uClinux, so when compiling, you need to ensure it is used. Normally, you

Figure 3-34. A Linux iPod on bootup

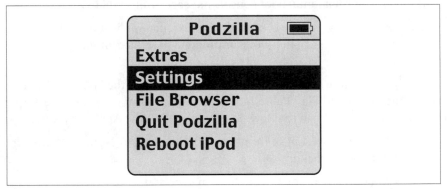

Figure 3-35. The Podzilla interface

would use the LDFLAGS variable in your *Makefile* to set this flag. The source package for Podzilla has an example of this:

```
LDFLAGS+=-elf2flt
```

So, to create a simple "hello world" application, use the following files:

```
---hello.c---
#include <stdio.h>
int main(int argc, char **argv)
{
    printf("Hello world!\n");
    return 0;
```

```
}
---Makefile---
CC=arm-elf-gcc
LDFLAGS=-elf2flt
hello: hello.o
        $(CC) $(LDFLAGS) -o hello hello.o
```

To install this application, simply copy it to the root filesystem on your iPod and set the executable bit. To execute it during the bootup of the iPod, you can modify the */etc/rc* file; just indicate the full path to your executable.

To develop graphic applications, use the Microwindows library (*http://www. microwindows.org*; free), which provides a free set of primitives for developing graphical applications. Included are :ipodloader (*http://sourceforge.net/project/ showfiles.php?group_id=73079&package_id=101451*); iPod Linux Kernel (*http:// sourceforge.net/project/showfiles.php?group_id=73079&package_id=73283*); and iPod Linux root filesystem (*http://sourceforge.net/project/showfiles.php?group_ id=73079&package_id=73279*).

Hacking the Hack

There is now an active community working on developing applications for the iPod and providing assistance to newcomers. Different people have different interests, from games (see Figure 3-36), text editors, and new codec support to speech synthesis; all are possible with the Linux kernel.

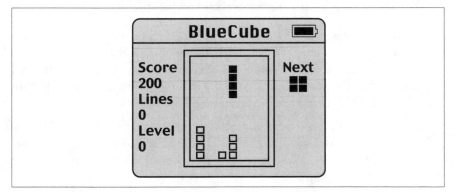

Figure 3-36. Tetris on the iPod?!

In addition to these user applications, core support for iPod features such as voice recording and FireWire disk support is also being improved to further extend the possibilities. Use this hack as a springboard from your Linux on iPod imagination. Just as with Apple, with Linux on the iPod, you can write any number of applications for the iPod.

—Bernard Leach

iTunes
Hacks 50–71

iTunes is the center of Apple's digital music universe. Just using the built-in tools, you can buy music, rip your current collection, manage your iPod, and much more. But you didn't buy this book to learn the basics; you bought it to understand how you can hack iTunes, taking it to the next level. This chapter covers a wide range of ways you can iTunes to do your bidding, from customizing its colors [Hack #66] to controlling its functionality [Hack #60].

iTunes Keyboard Shortcuts

The first rule of any power user is to use keyboard shortcuts. This hack introduces you to all the shortcuts available to iTunes users.

Apple engineers have been kind enough to include a veritable bounty of keyboard shortcuts in iTunes. In fact, after learning all of these shortcuts, you can toss your mouse out the window—well, not quite. However, Mac and Windows users alike can control iTunes much more quickly and easily with these keyboard shortcuts than by navigating with a mouse.

Tables 4-1 through 4-13 list the keyboard shortcuts available for iTunes. Windows users should substitute the ⌘ key with the Control key. Of course, you can also right-click (Windows) or Control-click (Mac) to display a list of commonly available options.

Table 4-1. Playback shortcuts

Action	Shortcut
Play the selected song immediately	Return
Listen to the next or previous album in a list	Option–right arrow or left arrow (or Option-click the Skip Forward or Skip Backward controls in the upper-left corner of the iTunes window)

Table 4-1. Playback shortcuts (continued)

Action	Shortcut
Rewind or fast-forward to the next song in a list	⌘-left arrow or right arrow (or click the Skip Forward or Skip Backward controls in the upper-left corner of the iTunes window)

Table 4-2. Library and playlist shortcuts

Action	Shortcut
Create a playlist from a selection of songs	Shift-click the Add (+) button (or drag the songs to the white area of the Source list)
Create a new Smart Playlist	Option-click the Add (+) button
Reshuffle the current playlist	Option-click the Shuffle button
Delete the selected playlist from your Source list without confirming you want to delete it	⌘-Delete
Delete the selected playlist and all the songs it contains from your library	Option-Delete
Delete the selected song from your library and all playlists	Option-Delete

Table 4-3. iTunes Music Store shortcuts

Action	Shortcut
Go to the next page in the Music Store	⌘-right bracket (])
Go to the previous page in the Music Store	⌘-left bracket ([)

Table 4-4. File and window shortcuts

Action	Shortcut
Check or uncheck all the songs in a list	⌘-click the checkbox next to a song
Change the song information columns you see	Control-click a column heading
Expand or collapse all the triangles in the Radios Stream's list	⌘-click a triangle
Shrink the iTunes window to show only the playback controls	Click the Zoom control in the upper-left corner of the iTunes window
Zoom the window to an ideal size	Option-click the Zoom control in the upper-left corner of the iTunes window
See the iTunes window resize while you are resizing it	⌘-drag the resize box in the lower-right corner of the window
Shrink the iTunes window to show only the playback controls	Click the zoom control in the upper-left corner of the iTunes window
In the Get Info window, see the info for the next or previous song in the list	⌘-N or ⌘-P
Go to the previous or next pane in the Get Info or Preferences window	⌘-click left bracket ([) or right bracket (])

Table 4-5. iPod shortcut

Action	Shortcut
Prevent iPod from automatically updating when you connect it to your computer	⌘-Option as you connect the iPod to your computer (hold the keys down until the iPod appears in the iTunes Source list)

Table 4-6. Audible shortcuts

Action	Shortcut
Go to the next chapter (if available)	⌘-Shift–right arrow
Go to the last chapter (if available)	⌘-Shift–left arrow

Table 4-7. iTunes menu shortcuts

Action	Shortcut
Open iTunes preferences	⌘-, (comma)
Hide the iTunes window	⌘-H
Hide all other applications	Option-⌘-H
Quit the iTunes application	⌘ C-Q

Table 4-8. File menu shortcuts

Aotion	Shortcut
Create a new playlist	⌘-N
Create a new playlist with the selected songs	Shift-⌘-N
Create a new Smart Playlist	Option-⌘-N
Add a file to the Library	⌘-O
Close the iTunes window	⌘-W
Import a song, playlist, or library file	Shift-⌘-O
Open the song or CD Info window for the selected song or CD	⌘-I
Show where a song file is located	⌘-R
Show the currently playing song in the list	⌘-L

Table 4-9. Edit menu shortcuts

Action	Shortcut
Undo your last action	⌘-Z
Cut the selected song's information	⌘-X
Copy the selected song's information	⌘-C
Paste the selected song's information	⌘-V
Select all the songs in the list	⌘-A
Deselect all the songs in the list	Shift-⌘-A

Table 4-9. Edit menu shortcuts (continued)

Action	Shortcut
Hide or show the Artist and Album columns	⌘-B
Hide or show the song artwork	⌘-G
Open the View Options window for the selected source	⌘-J

Table 4-10. Controls menu shortcuts

Action	Shortcut
Stop or start playing the selected song	Spacebar
Move to the next song	Up arrow
Move to the previous song	Down arrow
Play a song	Return
When a song is playing, play the next song in a list	Right arrow
When a song is playing, play the previous song in a list	Left arrow
Increase the volume	Up arrow
Decrease the volume	Down arrow
Mute the sound (song keeps playing)	Option-⌘–down arrow

Table 4-11. Visualizer menu shortcuts

Action	Shortcut
Turn the visualizer on or off	⌘-T
Make visual effects take up the entire screen (when visualizer is on)	⌘-F

Table 4-12. Advanced menu shortcuts

Action	Shortcut
Stream the audio file at a specific URL to iTunes	⌘-U

Table 4-13. Window menu shortcuts

Action	Shortcut
Put the iTunes window in the Dock (Mac only) or switch to mini iTunes player (Windows only)	⌘-M
View the iTunes window	⌘-1
View the Equalizer window	⌘-2

Control iTunes from the Finder   ⓜⓢⓔ

With a few extra tools, you can control iTunes from the Finder or any other application.

iTunes gives all of us an incredible amount of control over our digital music. However, most of us make our living doing things outside of iTunes, and often we get interrupted. Phone calls, obtrusive coworkers, and the almighty nature calls might conspire to force us to go back to iTunes and pause what's playing. Likewise, we might want to (gasp!) skip to the next track or switch to another playlist. Again, we have to stop what we're doing, switch to iTunes, and hit the fast-forward button or make a new selection.

Luckily, some smart and friendly developers have solved this problem by creating applications that allow you to control iTunes from the Macintosh Finder. For this hack, we are going to take a look at two of the available options: ByteController (*http://brainbyte.digitalhybrid.net*; donationware) and the aptly named SizzlingKeys4iTunes (*http://www.yellowmug.com*; free).

ByteController appears as a small menu item in the Finder menu bar, as shown on the left in Figure 4-1.

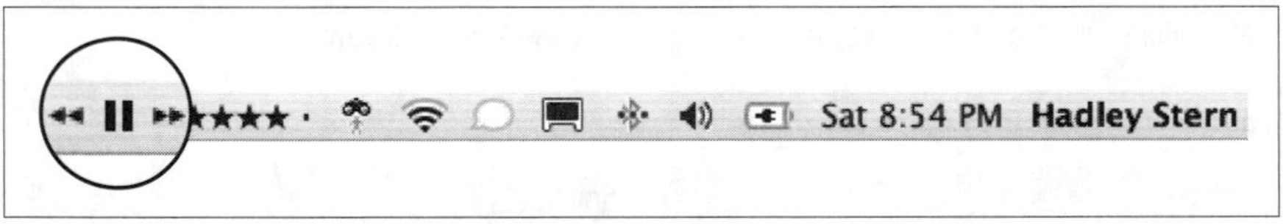

Figure 4-1. Play/Pause and more from the menu bar, using ByteController

To run ByteController, download the application and install in it your *Applications* folder. If you want, you can have ByteController launch upon login by Control-clicking on the ByteController's menu bar item and selecting Preferences from the drop-down menu. Two tabs will load: General and Hot Keys. Select the General tab and click Load at Startup to have ByteController always available.

The next tab, Hot Keys, lets you really become a power iTunes user. You can assign keyboard shortcuts to the Play, Next Song, and Previous Song ByteController items. To do so, tab to the field to which you want to assign a shortcut, enter a combination of keys, and then hit Enter. Voilá! You can now control iTunes from the Finder using your keyboard.

Your Mac comes preset with some keyboard shortcuts. Make sure the keyboard shortcuts you set up for iTunes don't conflict with the operating system's keyboard shortcuts. To check your operating system's shortcuts, go to System Preferences → Keyboard & Mouse and select the Keyboard Shortcuts tab.

ByteController is cool and all, but you might be thinking to yourself, "What if I want to show or hide iTunes from the Finder? Or mute my song instead of pausing it? Or even rate my songs using the keyboard?" This is where SizzlingKeys4iTunes comes in. Unlike ByteController, SizzlingKeys4iTunes's sole raison d'etre is controlling iTunes from the keyboard; therefore, it gives you more options.

To use SizzlingKeys4iTunes, first install the program in your *Applications* folder. Then, double-click on the SizzlingKeys.prefPane icon. System Preferences opens up, and a window pops up, asking you if you want to install the panel for all users or just the current user. Make your selection, and SizzlingKeys4iTunes is good to go.

The System Preferences panel (shown in Figure 4-2) is where you make all your selections for how SizzlingKeys4iTunes works. The Basic Controls tab allows you to set keyboard shortcuts for the following items:

- Play/Pause
- Next Track
- Previous Track
- Volume Down/Up
- Semi-mute
- Mute
- Show/Hide iTunes

SizzlingKeys4iTunes ships with default key combinations. To customize the application, in the SizzlingKeys4iTunes Preference Pane, click on the appropriate button for the item you want to customize; a window pops up for you to enter your own key combinations. SizzlingKeys4iTunes also lets you rate songs from the keyboard. Click the Rating tab and customize the hot keys in any way you see fit.

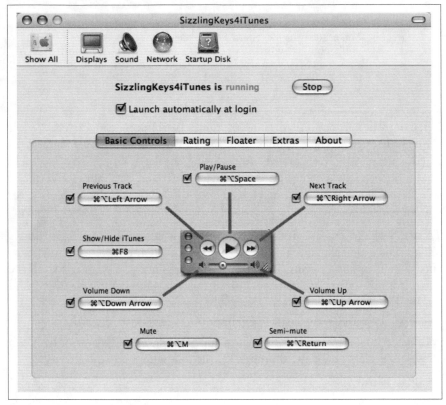

Figure 4-2. The SizzlingKeys4iTunes Preferences window

Clean Up Your ID3 Tags ⓜⓦⓛ

Keep Britney and Mozart separate by ensuring that the ID3 tags that describe your iTunes songs are correct.

When you insert a CD to be ripped in iTunes, it looks up the album information on the CD database (CDDB). All of the information about your CD magically appears in iTunes, which is very handy—except when the CDDB labels as Alternative music that you'd classify as Pop, or when information you think is important has been omitted. Back in the wild-west days of downloading from Napster, you could also find MP3s that someone else catalogued in an entirely different way. Suddenly finding that album or song you want in iTunes is like finding a digital needle in a haystack.

One song can contain a lot of information: the name of the song, the year it was made, and, thanks to the CDDB standard, a whole slew of additional useful information. Some tags get imported automatically when iTunes connects to the CDDB. Other tags (for example, Record Label) are there for you to fill in yourself. Following are lists of all the tags in the CDDB (see *http://www.gracenote.com/gn_products/cddb.html*).

Here are the Album data fields:

Album Title
> The album title—includes sort information (e.g., so that Pink Floyd's "The Wall" can be sorted under *W* instead of *T*)

Album Artist
> The artist's name—includes sort information (e.g., so that *Dave Matthews Band* can be sorted under *Matthews* instead of *Dave*)

Record Label
> The label or publisher of the CD

Year
> The year the CD was recorded or published

Genre
> The primary and secondary genres of the album

Credits
> A list of the album's principal musicians, composer, conductor, producer, etc.

Compilation
> A flag that you can set to indicate that tracks on the album have different artists

Number/Total Set
> Identifies a CD as a member of a box set

Language
> Displays information in the appropriate character set

Region
> Identifies where the CD was released

Certifier
> Identifies the authorized party (artist or label) who has certified the accuracy of the data

URLs
> Lists artist or fan sites, genre sites, movie sites for soundtracks, etc.

ISRC
> The International Standard Recording Code number for the CD

Notes
> General notes such as dedications, where a live set was recorded, etc.

And here are the Track data fields:

Track Title
> The title of the track—includes sort information (e.g., so that "The Late Greats" will appear under *L* instead of *T*)

Track Artist
> The artist's name—important for compilations such as soundtracks (also includes sort information)

Record Label
> The label that released the track—in a compilation, might differ from track to track

Year
> The year the track was recorded—in an anthology, might differ from track to track

Beats Per Minute
> The number of beats per minute, used for DJ syncing

Notes
> General track notes

Credits
> Lists credits for the entire album or for individual tracks (150 fields)

Credit Name
> Credits a person, company, or place (such as recording location)

Credit Role
> Credits a particular musical instrument, composer, songwriter, producer, recording location, etc.

Credit Notes
> Notes if an unusual instrument was used, if a track or segment appears courtesy of someone, etc.

Genres
> Musical genres can be entered for the entire album or applied to individual tracks

Metagenres (20)
> A general classification (e.g., Rock, Classical, New Age, Jazz)

Subgenres (251)
> The more specific style (e.g., Goth, Punk, Ska, Baroque, Choral, Ambient, Bebop, Ragtime)

Segments
> Useful for identifying classical pieces (which can cross track boundaries), musical pieces (groups of track movements), or famous or critical sections of a track; each segment can have its own name, notes, and credits

It's time to clean up those tags! The quickest way is within iTunes itself. First, select the song or group of songs whose tags you want to change, and then either Control-click (Mac) or right-click (Windows). A contextual menu will pop up, as shown in Figure 4-3. Select Get Info.

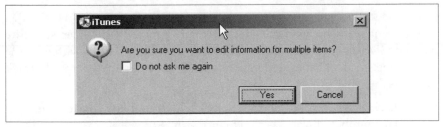

Figure 4-3. Selecting songs to edit

iTunes, being the polite and user-friendly application that it is, pops up a warning message that asks you, "Are you sure you want to edit information for multiple items?," as shown in Figure 4-4. If you think this warning is over-kill for a confident hacker like yourself, go ahead and click "Do not ask me again." If you are like me and you like being prompted before doing something potentially silly, just click the Yes button and proceed. But proceed with caution, because you are about to edit multiple items in one fell swoop.

iTunes
Are you sure you want to edit information for multiple items?
☐ Do not ask me again
Yes   Cancel

Figure 4-4. iTunes' polite warning message

Now, you'll see a window that displays all the fields in the ID3 tags associated with the songs you've just selected, as shown in Figure 4-5.

You can change or add any number of bits of information about your songs right here. Want to rate a song, add the year the album came out, or adjust the volume for the song? Simply make the appropriate changes in iTunes' ID3 window.

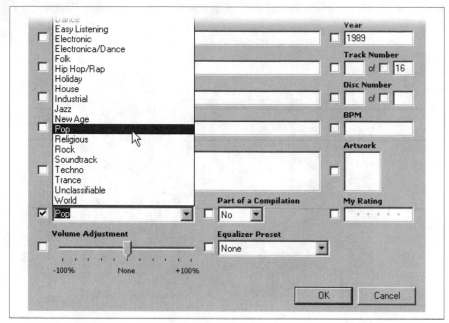

Figure 4-5. All the fields within an ID3 tag that you can change

iTunes has built in a great tool for editing ID3 tags, but if you want to take things to the next level, there are some great shareware and freeware tools out there. On the Macintosh side, some good choices are Chaotic Software's MP3 Rage (*http://www.chaoticsoftware.com*; $24.95; limited trial version available) and ID3X (*http://www.three-2-one.de/321apps*; free). For Windows, try Easy Tagger (*http://www.istoksoft.com/products.htm*; $25.00; limited trial version available) or MP3 Tag Tools (*http://massid3lib.sourceforge.net*; free).

These tools allow you not only to edit the ID3 tags, but also to use the ID3 tags to rename your MP3 files and even reorganize your folder structure based on ID3 tag information. By default, iTunes names tracks with only the song name. In the iTunes preferences you do have the option to add track numbers, but that's it.

In this hack, we'll look specifically at ID3X. This tool lets you rename your files in any number of ways, as shown in Figure 4-6.

Once you've downloaded the application and have it running, simply select an MP3 or series of MP3s to rename and hit OK. Now you have several options. For example, if you want to have your file name be Genre-Artist-Year, enter the following code in the Renaming Scheme window: %g-%b-%y. You also have options to include or remove numbers, spaces, and even vow-els! Before hitting OK, make sure to click the Try Out tab to see how the

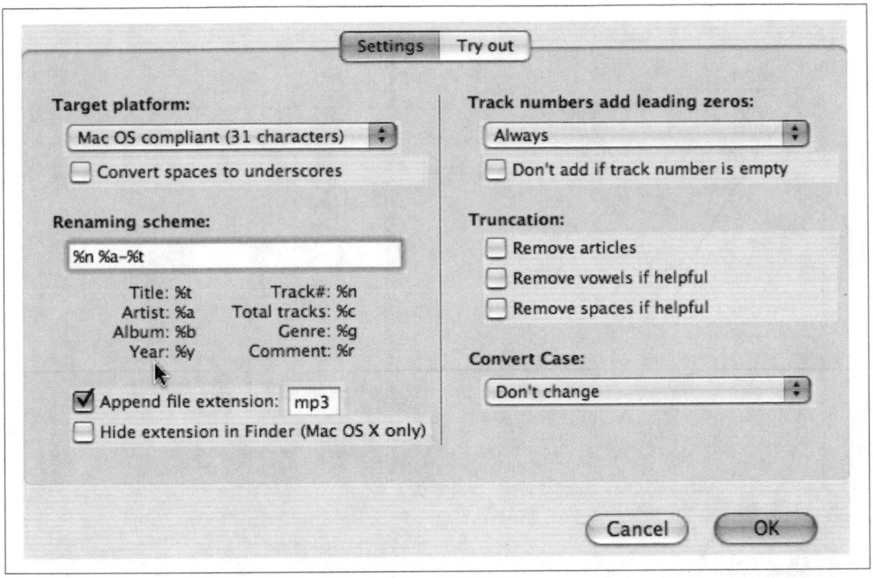

Figure 4-6. ID3X's file renamer

conversion will work. Once you are happy with your settings, just click OK and, like magic, your files will be renamed.

Another handy ID3X feature is the ability to organize your files in the Finder based on their ID3 tag information. By default, iTunes puts files in order of artist name and then, within those folders, by album name. Some of us prefer to organize our music by genres. Others insist, as if any other way were sacrilege, that organizing alphabetically is the only way to go. But where do The Shangri-Las go—under *S* or *T*? And what about artists like 10,000 Maniacs?! If you want to reorganize your digital music files, the information in ID3 tags will come to your rescue.

Pull down the menu in ID3X's main window and select "Batch sort to folder structure." Select the files you want to organize. Now you can choose how you want the folders to be organized. In Figure 4-7, I have decided to organize my music by Genre, Artist, and then Album. This means that ID3X will take the music files I have selected and reorganize them so that the upper-level folder is Genre. Within the Genre folders, my music will be organized by Artist, and within those folders it will be organized by Album name. You can also choose to move MP3 files, duplicate MP3 files, or just create aliases. You can choose to organize your files by Artist, Album, Year, Genre, Comment, ID3 version, or MP3 bit rate.

With organizational tools like ID3X, there is no excuse for your music to be disorganized. When Apple releases a 200-GB iPod, you'll be very happy that your ID3 tags are clean and organized. So get cleaning!

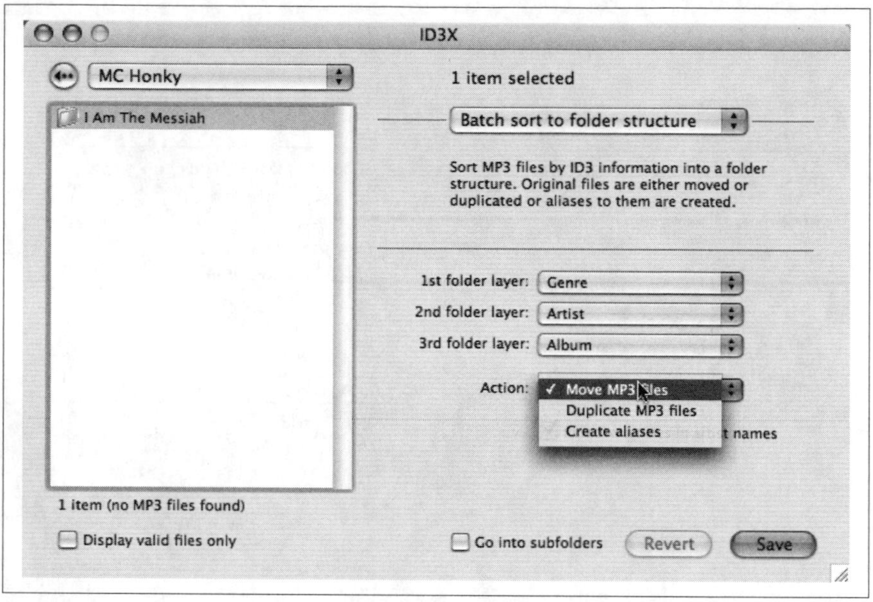

Figure 4-7. Organizing files using ID3 tag attributes

HACK #53   Import Lyrics into iTunes and iPod   ⓜⓦⓘ

For all you karaoke-obsessed individuals, there are a number of ways to incorporate song lyrics into an iPod and iTunes workflow.

Whenever "It's the End of the World as We Know It (And I Feel Fine)" by R.E.M. comes on the radio, are you and your friends prone to getting into near-violent arguments over what Michael Stipe is singing? Do you find yourself correcting your girlfriend when she is (incorrectly) singing along to songs in the car? Do you love to get drunk and serenade countless strangers at every karaoke event you trip across? If you answered yes to any of these questions, then this hack is for you. I'm going to walk you through a few available options to bring lyrics into iTunes and your iPod.

Sure, you could launch Mozilla, Internet Explorer, or Safari and manually look up the lyrics to your favorite songs on Absolute Lyric (*http://www. absolutelyric.com*) or a similar site, but then again, it is the twenty-first century. It's time to start acting more like The Jetsons and less like The Flintstones; it's time to automate.

"Search for Lyrics on Google" **[Hack #80]** presents one way to search for lyrics automatically while using iTunes. This hack provides a few good alternatives for Windows users, as well as another option for Mac users.

On Windows

Two good lyric-hunting options available to Windows users are Canto Pod and EvilLyrics.

Canto Pod. Canto Pod (*http://www.staylazy.net/canto*; donateware), powered by Sharedlyrics.net, is a lyric-searching program for all flavors of Windows (it will also run on any Mac running VirtualPC alongside a Windows-formatted iPod). On first launch of Canto Pod, you need to register for a free account with Sharedlyrics.net. After registering, you will be taken to a preferences pane where you select your iPod and enter your login name and password. After logging in, click Save, and you will be taken to the main Canto Pod page shown in Figure 4-8.

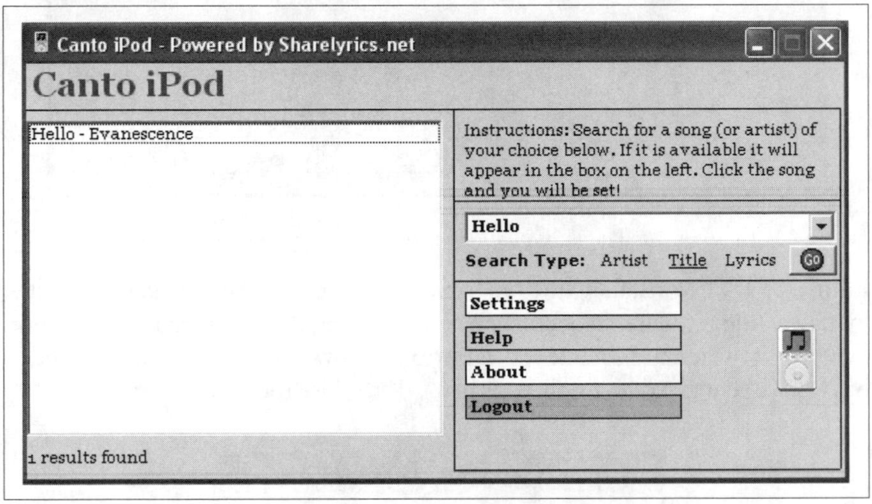

Figure 4-8. Canto Pod's main interface, searching for "Hello"

Once Canto Pod finds lyrics to your song in the Sharedlyrics.net database, you simply double-click the song you want, and Canto Pod uploads the lyrics to your iPod as a Contacts file. As an added bonus, it works with any generation of iPod. Unfortunately, however, at the time of this writing, the Sharedlyrics.net database seems to be a bit sparse.

EvilLyrics. EvilLyrics (*http://www.evillabs.sk/evillyrics/index.php*; donateware), a Windows program that works with a variety of players, including iTunes, is probably the most comprehensive and best working of all the lyric-oriented programs I've seen. To use it, download and install the program. Make sure that you check the box to install the iTunes plug-in during setup, as shown in Figure 4-9.

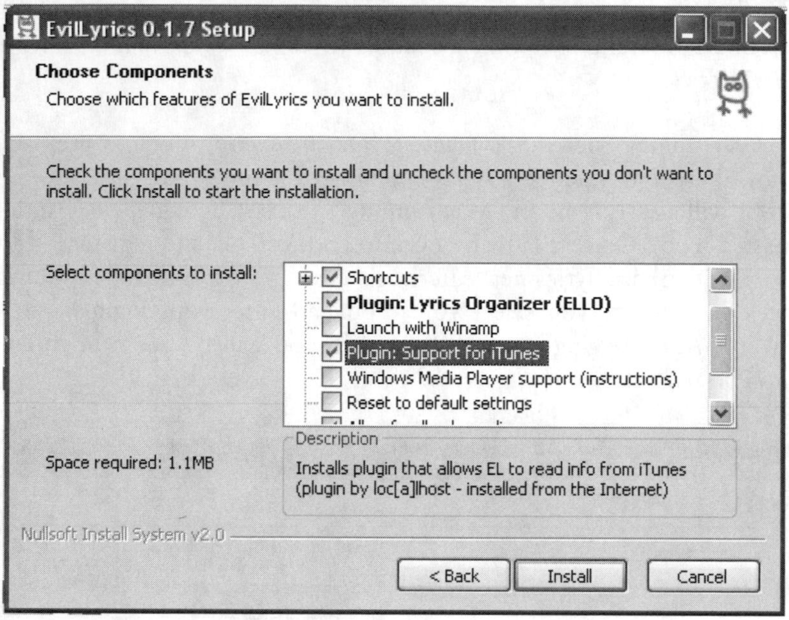

Figure 4-9. Checking the Plugin: support for iTunes option when installing EvilLyrics

Immediately after installing the program, you should update the karaoke index by navigating to the preferences pane and selecting the Advanced tab shown in Figure 4-10. Click the Update Index button and wait for a notice that the index has been updated. Click Apply and then OK to close the preferences pane.

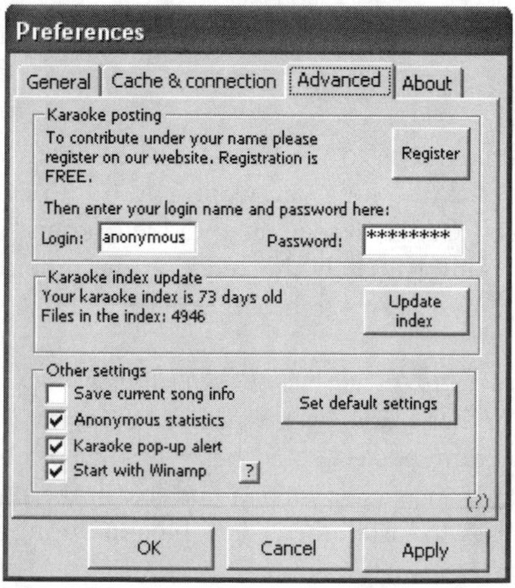

Figure 4-10. Updating the Karaoke Index under the Advanced Preferences tab

The interface is simple. You can either type in a search, or simply start play-ing a song in your player of choice while EvilLyrics is open; it automatically starts searching for matches to the currently playing song. After conducting a search, as shown in Figure 4-11, you can launch the results in your web browser of choice to see if there is an available timed karaoke version of the file and to see a rating of its timing by other users.

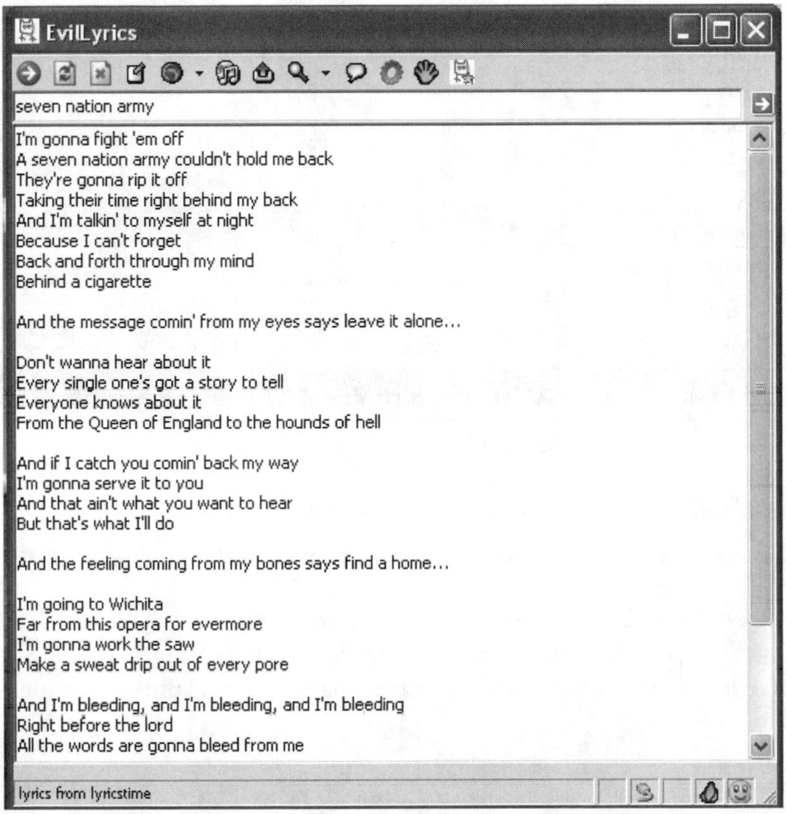

Figure 4-11. EvilLyrics's main interface, after searching for "seven nation army"

From the web page, you simply click "Import into EvilLyrics" to download the karaoke file. If you click on the in-browser option, the information for the current search shows up in your browser, as shown in Figure 4-12.

Once the file loads in EvilLyrics, click the magnifying glass to launch a little window with the lyrics. If you click this button at the beginning of the song, they should scroll along line by line, nicely in sync with the tune. Call all your friends over and throw a karaoke dinner party!

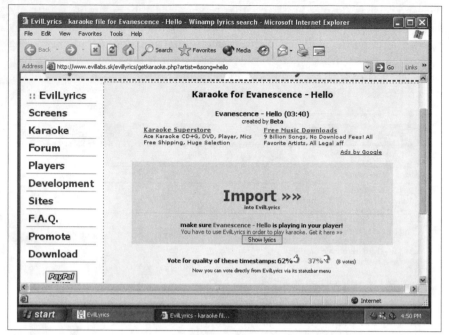

Figure 4-12. Downloading the karaoke file

On the Mac

Mac users have a couple lyric-searching options as well.

Google Lyric Search. The first option for Mac users is to check out "Search for Lyrics on Google" [Hack #80]. After running through the hack, you'll have the Google Lyric Search AppleScript available from iTunes, as shown in Figure 4-13.

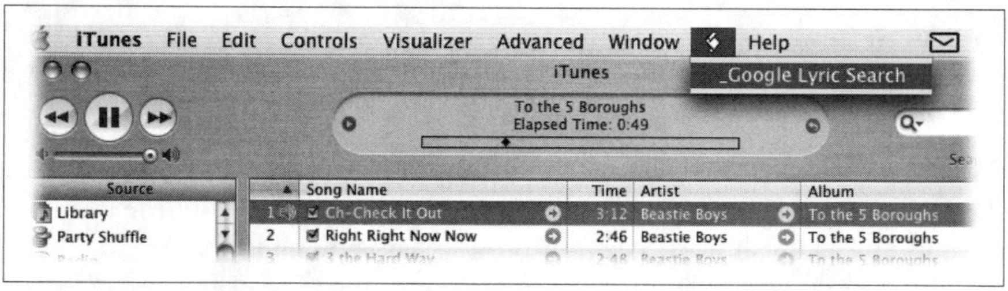

Figure 4-13. Beginning a search for the lyrics to the Beastie Boys' "Ch-Check It Out" with Google Lyric Search

Figure 4-14 shows the results of the search initiated in Figure 4-13.

This script will send a Google search string to Safari and return a results page listing all the hits.

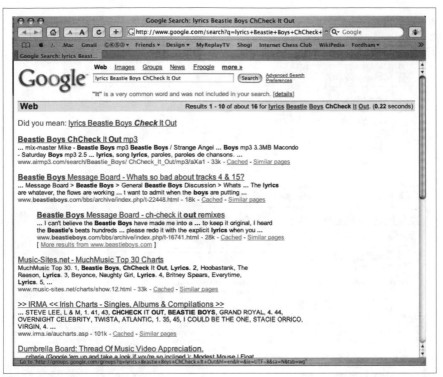

Figure 4-14. The search results from the Google Lyric Search–generated string for "lyrics Beastie Boys ChCheck It Out"

LyricTracker X. Another option for Mac users is LyricTracker X (*http://lyrictracker.com/main.php?action=x*; $10). Lyric Tracker X lets you search the LyricTracker database for song lyrics. If you pay $10 for this piece of shareware, you also have the ability to upload the lyrics you choose to your iPod's Contacts files. However, this is entirely dependent upon the Lyric-Tracker database containing the song lyrics for which you are searching (my search for "Ch-Check It Out" turned up empty).

The program also has an integrated chat feature for the LyricTracker community, an interface to submit lyrics, and a Most Requested Lyrics page. Figure 4-15 shows a successful search for Toad the Wet Sprocket, with the lyrics to "Pray Your Gods" opened up in the Query Results window, and a mouse-over of the button to upload the lyrics to your iPod.

Hacking the Hack

Mac and Windows users alike, remember that if you have a third- or fourth-generation iPod or iPod mini, you can simply save the lyrics to your favorite songs as plain-text files in your iPod's *Notes* folder for portable reading.

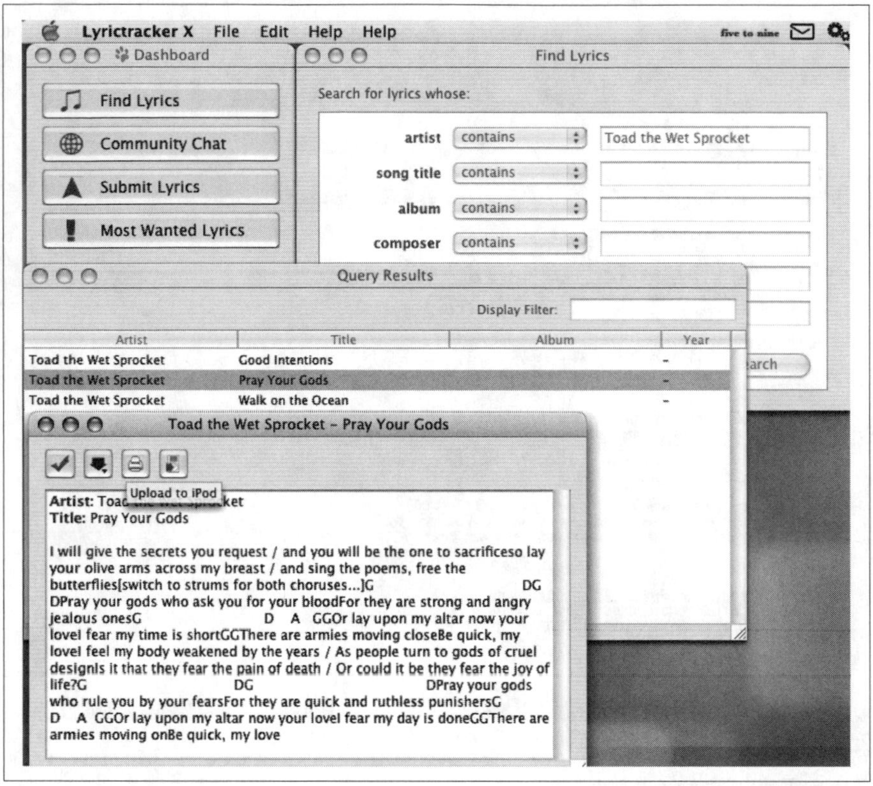

Figure 4-15. LyricTracker X's main menu, showing the Find Lyrics window, the Query Results window, and the Upload to iPod button selected in the individual song lyrics file

Consider including links to the song files on your iPod, so that you can pull up a song's lyrics on the iPod and click the link to begin playing that song as you read along. To find out how to create this type of link in your notes, read "Write Your Own iPod Book" **[Hack #39]**.

—C. K. Sample III

HACK #54 Extend Your Visualizer Options ◐◑◔

Get the most out of Apple's built-in visualizer, and get to know some cool third-party visualizer plug-ins.

You might not have discovered it yet, but there is a pretty cool *visualizer*—an engine for generating interesting patterns based on the pitch and rhythm of the currently playing track—built into iTunes. To see the visualizer do its thing, play a track and go to Visualizer → Turn Visualizer On. iTunes translates your music into some pretty psychedelic graphics. Go back to the Visualizer menu and select Full Screen, and the effect will fill your screen. The visualizer looks great from across the room on your computer or, even better, connected to your television. If you're having a party, you can even try connecting your laptop to a digital projector and projecting the visuals on a wall.

Apple has built in some pretty extensive customization options for the iTunes visualizer and has done a good job of hiding them. Try all these keyboard shortcuts on both the Macintosh and Windows versions of iTunes. To access these options, have a song playing in iTunes and Apple's visualizer turned on. Surprisingly, for Apple, the customization controls are not the most intuitive. There are three variables that control how the visualizer ends up looking: behavior, color, and color theme. The behavior variables have odd names like Uber Disco Lights, Kaleidoscope, and Melt-O-Rama. Color variables have equally wacky names like Hip-No-Therapy, Sunburst, and Dandelion Psyc. Color themes have names like Metal Brood, Cold Fire, and Dark Rainbow. Use the following keys to toggle between all the variables:

Q and W
> Control behaviors

A and S
> Control colors

Z and X
> Control color themes

Table 4-14 lists all the keyboard commands for the iTunes visualizer.

Table 4-14. iTunes visualization keyboard commands

Keystroke	Result
N	Switch between normal or high-contrast colors.
R	Display a random new visualization configuration.
C	Show current visualization configuration.
M	Elect configuration mode (random, user, freeze). Use "freeze" while toggling form, color, and effect.
Q/W	Toggle visualization behavior.
A/S	Toggle visualization effect.
Shift-0 through Shift-9	Save current configuration.
0–9	Display saved configuration.
D	Reset visualization to iTunes default. Be careful, because this deletes your custom configurations.
F	Toggle the frame rate display.
T	Toggle the frame rate capping.
H or ?	View the Help menu.
I	Display track info (Title, Artist, Album).
Left/right arrow	Go to previous/next song.
Up/down arrow	Increase/decrease volume.

You can use any combination of behaviors, colors, and color themes. But what if your favorite combination is Melt-O-Rama, Hip-No-Therapy, and Dandelion Psyc on weekdays but another combination on weekends? Fortunately, iTunes lets you save up to 10 combinations.

First you need to freeze your current configuration. Do this by hitting the M key until you get to Freeze Current configuration. Then, go back to adjusting the behaviors, colors, and color themes until you have the combination you want. To save the combination, hit the Shift key and a number from 0–9. Because this is a hackerific interface, you won't get the usual Apple user interface guidelines, such as messages like "Configuration accepted." In fact, you get no feedback whatsoever! But trust me, your configuration has stuck. Whenever you want your saved configuration to appear, just hit the appropriate number.

After a while, the built-in iTunes visualizer gets, well, old. Let's explore some visualizer plug-ins that offer a myriad of visual options. Currently, there are more options available for Mac users, but PC users, don't fear; you won't be left out (entirely) in the cold.

Mac Plug-ins

On the Mac side, there are a number of plug-ins available, including Volcano Kit (*http://volcanokit.com/volcanokit2/iTunesVis/index.php*; free), MT Space (*http://www.andrew.cmu.edu/~mtomczak/MTSpace/*; free), and G-Force (*http://www.soundspectrum.com*; free). Point your web browser to MacUpdate (*http://www.macupdate.com*) and enter "iTunes visual" in the search window to see more of your plug-in options.

Once you've downloaded your plug-in, installation is a snap. Quit iTunes, navigate to *<Your Home Folder>/Library/iTunes/iTunes Plug-ins*, and copy the file included with the download. Depending on your version of iTunes, there might not be an *iTunes Plug-ins* folder. If this is the case, just go ahead and create one, making sure you name it correctly.

Next time you launch iTunes, your installed visualizer plug-ins will be available under the Visualizer menu, as shown in Figure 4-16. Some plug-ins have options that you can play with. To access them, just click the Options button in the top-right corner of the iTunes window.

Take a peek at Figures 4-17 and 4-18 for some examples of Mac plug-ins. One of my favorites is the iTunes LED plug-in (*http://homepage.mac.com/graham.cox/LEDSA/Spectrum.html*; free), which mimics the visual feedback of old-school amplifiers.

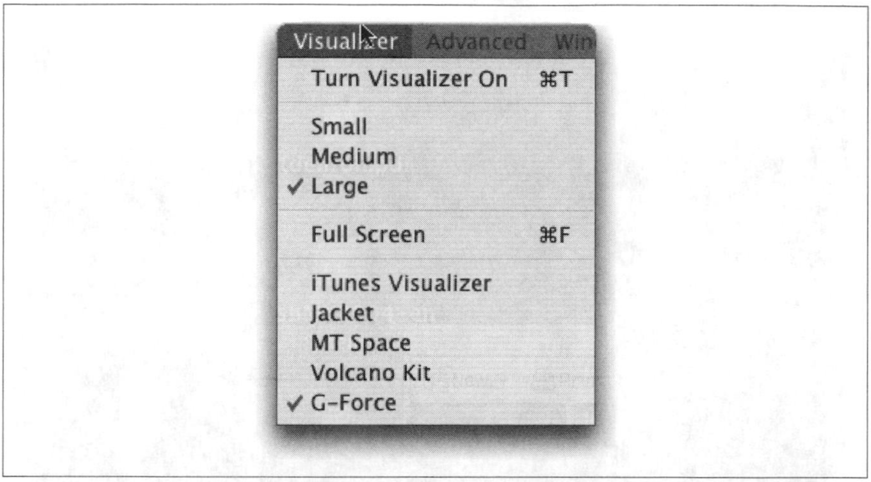

Turn Visualizer On   ⌘T

Small
Medium
✓ Large

Full Screen   ⌘F

iTunes Visualizer
Jacket
MT Space
Volcano Kit
✓ G-Force

Figure 4-16. Accessing all visualizers from the Visualizer menu

Figure 4-17. The Volcano Kit visualizer plug-in

Windows Plug-ins

On the Windows side, there are fewer options for visualizers. This will probably change soon, though, because iTunes for Windows came out quite a bit later than iTunes for the Mac. In the meantime, Windows users can enjoy the G-Force and WhiteCap visualizers from Sound Spectrum

Figure 4-18. iTunes LED—looks like an old-school amp, but it's iTunes!

(*http://www.soundspectrum.com*; free). Unlike on the Macintosh side, the G-Force download for Windows is an executable package that takes you through a few easy steps to complete the installation. You'll notice when you go through the installer that you can use G-Force in several other Windows audio players, including Windows Media Player.

Once you have installed the plug-in, two visualizers will appear in the iTunes Visualizer menu: G-Force and WhiteCap.

For some reason, the Windows plug-ins do not take advantage of the Options button. Instead, type the letter H, and a number of options appear that will allow you to optimize the look and feel of the visualizer.

Hacking the Hack

Now that you have all these funky visuals, it's time to think about how to display them. If you are having a party and want to make your music the centerpiece, you can display your visuals on your television or, if you have one, on a digital projector. If you're more of a loner and enjoy listening to music while working on your computer, with this hack you'll have more visual options to accompany your tunes.

Bulk-Rip CDs ⓜⓦⓛ

Convert your music to MP3s/AACs more efficiently.

Pouring your existing CD collection into your iTunes library and iPod is a time-consuming process. You have to open each CD jewel case, pop out the CD and put in it your computer, hit Import in iTunes, and wait. You might enjoy listening to those old CDs you barely remember buying, but it will still take quite a while to get through them all. Of course, you can buy digital tunes from the iTunes Music Store, but unless you have money to burn, you'll probably want to skip repurchasing music you already own.

One option is to use a service such as RipDigital (*http://www.ripdigital.com*) to do the dirty work for you. RipDigital will convert your CD music collection to AAC files for you. All you do is send them your CDs, and a few weeks later you get your CDs back along with all the digital files on a hard drive. It will cost you a lot more than this hack, though—around $1 a CD.

The other option is to turn your Mac into an AAC-ripping machine. The time savings are minimal if you are only ripping 10 CDs but get exponentially better as the bigger your collection is. This hack is particularly great for long flights where you are just sitting there twiddling your thumbs. You can use the time to rip dozens of CDs, and you won't even have to schlep the CDs along with you!

To get things going, all you'll need to have is Roxio's Toast Titanium (*http://www.roxio.com/en/products/toast/index*; $99.95) and a handy little AppleScript from this hack. You can use Toast to create the necessary disc images and the AppleScript to automatically rip any number of disc images in sequence.

Ripping by Hand

Roxio's Toast is a great tool for making disc images of CDs on the Mac. To get started, fire up Toast and insert a music CD that you want to rip.

If you plan on bulk-ripping your CDs in iTunes when you won't be connected to the Internet—say, when you're on a flight from New York to L.A. —you can have Toast get your CD's CDDB track info for you before you get on the flight. Then, using the rest of the steps in this hack, you can rip your CD in iTunes without actually having the CD in your drive. The CDDB information contains all the good stuff (album name, artist name, song names, etc.) that makes using iTunes such a pleasure. Toast will use the same Gracenote CDDB server (*http://www.gracenote.com/gn_products/cddb.html*)

that iTunes uses. If, however, you know you are going to be connected to the Internet when you rip the CDs in iTunes, you can skip this step.

To get your track info in Toast, go to Disc → Get Track Info.... Once you have the CDDB info, it's time to create the disc image in Toast. To create a disc image, go to File → Save as Disc Image. Toast will read the data off of the CD and create the disc image. Depending on the length of the audio CD, the processor speed of your machine, and the speed of your CD drive, creating the disc image takes anywhere between two and five minutes. A disc image is an exact mirror of the CD, so you will be creating large files (upwards of 700 MB). Want to bulk-rip 10 CDs? You'll need around 7 GB of space. Once you are done ripping them in iTunes, though, you can trash the disc images.

Once you have created your disc images, you can leave them on your hard drive until you are ready to rip. The best time to do this is when you are going to be using your laptop on the move. For example, if you commute by train or have a business flight coming up, preload a bunch of disc images and get ready to rip them.

Before opening iTunes, you need to mount all the disc images in Toast. Open Toast and select Utilities → Mount Disc Image. You can select multiple disc images from the dialog box. Hit OK. All of your disc images will mount, and they will look exactly like CDs to the Finder and to iTunes. Go ahead and open up iTunes. Your eyes do not deceive you! iTunes shows all the CDs in the Source window, as shown in Figure 4-19.

Figure 4-19. Yes, that is five CDs in iTunes!

To iTunes, your disc image is a regular CD. If you didn't import the CD's metadata in Toast using the CDDB and you have iTunes set up to do this automatically upon CD insert, iTunes will get the track info now. If you have your iTunes preferences set to import CDs to MP3s/AACs on CD insert, iTunes will go ahead and start importing the first CD automatically, but it will stop once the first CD has been imported. To import all your CDs one by one, after that just select each CD and hit Import.

Automated Ripping with AppleScript

The real power of creating disc images to rip later comes into play when you combine it with a little nifty AppleScript written by Doug Adams. *Rip CDs In A Row* (*http://www.malcolmadams.com/itunes/scripts/ss.php?sp=ripcdsinarow*) is an AppleScript that allows you to rip multiple CDs within iTunes in one pass. Install the script by quitting iTunes, opening up */Home/Library/iTunes*, and dropping the script in the *Scripts* folder. If you don't already have a *Scripts* folder, go ahead and create one. Now, when you open up iTunes there will be an AppleScript icon between the Window and Help menu items.

To bulk-rip your disc images, simply select Rip CDs In A Row from the AppleScript menu in iTunes. The pop-up window shown in Figure 4-20 will list all of your disc images.

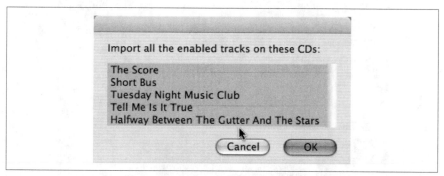

Figure 4-20. Selecting the CDs you want to rip from the Rip CDs In A Row dialog box

If you have mounted 5 discs, 5 albums will appear; if you have mounted 20 discs, 20 albums will appear. Either select all the albums or select only the ones you want to rip by holding down the Option key and clicking on the individual album titles. Hit OK, and watch iTunes go to work. One by one, iTunes will rip all of the albums you've selected without you having to do a thing! No switching CDs between ripping—just sit back, work on another project (or go to sleep), and let iTunes do the work for you!

Unless you have 10 CD drives hooked up to your Mac, you will still have to manually insert the CDs in your machine to make the disc images. However, this hack will save you some time and let you rip in the background while working. So, get ripping!

HACK   Work with Album Artwork   ⓜⓦⓛ
#56   Get all of your album artwork into iTunes quickly and easily.

When you buy a CD, you get not just the audio files, but a package consisting also of the album artwork and liner notes (often the lyrics, too)—not to mention something you can hold in your hand, which is a quality sorely lacking in the digital music world. While this hack won't have you turning over your monitor in your hands like a CD jewel case, it will inject some of that visual appeal into your iTunes collection.

The latest version of iTunes incorporates cover artwork into its interface. If you purchase a song from the iTunes Music Store, this artwork is downloaded for you right along with your AAC tracks. To view the album cover, just click the Show/Hide Song Artwork icon, as shown in Figure 4-21.

Figure 4-21. Viewing album artwork in iTunes

In all likelihood, though, you've not repurchased all your CDs as AACs from the iTunes Music Store. You're more likely to have ripped some portion of your collection to MP3s/AAC files, CD by CD [Hack #55]. While iTunes does gather and fill in the CD metadata for each track/album from the CDDB for you, it doesn't take the extra step of grabbing the album covers. That, I'm afraid, is left to you.

If you want to go the manual route, visit Amazon.com (*http://www.amazon. com*) or Allmusic (*http://www.allmusic.com*)—a fantastic source for information on music—search for your album, and drag the album artwork from your web browser to iTunes's song artwork pane. iTunes copies the artwork, and it will appear whenever you are browsing or listening to that album. Make sure you have all the songs associated with that album selected in iTunes, though, or the album artwork will be associated only with the single track you have highlighted.

Don't break out in a cold sweat wondering how you are going to find the time to search for all the album artwork in your collection; there are some nifty tools out there for both Macintosh and Windows that make easy work of automating this unenviable task.

On the Mac

On the Mac side, iTunes Catalog (*http://www.kavasoft.com/iTunesCatalog*; $9.99; limited trial version available) is a fantastic tool. Not only can you use it to import all your album artwork into iTunes, but it also comes in handy when you're creating a web page for your iTunes library [Hack #63]. In one fell swoop, iTunes Catalog grabs the artwork for all the albums in your library from Amazon and import it into iTunes. Now, that's service!

The limited trial version gives you a chance to evaluate the software, limiting you to artists starting with the letters A–E.

When you launch iTunes Catalog, it opens your iTunes library. Select Artwork → Copy All Artwork to iTunes to have iTunes Catalog download cover art for all of the albums in your library, drop the artwork files into iTunes, and associate them with the appropriate tracks from each album. Depending on the size of your library this can take quite a bit of time, but it is well worth the wait. The next time you open iTunes, all the artwork that iTunes Catalog could find on Amazon shows up as if by magic—or at least as if you'd bought the tracks from the iTunes Music Store.

Should you come across some music in your library for which Amazon doesn't have artwork, try finding the covers on Allmusic (*http://www. allmusic.com*) and (gasp!) manually adding the artwork. Another good source is Google's Image Search (*http://images.google.com*); just Google, drag, drop, and repeat as necessary.

On Windows

On the Windows side, life isn't quite as convenient, but some help is available. Launch Internet Explorer and browse to art4iTunes.com (*http://www.art4itunes.com*).

 Netscape and Opera won't let you drag and drop images directly from the browser into iTunes.

Then, go back to iTunes and select File → Export File List, as shown in Figure 4-22. From the Save As Type drop-down menu, select Plain Text.

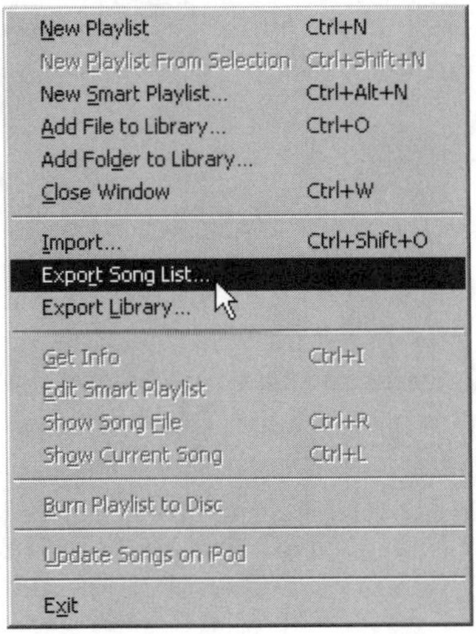

New Playlist	Ctrl+N
New Playlist From Selection	Ctrl+Shift+N
New Smart Playlist...	Ctrl+Alt+N
Add File to Library...	Ctrl+O
Add Folder to Library...	
Close Window	Ctrl+W
Import...	Ctrl+Shift+O
Export Song List...	
Export Library...	
Get Info	Ctrl+I
Edit Smart Playlist	
Show Song File	Ctrl+R
Show Current Song	Ctrl+L
Burn Playlist to Disc	
Update Songs on iPod	
Exit	

Figure 4-22. Exporting your song list from iTunes

Now, go back to art4iTunes.com in IE. Click the Choose File button and browse to the song list you just exported from iTunes, as shown in Figure 4-23. Click the Send File button to send your song list to art4iTunes.com. It'll take a few minutes as art4iTunes.com goes about collecting your album artwork for you; it actually uses Amazon.com in the background.

Once art4itunes.com is done, it opens a browser window listing all of your albums and tracks, along with cover artwork, where available. Getting the artwork from IE into iTunes is, I'm afraid, a manual process. However, it's a simple (if repetitive) task. Select an album or all its tracks in iTunes, switch to IE, and drag the artwork to the cover art pane in iTunes, as shown in Figure 4-24. Repeat as necessary.

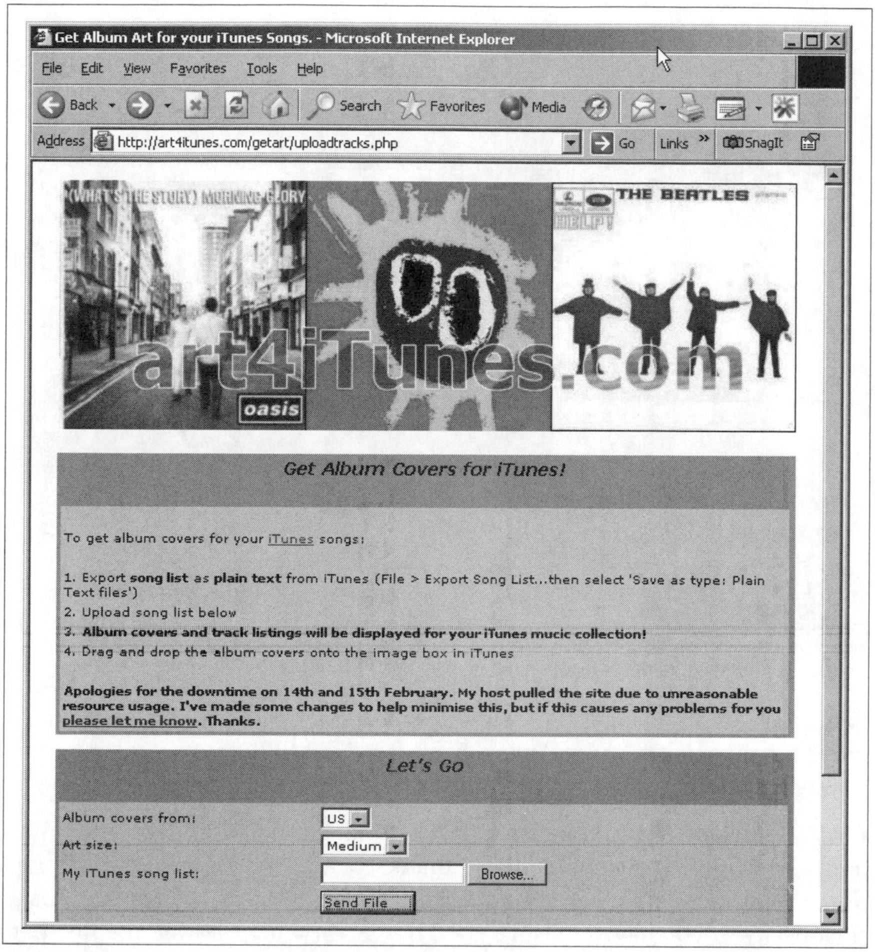

Figure 4-23. Uploading your song list to art4iTunes.com

Hacking the Hack

Now that you've got all your artwork in iTunes, there are a number of neat utilities out there that let you view your artwork outside of iTunes.

Mac users should be sure to check out Clutter **[Hack #56]** (*http://www.sprote. com/clutter/*; free), Playalong (*http://www.geocities.com/suitts/sw/playalong. html*; free), and OnDeck (*http://holocore.com*; free). Clutter places album covers on your desktop. You can organize them any way you want. To play an album, just double-click on a cover.

Figure 4-24. Dragging album covers from Internet Explorer into iTunes

Playalong places a small window on your desktop that shows the album cover for the current song playing, as well as its My Rating score and a link to buy the album from Amazon.com.

OnDeck displays your album cover in a Finder window and allows you to adjust the opacity of the window—thanks to the power of Quartz. If you don't want OnDeck's window to dominate the desktop, simply scale back the opacity. If you haven't been a good boy or girl and followed the first part of this hack, OnDeck will even go out and download the artwork for you.

On the Windows side, unfortunately, there currently aren't any such utilities available.

H A C K   Clutter Your Desktop with Music ⓜⓨⓞ
#57
Neatness sometimes just doesn't count, particularly when it comes to artistic expression. So, go ahead and clutter your desktop with click-to-play album covers from your iTunes library.

Remember when discs weren't compact? I'm talking about *albums*, those lovely black plastic platters cluttering your shelves and spinning away with the occasional crackle and pop on your turntable. If you've made the switch to all digital yet still wax nostalgic for thumbing through your old record collection—each record lovingly tended, all but scratch-free, and gently placed within its sleeve—and find iTunes a little too sterile, you're going to love Clutter (*http://www.sprote.com/clutter*; freeware).

This groovy little app from Sprote Research gives all the MP3s and AACs in your iTunes 4 library the tactile feel of those stacks and stacks of records, eight tracks, cassettes, and CDs you left behind in your frenzy to join the 21st century. Set aside any tendencies toward neatness you may have, toss album covers on your desktop like so many throw pillows, and just enjoy the colorful clutter, as shown in Figure 4-25.

Figure 4-25. Embracing the clutter and enjoying the color

When you first launch Clutter, a small Not Playing window appears (Figure 4-26, left). Launch iTunes, start playing any song in your library, minimize or hide iTunes, and bring Clutter to the front. Clutter's Now Playing window (Figure 4-26, right) sports the album cover (if available) in the formerly empty square. You have a nice set of play/pause, fast-forward, and rewind buttons, overlaid in music-video style with the artist, song, and album names (if defined in iTunes).

If no artwork appears and the album name is defined, select File → Find Cover On Amazon (⌘-F) to search for and download the associated album cover, as shown in Figure 4-27. If Amazon turns up nothing, you can also Google for something appropriate by using File → Search Google (⌘-G).

Figure 4-26. Clutter's Not Playing (left) startup and Now Playing (right) windows

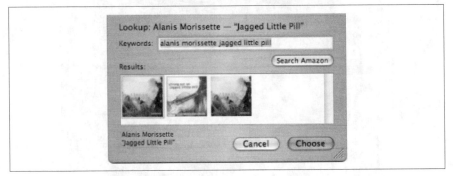

Figure 4-27. Finding cover art on Amazon

If you have an image on hand, you can simply drag it into the window. With your preferred cover art showing, you can use Clutter's File → Copy Cover to iTunes option to copy it over to iTunes if you like.

There are several other programs available—not to mention a handful of Konfabulator widgets [Hack #59] that display album covers. What separates Clutter from all those other programs is the ability to clutter your desktop with these works of art. That's right; throw them anywhere you like. Simply click on the album cover in the Now Playing window and drag it onto your desktop to add it to the mix.

> It took me just a few minutes to clutter my desktop with a rich assortment of colorful album covers. The only glitch I encountered was when Clutter gave a song from Guns N' Roses's "Greatest Hits" album the artwork from Fleetwood Mac's "Greatest Hits," even though the cover art was already defined in iTunes and both songs came from the iTunes Music Store. A quick Amazon search and replace corrected the problem.

Each of these covers is independent; you can move them around, stack them on top of one another, or organize them neatly in rows (if you really have to). Browse your desktop for something you want to hear, double-click the album cover, and it'll start playing in iTunes. If you can't find a particular cover in all the mess you've made on your desktop, you can cheat by Control- or right-clicking Clutter's Dock icon and selecting it from a list. Just try that with your physical album collection spread across your floor or real desktop!

Not sure what album a piece of artwork belongs to? Simply Control- or right-click on it to bring up a contextual menu containing all available information on the album: the artist and album name, along with the titles of all the songs from the album, are all available right there on the menu. Just choose your favorite song to jump right to it.

If you switch back over to iTunes, you'll see that Clutter has its own playlist that contains the currently playing album.

> There's even better news. According to a little benchmarking I did with top, Clutter takes up practically none of your processor power (unless it is searching for album artwork that it doesn't already have loaded, in which case the load is still minimal). Its memory footprint can be somewhat large for a small program (in my case, 131 MB of virtual memory!), depending upon how many albums you have open, but with something this cool, who cares?

Before Panther and Exposé, I hated windows cluttering my desktop, and as a result, I never really got into Clutter. Now, however, I can easily shuffle through all of my albums, or push them all out of the way with a mouse gesture or a keystroke whenever I want. And any song I want to hear is simply a couple of clicks away; I no longer have to scroll through a long alphabetical list in iTunes to find it.

I have my albums again!

—*C. K. Sample III*

Make Your Playlists Smart ⓂⓌⓁ

Take your playlists to the next level by mastering Smart Playlists.

Smart Playlists are a powerful and underused feature in iTunes. These special playlists are updated automatically, depending on a simple set of criteria. The ability to create playlists by mixing music tracks from different albums and genres has always been one of the great features of iTunes, and Smart Playlists take this to the next level.

Make Your Playlists Smart

Introduced in iTunes 3, Smart Playlists let you personalize your listening experience by creating music lists that automatically update based on user-specified criteria such as My Rating, Last Played, Comment, and Play Count. Some attributes about a track that can be used as criteria for creating a Smart Playlist (such as Song Name) are static, while others (such as Play Count) are dynamically updated to reflect track status. Smart Playlists have something to offer every listener.

To rate songs on the iPod, press the center (wheel) button two times. The first time will put the wheel into jog mode, and the second into rating mode. Once there, you will see the stars on the screen. Spin the wheel to increase or decrease the star rating. Make sure that iTunes is set to one of the two automatic transfer modes in the iPod Options screen. Otherwise, you will not be able to easily transfer Play Counts, Ratings, and Play Dates back to iTunes.

The Smart Playlist dialog (shown in Figure 4-28) is accessed from the iTunes File menu and can be broken into three distinct areas: the Match Line, the Criteria Lines, and the Limiter Area. The Match Line determines how the criteria are evaluated. It will change contextually depending on the Criteria Lines. When multiple criteria are specified, the Match Line will display the any/all pop-up. Otherwise, there will be no pop-up in this area.

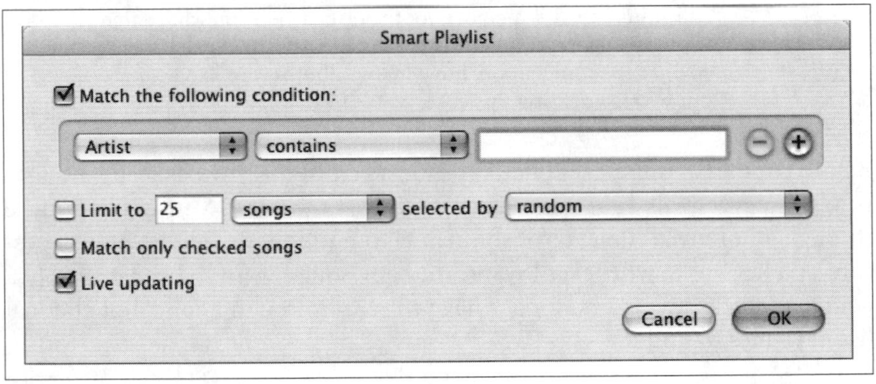

Figure 4-28. The Smart Playlist dialog

Start by making your selections from the pop-up menus in the Criteria Lines area, choosing the desired attributes, operators, and values. The Criteria Line initially displays only one line. Press the + button to add additional criteria lines. The Match Line settings will determine how the criteria are evaluated.

The real power of Smart Playlists comes from combining various rules. To add a rule, or Criteria Line, simply click the + icon. There is virtually no limit to the number of Criteria Lines you can have. Each rule is interpreted as a Boolean operator, meaning that a match or true result will display the track, while a false result or nonmatch will not display the track.

After you've chosen your criteria, the Limiter Area allows you to limit the number of results returned by the Smart Playlist.

Track Attributes

Understanding the meaning of the many track attributes is important to get the most out of Smart Playlists. Attributes are always examined on a per-track basis in iTunes, regardless of the source of the music (e.g., CD, iTunes Music Store download, or analog recording). The only attribute that groups CD tracks together is Album Name. Tracks can just as easily be grouped by Artist, Genre, Year, or Play Count. Figure 4-29 shows the iTunes drop-down menu listing the track attributes you can use for building Smart Playlists. Table 4-15 describes all the attributes.

Figure 4-29. Drop-down menu of the track attributes that can be used to build Smart Playlists

Make Your Playlists Smart

Table 4-15. Track attributes

Attribute name	Description
Album	The album on which the track was released.
Artist	The artist who recorded the track.
BPM	Beats per minute, or tempo. This is a numerical value describing the number of musical beats in one minute. The value is not calculated by iTunes and is not included with songs purchased from the iTunes Music Store. It must be entered manually or calculated by a third-party application.
	Although it has a strange interface, the application Ask the DJ (*http://www. wildbits.com/askthedj/purchase.html*; $29; free trial version available) effectively calculates BPM. Once the BPM attribute is written to your tracks, you can create excellent workout playlists.
Bit Rate	The number of kilobits per second (kbps) used to represent the track. The higher the bit rate, the higher the resulting audio quality and the larger the file size. Music files are typically 128 kbps or higher, while audio books and other spoken-word content are often 96 kbps or lower.
Comment	A *user-defined* field, which means you can do whatever you want with it. This is a great place to put keywords or extra information about tracks. For example, you may record the source of music files in the Comment field (e.g., my CD collection, bought from iTunes Music Store, ripped from DAT tree, borrowed from girlfriend, sampler CD from club, promo, etc.).
Grouping	Used to group multiple movements in single larger classical pieces. Many users have developed individualized schemes involving grouping, such as subcategorization by genre or specially featured performer.
Kind	The audio file format. Current supported formats are AAC Audio File, Protected AAC Audio File, AIFF Audio File, Apple Lossless Audio File, Audible File, MPEG Audio File, MPEG Audio Stream, Playlist URL, and WAV Audio File.
Last Played	iTunes records the date and time when you play a track. Note that this is written only after a song has completed playing, not when the player is skipped to the next song.
My Rating	Rate your music collection by assigning 0–5 stars in iTunes or on an iPod (third-generation or dockable and newer).
Play Count	A *musical odometer*: keeps track of how many times you listen to each song.
Playlist	Includes or excludes tracks contained within other playlists (new in iTunes 4.5). This parameter allows for nesting and extremely complex mixed-Boolean Smart Playlists.
Sample Rate	Number of samples of a sound taken each second to represent a sound digitally. The more samples taken per second, the more accurate the digital representation of the sound can be. The sample rate for CD-quality audio is 44,100 samples per second. This sample rate can accurately reproduce audio frequencies up to 20,500 Hertz (cycles per second), covering the full range of human hearing.
Size	File size in megabytes.
Song Name	Name attribute of the track.
Time	Total duration of the track.
Track Number	Track number as assigned per album (e.g., 7 of 10).
Year	Year of track release.

Additional Attributes

Now, we're on to the final set of Smart Playlist attributes to consider when creating a Smart Playlist. These variables limit playlist size and are important for portable audio players, ease of viewing in iTunes, and building CDs.

Here are the attributes to consider for limiting your playlists:

Limit to 25 songs selected by random
 This line allows you to limit the size of the playlist and choose how the selection is made.

Songs
 Song limits create manageable lists, which can be scrolled through visually.

Minutes & Hours
 Timed lists are great for creating CDs. Try limiting to 74 minutes for the perfect CD-sized playlist.

MB (megabytes) & GB (gigabytes)
 File-size limitations are important for portable music players, such as the iPod. Why let iTunes randomly fill your iPod mini when you can create four different 1-GB Smart Playlists, tailored to your taste?

Selected by:
 This pop-up menu specifies how the song selector sorts the list. Choices include Random, Album, Artists, Genre, Song Name, Highest Rating, Lowest Rating, Most Recently Played, Least Recently Played, Most Often Played, Least Often Played, Most Recently Added, and Least Recently Added.

Match only checked songs
 This selector is handy for omitting tracks from playback by iTunes or iPod. Uncheck songs in the iTunes Library, and they won't show up in the playlist. (Unchecked songs do not play in iTunes by default. They play only when double-clicked.) Try unchecking holiday songs, exceptionally long tracks, or other content that you don't often access.

Live Updating
 Checking this box will allow your Smart Playlists to update on the fly. It's a good thing it's checked by default, because if it's unchecked you'll need to manually refresh the list by selecting all the tracks and pressing the Delete key. All the examples given in the next section should have this box checked.

Smart Playlists

Let's take a look at how the attributes can be used to build selection criteria for Smart Playlists. Create a new Smart Playlist by selecting New Smart

Playlists from the File menu in iTunes. Fill the criteria in the following sections into the resulting dialog box and click OK. The new playlists you create will appear in the Source column on the left side of the iTunes window.

Artist name. Want all the songs by a particular artist or DJ gathered into a playlist? Create a Smart Playlist with the following attributes (iTunes will automatically suggest naming it by the Artist Name):

```
Artist - contains - Artist Name
```

This will match all instances of the Artist Name, including those that feature other artists, remixes, and, quite often, covers.

Workout. These Smart Playlists are excellent to put on the iPod for use in the gym. Try creating a Smart Playlist for each of the following ranges (you may want to adjust them depending on your fitness level).

Warm up
```
BPM - is in the range - 125 to 13
Limit to 5 minutes selected by random
```
Walk
```
BPM - is in the range - 136 to 140
Limit to 5 minutes selected by random
```
Run
```
BPM - is in the range - 141 to 150
Limit to 5 minutes selected by random
```

Repeat the Walk and Run playlists as many times as desired.

High school tunes. Combining comment information with years and ratings can create excellent nostalgic playlists. Try this:

```
Comment - contains - my CD collection
Year - is in the range - start of high school to end of high school
```

Rockin' in the free world. So, what do you do if you want a general rock list? One approach might be to do this:

```
Match - any - of the following conditions
Genre - is - Hard Rock
Genre - is - Indie Rock
Genre - is - Progressive Rock
Genre - is - Southern Rock
Genre - is - Rockabilly
Genre - is - Psychedelic Rock
Genre - is - Latin Rock
Genre - is - Rap Rock
```

But why not use a nested Smart Playlist and make life easier?

```
Genre - contains - Rock
Last Played - is not in the last - 1 day
```

Lose the streams. To keep streaming stations and tracks out of shuffle-mode playlists, try this:

```
Kind - is not - MPEG Audio Stream
Kind - is not - Playlist
```

Fresh mix. Ratings are one of the best attributes. If you've rated your songs and are tiring of hearing the same songs over and over, try this:

```
My Rating - is greater than - 3 Stars
Last Played - is not in the last - 2 weeks
```

Never been listened to. Weed out the songs you've never listened to with this list:

```
Play Count - is - 0
```

Clean tracks. The "Lose the Streams" playlist specifies a method for excluding streaming tracks. Prior to the introduction of the Playlist attribute, this exclusion criterion had to be added to each Smart Playlist where streaming tracks needed to be excluded. Now, we can create nested playlists to exclude undesirable tracks from multiple playlists.

Create a Smart Playlist called "Clean Tracks" to match any of the following conditions:

```
Kind - is not - MPEG Audio Stream
Kind - is not - Playlist
Genre - does not contain - Christmas
Genre - does not contain - Holiday
Genre - does not contain - Audio Book
Bit Rate - is greater than - 96kbps
Time - is less than - 10 minutes
Match checked songs only
```

Now, you can add the following line to any other Smart Playlist:

```
Playlist - is - Clean Tracks
```

Setting the attribute in this way will apply the "Clean Tracks" logic with only one step, essentially nesting the logic and eliminating the need to apply all the attributes to additional Smart Playlists.

A word about mixed Boolean operators: iTunes *does* let you use mixed Boolean operators (AND/OR) to select parameters for Smart Playlists, but the choice appears only after you've added a second line of variables to the playlist. A small all/any pop-up menu will appear at the top, where "Match the following condition" is located, changing the line to read "Match any/all of the following conditions."

Mixed all/any behavior was not possible using Smart Playlists until iTunes 4.5, when the Playlist track attribute was introduced. Using Playlist, it became possible to nest playlists and create complex selectors.

Live hour. On the iTunes web site, Apple suggests using keywords to create a simple romantic Smart Playlist:

```
Name - contains - love
```

Building on this concept, you can gather all live songs from your library and do a *live hour* (although if you are a big fan of the group Live and you don't have any of their live recordings, you might want to add `Artist - is not - Live`):

```
Match - any - of the following conditions
Name - contains - live
Album - contains - live
Comments - contains - live
Limit to - 1 hour - by random
```

Hacking the Hack

Smart Playlists revolutionized the way we play our music. Their introduction in iTunes changed not only the way we listen to music, but also the way we think about it. If you can imagine a Smart Playlist, iTunes can build it for you and keep it fresh to boot.

If you're a Mac user, getting the techniques of Smart Playlists under your belt now will make you much more productive as the feature is added to more and more Apple apps. It is no surprise to Smart Playlist users that Tiger (Mac OS X 10.4) has introduced them to the Finder, Mail, and more.

—*David Bills*

Konfabulate Your iTunes

Use Konfabulator widgets to perform a wide range of iTunes tasks right from your desktop.

Having your music playing through iTunes is the bomb—until your mother-in-law calls. If you are working in another application, you have to switch to iTunes and then click the Pause button. No, it doesn't seem arduous, but after the tenth time it gets to be a pain. This hack not only helps you to pause iTunes from any application, but it also introduces you to some pretty nifty utilities for doing a myriad of iTunes tasks right from your OS X desktop.

Konfabulator (*http://konfabulator.com*; $25.00; trial version available) is a JavaScript runtime engine for Mac OS X. What makes it sing are *widgets*: little pieces of code that do any number of things (alarm clocks, calculators, weather forecasters, and much, much more). To check out some widgets, go to the Gallery section of the Konfabulator web site.

A number of iTunes- and iPod-specific widgets are available from the Konfabulator web site. For this hack, we are going to look at iPod Mini (*http://www.widgetgallery.com/view.php?widget=35978*; free), TuneRater (*http://www.widgetgallery.com/view.php?widget=35857*; free), iTunes volume hotkey (*http://www.widgetgallery.com/view.php?widget=35902*; free), and Name that iTune! (*http://www.widgetgallery.com/view.php?widget=35930*; free).

After you've downloaded widgets, you will need to install them. Widgets, by default, are kept in */User/Documents/Widgets* (when you install Konfabulator, the folder is created for you). Just drag and drop the downloaded widgets into the *Widgets* folder and launch Konfabulator. After Konfabulator launches, a menu will be added to your Finder menu bar, as shown in Figure 4-30.

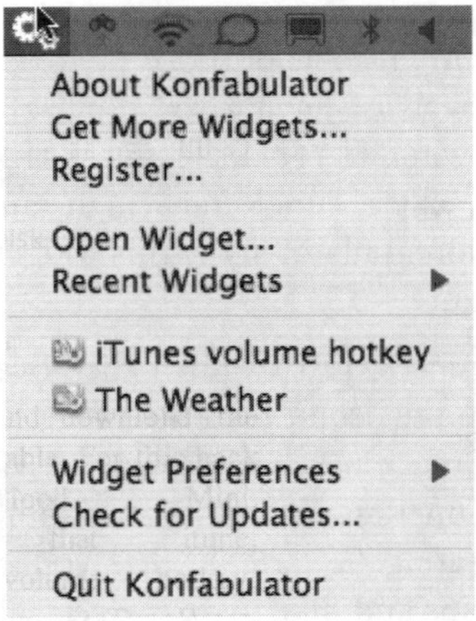

Figure 4-30. The Konfabulator menu bar

iPod Mini

Select Open Widget and open up the iPod Mini widget. One of the hottest MP3 players in existence will appear on your desktop, as shown in Figure 4-31.

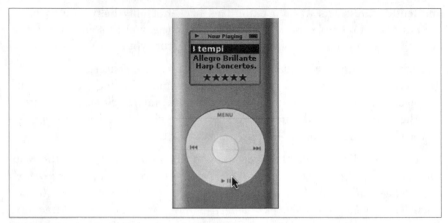

Figure 4-31. An iPod Mini widget on your desktop

Just like in the real iPod mini, you can use the Play, Rewind, and Fast-Forward buttons (the menu bar is inactive). The iPod Mini widget is just one of many desktop interfaces people have written for Konfabulator and iTunes. It also isn't the most space-conscious one; if you want a small widget, check *http:// www.konfabulator.com* for some other cool options.

TuneRater

TuneRater is a widget with a single purpose: to make it easier for you to rate your iTunes songs. Instead of having to stop working on that important Excel spreadsheet and switch to iTunes to rate a song, you can just click the star rating right on the widget. TuneRater will instantly update the song info within iTunes. In true Konfabulator style, this widget comes with some great options, as shown in Figure 4-32.

To access widget preferences, just Control-click over the widget and select Widget Preferences from the drop-down menu (or click on the Konfabulator menu item → Widget Preferences and select the widget whose preferences you want to change). TuneRater will let you skip a song immediately once you've given it a bad rating (a variable that you can also adjust). It also includes a number of skins and, like most widgets, allows you (thanks to the power of Mac OS X Quartz) to adjust the opacity of the widget.

iTunes "volume hotkey"

Widgets aren't just about little things that show up on your desktop. Using the Konfabulator framework, iTunes volume hotkey brings you the ability to control iTunes from any application. When you open the widget, the window shown in Figure 4-33 appears on the desktop to tell you how the widget works.

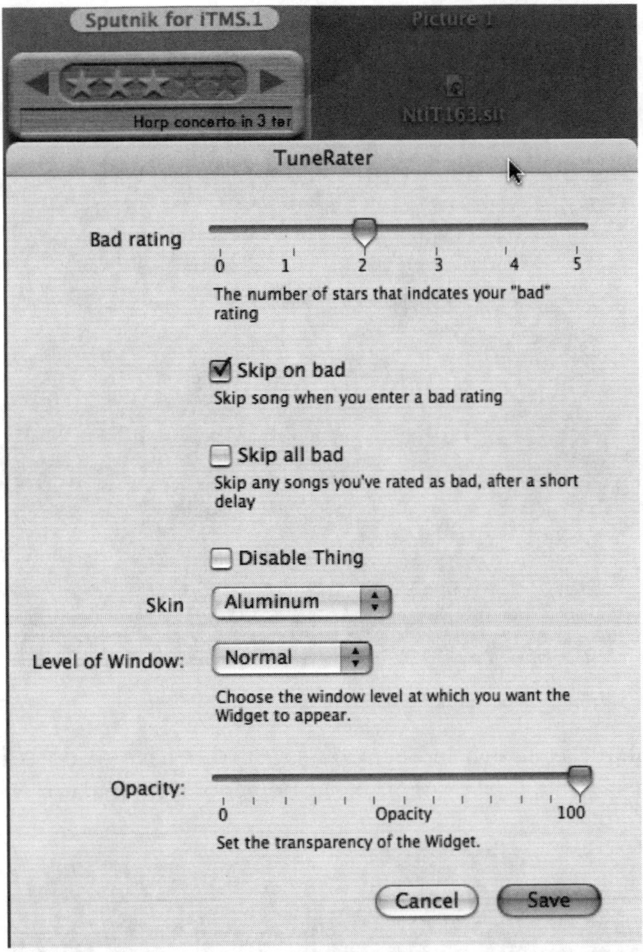

Figure 4-32. The TuneRater widget

The default control keys are ⌘-F13 for volume down, ⌘-F14 for volume up, ⌘-F15 for volume mute, and ⌘-Option-F15 for volume low. You cannot customize these options from this pop-up window! Instead, select "iTunes volume hotkey" from the Widget Preferences in the Konfabulator menu bar. Any changes made there will take effect immediately.

Name that iTune!

Konfabulators can also be just plain old fun, too, like the Name that iTune! widget. Once you open the widget, it will randomly play songs from your

Figure 4-33. Setting up your hotkey preferences

iTunes library, as shown in Figure 4-34. All you have to do is name that tune. It's a silly but good example of the power of Konfabulator widgets.

Figure 4-34. How well do you know your music?

Once you start playing with some widgets, you'll inevitably find some you can't live without when listening to music on your Mac. So, get Konfabulating!

Use Java to Expand iTunes Functionality   ⓜⓧⓛ

HACK
#60

MyTunes is an easy-to-use and extensible framework you can use to build upon iTunes' built-in functionality. With a little help from Java, you can even run iTunes remotely from another machine.

AppleScript fans have had hooks in iTunes for several years, which makes the information in your music library accessible to other scriptable applications. And while AppleScript can be glued together with other components in OS X (in the Terminal, via the /usr/bin/osascript command and AppleScript's do shell script command), attempting to provide your music information to nonscriptable applications or resources (e.g., a web site powered by PHP and MySQL) has traditionally been done in hack-and-scratch ways.

MyTunes fills that void by providing an easy-to-use and extensible framework that allows you to access and manipulate your iTunes library via Java. This hack introduces you to MyTunes and describes the basic concepts of how and why it works the way it does.

Introducing MyTunes

MyTunes has been around for several years in a previous form. It was originally an AppleScript that created an XML-ish file from the iTunes library, which was then parsed by a Perl script to load into a MySQL database (hence the name: *MySQL + iTunes = MyTunes*).

However, iTunes Version 4 creates a file called *iTunes Music Library.xml* in your music library folder, so the first half of MyTunes' original purpose is no longer necessary. And because the Perl script had to be rewritten to parse the new file that is automatically maintained by iTunes, I overhauled the package to make it do so.

The *iTunes Music Library.xml* file contains just about every piece of data you could possibly want to know about your music collection, including:

Application data
    Version and library location

Tracks
    Name, artist, album, length, rating, comments, etc.

Playlists
    Name, whether the playlist is *smart*, and all tracks that belong to it

To see what other information is included, open it in your favorite text editor and take a peek.

Later in this hack, we'll walk through an example of how the bigger and better MyTunes accomplishes the task previously completed by its predecessor and, in doing so, provides a reusable framework to avoid rewriting the meat and potatoes; instead, we'll be spending our time *using* the information, rather than *retrieving* the information. But before we start playing around with MyTunes, we'll need to install the necessary components that comprise the package.

Downloading and Installing MyTunes

As with any other time that you deal with XML, the first thing you'll need is an XML parser. MyTunes uses the Apache Software Foundation's Xerces parser (*http://xml.apache.org/dist/xerces-j/*; free). You'll also need Apache's XMP-RPC library (*http://ws.apache.org/xmlrpc/*; free) to take advantage of the new remote control features available.

The latest version of MyTunes is available as a free download from *http://www.macdevcenter.com/mac/2003/09/03/examples/mytunes.zip*.

Be sure to add these files to your CLASSPATH (refer to *http://java.sun.com/j2se/1.4.2/docs/tooldocs/windows/classpath.html* to set up the CLASSPATH environment variable), or place all the JAR files in the */Library/Java/Extensions/* folder, so that all classes will be automatically made available to your Java applications.

Customizing MyTunes

A configuration file holds all necessary parameters; all classes in the package that have parameterized variables will look for the configuration file *~/.mytunes.xml*. Once you've downloaded the sample to your desktop, place it in the proper location with the following command:

```
mv ~/Desktop/mytunes.xml ~/.mytunes.xml
```

You'll notice that it won't show up when you view your home directory in the Finder. This is because every file that has a period (.) as the first character in its name is hidden. In order to view and edit the file, you'll have to use the Terminal in conjunction with a text editor such as emacs (*http://www.gnu.org/software/emacs/emacs.html*), vi (*http://www.vim.org*), or pico (*http://www.washington.edu/pine/faq/whatis.html#2.2*):

```
emacs ~/.mytunes.xml
```

The configuration file should look similar to Figure 4-35.

As you can see from Figure 4-35, MyTunes has several groups of properties:

Figure 4-35. Sample configuration file for the MyTunes package

library
> Location of the *iTunes Music Library.xml* file

remote.*
> Features with remote control (via XML-RPC)

mysqlimport.*
> Chord that will be created

Opening MyTunes

Once you have installed the necessary components and have set the proper values in your configuration file, open a Terminal window and enter the following command:

```
java com.fivevoltlogic.mytunes.MyTunesLibrary
```

You should see something similar to Figure 4-36.

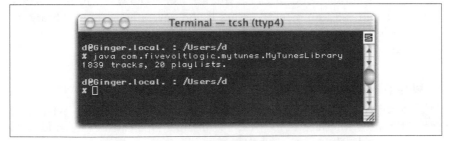

Figure 4-36. Sample output from MyTunesLibrary

If you receive a `ClassNotFoundException`, then one (or more) of the JAR files is missing from */Library/Java/Extensions* or the location you specified in your `CLASSPATH`.

One other problem that you might run into is a thrown `java.io.IOException`. This arises if you are not connected to the Internet when using `MyTunesLibrary`. Because the *iTunes Music Library.xml* file's Document Type Declaration (DTD)—the guide that describes how a particular XML document is constructed—is declared as `PUBLIC` it is located on Apple's servers. Thus, the XML parser attempts to load the document from this location via the internet and throws a `java.io.IOException` since the file can't be accessed.

Looking at the sample output, we can see that I currently have 1839 tracks and 20 playlists in my iTunes library. However, this is the only information that `MyTunesLibrary` provides on its own. While `MyTunesLibrary` parses the information in the library (track names, albums, the playlists to which songs belong, etc.), the class doesn't actually do anything with the data. This separation of logic allows us to reuse the class in different applications without rewriting the bulk of the code (which consists mainly of parsing the XML file to extract the desired information).

With that in mind, in order to use the information made available to us, we have to create a class with appropriate methods invoked by `MyTunesLibrary` as callbacks. For anyone who has worked with SAX before, the `ContentHandler` interface should spring immediately to mind; with SAX, we receive notifications when we've reached XML elements, text, or other items.

Design Considerations

While MyTunes' callback structure is similar to the Simple API for XML (SAX), the XML file is actually parsed with Document Object Model (DOM). The reasoning behind this choice derives from the nonsemantic markup in *iTunes Music Library.xml*; the entire library is described by approximately 10 tags, which makes keeping track of our location in the file while parsing problematic. Because you are using DOM, there is a chance that you could run into memory issues if you have a large music library. In the event that you do run into memory errors, try increasing the memory allocated to your Java Virtual Machine (JVM) to fix the problem.

Extending Chord

The `com.fivevoltlogic.mytunes.Chord` class is to MyTunes what the `ContentHandler` interface is to SAX; `Chord`'s methods can be overridden to suit your needs. As mentioned earlier, we'll create a `Chord` to populate a MySQL database with the information from your iTunes library. While the design could be improved in many ways, it serves as an excellent starting point, and after reading and walking through the following steps, you'll be confident and knowledgeable enough to use MyTunes in any way that you could want.

 This hack assumes you already have MySQL up and running on your Mac and a basic level of competency in using and administrating the server. If this is not the case, Marc Liyonage (*http://www.entropy.ch/home/*) has an excellent tutorial for installing the MySQL server on OS X. In addition to *xerces.jar* and *mytunes.jar*, you'll need a JDBC driver to connect to the MySQL database that you're populating. MySQL Connector/J will do exactly that. Again, extract and place the JAR file in */Library/Java/Extensions/* and you'll be ready to go.

The first step is to create the database tables that will hold the desired information. Here is a MySQL script that will accomplish that task:

```
# attempt to delete tables named Playlists, PlaylistTracks, or Tracks that
# already exist
# if your database already has table(s)
#
DROP TABLE IF EXISTS Playlists;
DROP TABLE IF EXISTS PlaylistTracks;
DROP TABLE IF EXISTS Tracks;

# holds all information regarding an iTunes track
#
#
#
#
CREATE TABLE Tracks (    trackId INT UNSIGNED NOT NULL,
                         trackAlbum VARCHAR(128),
                         trackArtist VARCHAR(128),
                         trackBitRate INT DEFAULT 128,
                         trackComment VARCHAR(128),
                         trackComposer VARCHAR(128),
                         trackDateAdded DATETIME,
                         trackDateModified DATETIME,
                         trackDiscCount SMALLINT DEFAULT 1,
                         trackDiscNumber SMALLINT DEFAULT 1,
                         trackDuration SMALLINT UNSIGNED NOT NULL,
                         trackEqualizer VARCHAR(32),
                         trackGenre VARCHAR(128) DEFAULT "",
                         trackKind VARCHAR(32),
                         trackLocation VARCHAR(128) NOT NULL,
                         trackName VARCHAR(128) DEFAULT "",
                         trackPlayedCount SMALLINT UNSIGNED DEFAULT 0,
                         trackPlayedDate DATETIME,
                         trackRating SMALLINT UNSIGNED DEFAULT 0,
                         trackSampleRate INT DEFAULT 44100,
                         trackSize INT,
                         trackCount SMALLINT DEFAULT 0,
```

```
                        trackNumber SMALLINT DEFAULT O,
                        trackYear SMALLINT DEFAULT O,
                        trackCurrent ENUM("true", "false"),

                        PRIMARY KEY(trackId),
                        INDEX(trackId)
);
# holds all the information regarding an iTunes playlist
# EXCEPT for the tracks that it contains; because a playlist can
# (and should) have more than track, we'll need a separate table
# to map this relationship
#
CREATE TABLE Playlists (    playlistId SMALLINT UNSIGNED,
                            playlistName VARCHAR(32),
                            playlistSmart enum("true", "false"),
                            playlistCurrent enum("true", "false"),

                            PRIMARY KEY(playlistId),
                            INDEX(playlistId)
);


# maps the many-to-one relationships between Tracks and Playlists
#
CREATE TABLE PlaylistTracks (    playlistId SMALLINT UNSIGNED NOT NULL,
                                 trackId INT UNSIGNED NOT NULL,
                      trackIndex SMALLINT UNSIGNED NOT NULL,

                            PRIMARY KEY(playlistId, trackId,
trackIndex),
                            INDEX (trackId)
);
```

Three tables are created (see the script for details on the columns that will be created in each table to correspond to the fields of the Track and Playlist beans), two of which are self-explanatory:

Tracks
: Holds information about an iTunes track.

Playlists
: Holds information about an iTunes playlist.

PlaylistTracks
: Maps Tracks to a Playlist. This table is necessary to describe the many-to-one relationship between Tracks and Playlists.

To create the tables in the FVL database (as an example), open the Terminal and type the following command:

```
mysql FVL < mytunes.mysql
```

With the database ready to go, the next step is to extend the Chord class to populate the database with the information it receives. Here's the resulting class:

```
/
****************************************************************************
**************************
*
* FILE:        MySQLImport.java
* AUTHOR:      David Miller  http://www.sqlmagic.com/d/
* ABOUT:       Describes of how to extend com.fivevoltlogic.mytunes.Chord to
*              provide customized functionality.
* DATE:        September 1, 2003
*
****************************************************************************
**************************/

import com.fivevoltlogic.mytunes.*;
import java.io.IOException;
import java.util.List;
import java.sql.*;

public class MySQLImport extends Chord {

    // sql classes to provide connection, query, and
    private Connection con;
    private PreparedStatement insertTrack,
                              insertPlaylist,
                              insertPlaylistTrack;
    private ResultSet rs;
    private Statement stmt;

    public MySQLImport() throws SQLException, ClassNotFoundException,
IllegalAccessException, java.lang.InstantiationException, IOException {

        // will read the values in from ~/.mytunes.xml;
        // these properties will be stored in the props Properties instance
        super();


        // connect to the database with the appropriate parameters
        Class.forName((String)props.get("mysqlimport.driver")).newInstance(
);
        this.con = DriverManager.getConnection("jdbc:mysql://" + (String)
props.get("mysqlimport.host") + "/" + (String) props.get("mysqlimport.
database") + "?user=" + (String) props.get("mysqlimport.user") +
"&password=" + (String) props.get("mysqlimport.password"));
        this.stmt = con.createStatement();
    }

    public void onStart() {

        try {
```

```
                // clear all existing information from the database
                this.stmt.executeUpdate("DELETE FROM Tracks");
                this.stmt.executeUpdate("DELETE FROM Playlists");
              this.stmt.executeUpdate("DELETE FROM PlaylistTracks");

                // prepare statements for queries
                // refer to mytunes.mysql to see the details on the tables
                this.insertTrack = con.prepareStatement("INSERT INTO Tracks
VALUES(" +
                        "?, " +     // 01 trackId
                        "?, " +     // 02 trackAlbum
                        "?, " +     // 03 trackArtist
                        "?, " +     // 04 trackBitRate
                        "?, " +     // 05 trackComment
                        "?, " +     // 06 trackComposer
                        "?, " +     // 07 trackDateAdded
                        "?, " +       // 08 trackDateModified
                        "?, " +     // 09 trackDiscCount
                        "?, " +     // 10 trackDiscNumber
                        "?, " +     // 11 trackDuration
                        "?, " +     // 12 trackEqualizer
                        "?, " +     // 13 trackGenre
                        "?, " +     // 14 trackKind
                        "?, " +     // 15 trackLocation
                        "?, " +     // 16 trackName
                        "?, " +     // 17 trackPlayedCount
                        "?, " +     // 18 trackPlayedDate
                        "?, " +     // 19 trackRating
                        "?, " +     // 20 trackSample
                        "?, " +     // 21 trackSize
                        "?, " +     // 22 trackCount
                        "?, " +     // 23 trackNumber
                        "?, " +     // 24 trackYear
                        "'false'" +    // 25 trackCurrent
                        ")");

                this.insertPlaylist = con.prepareStatement("INSERT INTO
Playlists VALUES("
                        "?, " +         // 01 playlistId
                        "?, " +         // 02 playlistName
                        "?, " +         // 03 playlistSmart
                        "'false'" +     // 04 playlistCurrent
                        ")");

                this.insertPlaylistTrack = con.prepareStatement("INSERT INTO
PlaylistTracks VALUES("
                        "?, " +         // 01 playlistId
                        "?, " +         // 02 trackId
                        "? " +          // 03 trackIndex
                        ")");

        } catch (Exception e) { this.onError(e.getMessage()); }

    }
```

```java
public void onTrack(Track t) {

    try {

        // get the information about the track and populate the
PreparedStatement with the values
        this.insertTrack.setInt(1, t.getId());
        this.insertTrack.setString(2, t.getAlbum());
        this.insertTrack.setString(3, t.getArtist());
        this.insertTrack.setInt(4, t.getBitRate());
        this.insertTrack.setString(5, t.getComment());
        this.insertTrack.setString(6, t.getComposer());

        // convert the XML date format into an SQL format
        if (t.getDateAdded() != null) {
            this.insertTrack.setTimestamp(7, new Timestamp(t.
getDateAdded().getTime()));
        }

        // convert the XML date format into an SQL format
        if (t.getDateModified() != null) {
            this.insertTrack.setTimestamp(8, new Timestamp(t.
getDateModified().getTime()));
        }

        this.insertTrack.setInt(9, t.getDiscCount());
        this.insertTrack.setInt(10, t.getDiscNumber());
        this.insertTrack.setInt(11, t.getDuration());
        this.insertTrack.setString(12, t.getEqualizer());
        this.insertTrack.setString(13, t.getGenre());
        this.insertTrack.setString(14, t.getKind());
        this.insertTrack.setString(15, t.getLocation());
        this.insertTrack.setString(16, t.getName());
        this.insertTrack.setInt(17, t.getPlayedCount());

        // convert the XML date format into an SQL format
        if (t.getPlayedDate() != null) {
            this.insertTrack.setTimestamp(18, new Timestamp(t.
getPlayedDate().getTime()));
        } else {
            this.insertTrack.setTimestamp(18, null);
        }

        this.insertTrack.setInt(19, t.getRating());
        this.insertTrack.setInt(20, t.getSampleRate());
        this.insertTrack.setInt(21, t.getSize());
        this.insertTrack.setInt(22, t.getTrackCount());
        this.insertTrack.setInt(23, t.getTrackNumber());
        this.insertTrack.setInt(24, t.getYear());


        // execute the query
```

```
                                insertTrack.executeUpdate( );

                    } catch (SQLException e) { this.onError(e.getMessage( )); }

            }

            public void onPlaylist(Playlist p) {

                    try {

                            // note: Playlist.isSmart( ) always returns false,
                            // as this feature isn't complete yet
                            String b = new Boolean(p.isSmart( )).toString( );
                            insertPlaylist.setInt(1, p.getId( ));
                            insertPlaylist.setString(2, p.getName( ));

                            // as of right now, we don't check to see if a playlist is smart
            or not,
                            // so we'll default to false for now...
                            insertPlaylist.setString(3, "false");

                            // execute the query
                            insertPlaylist.executeUpdate( );

                            // get a list of the database ids of all tracks in this
            playlist,
                            List tracks = p.getTracks( );
                            for (int i = 0; i < tracks.size( ); i++) {

                                    // prepare the statement
                                    int t = ((Integer)tracks.get(i)).intValue( );
                                    insertPlaylistTrack.setInt(1, p.getId( ));
                                    insertPlaylistTrack.setInt(2, t);
                                    insertPlaylistTrack.setInt(3, i + 1);

                                    // insert the query
                                    insertPlaylistTrack.executeUpdate( );
                            }

                    } catch (Exception e) {
                            this.onError(e.getMessage( ));
                    }

            }


            // simply echo the error to the screen
            public void onError(String message) {
                    System.out.println("error: " + message);
            }


            // close the database connection
```

```
public void onFinish( ) {
    try {
        con.close( );
    } catch (SQLException e) { this.onError(e.getMessage( )); }
}


// if we have a command-line argument, we interpret it to be the path
// to the user's config file; if there are no command-line arguments,
// look for the config file at ~/.mytunes.xml
public static void main(String[] args) {

    try {

        if (args.length != 0) {

            System.out.println("Usage: java MySQLImport");
            System.exit(0);

        } else {

            // create an instance of MyTunesLibrary and set
            // an instance of this class to be the handlers
            MyTunesLibrary lib = new MyTunesLibrary( );
            lib.setHandler(new MySQLImport( ));

            // begin parsing, at which point this class's methods
            // will be invoked as callbacks throughout the process
            lib.parse( );
        }

    } catch (IOException e) {
        System.out.println("io: " + e.getMessage( ));
    } catch (SQLException e) {
        System.out.println("sql: " + e.getMessage( ));
    } catch (org.xml.sax.SAXException e) {
        System.out.println("sax: " + e.getMessage( ));
    } catch (ClassNotFoundException e) {
        System.out.println("cnf: " + e.getMessage( ));
    } catch (InstantiationException e) {
        System.out.println("i: " + e.getMessage( ));
    } catch (IllegalAccessException e) {
        System.out.println("iae: " + e.getMessage( ));
    }
}
}
```

Upon running the Chord class, you should receive no output. However, upon checking your database, you'll see that the information has been properly stored.

And now that our information is stored in a SQL database, we can view the number of tracks in our iTunes music library, as shown in Figure 4-37.

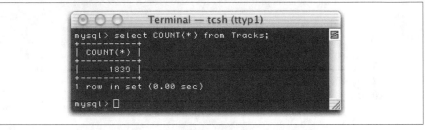

Figure 4-37. Viewing the number of tracks in the iTunes music library

We can also run a variety of queries on our music data. This query returns all information from all tracks by either Bran Van 3000 or The Weakerthans:

```
select * from Tracks where trackArtist="Bran Van 3000" or trackArtist="The
Weakerthans"
```

And this query returns the database ID for all tracks that are shorter than three minutes and have a rating of four or five stars:

```
select trackId from Tracks where trackDuration < 180 and trackRating > 80
```

Controlling iTunes Remotely

The previous section showed how to create a Chord to populate a MySQL database with information from the iTunes library. However, the com.fivevoltlogic.mytunes package contains several utility classes that are not related to the library. As you can probably guess by the heading of this section, MyTunes also allows you to control iTunes via Java.

If you open iTunes' dictionary in Script Editor and compare it to the com.fivevoltlogic.mytunes.Remote API, you'll see there is a similarity between the two. There's good reason for this: the majority of Remote's methods are actually just wrappers around iTunes' available AppleScript commands. Commands such as pause( ), backTrack( ), nextTrack( ), playPause( ), previousTrack( ), and stop( ) are self-explanatory. Here are a couple commands that might require a bit more information:

playTrack(int)
    Plays a track with the corresponding database ID from the library

playArtist(String)
    Plays the first track in the library with the corresponding artist

When one of these methods is invoked, a file is created in the directory indicated by the System property java.io.tmpdir (which, by default, evaluates to /*tmp*). The contents of this file are merely an AppleScript that will be passed as an argument to the /usr/bin/osascript command. For example, create an instance of Remote and invoke the playPlaylistTrack(playlist, track) command, as in this example:

```
import com.fivevoltlogic.mytunes.Remote;

public class RemoteTest {

    public static void main(String[] args) {

        try {

            Remote r = new Remote( );

            // we need two arguments to for this method:
            // (1) the playlist index, and
            // (2) the track number
            if (args.length != 2) {
                System.out.println("Usage: PlaylistTrack [playlist index]
[track number]");
                System.exit(0);
            }

            if (! r.playPlaylistTrack(Integer.parseInt(args[0]), Integer.
parseInt(args[1]))) {
                System.out.println("Unable to play track");
            }

        // if we aren't able to instantiate a Remote object
        // a basic exception will be thrown
        } catch (java.lang.Exception e) {
          System.out.println("Error: " + e.getMessage( ));
        }
      }
    }
```

A file named *mytunes.remote* will be created containing the following text:

```
tell application "iTunes"
  play (track 4 of playlist 1)
end tell
```

This file is then passed as an argument to the /usr/bin/osascript command.

Following the completion (successful or not) of the method's execution, the temporary file is deleted to allow the next command to be executed. Because iTunes is controlled in this manner, the method must be synchronized.

You have been introduced to all classes in the com.fivevoltlogic.mytunes package but one. You saw how to control iTunes from a Java class that is running on the local machine (localhost); the next step is to control iTunes from a different machine. And since we're using Java and XML as our foundation, there are three ways to implement this feature:

- XML Remote Procedure Calling (XML-RPC)
- Simple Object Access Protocol (SOAP)
- Remote Method Invocation (RMI)

All three frameworks are under the same general umbrella called distributed computing. And of the three choices there are a variety of reasons to choose one over the others in certain situations. RMI's main drawback is that both sides of the communication line must be written in Java. While this isn't necessarily bad, the client, ideally, shouldn't be tied to just one language. And because XML-RPC is easier than SOAP to get up and running, we'll use it as our transport from client to server and back again. For a more detailed description and comparison of the protocols, see *Java and XML*, by Brett McLaughlin (O'Reilly).

The first step is to get the server up and running. If you like, you can specify a port that the server should listen to; by default, it uses the property given in *~/.mytunes.xml*.

Once BaseStation is listening, we'll need to create a client to talk to the server. Because of XML-RPC's simplicity, this can be done in a matter of minutes.

For Eric Kidd's introduction to XML-RPC, see *http:// xmlrpc-c.sourceforge.net/xmlrpc-howto/xmlrpc-howto.html*.

The source for RPCTest.java is available at *http://www.macdevcenter.com/pub/ a/mac/2003/09/03/RPCTest.java*. Because both the server and client run on the same machine, this example isn't very practical. But if you have two or more Macs on a network, it is easy to control another Mac to behave as a jukebox. Throw this into a servlet (see *http://developer.apple.com/internet/java/tomcat1. html* on Apple's Developer Connection to get Apache Tomcat up and running on OS X) and you've got remote control of iTunes from a web interface.

Updating MyTunes Features

Most of the desired features of MyTunes are in place. However, several issues remain to be addressed. For example:

- The isSmart( ) method of the Playlist class always returns false.
- Playlists are dealt with in the order in which they are located in the XML file; hence, their getId( ) method returns a value based on that, which has nothing to do with the index of the playlist in iTunes' sorting order.

These changes and additions will be incorporated into the package as time permits. If you're interested in the package, stay tuned to the project's home page (*http://www.sqlmagic.com/d/mytunes/*) for updates and changes as they are released.

—David Miller

Control iTunes with Perl

#61   Use the Mac::iTunes Perl module to control iTunes from scripts and from other machines

When I started to work with iTunes AppleScripts, I wanted them to be as easy to write as Perl scripts, even though they were not. After a while, I decided to fix that by writing a Perl module to handle the AppleScript portions of iTunes. I already had a MacOSX::iTunes Perl module that I used to parse the binary format of the *iTunes Music Library.xml* file. I needed to add AppleScript support to it.

On the suggestion of Chris Nandor, the caretaker of MacPerl and author of Mac::Carbon, I changed the name of my distribution to Mac::iTunes and added the Mac::iTunes::AppleScript module, which wrapped common AppleScripts in Perl functions. The meat of the module was the _osascript routine, which creates an AppleScript string and calls osascript:

```
sub _osascript
        {
        my $script = shift;

        require IPC::Open2;

        my( $read, $write );
        my $pid = IPC::Open2::open2( $read, $write, 'osascript' );

        print $write qq(tell application "iTunes"\n), $script,
                        qq(\nend tell\n);
        close $write;

        my $data = do { local $/; <$read> };

        return $data;
        }
```

The Mac::iTunes::AppleScript module works much like the osascript command-line tool. Indeed, the first version simply created a script string (called osascript) with that script and captured the output, if any, for parsing. About the same time I finished the first version, Nathan Torkington needed Perl access to AppleScript and convinced Dan Sugalski to write Mac:: AppleScript. With that module, Perl could work with AppleScript without calling an external program. I replaced the _osascript routine with tell( ), which uses the RunAppleScript function from Mac::AppleScript:

```
sub tell
        {
        my $self    = shift;
        my $command = shift;

        my $script =
                qq(tell application "iTunes"\n$command\nend tell);

        my $result = RunAppleScript( $script );

        if( $@ )
                {
                carp $@;
                return;
                }

        return 1 if( defined $result and $result eq '' );

        $result =~ s/^"|"$//g;

        return $result;
        }
```

Once I have tell( ), I simply feed it an AppleScript string, which it runs and then returns the result. For example, iTunes can play Internet streams. The AppleScript way to say this uses open location:

```
tell application "iTunes"
        open location "http://www.example.com/streaming.mp3"
end tell
```

In Mac::iTunes::AppleScript, I wrapped this little script in a method, named open_url( ), which takes a URL as an argument and uses tell( ) to run it:

```
sub open_url
        {
        my $self = shift;
        my $url  = shift;

        $self->tell( qq|open location "$url"| );
        }
```

Most of the AppleScript commands for iTunes have a corresponding method in Mac::iTunes::AppleScript. Now I can use the full power of Perl, even though I am really using AppleScript behind the scenes.

iTunes, Perl, and Terminal

Just as I ran AppleScripts from the Terminal window with osascript, I can now run Perl programs that interact with iTunes. I want to play streaming media with few keystrokes and without going to the iTunes Open Streaming... menu item; that's just too much work when I do not want to switch applications.

I created a simple program, named `stream`, using `Mac::iTunes`. I create an iTunes controller object and then call the `open_url( )` method with the first command-line argument. Perl tells iTunes to play the MP3 stream, and even though iTunes starts to do something, it stays in the background while I continue whatever I am doing. I can even use this program from shell scripts:

```
#!/usr/bin/perl
use Mac::iTunes;
my $controller = Mac::iTunes->controller;
$controller->open_url( $ARGV[0] );
% stream http://www.example.com/streaming.mp3
```

Small scripts do not have much of an advantage over the equivalent Apple-Scripts, but as things get more complex, Perl starts to shine.

I have been using Apple's AirPort for a while. We swear by it in my household, and my guests like to bring their laptops and wireless cards when they visit. The AirPort has raised our computer expectations: we want to be able to do any task from anywhere in the house. However, when it comes to playing music, we have a problem. Which computer is hooked up to the stereo? I do not like listening to music on the built-in speakers of my laptop, so I have another Mac hooked up to my stereo and a large external hard drive filled with MP3s.

I cannot carry that computer around my apartment. Even if I could, I want it to just play music and perhaps perform other silent tasks. I should not have to interrupt my music because I decide to change something on the Mac I am working on. I want the music to keep playing even if I restart the iTunes on my laptop, which I do frequently while developing `Mac::iTunes`.

I need to control this central MP3 player remotely. I could create a command-line tool to control iTunes and then log in the machine with `ssh`, but not everyone who wants to control iTunes likes using the Terminal. I need a more pleasing interface. Since Mac OS X comes with the Apache web server (which runs by default), I can write a CGI script to control iTunes:

```
#!/usr/bin/perl
# $Id: ch04,v 1.17 2004/09/16 19:35:31 jamie Exp andrews $
use strict;

use CGI qw(:standard);
use Mac::iTunes;
use Text::Template;

my $Template = '/Users/brian/Dev/MacOSX/iTunes/html/iTunes.html';

=head1 NAME
```

```
iTunes.cgi - control iTunes from the web

=head1 SYNOPSIS

=head1 DESCRIPTION

This is only a proof-of-concept script.

=head1 AUTHOR

brian d foy, E<lt>bdfoy@cpan.orgE<gt>

=head1 COPYRIGHT

Copyright 2002 brian d foy, All rights reserved

=cut

my $controller = Mac::iTunes->new( )->controller;

my $command      = param('command');
my $playlist     = param('playlist') || 'Library';
my $set_playlist = param('set_playlist');

if( $command )
        {
        my %Commands = map { $_, 1 }
                qw( play stop pause back_track);
        $controller->$command
                if exists $Commands{$command};
        }
elsif( $set_playlist )
        {
        $controller->_set_playlist( $set_playlist );
        $playlist = $set_playlist;
        }

my %var;

$var{base}
        = 'http://10.0.1.2:8080/cgi-bin/iTunes.cgi';
$var{state}     = $controller->player_state;
$var{current}   = $controller->current_track_name;
$var{playlist}  = $playlist;
$var{playlists} = $controller->get_playlists;
$var{tracks}
        = $controller->get_track_names_in_playlist(
                $playlist );

my $html = Text::Template::fill_in_file(
        $Template, HASH => \%var );

print header( ), $html, "\n";
```

On the first run without input, the script creates an iTunes controller object, sets the starting playlist to *Library* (the iTunes virtual playlist that has everything iTunes knows about), and then asks iTunes for a lot of state information, including the names of tracks in the playlists, the names of the playlists, and what iTunes is currently doing (e.g., playing or stopped). The script uses `Text::Template` to turn all of this into HTML, which it sends back to a web browser, as shown in Figure 4-38.

Figure 4-38. The Mac::iTunes CGI interface

The template file I use is in the *html* directory of the `Mac::iTunes` distribution. If you have any design skills, you'll surely want to design something more pleasing. The code is separated from the presentation.

I have a small problem with this approach. To tell an application to do something via AppleScript, the telling program has to be running as a logged-in user. The web server is set up to run as the unprivileged pseudo-user *nobody*, so this CGI script will not work from the stock Apache configuration. This is not much of a problem, since I can make Apache run under my user. On my machine, I run a second Apache server with the same configuration file, save for a couple of changes.

First, I have to make the web server run as my user, so I change the User directive. Along with that, I have to choose another port, since only root can use port numbers below 1024 and Apache expects to use port 80. I choose port 8080 instead. I will have to pass this nonstandard port along in any URLs, but my CGI script already does that. As long as I use the web interface without typing into the web browser's location box, I will not have to worry about that.

```
User brian
Port 8080
```

I also have to change any file paths that Apache expects to write to. Since Apache runs as my user, it can create files only where I can create files:

```
PidFile "/Users/brian/httpd-brian.pid"
```

Once everything is set up, I access the CGI script from any computer in my home network, Mac or not, and I can control my central iTunes.

iTunes, Perl, Apache, and mod_perl

CGI scripts are slow. Every time I run a CGI script, the web server has to launch the script and the script has to load all of the modules that it needs to do its work. I have another problem with Mac::iTunes, though. The first call to Mac::AppleScript's RunAppleScript() seems to be slower than subsequent calls. I pay a first-use penalty for that. To get around that, I want to keep my iTunes controller running so that I don't have to pay this overhead over and over again.

I created Apache::iTunes to do just that. I could run my CGI script under Apache::Registry, but I like the native Apache interface better. I configured my web server to hand off any requests of a URL starting with *iTunes* to my module. I used PerlSetEnv directives to configure the literal data I had in the CGI version:

```
<Location /iTunes>
SetHandler perl-script
PerlHandler Apache::iTunes
PerlModule Mac::iTunes
PerlInitHandler Apache::StatINC
PerlSetEnv APACHE_ITUNES_HTML /web/templates/iTunes.html
PerlSetEnv APACHE_ITUNES_URL http://www.example.com:8080/iTunes
PerlSetEnv APACHE_ITUNES 1
</Location>
```

The output, shown in Figure 4-39, looks a little different from the CGI version, because I used a different template that included more features. I can change the look and feel without touching the code.

I tend to like the mod_perl interface more. Instead of passing variables around in the query string, the URL itself is the command and is simple, short, and without funny-looking characters:

```
http://www.example.com/iTunes/play
http://www.example.com/iTunes/stop
```

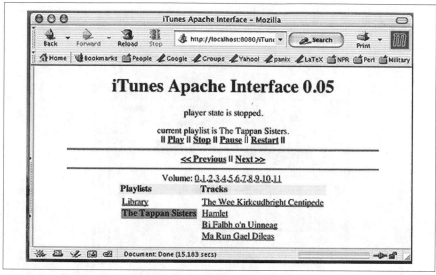

Figure 4-39. Mac::iTunes mod_perl interface

iTunes, Perl, and Tk

As I was working on Apache::iTunes, I was also working on a different project that needed Tk. I was programming things on FreeBSD, but I like to work on my Mac. That's easy enough, since I have XDarwin and OrobosX installed.

Since I had been away from the Tk world for a while, I was referring to *Mastering Perl/Tk* (O'Reilly) quite a bit. As I was flipping through the pages on my way to the next thing I needed to read, I noticed a screenshot of iTunes. It was not really iTunes, though; Steve Lidie had taken the iTunes look and feel as a front end for his MP3 player example.

I already had all of the back-end stuff to control iTunes, and none of it was tied to a particular interface. Even my CGI script could output something other than HTML, such as plain text or even a huge image. I could easily add a Tk interface to the same thing—or so I thought.

Controlling iTunes is easy. Controlling it from a web page is easy. Controlling it from Tk, which has a persistent connection to whatever it hooks up to, was harder. Since I had the persistent connection, I could reflect changes in iTunes instantaneously. In the web versions, if somebody else changed the state, such as changing the song or muting the volume, the web page would not show that until I reloaded. The Tk interface could show it almost instantaneously. In reality, I could get the Tk interface to poll iTunes for its state only every three and a half seconds or so before it took a big drop in performance. But that's good enough for me. Check out the Tk interface in Figure 4-40.

Figure 4-40. Mac::iTunes Tk interface

The *tk-itunes.pl* script comes with `Mac::iTunes`. Someday, I might develop a skins mechanism for it; all I (or somebody else) need to do is make the colors configurable. The script already uses a configuration file, although I can configure only a few things at the moment.

Final Thoughts

Perl can interact with Aqua applications through AppleScript. With `Mac::iTunes` as a back end, you can create multiple interfaces to iTunes that you can use on the same computer or on other computers on the same network. Everyone in your house, or within range of your AirPort, can control your iTunes.

—brian d. foy

HACK #62   Upload a Graphic of Your Currently Playing Song ⓜⓥⓒ

> With Now Playing, you can upload to your web site a .png file that shows which track you are currently listening to in iTunes.

Blogs are great. Blogs that have graphics that update automatically to show which song you are listening to are even better! With this hack you will be able to post a graphic (automatically updated every 15 seconds) that will show the song you are currently playing in iTunes. You can use any number of template graphics or design your own.

This hack uses a program called Now Playing (*http://www.big.or.jp/~crane/soft/nowPlaying/*; free). Yes, that is *.jp*; most of the site is in Japanese, and there is only one help file in English. Don't worry, though; Now Playing spits out titles in English, and if you read this hack closely, you'll have all the knowledge you need to get the most out of the application.

Now Playing has a one-window interface with four tabs: Theme, Network, Filter, and Etc (shown in Figure 4-41).

Figure 4-41. Now Playing's interface

The Theme panel is where you select the look of your graphic. You can select any of the more than 10 available themes. A preview loads in the window below. Within any particular theme, you can adjust the display font used by clicking on the Define button. Select any font you want and preview how it looks within the window.

Now that you have determined the look and feel of your graphic, it's time to tell Now Playing your server settings. You do this in the Network panel. Now Playing will play nicely with three server protocols: FTP, .Mac, and WebDav. If you want to post your image on your web site, enter your FTP server name, your username, and your password. In the Path field, enter where you want the *.png* file that Now Playing creates to reside. On a typical server setup, this location would be your Images folder.

If you want to host the *.png* on your .Mac site, enter your .Mac username and password. Now Playing will only work with .Mac if you don't provide a path (i.e., don't put the *.png* within a folder on your server; just keep it at the uppermost level). WebDav settings are similar to FTP settings; you'll need to provide a server and a username and password.

The final button on the Network panel is the Automatic Uploading button. This is where the fun begins. Sure, you could keep Now Playing open and hit Upload Now every five seconds, but that isn't fun, is it? Turn on Automatic Uploading, and Now Playing does your grunt work for you. Every 15 seconds, Now Playing will check what is playing in iTunes, pass on that data to create a *.png* file on the fly, and upload it to your server. Very cool.

The Filter tab allows you to exclude certain items. Don't want your friends to know that you listen to Milli Vanilli all day? Just exclude them in the Artist field. You can also exclude whole genres.

The final tab, Etc, allows you to adjust the transparency of the widget that Now Playing displays on your desktop.

To display your image on your web page, use a regular old HTML image tag. Place the tag in your HTML code in the spot where you want the *.png* to show up. That's it! Every time your visitors come to your web page, they will be able to see what you are enjoying in iTunes at that very moment!

HACK #63 Create a Web Page to Display Your iTunes Library ⓂⓌⓁ

Want to share your excellent taste in music with your buddies? This hack will show you how to take your iTunes library data and export it as a web page for all the world to see.

Back in the day, you used to show with pride your immense CD collection (or, if you go way back, your LP collection). Now that so many of us have iPods, it is hard to share with your friends and family your excellent taste in music. This hack will allow you to show off your digital tunes in a digital fashion on the World Wide Web.

On the Mac

First, get hold of Kavasoft's iTunes Catalog (*http://www.kavasoft.com/iTunesCatalog/index.html*; $9.99; free demo available). After downloading and installing the program, go ahead and launch it. The free demo will work on letters A–E of your collection. You can always try this hack out, and if you love what iTunes Catalog does for you, go ahead and purchase it.

If you've purchased music from the iTunes Music Store, the associated cover artwork should be in iTunes, and if you've already taken a stab at "Work with Album Artwork" [Hack #56], you should have all your album artwork in iTunes. If you haven't yet, go take a peek at the hack and import all your album artwork into iTunes. You don't have to have the artwork available for this hack to work, but your web page will look a lot snazzier if you do. If you already have some artwork in iTunes, you can import your artwork into iTunes Catalog from there. Otherwise, iTunes Catalog will attempt to retrieve your artwork from Amazon.com. Depending on the size of your iTunes library and the speed of your Internet connection, this can take anywhere from a minute to half an hour.

Once iTunes Catalog has your artwork, you can publish a listing of your entire iTunes library to the Web! If you have a .Mac account, with one click you can post your catalog to your .Mac site. Otherwise, you can publish your catalog to the shared folder on your Mac, or save it as an HTML file and FTP the file to your web site.

iTunes Catalog uses OS X's .Mac system preferences. If you haven't set up your Mac to work with your .Mac account, you need to do so before publishing through iTunes Catalog. To access your .Mac account, simply go to System Preferences under the Apple menu (or in your *Applications* folder if you are still running Jaguar or—gasp!—Puma) and select .Mac. To allow your computer to connect to your .Mac account, enter your .Mac username and password, as shown in Figure 4-42. That's it!

Figure 4-42. The .Mac preferences window in System Preferences

If you don't have a .Mac account and want to get one, all
you have to do is click the Sign Up button.

Now that your machine knows what your .Mac account is, you are ready to
publish your catalog. Go to iTunes Catalog → Preferences and select the
Publishing tab, shown in Figure 4-43. By default, iTunes Catalog names
your file *Music.html*.

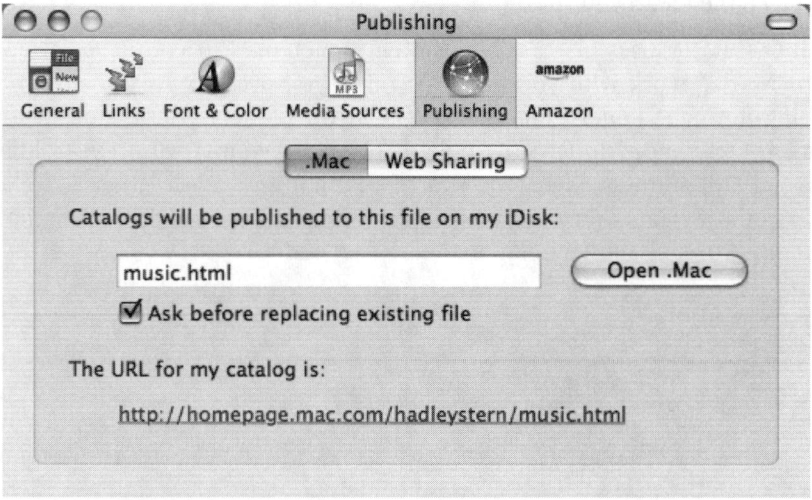

General	Links	Font & Color	Media Sources	Publishing	Amazon	

Publishing

.Mac   Web Sharing

Catalogs will be published to this file on my iDisk:

music.html   Open .Mac

☑ Ask before replacing existing file

The URL for my catalog is:

http://homepage.mac.com/hadleystern/music.html

Figure 4-43. Getting ready to publish your catalog

iTunes Catalog also shows you the URL of your catalog in the Preferences
window, which is handy. Before publishing, take a look at the Links tab in
the Preferences window. If you have a favorite site (say, MTV.com) that
you'd like your friends to go to when they click on an artist within your catalog, you can specify it here. Apart from the myriad of options iTunes Catalog presents, you can also add your own sites by clicking the New Link
button and entering the pertinent information.

Under the General tab in Preferences, iTunes Catalog also allows you to
specify how artists and compilations are arranged.

Now you are ready to publish your catalog to your .Mac account! Just click on
the Publish on .Mac button in iTunes Catalog, and the program compiles your
catalog into an HTML page complete with album images. If an album cover
isn't available on Amazon.com, iTunes Catalog substitutes a nice, shiny
iTunes logo. Your friends will be able to see the size of your collection, the
dates the albums were released, and much more, as shown in Figure 4-44.

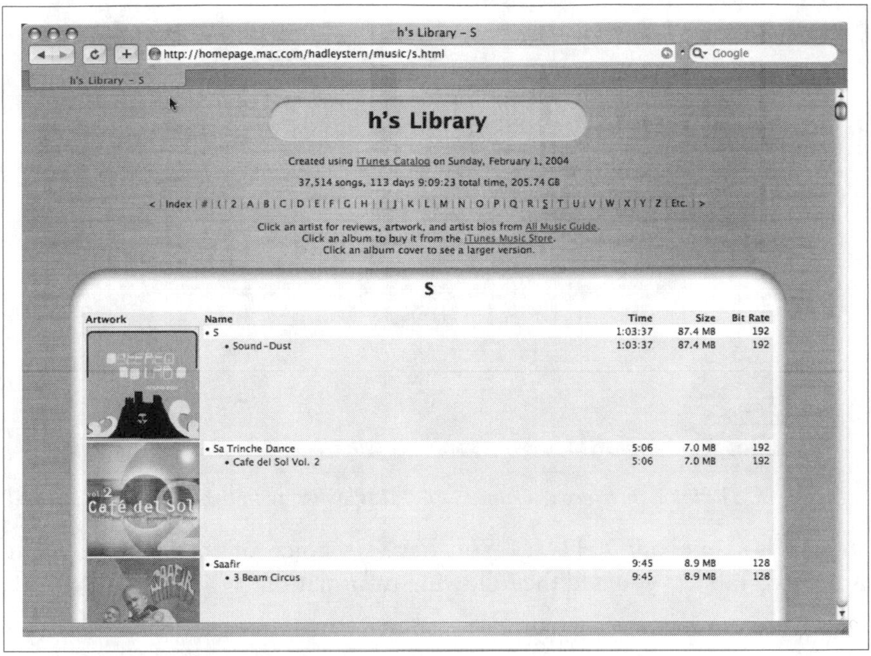

Figure 4-44. Your library on the Web

On Windows

iTunes Catalog is a snazzy way to let the world know of your eclectic (and, of course, good) taste in music. But what if you are on a PC?

Windows users don't have the luxury of iTunes Catalog. While your web page won't have the album covers and link-love that iTunes Catalog provides, you can still create an XHTML-compliant web page from your iTunes library.

The software that will help you do it is iTunes XHTML Playlist (*http://spark. is-a-geek.net/itunesxhtmlplaylist/*; free). Download and install the program, then open up iTunes and select your library. Go to File → Export Song List, and save the file in text format. Then, open iTunes XHTML Playlist. The program's main interface (shown in Figure 4-45) has three tabs: Format, Themes, and Advanced.

The Format tab lets you choose which of the following to include on your library web page: Name, Artist, Composer, and Album. You can also adjust the maximum character count of each item. The Theme tab is pretty straightforward because your page is going to be rendered in web

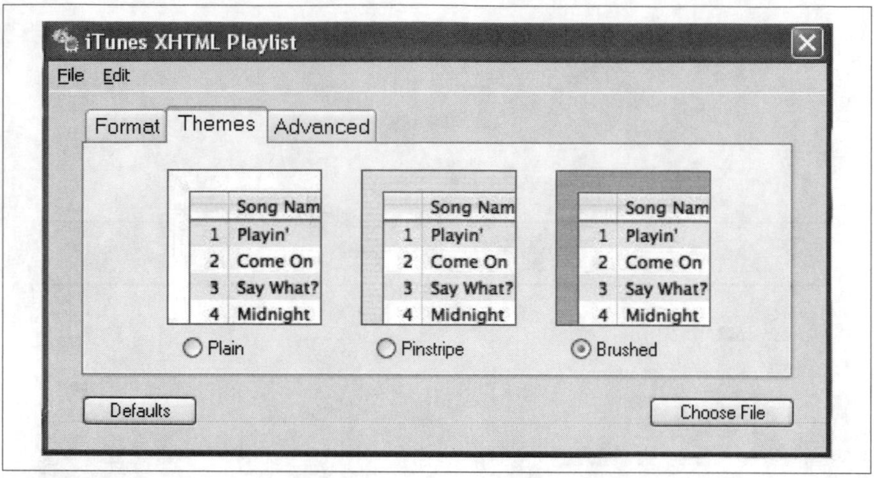

Figure 4-45. *The main interface of iTunes XHTML Playlist, with the Themes tab selected*

standards–compliant XHTML. You have a choice of three themes. The Advanced tab lets you add the following information:

Genre	Bit Rate
Size	Sample Rate
Time	Kind
Disc Number	Equalizer
Track Number	Play Count
Year	Last Played
Date Modified	My Rating
Date Added	

You are now ready to export your web page. Click the Choose File button in the lower-right corner of the interface. iTunes XHTML Playlist will prompt you to choose a source file. Browse to your exported iTunes song list and open it. You will be prompted to choose a location to save your HTML page. Click OK, and iTunes XHTML Playlist will do its magic. You will notice that the export is very speedy. At the end, you will have one HTML file (the program includes CSS stylesheet information within the HTML file).

Open the file, and you should see your iTunes library's contents laid out in a nice and tidy web page. That's it! Now, you can email the page to your friends or post it on your web site.

Your music collection is a reflection of who you are. With this hack, you can share your unbelievably sound taste in music with your friends. So, get exporting!

Create Links to the iTunes Music Store 🔵🔵🔵

Send your friends a link to that new song you love and make it easy for them to buy it, all in one click.

One of the many brilliant (yes, brilliant) things about the iTunes Music Store is that, even though it is its own application, Apple has built some web-like functionality into it. Want to go back a page? Use the same keyboard shortcut you would use in Safari, ⌘-[.

As discussed in "Get at iTunes Music Store Metadata" [Hack #71], the Music Store uses web-friendly conventions such as XML. Even though the iTunes Music Store functions outside the paradigm of the World Wide Web, Apple has made it easy to create links to its store. The store-specific hyperlinks can be embedded in HTML web pages or emailed along to a friend, just like any other URL. The difference is that when your friend clicks on the URL, her web browser won't open. Instead, iTunes will open up on her machine and go to the Music Store and the artist or song to which you linked. Of course, this requires that your friend has iTunes on her machines, but who doesn't these days?

The quickest way to get a link is to Control-click or right-click on a song in the iTunes Music Store. A contextual menu pops up. Select Copy iTunes Music Store URL and simply paste the URL into an email or HTML page. Apple also provides a link-maker that lets you quickly create links through the Web (*http://www.apple.com/itunes/linkmaker/*). Link Maker provides not only the iTunes URL, but also the wrapper HTML and the link to the album cover image. This is great if you want to post a few of your favorite songs or albums on your blog. The cover art shows up, and when users click on it they will be sent to the iTunes Music Store, where they can purchase that song/album.

The first page of the Link Maker lets you search by song, album, or artist name, as shown in Figure 4-46.

Let's go ahead and enter "Hancock" in the artist field. iTunes Link Maker spits back all the Hancock songs that are on the iTunes Music Store and categorizes them by song, album, and artist. Notice that at the end of each category column is that now-familiar iTunes arrow. Link Maker gives you three options for creating links: you can link directly to a song, an album, or an artist. Click on the corresponding arrow, and Link Maker will create code specific to the category. In other words, if you want a link to the Herbie Hancock artist page on the iTunes Music Store, click on the Artist arrow. Want to link to a specific album? You guessed it; hit the arrow next to the

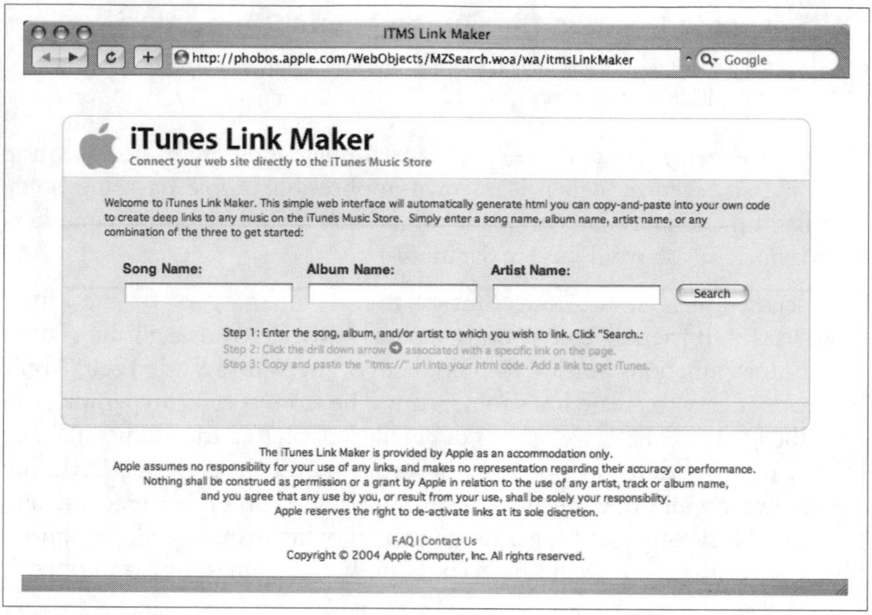

Figure 4-46. The iTunes Link Maker main page

album title. A song link will take a user to the album *and* will highlight the selected song.

Make your selection by clicking on the appropriate arrow. As shown in Figure 4-47, I've decided to link to the Herbie Hancock song "Shooz," which appears on "Dis is Da Drum." Link Maker provides the HTML code for the link. To use it, simply copy and paste the code into your HTML page.

You can use the code in a few ways. Figure 4-48 shows a couple different options. The code that Link Maker spits out is an image surrounded by an href tag. Apple expects you to use it like the first sentence in Figure 4-48— "I love this album by Herbie Hancock"—with the button right after. However, you can also use it as a regular web link by stripping out the button image and replacing it with your copy, as the second example shows. Finally, check out that sweet iTunes Download button!

If you want to quickly inform a friend of a new song you've discovered, copying the URL from iTunes and pasting it into an instant message (IM) is the way to go. If you want to show all the readers on your blog a new song, artist, or album you've discovered, use the Link Maker. Happy linking!

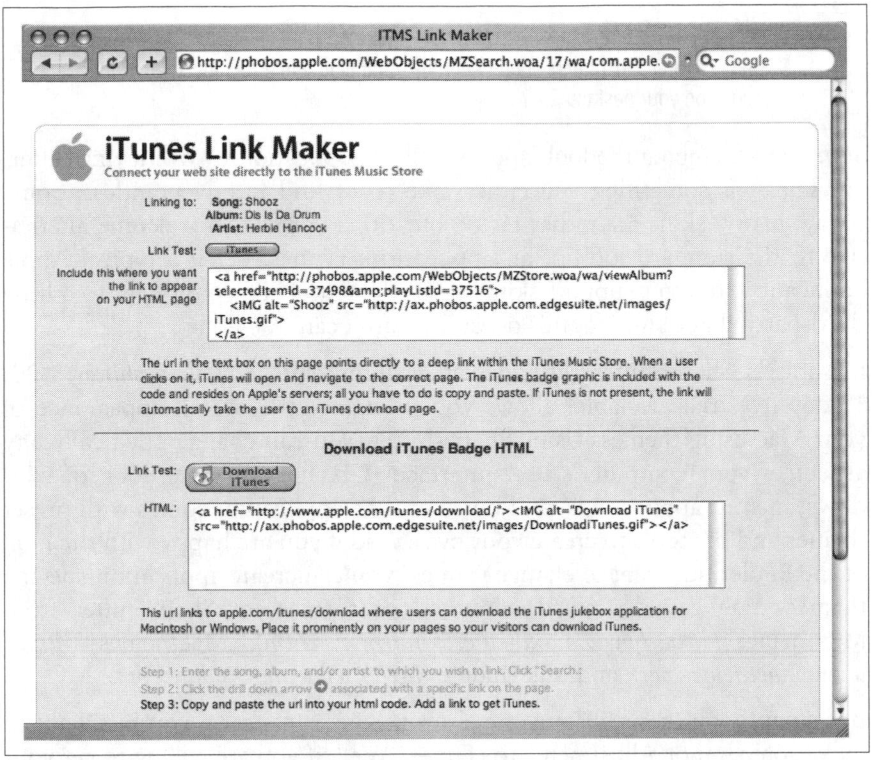

Figure 4-47. Copying and pasting the provided code to your web page

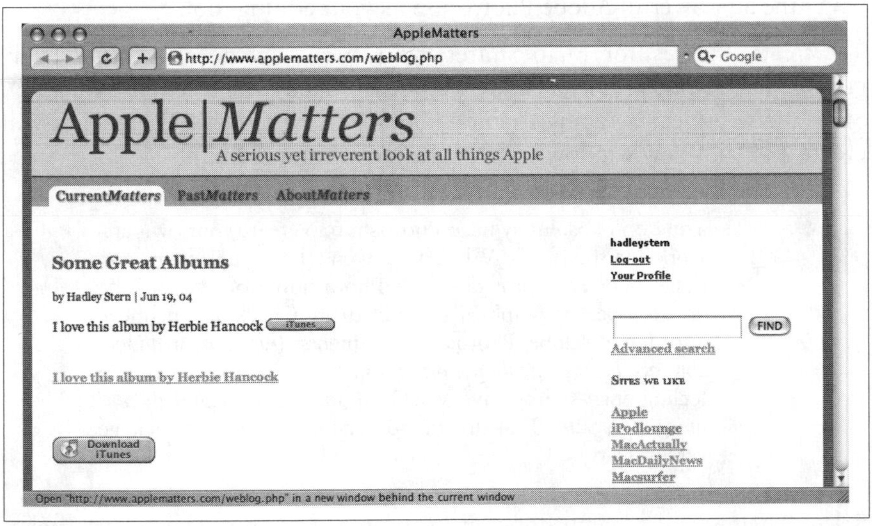

Figure 4-48. iTunes links on a web page

Skin iTunes with ShapeShifter ⓜⓢⓛ

Modify iTunes to match your décor by changing the graphics that render iTunes on your desktop.

Skinning—changing the look and feel of an application by overlaying different *skins*—is something you either take to or find utterly pointless. Some (okay, many) skins are rather tacky, but others provide a welcome alternative to the standard look of an application. iTunes, being a typical Apple application, doesn't support skinning by default. Thanks, though, to a little third-party shape shifting, this doesn't mean it can't be done.

Unsanity's ShapeShifter (*http://www.unsanity.com/haxies/shapeshifter*; $20; 15-day free trial available) allows you to change the overall appearance of your Mac using themes. Using Shapeshifter, you can change practically any aspect of your computer's user interface (UI), including the look of windows, menus, applications, and buttons. The application comes with preset themes and the tools to create your own. And if you are happy with the look of the Finder but want to change iTunes, you can create application-specific themes. You can download a myriad of themes for ShapeShifter from Maxthemes (*http://www.maxthemes.com/themes.htm*), Macthemes (*http://www.macthemes.net*), and MacUpdate (*http://www.macupdate.com*).

But what if you don't like anyone else's themes, or what if you just want to make some minor adjustments to iTunes? Well, if you are willing to get your hands a little pixel-dirty, you can change iTunes to your heart's content using the all-powerful Adobe Photoshop as your editing tool.

To create themes for ShapeShifter, you need ThemePark (*http://www.geekspiff.com/software/themepark/*; $20.00; limited trial version available). Start a new project by going to File → New → New GuiKit. ThemePark will create a default new window showing just a Themes column.

> You don't absolutely need Photoshop to create your own artwork for this hack. While you won't have the integration that ThemePark provides with Photoshop, you will still be able to open up graphics and edit them. Check out the more affordable Adobe Photoshop Elements (*http://www.adobe.com/products/photoshopel/main.html*; $99.00) or, if you are feeling open-soucry, give MacGimp (*https://www.archei.com/macgimp/*; $29.00 for download version; $49.95 for package version) a try.

Select Theme, and a menu pops up in the next column (ThemePark works in a similar fashion to Mac OS X's column view).

Click Add, and a new Theme called My Spiffy Theme appears in the second column, as shown in Figure 4-49.

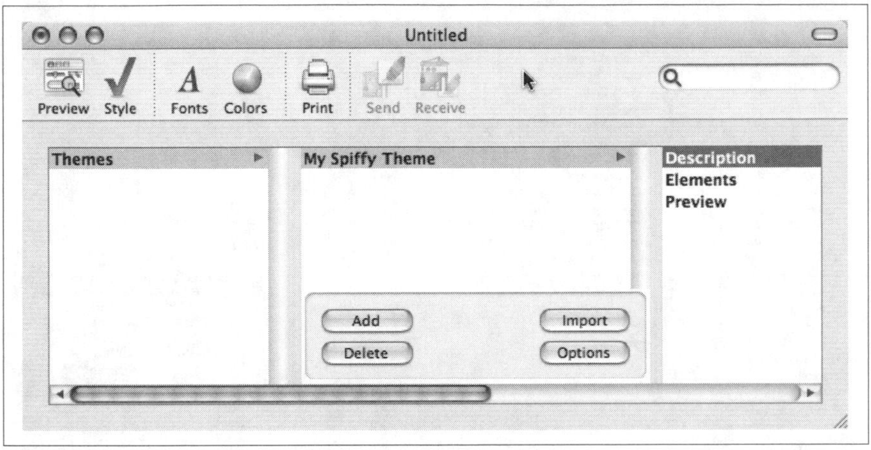

Figure 4-49. ThemePark's default Untitled window

Navigate to Elements → Application Skins, select iTunes from the drop-down menu, and click Add. You now have access to all the graphic files that make iTunes look the way it does! For example, scroll down the list of graphic files in the iTunes column and select Play. As in Mac OS X's column view, Theme-Park will load the graphic that iTunes uses for the Play button.

To edit the Play button with Photoshop, just Control-click on it and select Send to Photoshop from the drop-down menu, as shown in Figure 4-50. The graphic will now open up in Photoshop, where you can make any number of changes (such as adjusting the hue and saturation, adding elements, or starting from scratch and building your own arrow). Once you have made your edits in Photoshop, go back to ThemePark. Control-click on the graphic, and this time select Retrieve from Photoshop. ThemePark will now update the iTunes element.

UsingThemePark you can change every aspect of iTunes, including arrows, buttons, window chrome, and more. You might want to customize only a few elements, but the choice is yours.

Once you are finished with the design phase, you need to export the file as a ShapeShifter theme. First, save your ThemePark file (in case you want to make edits or additions in the future) by selecting File → Save. You have now saved the source ThemePark file. Much like Photoshop has a native *.psd* file format that you use to create your web artwork and then export to *.gif*, ThemePark has its own file format. Now that you have saved your ThemePark file, you need to export a file that can work with

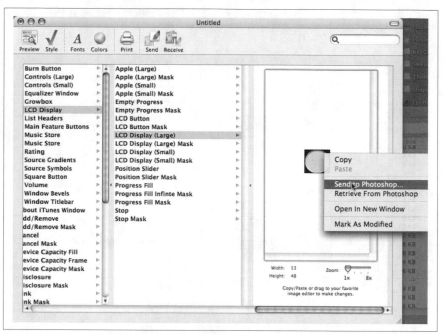

Figure 4-50. Sending your graphic to Photoshop for editing

ShapeShifter. Select File → Export Theme → For ShapeShifter and select your *Documents* folder as the destination.

Launch System Preferences, select the ShapeShifter panel under the Other grouping, and select the Theme tab. Click the + icon in the lower-left corner of the window, navigate to the theme file you just exported, and click the Open button, as shown in Figure 4-51.

The next time you open up iTunes, the interface changes you made in your theme will appear.

There are some aspects of iTunes that ShapeShifter can't get to, such as the scroll bars and the background color of the tables. That doesn't mean, though, that they're completely out of reach; take a gander at "Alter the iTunes Look and Feel by Resource Hacking" **[Hack #66]** for even more iTunes UI hacking tips.

HACK #66 Alter the iTunes Look and Feel by Resource Hacking ●◉◐

Alter iTunes's resource file to change the way the iTunes interface looks.

All applications use computer code to describe how they look. With a little work, you can get to the code that makes iTunes looks the way it looks and

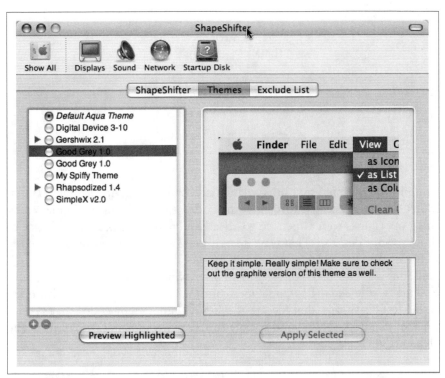

Figure 4-51. Activating your theme in the ShapeShifter System Preferences panel

alter it to your heart's content. This method isn't as simple as "Skin iTunes with ShapeShifter" [Hack #65]. However, your efforts will be rewarded, because you will be able to change elements of the iTunes UI that ShapeShifter cannot touch.

For this hack, we'll open up the iTunes resource file and change the code of hex values to adjust the appearance of the iTunes GUI. In order to open and edit the resource file, you need HexEdit (*http://hexedit.sourceforge.net*; free).

A typical Mac OS X application is not a single executable file but rather a bundle of files that contain their own executable binaries to make things tick. Apple hides all this from us, so that all we see is one tidy iTunes icon. However, with a little hacking, we can get to an application's executable binaries.

To find the executable file we want to hack, first open iTunes' package contents. Make sure iTunes is closed and Control-click on the iTunes application icon in the Finder. A contextual menu will pop up. Select Show Package Contents, and you will see a list of files usually kept hidden from you, as shown in Figure 4-52.

Figure 4-52. iTunes package contents

The file we are interested in is a Unix executable file, */Applications/iTunes/Mac OS/iTunes*. Because this file is the code behind iTunes, if we mess anything up, iTunes won't open, so go ahead and make a backup copy (Option-drag) to your desktop. That way, if anything goes awry, you can simply copy it back and, Bob's your uncle, it'll be good as new. When you launch HexEdit, you'll be taken directly to an open window. Navigate to the iTunes executable file and click the Open button. Figure 4-53 shows the open resource file. Within this file are the hexadecimal color codes that iTunes uses for its interface; find and change them, and you'll alter the colors of the elements in iTunes.

```
 ● ● ●                    iTunes – Data
Len: $0047A87C | Type/Creator:        /     | Sel: $00000000:00000000 / $00000000
00000000: FE ED FA CE 00 00 00 12 00 00 00 00 00 00 00 02   ................
00000010: 00 00 00 56 00 00 2C 34 00 00 00 95 00 00 00 01   ...V..,4........
00000020: 00 00 00 38 5F 5F 50 41 47 45 5A 45 52 4F 00 00   ...8__PAGEZERO..
00000030: 00 00 00 00 00 00 00 00 00 00 10 00 00 00 00 00   ................
00000040: 00 00 00 00 00 00 00 00 00 00 00 00 00 00 00 00   ................
00000050: 00 00 00 04 00 00 00 00 00 00 02 9C 5F 5F 54 45   ............__TE
00000060: 58 54 00 00 00 00 00 00 00 00 00 00 00 00 10 00   XT..............
00000070: 00 3E C0 00 00 00 00 00 00 3E C0 00 00 00 00 07   .>.......>......
00000080: 00 00 00 05 00 00 00 09 00 00 00 00 5F 5F 74 65   ............__te
00000090: 78 74 00 00 00 00 00 00 00 00 00 00 5F 5F 54 45   xt..........__TE
000000A0: 58 54 00 00 00 00 00 00 00 00 00 00 00 00 47 58   XT............GX
000000B0: 00 3A 56 C8 00 00 37 58 00 00 00 02 00 00 00 00   .:V...7X........
000000C0: 00 00 00 00 00 00 04 00 00 00 00 00 00 00 00 00   ................
000000D0: 5F 5F 70 69 63 73 79 6D 62 6F 6C 5F 73 74 75 62   __picsymbol_stub
000000E0: 5F 5F 54 45 58 54 00 00 00 00 00 00 00 00 00 00   __TEXT..........
000000F0: 00 3A 9E 20 00 00 E2 B0 00 3A 8E 20 00 00 00 02   .:. .....:. ....
00000100: 00 00 00 00 00 00 00 00 00 80 00 04 08 00 00 00   ................
00000110: 00 00 00 24 5F 5F 63 73 74 72 69 6E 67 00 00 00   ...$__cstring...
00000120: 00 00 00 00 5F 5F 54 45 58 54 00 00 00 00 00 00   ....__TEXT......
00000130: 00 00 00 00 00 3B 80 D0 00 00 05 B0 00 3B 70 D0   .....;.......;p.
00000140: 00 00 00 03 00 00 00 00 00 00 00 00 00 00 00 02   ................
00000150: 00 00 00 00 00 00 00 00 5F 5F 63 6F 6E 73 74 00   ........__const.
00000160: 00 00 00 00 00 00 00 00 5F 5F 54 45 58 54 00 00   ........__TEXT..
```

Figure 4-53. The code that makes iTunes tick

Before changing any colors, you'll need to figure out what you want them to be. Digital colors can be described in several ways: RGB (Red, Green, Blue), HSB (Hue, Saturation, Brightness), and, for the purpose of this hack, by hexadecimal values. The hexadecimal system is unique to describing color on the computer and is a base-16 number system. Don't worry; you don't need to know the ins and outs of hex colors to get this hack going (although it helps to have a little background so these strange numbers don't throw you off).

To determine which colors to use, open DigitalColor Meter, which is included with Mac OS X and is located at */Applications/Utilities/DigitalColor Meter*. Using this tool, you can find out the color of any pixel on your screen. The iTunes executable file uses color in the 16-bit hexadecimal color format, which DigitalColor Meter can translate. Just select "RGB As Hex Value, 16-bit" from the pull-down menu.

Now, as you drag your mouse around your screen, you'll notice that Digital-Color Meter picks up and displays the color values of the individual pixels, as shown in Figure 4-54.

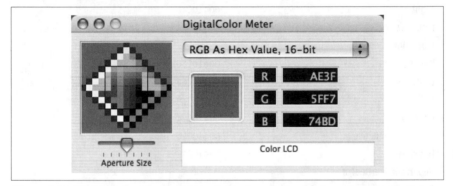

Figure 4-54. DigitalColor Meter, picking up the hexadecimal values of any pixel on the screen

If you are just playing around with this hack, you can open a colorful web page and capture a color that interests you. You can lock in a particular color at any time by pressing ⌘-L; DigitalColor Meter won't track new colors as you move your mouse about until you unlock it again with another ⌘-L.

Once you've chosen your hexadecimal color code, it's time to paint iTunes with it by entering the code into the iTunes executable file you have open in HexEdit. Use the code references in Table 4-16 to find the element you want to adjust.

 Make sure to read through the rest of the hack before you get started. Making changes willy-nilly will render your iTunes unworkable.

Table 4-16. Code references for elements to adjust in iTunes

Element	Code
Backgound	00375C10
Active levels	00375C20
Background of songs	003D4C00
Vertical bars that separate columns	003C4F30
Etched text colors	
Front	003BA338
Back	00410C84
Content frame colors	
Top	00410C32
Bottom	00410C34
Left	00410C3C
Right	00410C44
Inside	00410C2A
List colors	
White	00410C6C
Light sky	00410C64
Select	
Underline	00410C74
Select and inactive	00410C54
Underline	00410C7C
Separator (vertical)	
Select	003FEFA0
Select and inactive	003FEFA8
Text (Select)	003ED064
LCD level indicator colors	
Levels background	003B8E70
Inactive levels	003B8E68
Actual levels Top	003B8E60
Actual levels	003B8E58
Background	003B8E50
Window titles text colors	
Inactive	003BA340

For this example, let's change the background of the LCD in iTunes. The code we need to find is 003B8E50.

This is not the hex value of our new color; it's the line of code we need to find in the iTunes executable file.

Switch to HexEdit, go to Find → Go To Address, and enter 003B8E50, as shown in Figure 4-55. Make sure to select Hex before clicking Go!

```
○ ○ ○  Go To Address

Address:  003B8E50

  Entry:  ● Hex ○ Decimal

          GO
```

Figure 4-55. The Go To Address window in HexEdit

HexEdit takes you to the exact spot at which the address begins. You will notice that the starting point might be at the first line of code, or it might be in the middle. This doesn't matter; you need to start hacking at the place HexEdit puts the insertion point.

Now, we are ready to enter the hexadecimal value from DigitalColor Meter. If you just type in the numbers, however, the iTunes file will become corrupt. It is important to select each value, enter the new hex code, and then select the next value. Lather, rinse, and repeat. Here are the hex values from Figure 4-54 that we are going to use:

```
R (the Red channel): AE3F
G (the Green channel): 5FF7
B (the Blue channel): 74BD
```

Starting with the Red values, select the first chunk of code after the insertion point and type AE, as shown in Figure 4-56. Move over to the right, select the next chunk of code, and enter AE again. Make sure to select the code before you change it!

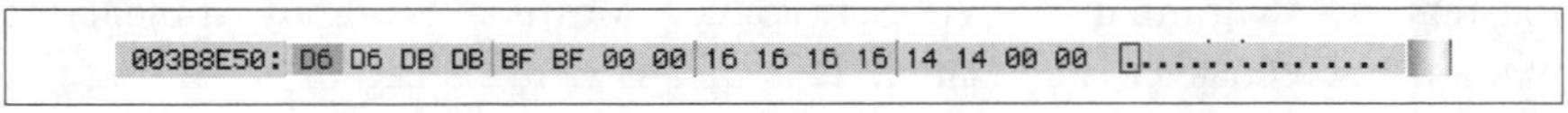

```
003B8E50: D6 D6 DB DB BF BF 00 00 16 16 16 16 14 14 00 00  [].............
```

Figure 4-56. Editing the hex values in HexEdit

Do the same for the other two channels, always repeating the value twice. Once you have finished, save the file and quit out of HexEdit. Start up iTunes and, if you did everything correctly, your changes will show up. So if you don't like the colors iTunes uses, with this hack, now you know how to change them!

Hacking the Hack

If you have the pixel-pushing skills—and Adobe Photoshop or another pixel image editing tool—go ahead and design your ideal iTunes interface in Photoshop. First, take a screenshot of your current iTunes window. Then, open it in Photoshop. Using Photoshop, color iTunes the way you want it to appear. Don't worry about being overly precise in Photoshop, because you are really just creating a sketch. Select different elements and use Adjust → Hue and Saturation until you are satisfied with the result. You'll still need to use DigitalColor Meter to find out the RGB values as 16-bit hex values.

H A C K   Use the iTunes Visualizer as a Screensaver

#67   Using ScriptSaver, you can replace that boring default Apple screensaver with the fanciful iTunes visualizer.

The visualizer included with iTunes just begs to be used as a screensaver. This hack uses a little AppleScript magic and a utility called ScriptSaver to make this possible. Combine this hack with "Extend Your Visualizer Options" **[Hack #54]**, and your Mac can display any number of visual options when it's inactive.

ScriptSaver (*http://homepage.mac.com/swannman/*; free), written by Matthew M. Swann, is a screensaver module that, when activated, executes an Apple-Script. There are many potential uses of ScriptSaver, limited only by your hacker imagination. When your Mac goes into screensaver mode, you can use ScriptSaver to have it set an away message in iChat, pause iTunes, back up files, or, as in the case of this hack, activate iTunes's visualizer mode.

To install ScriptSaver, expand the *.sit* file after downloading it and open */System/Library/Screen Savers*. Copy the *ScriptSaver.saver* file into this folder. Open System Preferences and click on the Desktop & Screen Saver icon. Click the Screen Saver tab, and you will see that ScriptSaver is now one of your options for a screensaver.

In and of itself, ScriptSaver doesn't do anything as a screensaver—no flying toasters, no swimming fish. All ScriptSaver does is execute an AppleScript when the screensaver is activated. This means that instead of activating the Flurry screensaver, for example, ScriptSaver makes a call to an AppleScript. Like any other screensaver, you set the parameters that indicate when Script-Saver should activate via Screen Saver preferences.

For this hack to work, we need to write, save, and point ScriptSaver to an AppleScript. This snippet of code originally appeared at the Mac OS X Hints site (*http://www.macosxhints.com/article.php?story=20040205044431199*). So, let's get scripting!

For an AppleScript primer, check out "Tame iTunes with AppleScript" **[Hack #72]**.

First, open Script Editor (*/Applications/AppleScript/Script Editor*). When you open Script Editor, an untitled window appears. Here is the code that activates iTunes as a screensaver:

```
property theModule : "Random"
tell application "iTunes"
    if player state is playing then
        set full screen to true
        set visuals enabled to true
    else
        do shell script "/System/Library/Frameworks/ScreenSaver.framework/
Resources/ScreenSaverEngine.app/Contents/MacOS/ScreenSaverEngine -module \""
& theModule & "\""
    end if
end tell
```

Before configuring ScriptSaver to run the AppleScript, let's take a look at what the code is doing. First, the code checks whether iTunes is open. If it is, the code tells iTunes to turn on visuals and set the screen mode to Full. If iTunes is not open, the AppleScript instructs Screen Saver to turn on Random mode. If you have a favorite screensaver (for example, Forest), substitute the name of the screensaver in the first line of the AppleScript code. Save the script **[Hack #72]**.

Go back to System Preferences → Desktop & Screen Saver. Click the Script-Saver icon in the menu of available screensavers on the left side of the window. Click on the Options button to bring up the ScriptSaver settings, as shown in Figure 4-57.

For this hack, the only field we are concerned with is the Activation Script field. Click the Choose button, navigate to your saved script, and click the OK button. You have now instructed ScriptSaver to run your script whenever the screensaver is activated. If iTunes is playing when the screensaver kicks in, your screen is replaced with the iTunes visualizer. If you've installed any third-party screensavers from "Extend Your Visualizer Options" **[Hack #54]**, whichever visualizer you have selected in iTunes shows once the screensaver is activated.

Hacking the Hack

Treat this hack as a springboard for your iTunes imagination. Want a particular song to come on, to pause whatever's playing, or to initiate any other scriptable action? Go for it! You'll notice that ScriptSaver also lets you run a

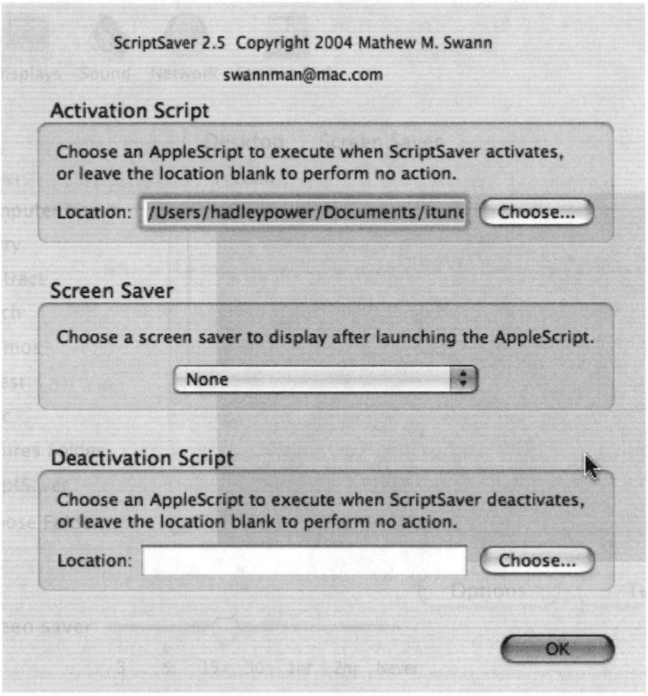

ScriptSaver 2.5 Copyright 2004 Mathew M. Swann

swannman@mac.com

Activation Script

Choose an AppleScript to execute when ScriptSaver activates,
or leave the location blank to perform no action.

Location: /Users/hadleypower/Documents/itune   [Choose...]

Screen Saver

Choose a screen saver to display after launching the AppleScript.

[None   ‡]

Deactivation Script

Choose an AppleScript to execute when ScriptSaver deactivates,
or leave the location blank to perform no action.

Location: [   ]   [Choose...]

[OK]

Figure 4-57. The ScriptSaver options window

script when your machine is awakened from screensaver mode. This means
you can have a script that pauses iTunes when the screensaver activates and
another script that plays iTunes when the screensaver is deactivated. To
pause iTunes, use the following script:

```
tell application "iTunes"
    pause
end tell
```

Save the AppleScript and tell ScriptSaver to activate it when screensaver
mode turns on. Now, here's the script to play iTunes once you wake your
Mac from screensaver mode.

```
tell application "iTunes"
    pause
end tell
```

Make the second script the deactivation script in ScriptSaver, and bingo,
when you exit screensaver mode, iTunes will resume playing right where it
left off.

Turn iTunes into a Trivia Player

Turn your Mac into a single- or two-player music trivia machine for a more active listening experience.

If you're fond of not only listening to your music but also knowing facts about the artist and album, a large iTunes music library is a veritable treasure trove of music trivia.

Name that iTune! (*http://homepage.mac.com/jonn8/as*; donationware) plays random songs from your iTunes library and prompts you with questions. All the questions are multiple choice; to answer, just click the correct button. If you get it right, Name that iTune! proceeds to the next question. If you get it wrong, you still have a chance to select any of the remaining answers, as shown in Figure 4-58.

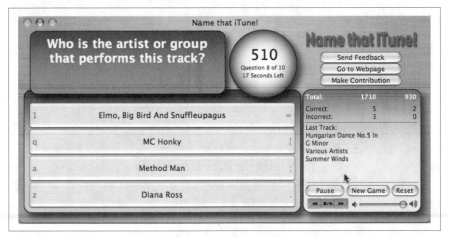

Figure 4-58. A Name that iTune! game in process

When you launch Name that iTune!, you are greeted with the settings window shown in Figure 4-59.

Here's a quick run-down on the settings:

Time Per Question
Specify how long a player has to answer the question (20, 40, or 60 seconds).

Use Playlist
Select the iTunes playlist you want Name that iTune! to use. You can use the playlist features to set up trivia-specific playlists. Got some buddies over from high school? Set up an "80s" playlist. Want to test your

Figure 4-59. The Name that iTune! preferences window

kids' abilities to tell the difference between a Bob the Builder track and a Sesame Street track? Use a "Kids" playlist.

Game Length
Specify the number of questions in your trivia game (10, 25, or 100 questions).

Question Types
Indicate a question type (track title, artist, album, or year).

Play Tracks from Beginning
Activate to make the game a little easier. By default, Name that iTune! starts playing in the middle of the song. Since it is often easier to recognize songs by their beginnings, turning on Play Tracks from Beginning makes the game a little less difficult.

Penalize for Incorrect Answers
Deduct points for incorrect answers to make things substantially harder.

Single Player or Two Players
Specify whether there will be one or two players and, if two, which keys each player must press to indicate a correct answer.

Once you have set things up as you'd like them, hit the Play button and let the games begin.

Single-Player Mode

Let's assume you are in single-player mode. When you hit Play, Name that iTune! will throw its first question at you while playing a track of music. For example, in Figure 4-59, Name that iTune! is playing a song from the album "The Love Below" and asking for the name of the song. The timer shows that there are 17 seconds left to answer the question. To answer it, use the mouse to select the song you think it is. If you are correct, Name that iTune! lets you know and moves on to the next track.

Two-Player Mode

Two-player mode works in a similar way to single-player mode: a track is played and a question is asked. The difference is that either you or your friend can answer in a head-to-head music trivia battle. Unlike in single-player mode, you do not use the mouse to answer. Instead, use the keys indicated (which can be adjusted in the settings) in the track answer window shown in Figure 4-60.

Figure 4-60. Name that iTune! in two-player (keys for player one on the left and player two on the right)

The first person who knows the answer has to press the correct key on the keyboard. This is why the default keys for players one and two are set up the way they are. Player one uses the keys 1, Q, A, and Z to indicate answers 1, 2, 3, and 4, respectively. Player two uses the equals sign (=), left bracket ([), semicolon (;) and period (.). Take a gander at your keyboard, and you will notice that player one's keys are on the left side of the keyboard, while player two's are on the right. This is so two people can share the same keyboard and still enter their answers as quickly as possible. If you are correct, Name that iTune! gives you points. Wrong? If you set the program to deduct points for incorrect answers, points will be deducted from your score.

Name that iTune! builds in some basic iTunes controls—volume slider, rewind, play, pause, and fast-forward—for in-play convenience.

Load up some esoteric tracks and have some fun. Name that iTune! is a great way to test your musical knowledge or lack thereof.

Hack Kung-Tunes into a Dynamic Server ⓂⓋⒸ

Turn the Kung-Tunes utility into a server-side PHP machine and take the public display of your listening habits to the next level.

Say you're working at your Mac while listening to some cool song and thinking "Wouldn't it be cool if I could share what I'm listening to with my blog readers?" Well, you can! iTunes includes extensive AppleScript support, so why not write a script so you can share information about the songs you're currently playing?

Kung-Tunes (*http://kung-foo.tv/kung-tunes*; donationware) is a utility that retrieves the information about the currently playing track in iTunes and uploads it to a web server. For information on setting up Kung-Tunes, visit *http://www.kung-foo.tv/blog/archives/000324.php*. Also, check out "Upload a Graphic of Your Currently Playing Song" **[Hack #62]** for another way to let your friends know what you are listening to right now.

Kung-Tunes is an extreme example that takes sharing listening info to the next level. It periodically checks whether iTunes is playing and then asks for details about the currently playing track. These details are then inserted into a highly customizable template and saved to a local file. Optionally (that is, if your Mac is not also your server), this file is submitted to your web server via FTP or HTTP, as shown in Figure 4-61.

Figure 4-61. Kung-Tunes, showing the currently playing song and the upload status

Kung-Tunes comes with instructions for setting up a basic HTML template and using the FTP upload method. This hack takes the functionality of Kung-Tunes up a notch and provides server-side support for even more customizability. Instead of uploading a single static file, you will employ a server-side script to store song data on the server. This gives you the advantage that you can display your listening preferences anywhere on your web site. Because FTP can be slow and is fickle on some servers, we'll use HTTP transfer in this hack.

First, you need to set up Kung-Tunes so that it submits iTunes data over HTTP to a PHP script that you will put on your server. Open Kung-Tunes and select the Preferences item from the Application menu. Click to reveal the Upload pane (shown in Figure 4-62), in which the following four changes have to be made. Set the upload method to HTTP and set the URL so that it points to the file *kt.php* on your server (you will create this file later) and set the location and name of the local file to */private/tmp/* and *newtrack* (or whatever you want it to be; it really doesn't matter).

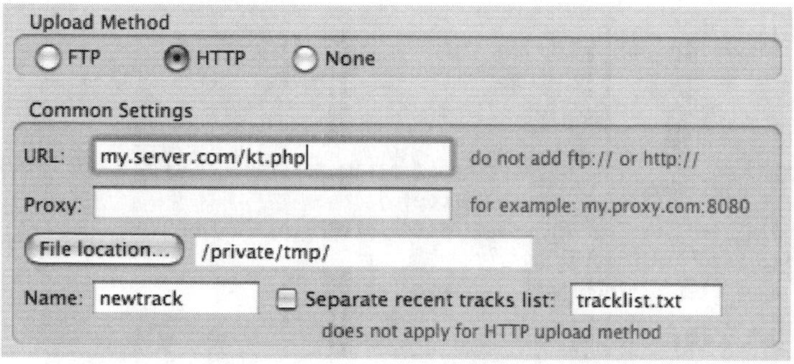

Figure 4-62. Upload settings in the Kung-Tunes Preferences dialog

Click Save to dismiss the Preferences dialog, and then choose Formats from the Application menu. Clear all text fields, set the name to HTTP, and enter the following text in the "Format for currently playing track" field:

```
code=secret&t=^t&p=#p^p#p&a=#a^a#a
```

Click Add and press the Save button to dismiss the dialog. This format string captures the information of the currently playing track that will be sent as parameters to a PHP script. For demonstration purposes, we'll use only the title (^t), artist (^p), and album (^a) placeholders (for a full list, see the Formats dialog). Since values for artist and album cannot be set in iTunes, you wrap them in # flags, allowing Kung-Tunes to strip them so that you will not be sending the placeholders themselves. Titles are always set, so you do not have to wrap that field with flags.

The Code

We need to accomplish two tasks. First, upload your current track data to your web site. Then, use that data to display what you are listening to on your web site.

Uploading your current track data. Now that you've set up Kung-Tunes to speak HTTP, you need something on your server that can actually do something with the data it gets. You will be using a simple PHP script that can not only process submission of a new song but also display what it has received so far, depending on whether it is called by a browser or by Kung-Tunes.

Save the following code as a file named *kt.php*. Upload this file to your server in the directory you specified in the Kung-Tunes upload preferences. Also upload an empty file named *kt.txt* and set its permissions to be readable and writable by everyone.

```php
<?
if ( $_SERVER['REQUEST_METHOD'] == 'POST' )
  processSong( $HTTP_POST_VARS );
else
  displaySongs();

function processSong( $var_list )
{
  extract( $var_list ); // get post parameters and check
  if ( is_null($t) or is_null($code) )
    die( "<error>Invalid usage of script</error>" );
  if ( $code != 'secret' )
    die( "<error>Incorrect password</error>" );

  // read old song list into array
  $tunes = file( 'kt.txt' );
  // forget last element if there are already more than 20 songs
  1f ( count($tunes) >= 20 ) array_pop( $tunes );
  // create a new string with the song details
  $t = date("m/d, G:i").' || '.$t.' || '.$p.' || '.$a."\n";
  // add new string to array
  array_unshift( $tunes, $t );
  // merge array into string
  $t_str = join( '', $tunes );
  // write to file
  $tfile = fopen( 'kt.txt', "w" );
  fwrite( $tfile, $t_str );
  fclose( $tfile );
}

function displaySongs()
{
  echo "<table>\n";
  echo "<tr> <th>time</th><th>band</th><th>song</th><th>album</th></tr>";
  // read song list into array
  $tunes = file( 'kt.txt' );
  foreach( $tunes as $song )
  {
    $bits = explode( ' || ', $song );
    echo '<tr>';
    for ( $i = 0; $i < 4; $i++ )
      echo "<td>$bits[$i]</td>";
    echo "</tr>\n";
  }
```

```
        echo "</table>\n";
    }
?>
```

The code has two main routines: processSong( ) and displaySongs( ). The first is called when the script is called by Kung-Tunes and updates the data on the server. The second routine is called by the browser and outputs a formatted list of songs that have been stored on the server.

When the script is called by Kung-Tunes, it first checks if there is a title (t) and a code parameter. You use the code parameter to authorize usage of the script, so that you will not be embarrassed by other people submitting a series of Britney Spears songs to the script. If the code parameter does not match the password string set in the script, it will bail out.

If the parameters are valid, their values are simply saved to the *kt.txt* text file. This file stores the last 20 songs played and also prepends each song with the date on which it was added. If the script is called via the browser, it reads in this song list file and displays the contents as a basic HTML table.

Displaying track data on your site. The hack doesn't stop here, of course. Thanks to PHP and having your song data available on your server, the possibilities are endless. You could, for example, display the most recently played song on your web page (provided its filename ends in *.php*), using the following code snippet:

```
<?
$tunes = file('kt.txt'); // read file into array
$bits = explode(" || ", $tunes[0]); // only use topmost item
$songTimePlayed = $bits[0];
$songTitle = $bits[1];
$songArtist = $bits[2];
$songAlbum = $bits[3];

echo "<h3>latest <a href=\"http://www.kung-foo.tv/kung-tunes\">iTunes</a>
    song</h3>";
echo "<p>$songTimePlayed<br />$songTitle<br />\n";
if ( $songArtist != "" )
    echo "<br /><a href=\"http://www.amazon.com/exec/obidos/external-search¬
    102-6473795-0973730?mode=music&amp;keyword=$songArtist\">$songArtist</a>¬
    \n";
if ( $songAlbum != "" )
    echo "<br /><a href=\"http://www.amazon.com/exec/obidos/external-search¬
    102-6473795-0973730?mode=music&amp;keyword=$songAlbum\">$songAlbum</a>\n";¬
    echo "</p>\n";
?>
```

Let's test what you have so far. Launch Kung-Tunes and open the Preferences dialog. Edit the Runtime options to look like Figure 4-63. This tells Kung-Tunes to start up automatically and to upload info any time a different song is playing. If Kung-Tunes is not running yet, press "Start timer" in the main window.

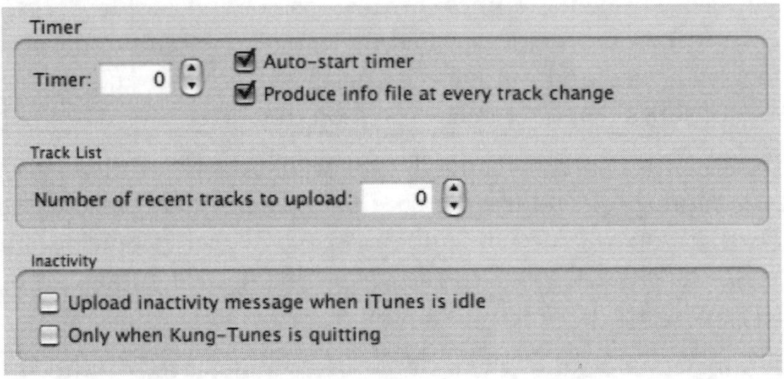

Timer

Timer: 0 ⏏ ☑ Auto-start timer
              ☑ Produce info file at every track change

Track List

Number of recent tracks to upload: 0 ⏏

Inactivity

☐ Upload inactivity message when iTunes is idle
☐ Only when Kung-Tunes is quitting

Figure 4-63. Timer settings in the Kung-Tunes Preferences dialog

To see what's happening under the hood, open Window → Console and Kung-Tunes will provide a detailed transcription report. This is useful for debugging the PHP script, because any error messages returned from the server will be shown in this console.

—Adriaan Tijsseling

Put the Ogg in iTunes ⓜⓝⓛ
#70

Turn iTunes into an Ogg Vorbis–playing application and enjoy the fruits of open source ripping and playing.

The MP3 and AAC file formats are just two ways of compressing large CD music files. They also happen to have licensing fees attached to them. Say, for example, you wanted to write an MP3 player; you'd have to pay a license fee to develop the application! Ogg Vorbis, on the other hand, is an open source codec, much like Linux is an open source operating system. Just as back in the day when audiophiles debated the efficacy of different chassis systems for turntables, now audiophiles (and geeks) argue about which codec is better. Some argue, quite vociferously, that Ogg Vorbis files just sound better. Not only that, but some bands that post files to download on the Internet post only in the Ogg Vorbis format. If you want to find out for yourself but don't want to give up on iTunes, this hack enables you to listen to Ogg Vorbis files in iTunes.

First you need to download the Ogg Vorbis decoder plug-in for QuickTime (*http://www.illadvised.com/~jordy/*; free). It works with QuickTime 6.2 and with Mac OS X 10.2 and later. Once you have downloaded the plug-in, quit iTunes. Navigate to the disk image folder: *QuickTime Vorbis Component*. In there, you will find a file called *OggVorbis.qtx*. iTunes uses QuickTime behind the scenes to play your MP3s and AAC files. By adding the Ogg Vorbis plug-in to the QuickTime library, you enable iTunes to play Ogg Vorbis files.

To do this, put the file *OggVorbis.qtx* in the *QuickTime* folder in the root *Library* directory. Now, when you launch iTunes, you will be able to play Ogg Vorbis files. However, the plug-in won't allow you to rip CDs to Ogg Vorbis files. An application for the Mac called Tenc (*http://zentrallabor. neoscientists.org*; free) lets you rip Vorbis files. The one caveat is that you won't be able to grab the CD song titles, artist name, etc. from the CDDB that iTunes uses.

If you are using Windows, you can try NeoNapster (*http://www.neonapster. com/na.html*; free), which will look up CD song titles and other information to rip your Ogg Vorbis tracks. If you feel really adventurous, hop onto the fountain of everything open source, Linux. Using any number of utilities that you can find at *http://www.vorbis.com/download_unix_1.0.1.psp*, you can rip Ogg Vorbis files under Linux to your heart's content.

It's a big world out there in digital music, and MP3 and AAC files are just two of many possible file formats. Using this hack, you can experiment with the sound quality of Ogg Vorbis files right within iTunes. Just don't try to transfer those files to your iPod, because it won't play them!

HACK #71 Get at iTunes Music Store Metadata ⓂⓂ●

Take a peek at the iTunes Music Store metadata and use the metadata for your own web applications.

Apple's iTunes Music Store (iTMS) is more than just a place to buy DRM-restricted songs for $0.99 apiece; it is also a massive audio information repository. This searchable database contains loads of valuable metadata about each song track and album—song and album name, publication date, and record label, to name but a few—not to mention a free 30-second preview for each track and a thumbnail image of each CD cover. Of course, a major limitation is that to search this trove of information you need the iTunes application, which means you need to be sitting in front of a Mac OS X or Windows 2000/XP machine. Here are just some of the possible actions that this limitation precludes:

- Browsing the iTunes Music Store from your cell phone
- Querying the iTMS from Linux or (gasp!) Mac OS 9
- Borrowing thumbnail images and preview clips for use in your own applications

- Crosschecking iTunes tracks against RIAA Radar (*http://www. magnetbox.com/riaa/*) to avoid buying RIAA-owned tracks (see *http:// www.riaa.com*)
- Developing a full-blown iTMS client for your favorite platform

There are many other desirable actions like these, all singing the same refrain: it sure would be nice to be able to access the iTMS from anywhere.

Thankfully, there is a solution, and it's called (appropriately enough) iTMS-4-ALL.

iTMS-4-ALL

iTMS-4-ALL (*http://hcsoftware.sourceforge.net/jason-rohrer/itms4all/*; free) is a Perl-based CGI script that lets you search the iTMS from any web browser. In addition to being a useful search tool in its own right, the script serves as an example of how to interact with Apple's Store server.

You can download and run iTMS-4-ALL on your own web server or just take it for a spin at *http://itunes.punboy.net/cgi-bin/itms4all.pl*. Figure 4-64 shows iTMS-4-ALL in action.

The iTMS Protocol

Before diving into the code for this hack, let's examine the details of the iTMS protocol. How does your iTunes client communicate with Apple's Music Store server? What kind of information is exchanged that might be useful to us? Here is what we know so far:

- iTunes communicates with Apple almost exclusively through HTTP.
- iTunes authentication (logging in so you can actually buy something) happens not through HTTP, but instead through HTTPS. For some reason, iTunes will not direct its HTTPS requests through a web proxy, even though other applications (such as Internet Explorer) will.
- iTunes fetches gzipped (i.e., compressed using the GZIP format) XML files from Apple to lay out its GUI (to display the storefront, genre pages, and search results).
- Every gzipped XML file is encrypted with AES-128 (Rijndael) in CBC mode. The CBC initialization vector is included as one of the HTTP headers (x-apple-crypto-iv). In other words, you essentially need two 128-bit strings to decrypt the XML: the first one (the initialization vector) is provided right in the HTTP response, while the second one (the AES key) is supposed to be a secret shared by Apple's server and your iTunes client.
- The secret AES key used by Apple and your iTunes client is 8a9dad399fb014c131be611820d78895. This secret key is used over and

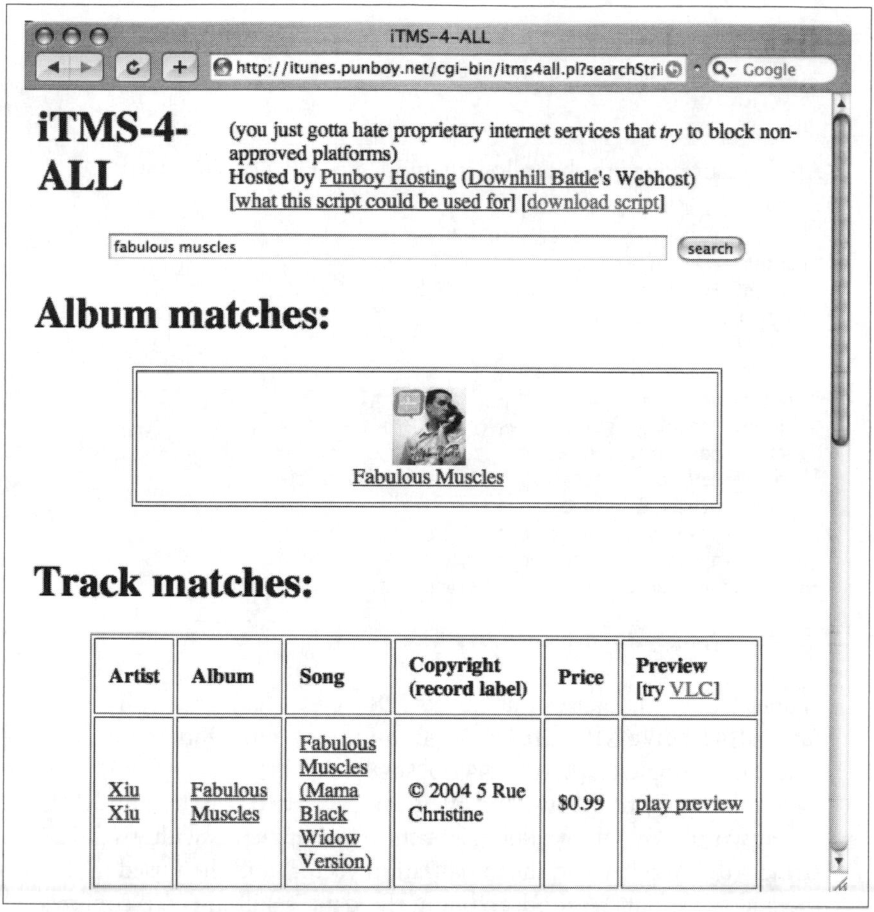

Figure 4-64. iTMS-4-ALL in action

over, though a fresh initialization vector is selected for each communication. (Sean Kasun gleaned this key from the iTunes application).

Fetching information from Apple (for example, searching for "Xiu Xiu," a flamboyant post-rock band) involves the following steps:

1. iTunes sends the following HTTP (web) request to *phobos.apple.com* on port 80:

```
GET /WebObjects/MZSearch.woa/wa/com.apple.jingle.search.DirectAction/
search?term=Xiu%20Xiu HTTP/1.1
User-Agent: iTunes/4.2 (Macintosh; U; PPC Mac OS X 10.2)
Accept-Language: en-us, en;q=0.50
Cookie: countryVerified=1
Accept-Encoding: gzip, x-aes-cbc
Connection: close
Host: phobos.apple.com
```

The User-Agent header is important: Apple will not return information to non-iTunes agents.

2. Apple responds with the following wodge of HTTP:

```
HTTP/1.1 200 Apple
Date: Fri, 16 Apr 2004 13:55:07 GMT
Content-Length: 4320
Content-Type: text/xml; charset=UTF-8
Cache-Control: no-cache
Connection: close
Server: Apache/1.3.27 (Darwin)
Pragma: no-cache
content-encoding: gzip, x-aes-cbc
x-apple-max-age: 3600
x-apple-crypto-iv: 19953b75e9846ea59715be906cdca0c8
x-apple-protocol-key: 2
x-apple-asset-version: 2118
x-apple-application-instance: 20
Via: 1.1 netcache04 (NetCache NetApp/5.2.1R3)

[-- encrypted gzip archive starts here --]
```

3. iTunes then initializes an AES-128 CBC cipher with its key (8a9dad399fb014c131be611820d78895) and the initialization vector provided by x-apple-crypto-iv (19953b75e9846ea59715be906cdca0c8). iTunes decrypts the GZIP archive and then un-gzips it to get the raw XML. In other words, the decryption algorithm is initialized with two 128-bit strings (the AES key and the initialization vector) and then used to decode the encrypted data. After decryption, the data is still in GZIP-compressed form and needs to be decompressed before it can be used.

The full XML document for search results is too long to show here (one example is 72 KB of text when uncompressed). The XML includes lots of layout information, so Apple can change the way results are displayed to the user without upgrading the iTunes client. The dict entries near the end of the document contain information for each track matching your search. These entries are *dictionaries* (think about looking up something in the dictionary: you want a definition associated with a particular word) that map various key names to pieces of metadata. Here is an example dict entry:

```
<dict>
<key>kind</key><string>song</string>
<key>artistName</key> <string>Xiu Xiu</string>
<key>artistId</key><string>3208396</string>
<key>bitRate</key><integer>128</integer>
<key>buyParams</key><string>productType=S&salableAdamId=5390052&price=990¬
    </string>
```

```
<key>price</key><integer>990</integer>
<key>copyright</key><string>_ 2004 5 Rue Christine</string>
<key>dateModified</key><date>2004-03-10T06:44:25Z</date>
<key>discCount</key><integer>1</integer>
<key>discNumber</key><integer>1</integer>
<key>duration</key><integer>179164</integer>
<key>explicit</key><integer>0</integer>
<key>fileExtension</key><string>m4p</string>
<key>genre</key><string>Alternative</string>
<key>genreId</key><integer>20</integer>
<key>playlistName</key><string>Fabulous Muscles</string>
<key>playlistArtistName</key><string>Xiu Xiu</string>
<key>playlistArtistId</key><integer>3208396</integer>
<key>playlistId</key><string>5390070</string>
<key>previewURL</key><string>http://a1535.phobos.apple.com/Music/y2004¬
    /m02/d06/h14/s05.ojrmonwq.p.m4p</string>
<key>previewLength</key><integer>30</integer>
<key>relevance</key><string>1.0</string>
<key>releaseDate</key><string>2004-02-17T08:00:00Z</string>
<key>sampleRate</key><integer>44100</integer>
<key>songId</key><integer>5390052</integer>
<key>comments</key><string></string>
<key>trackCount</key><integer>10</integer>
<key>trackNumber</key><integer>2</integer>
<key>songName</key><string>I Luv the Valley OH!</string>
<key>vendorId</key><integer>1143</integer>
<key>year</key><integer>2004</integer>
</dict>
```

Just look at all that lovely metadata! The album name (Fabulous Muscles) is provided under the playlistName key, while the song name (I Luv the Valley OH!) is tagged with the songName key. Of particular interest is the previewURL, which in this case is *http://a1535.phobos.apple.com/Music/ y2004/m02/d06/h14/s05.ojrmonwq.p.m4p*; this URL can be fetched by any web browser (baked into iTunes or not) and played on most platforms (Mac, Windows, Unix, etc.) using VideoLAN's VLC media player (*http:// www.videolan.org*; free).

In addition to the metadata included in each dict entry, the search results also include CD cover thumbnails, which appear in the XML as URLs for JPEG files. In our example results, the cover JPEG for *Fabulous Muscles*, shown in Figure 4-64, has the URL *http://a1.phobos.apple.com/Music/y2004/ m02/d06/h14/s05.kmxqqbbr.60x60-75.jpg*. The current iTunes Music Store incarnation includes up to four thumbnails with each set of search results.

This is the protocol that iTunes uses to interact with the iTMS server, but how do you interact with the server *sans* iTunes? Here is where you get to start hacking.

The Code

With knowledge of the protocol in hand, you can now start writing code to fetch search results from Apple and access the XML-formatted metadata.

Searching the iTMS with wget. wget is a command-line agent for grabbing data off the Web. In general, if you pass a URL to the wget command, wget will download the contents pointed to by the URL and save them to disk. wget is standard issue on most Unix-like platforms, including Mac OS X, and you can also download it for Windows platforms from various sources (try Googling for "wget for Windows").

You can grab encrypted iTMS data from Apple yourself with wget, but you need to specify an iTunes User-Agent header to override wget's default User-Agent header:

```
$ wget http://phobos.apple.com/WebObjects/MZSearch.woa/wa/ ¬
    com.apple.jingle.search.DirectAction/search?term=Xiu%20Xiu -U ¬
    "iTunes/4.0 (Macintosh; U; PPC Mac OS X 10.2)"
```

Of course, the fetched file is encrypted with AES, as described above. Unfortunately, there are no standard-issue tools for decrypting these files, so we need to resort to some relatively simple Perl code to go any further.

Cryptography programming in Perl. To decrypt AES-128 CBC, you need two nonstandard Perl modules: Crypt::CBC and Crypt::Rijndael. Both modules can be downloaded from CPAN (*http://www.cpan.org*).

> In case you are wondering, Rijndael is another name for AES, since the Rijndael algorithm was selected as the AES standard.

CBC.pm is pure Perl, but the Rijndael module must be compiled for your platform. Compilation instructions are included with the module package that you download from CPAN. Once installed, these modules can be included in your Perl program as follows:

```
use Crypt::CBC;
use Crypt::Rijndael;
```

You can get the encryption initialization vector (IV) for the x-apple-crypto-iv HTTP header, as described previously. Apple picks a fresh IV for each response, and you must use the IV included with a response to decrypt that response. Assume the IV is 19953b75e9846ea59715be906cdca0c8. You can set up variables for the key and IV as follows:

```
my $iTunesKeyHex = "8a9dad399fb014c131be611820d78895";
my $ivHex = "19953b75e9846ea59715be906cdca0c8";
```

The CBC module requires that both keys and IVs be in binary form, though we currently have them in hex-encoded form. We can pack our key and IV into binary form as follows:

```
my $iTunesKeyBinary = pack( "H*", $iTunesKeyHex );
my $ivBinary = pack( "H*", $ivHex );
```

Using these binary values, you can create a Rijndael CBC cipher as follows:

```
my $cipher = Crypt::CBC->new( { 'key'              => $iTunesKeyBinary,
                                'cipher'           => 'Rijndael',
                                'iv'               => $ivBinary,
                                'regenerate_key'   => 0,
                                'padding'          => 'standard',
                                'prepend_iv'       => 0
                              } );
```

You can think of this initialized cipher object as a black box that takes encrypted data as input and outputs decrypted data. Assuming that you have your encrypted GZIP data stored in a variable called $encryptedSearchResults, you can finally decrypt the results as follows:

```
my $decryptedSearchResultsGZIP =
    $cipher->decrypt( $encryptedSearchResults );
```

Now, your results can be decompressed with GZIP, producing raw XML that you can peruse, parse, and otherwise enjoy.

iTMS-4-ALL. iTMS-4-ALL is a Perl-based CGI script that pulls all of the aforementioned pieces together into a user-friendly package. The script can be installed on any web server that supports CGI and Perl and then accessed from any web browser. The user interface for searching the iTMS was shown earlier in Figure 4-64. If you want to explore the script right away, you can download the code from *http://hcsoftware.sourceforge.net/ jason-rohrer/itms4all/*. A live installation of the script is also available on that page, so you can search the iTMS from your browser without installing anything.

The HTML user interface generated by iTMS-4-ALL is basic by design: it works in all web browsers, including text-mode applications such as Lynx and the palmtop microbrowsers present on cell phones. Thus, iTMS-4-ALL not only unshackles iTMS searching from the officially supported iTunes platforms, it also enables searching away from the desktop. You can now browse the iTunes store while sitting on the bus.

Installing the script on your own web server is relatively painless. All necessary Perl modules are included with the download package, and a script is provided to compile the modules for your server's platform. After running the compilation script, you need to copy the files into your web server's *cgi-bin* directory. For example, if your server keeps CGI scripts in */httpd/cgi-bin*, you would type:

```
cp -r itms4all.pl Crypt IO auto /httpd/cgi-bin
```

Finally, you need to make sure that your web server has permission to execute your script. For most common server setups, you can grant permission with the following command:

```
chmod o+x /httpd/cgi-bin/itms4all.pl
```

This command grants execution permission (x) to the *other* users (o), including your web server. Now you are ready to test the script. If your server had the address *http://www.myserver.com*, you could run the script by pointing your browser to *http://www.myserver.com/cgi-bin/itms4all.pl*.

—Jason Rohrer

## CHAPTER FIVE

AppleScript for iTunes
Hacks 72–92

If you are a meticulous iTunes user, you probably spend a lot of time doing iTunes housekeeping tasks, such as tidying track names, arranging playlists just so, researching artist information, and moving tracks to your iPod.

Wouldn't it be great if you didn't have to spend so much time doing all those chores? The good news is, you don't! Many of the repetitive tasks you now do by hand can be done much quicker with AppleScript, a programming language built into your Mac's operating system.

"But I'm no computer programmer!" you say. Well, here's more good news: you don't have to be. AppleScript is not that difficult to learn and use. Yes, there is a learning curve, but the curve's not as steep as learning, say, Perl or even JavaScript. Another bonus is that to use AppleScript with iTunes, you don't have to learn every single thing about AppleScript. You only have to learn about the stuff that works with iTunes.

This chapter contains a brief introduction to AppleScripting and over 20 diverse and useful AppleScript hacks. Each script is ready to run; simply copy it into Script Editor and save it to your iTunes Scripts folder. Plus, each hack explains the routines in such a way that you'll be able to reuse many of them in your own AppleScript scripts for iTunes.

HACK #72   Tame iTunes with AppleScript

Whether you need an AppleScript refresher or you are a willing AppleScript newbie, this hack provides the AppleScript basics you'll need to understand the rest of the scripts in this chapter.

AppleScript is a simple but powerful programming language that lets you control applications on your computer and automate the tasks that they perform. Basically, an AppleScript *script* is a list of instructions. When you activate the script, the instructions are carried out. Additionally, a script is able to perform computations that allow it to make decisions about how its instructions are executed.

You write, test, and save AppleScript scripts with *Script Editor*, an application that comes installed with your Macintosh operating system. Scripts are saved as files and can be run like applications or, even simpler, like menu commands. As you will see, the language used to write AppleScript is much more English-like than other programming languages, which makes Apple-Script relatively easy to learn and use.

> Unlike scripts written in other scripting languages (such as Perl or JavaScript) that can be written and saved using any text editor and can run on other computer platforms, Apple-Script scripts can be written only with an AppleScript editor and can be used only on a Mac. Apple provides Script Editor as part of the operating system, but there are a couple other script editors available as well—most notably, Script Debugger, a commercial product (*http://latenightsw.com*; $189.00; demo available), and Smile (*http://www.satimage.fr/ software/en/softx.html*; free).

Using AppleScript, you can perform automated iTunes tasks that otherwise would be repetitive, time-consuming, or just plain difficult. For example, you can create scripts that clean up the text in track tags **[Hack #74]**, create playlists **[Hack #82]**, export artwork **[Hack #86]**, send track tag information to other applications **[Hack #80]**, and **[Hack #87]**, control the playing of tracks **[Hack #88]**, send files to iPod **[Hack #83]**, and much, much more.

> This hack is a crash course in some of the AppleScript you should know to understand the hacks in this chapter. For a comprehensive guide to AppleScript, take a gander at *Apple-Script: The Definitive Guide*, by Matt Neuburg (O'Reilly).-

Writing AppleScript Scripts with Script Editor

Script Editor is located on your computer in */Applications/AppleScript*. When you run Script Editor and create a new Script Editor document (File → New) you might notice how similar it looks to a text editor (see Figure 5-1). As in a text editor, the document window is where you will enter and edit text that will eventually become a script.

The Script Editor toolbar contains a default set of four buttons:

Record

> Lets you start recording your actions in the Finder and any other Apple-Script-aware applications, although not all of these applications are

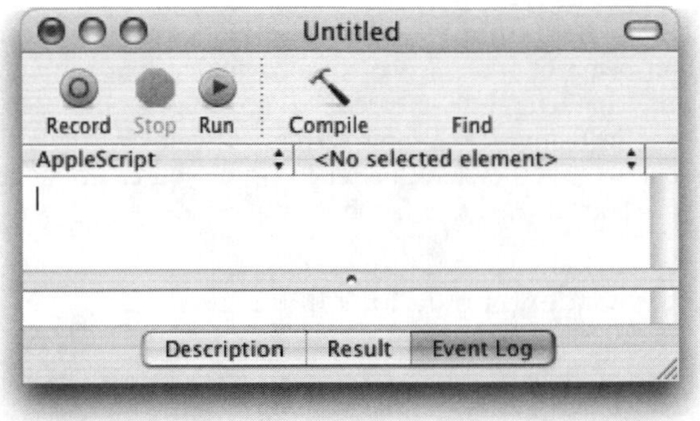

Figure 5-1. Script Editor is quite similar in appearance to a text editor such as TextEdit

recordable (including iTunes). We will not be using this function much, if at all.

Stop

Stops execution of the script or halts recording if it is active. Pressing ⌘-. (that's the Command key and the period) also aborts the running of a script.

Run

Executes the current script.

Compile

Tells Script Editor to check the script for correct syntax before running it. This does not check if the script actually works, just whether it's constructed properly.

Along the bottom of the Script Editor window are three tabs that determine what is displayed in the lower half of the window. The Description tab contains a text description from the author of what the script does, displayable as a splash screen at startup. I also use it for temporarily parking snippets of code or copy-and-pasted text. The Result tab displays the last result computed by the running script. Event Log is a running display showing the results of a running script and logged results—very handy for debugging. You will use the Event Log window often while writing AppleScript scripts.

For the purposes of introduction, we're going to create, save, and run a simple script to use with iTunes. We'll get into more detail about the language momentarily.

Type the following text into the Script Editor window:

```
tell application "iTunes"
  play playlist "Library"
end tell
```

Hit the Return/Enter key on your keyboard to end each line
and begin another. You will also notice that the continuation character ( ), created by pressing Option-Return, is
used in many of the later scripts to segment single lines of
code so that they look better in print; you can omit them in
your code if you like.

Your Script Editor window should look like Figure 5-2.

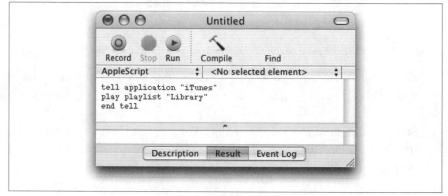

Figure 5-2. An AppleScript script in the Script Editor window

When you first enter text into a Script Editor window, it's only text. But click
the Compile button (or press ⌘-K), and Script Editor will check the script's
syntax for any errors and format it nicely for you, as shown in Figure 5-3.

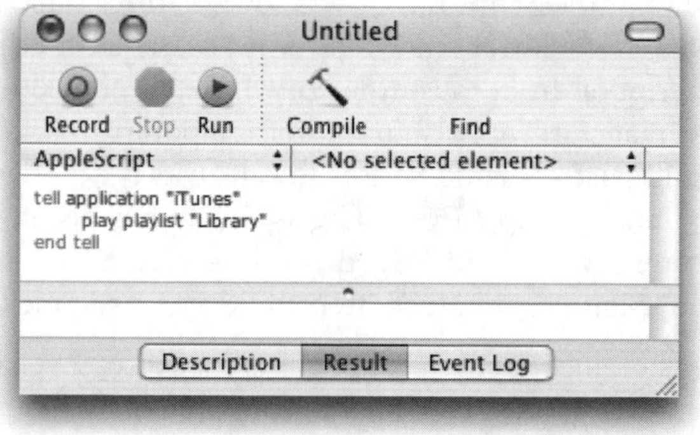

Figure 5-3. Script Editor, compiling and formatting the text

You now have a script that you can run and save.

To use a script from iTunes's Scripts menu, you need to save it as a *compiled* script (see the sidebar "Save As...").

Save As...

A *compiled script* is one that has the proper syntax and whose commands work properly on your computer. However, it is not a freestanding application. It can be run only by Script Editor or within an application that has a Scripts menu and script interpreter (such as iTunes), or by using the optional systemwide Scripts menu, installable by running the Install Script Menu AppleScript applet located in */Applications/AppleScript/*. For this option, select Script from the File Format drop-down box in the Save As... dialog.

A *script saved as an application* is self-contained and can be run by double-clicking it in the Finder, as with any other application. Sometimes, Apple-Script applications are called *applets*. Applets can also be activated from iTunes's Scripts menu. For this option, select Application from the File Format drop-down box in the Save As... dialog.

A *stay-open application* is an AppleScript applet that just doesn't quit—literally. In general, this is a type of script application that runs in the background indefinitely, watching for a particular condition or changes to a condition. For instance, a stay-open applet can be used to detect when a new track has started playing in iTunes and then perform some task. The script Current Track to iChat Status **[Hack #87]** is a stay-open applet. For this option, select Application from the File Format drop-down box in the Save As... dialog, and check the Stay Open checkbox.

Scripts can also be saved as *text files* in Script Editor. However, these text files can only be read by Script Editor, not by regular text editors. Script Editor doesn't try to compile a script before saving it as text, so often it's convenient to save an unfinished script this way. For this option, select Text from the File Format drop-down box in the Save As... dialog.

We will be working with compiled scripts at first. Later, you will see scripts saved as applets and stay-open applications.

1. Select File → Save As....
2. In the Save As... box, enter the name for your script—*Play Library* is as good as anything else.
3. Select either the non–user-specific */Library/iTunes/Scripts* folder or the */Users/username/Library/iTunes/Scripts* folder as the destination folder for your script (if either folder doesn't exist, simply create it).
4. Choose Compiled from the File Format menu, and click the Save button.

The script is available in the iTunes Scripts menu, as shown in Figure 5-4.

Go ahead and give it a whirl.

Figure 5-4. The Play Library script in the iTunes Scripts menu

AppleScript for iTunes: A Primer

The language of AppleScript is pretty similar to everyday language (though with a stricter-than-English grammar), so you won't have to learn too many new *code words*. This also makes it much easier to explain. Usually, a line of AppleScript does exactly what it says it will do.

tell statements. Type this fairly simple sentence into Script Editor, and then activate it by pressing the Run button:

```
tell application "iTunes" to play
```

This is a tell statement; it *tells* a particular application to do something. In this case, it tells iTunes to start playing. tell statements contain *objects* and *commands*, which are very much like nouns and verbs, respectively. When you want to perform several commands on one targeted application, you can use just one tell statement around a block of other commands, terminated by an end tell:

```
tell application "iTunes"
    set sound volume to 40
    set EQ enabled to true
    play
end tell
```

Sometimes, this is called a *compound* tell statement or a tell *block*. Usually, all of a script's commands and computations occur within just one set of tell statements.

Objects and references. An AppleScript *object* is a *thing* that is scriptable. In the case of iTunes, this includes a playlist, a track, an audio source, and so on. AppleScript identifies an object in a scriptable application by using a *reference* to it. A reference is an unambiguous pointer to a very specific thing. Observe the middle line in the following script:

```
tell application "iTunes"
    play track 7 of user playlist "Sparkle and Fade"
end tell
```

In this script, the phrase `track 7 of user playlist "Sparkle and Fade"` is a reference to a specific track in a specific playlist in the application iTunes. The word of is used in a reference to unambiguously connect a particular object to its *container*; in the previous code snippet, the user playlist named "Sparkle and Fade" is the container of track number 7.

Additionally, an object can contain *properties*. For example, `name` is a property of the track object; the value of `name` is the text of the track's Song Name. You can specify a particular property of an object using a reference as well. In the following script, the statement in the second line references the name of a particular track in a particular playlist:

```
tell application "iTunes"
  name of track 7 of user playlist "Sparkle and Fade"
end tell
```

Often, rather than typing the same reference over and over whenever you need it in the script, you can store the reference in a *variable*. A variable is a user-named holder for a value. The value in this case will be a reference. In the following example, I store a reference to the playlist called "Mom's Favorites" in a variable I have chosen to name `thisPlaylist`:

```
tell application "iTunes"
  set thisPlaylist to playlist "Mom's Favorites"
end tell
```

Later in the script, whenever I want to refer to the playlist "Mom's Favorites," I can simply use the variable `thisPlaylist` instead.

get and set (and sometimes copy). You can retrieve the value of a variable or property with the AppleScript command get, and you can assign a new value to a variable or property with set:

```
tell application "iTunes"
  -- get a value
  copy (get name of track 12 of playlist "Favorites") to trackName
  -- and set one
  set name of track 4 of playlist "Favorites" to "Everlong"
end tell
```

In AppleScript, a line starting with a pair of dashes (--) is a comment, there for your own reference and the edification of others reading your code. The AppleScript interpreter ignores comments, so we encourage you to comment liberally.

The AppleScript copy command, which I used in the statement with get in the previous example, is similar to the set command. Notice that their syntax appears inverted. A set statement assigns a variable to a value:

```
set thisVariable to someValue
```

whereas copy assigns a value to a variable:

```
copy someValue to thisVariable
```

Because there are some situations in which their usages are not interchangeable (situations that are a bit too advanced to explain here) I got into the habit of using set exclusively. You should, too.

Conditionals. You can determine how the script will behave by testing whether certain conditions are met by way of a *conditional statement*. By far, the most common conditional across programming languages is the if...then statement—literally, "if the *result* of an *expression* is *true*, then do something."

The following snippet of code tells iTunes to play if it is currently paused:

```
tell application "iTunes"
    if player state is paused then play
end tell
```

And this bit of code instructs iTunes to delete the "Black Sea" playlist if it is empty (literally, "if the number of tracks is zero"):

```
tell application "iTunes"
    if (count tracks of playlist "Black Sea") is 0 then delete playlist "Black
Sea"
end tell
```

In much the same way that you can group together several statements in a tell block, you can also create *compound conditional statements*, causing all of the enclosed statements to be run if the if condition is true.

This code checks to see if the playlist "Mom's Favorites" is set to shuffle. If not (that is, if the statement shuffle of playlist "Mom's Favorites" is false is *true*), iTunes is instructed to turn on shuffling for "Mom's Favorites" (i.e., set the shuffle property to true) and play it:

```
tell application "iTunes"
    if shuffle of playlist "Mom's Favorites" is false then
        set shuffle of playlist "Mom's Favorites" to true
        play playlist "Mom's Favorites"
    end if
end tell
```

A compound block ends with an end if statement.

> Notice that the if...end if block is contained within the tell...end tell block. This is called *nesting* and is rather common practice in scripting logic.

You can also use else to provide an alternative task if the initial if condition is not true. Here, for example, if mute is not true (i.e., audio is not muted), go ahead and mute the sound now:

```
tell application "iTunes"
  if mute is true then
    set mute to false
  else -- if mute is not true
    set mute to true
  end if
end tell
```

The else terminates the initial if block in much the same manner an end if would, but further states that there's an alternative coming up. The end if then closes the else block.

When an if statement offers an alternative using an else statement, the flow of the script is said to *branch* to either the if or the else clause.

You can offer more alternatives using else if:

```
tell application "iTunes"
  if player state is paused then
    play
  else if player state is playing then
    pause
  else
    quit
  end if
end tell
```

In this script, there are three possible branches. If neither of the conditions in the if or else if statements are true, then the final else clause is executed no matter what. You can use as many else if clauses as you require.

Repeat loops. A *repeat loop* iterates over a set of statements a certain number of times, on each item in a collection of objects, or while a certain condition is true. AppleScript provides repeat loops for each of these occasions.

In the course of the hacks in this chapter, we will most often be using a repeat loop to perform a set of tasks on each item in a list. A *list*, as the name suggests, is a collection of *items* (strings, numbers, object references, other lists, etc.) delimited by commas and held within braces, like so:

```
-- text strings:
{"Come Together", "Something", "Maxwell's Silver Hammer"}

-- numbers:
{1, 456, 27}

-- references:
{file track id 4100, file track id 4099, file track id 4098}
```

```
-- combination:
{2,"cute to be",4,"got","ten"}
```

The lists you use in your interactions with iTunes usually contain track or playlist references.

To briefly illustrate how various repeat loops work, let's suppose you want to change the artist's name for every track in a playlist to Talking Heads. The first task is to get the list of tracks in the playlist. The following code sets a variable called theList to a list of references to every track in the "Talking Heads Songs" playlist:

```
tell application "iTunes"
    set theList to every track in the playlist "Talking Heads Songs"
end tell
```

Each track reference in theList is an *item* of that list. Now we can loop through each item in the following ways.

Here, each item in theList is assigned to the variable thisTrack on each loop:

```
tell application "iTunes"
    set theList to every track in the playlist "Talking Heads Songs"
    repeat with thisTrack in theList
        set thisTrack's artist to "Talking Heads"
    end repeat
end tell
```

Here, the variable i is automatically incremented on each loop and is used to target each item in the list successively:

```
tell application "iTunes"
    set theList to every track in the playlist "Talking Heads Songs"
    repeat with i from 1 to (count items in theList)
        set artist of item i of theList to "Talking Heads"
    end repeat
end tell
```

This repeat loop references the tracks in the playlist directly and does not use the list variable at all:

```
tell application "iTunes"
    repeat with i from 1 to (count every track of playlist
    "Talking Heads Songs")
        name of track i of playlist "Talking Heads Songs"
    end repeat
end tell
```

Many of the scripts in this book use variations of these repeat blocks. I provide greater detail when discussing a script that uses a repeat loop.

Consulting the dictionary. An application's AppleScript Dictionary describes all the objects and commands that the application understands. It's generally useful to take a look at the Dictionary before you start scripting. You can access iTunes's AppleScript Dictionary, shown in Figure 5-5, in one of two ways: click on Open Dictionary in Script Editor's File menu and select iTunes from the list of applications that appears, or drag the iTunes icon to Script Editor's icon in the Finder or the Dock.

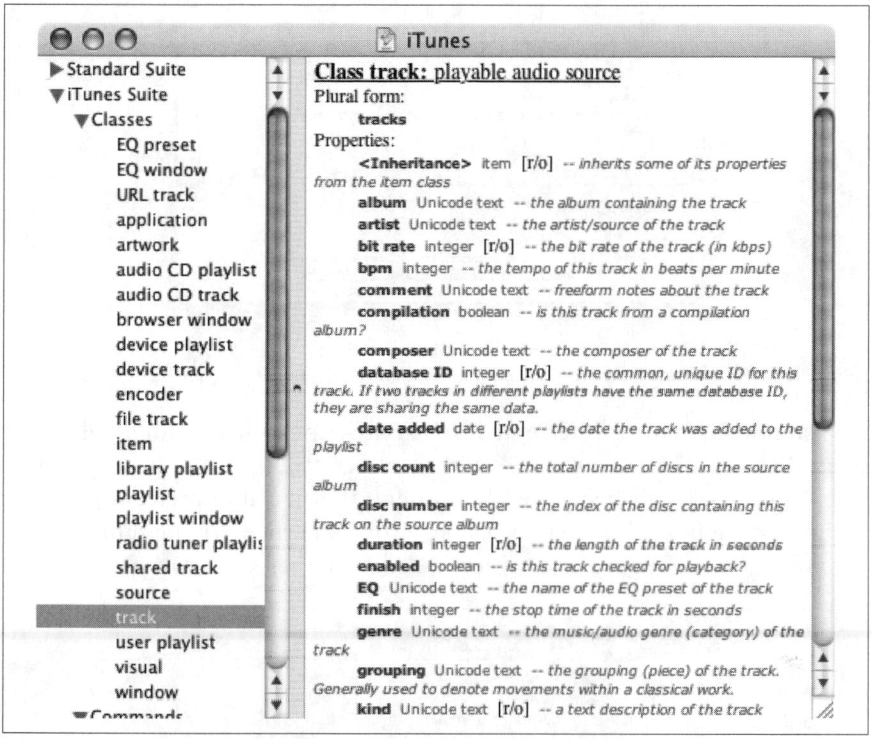

Figure 5-5. iTunes 4.5's AppleScript Dictionary

In Figure 5-5, the column on the left side of the window lists the various AppleScript classes (objects) and commands that iTunes understands. The track object is selected, and its properties are displayed in the right column.

Basic Debugging

No matter how well you know your AppleScript syntax, your script *will* generate errors while you are developing it and trying to get it to work properly. Script Editor has a couple features that will help you observe how a script is working so that you can see results, spot trouble, trap errors and problems, and eliminate a lot of the guesswork (although guesswork will always go on!).

You will want to be able to see the final results of any script actions, so click on the Result tab. You can resize this window so that you have easy visual access to it while working on your script in the main Script Editor window. The Result window always displays the *last* result from the Script window, as shown in Figure 5-6.

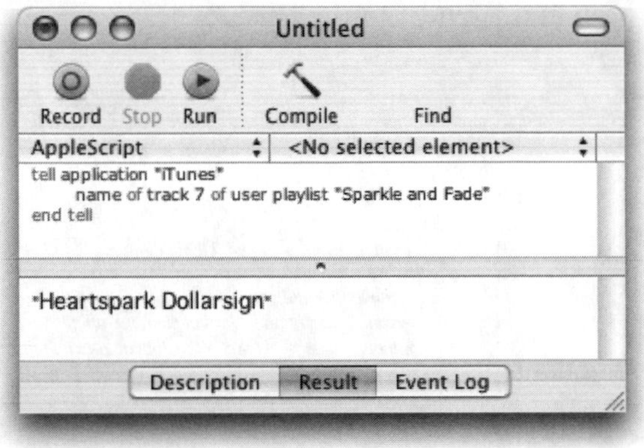

Figure 5-6. The Result window

To see how a script is interpreted by AppleScript as it's running, click the Event Log tab. When you run a script from Script Editor, the Event window (see Figure 5-7) will display each command as it's interpreted by Apple-Script and each result (when available). This is particularly helpful in refining your syntax or figuring out where a bad script has gone wrong.

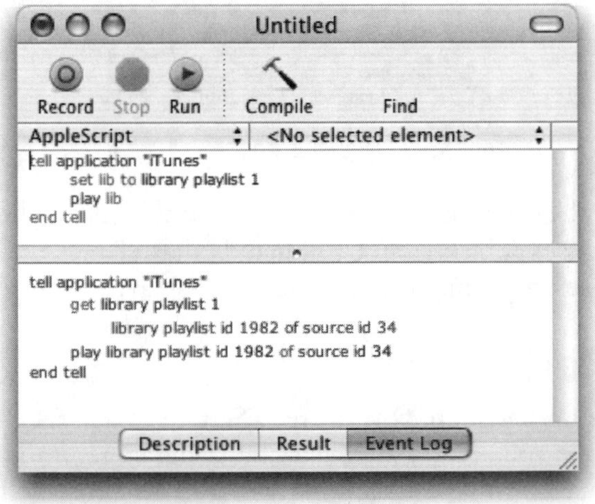

Figure 5-7. The Event window

The iTunes Scripts Menu

You need to put AppleScript script files for use with iTunes in a special folder so that they will be accessible from the iTunes Scripts menu.

To make iTunes scripts available to all users of your Mac, create a folder called *Scripts* in the */Library/iTunes* folder.

To make iTunes scripts available only to a particular user of your Mac (most likely you), make a *Scripts* folder in that user's personal */Library/iTunes* folder (i.e., */Users/username/Library/iTunes*, where *username* is the user's login name).

After creating the *Scripts* folder, the next time you launch iTunes you will see the AppleScript menu bar icon appear magically between the Window and Help drop-down menus.

Compiled and application scripts in the *Scripts* folder will appear in iTunes's Scripts menu. Scripts saved as an Application Bundle cannot be accessed via the iTunes Scripts menu. (We will be using and writing both compiled and application scripts.)

You can organize your scripts to some degree by placing them in folders inside your *Scripts* folder—one folder deep. You can also use aliases to scripts that are stored outside the *Scripts* folder. This might be helpful to you in the Finder, but the scripts will still appear in one long list in the iTunes Scripts menu.

Another trick for staying organized in the Scripts menu is to use various alphanumeric prefixes in your script names, such as spaces, underscores, bullets (Option-8), or degrees (Shift-Option-8). This groups like-prefixed scripts together by various alphanumeric strata in the Scripts menu. I am not aware of a maximum limit on the number of scripts you can put in your *Scripts* folder. I have had as many as 288, and no evil was visited upon me.

Alternatives to the iTunes Scripts Menu

In addition to iTunes' Scripts menu, you can also use the systemwide Scripts menu. This is handy for accessing iTunes scripts if iTunes is not the front-most application. You add scripts to the Finder's Scripts menu by putting them in */Library/Scripts* (for all users) or */Users/username/Library/Scripts* (for individual users). As with iTunes, once you create the folder, a drop-down menu with the AppleScript icon appears in the Finder menu bar.

> If the Scripts menu was not installed with your system, download it for free from Apple at *http://www.apple.com/ applescript/scriptmenu*. The installer should also be located in */Applications/AppleScript/*. Simply run the *Install Script Menu* script located within that folder to install the system-wide Script menu.

You can drag and drop AppleScript applets (scripts saved as self-contained applications) to the Finder's toolbar for easy access.

Dock and launcher applications are handy for firing scripts, too. I use the venerable DragThing (*http://www.dragthing.com*; $29.00; trial version available) to run compiled scripts.

There are also several applications that allow you to assign shortcut keys to AppleScript applets. These include iKey (*http://scriptsoftware.com/ikey/*; $20.00; free trial version available) and QuicKeys (*http://www.cesoft.com/ products/quickeys.html*; $99.95; trial version available).

Final Thoughts

You now have the basic tools for manipulating iTunes with AppleScript, and the scripts that lie ahead will reveal to you the range of tasks that you can accomplish with it. We will discuss each new concept as it comes.

—Doug Adams

HACK #73   Swap Song Name and Artist   Ⓜ Ⓧ Ⓔ

Correct that irritating problem of' song names and artist names being reversed.

The first time you find a track in iTunes that somehow has gotten its Song Name and Artist reversed, you open up its Get Info window and do some cutting, copying, pasting, and typing to effect repairs. It's kind of a drag. When you see the same problem with another track, you begrudgingly do the swap a second time and hope that you won't have to go through all that again. But when you notice it a third time, don't lose your temper. Just break out the AppleScript.

The Code

This script gets the text from the `name` and `artist` properties of each of the selected tracks—or, if no tracks are selected, all the tracks in the selected playlist—and swaps them:

```
tell application "iTunes"

    -- act on particular tracks or all tracks currently displayed
```

```
if selection is not {} then
  set sel to selection
else
  set sel to file tracks of view of front window
end if

-- loop through each selected track
repeat with aTrack in sel
  tell aTrack
    set temp1 to (get name)
    set name to (get artist)
    set artist to temp1
  end tell
end repeat

end tell
```

The first thing the script does is determine which tracks the user has selected for swapping. If none are selected, the script acts on all the tracks of the currently selected playlist. In either case, the list of tracks to be acted upon by the script is stowed away in a variable called sel.

Next, the script moves on to a repeat loop [Hack #72] to process each item in the sel list, stuffing each track into an aTrack variable. Since aTrack is a reference to an object, you can tell it to do things (in this case, swap some of its properties).

A temporary variable, temp1, is set to the name property of the aTrack object. That safely stowed away, the name is replaced with the artist property. Then, to complete the swap, the artist property is set to the original name of the track, now held in the temp1 variable.

When the repeat block has looped through the contents of sel, the name and artist properties of each track will have been swapped.

Running the Hack

Enter the code into Script Editor [Hack #72]. Save it to your iTunes *Scripts* folder as a compiled script (i.e., set the File Format in the Save As... dialog to Script) named *Swap Song Name and Artist*.

Now, in iTunes, select any tracks on which you want the script to act and select Swap Song Name and Artist from the iTunes Scripts menu. The Song Name and Artist of each track will be swapped before your very eyes. If you make a mistake and swap the tags of a track or tracks that didn't need swapping, select the mis-swapped tracks and run the script again to swap the tags back.

—Doug Adams

HACK
#74   **Clean up "Artist - Song Name"-Style Titles**
Ⓜ◐◉

> Split song names of the form "The Beatles - Can't Buy Me Love" into
> separate artist and song names.

Sometimes, you'll encounter a Song Name in iTunes that incorporates the
Artist as well as the Song Name of the track, typically like this: "The Beatles
- Can't Buy Me Love." I don't care too much for this arrangement, but I ran
into it so often that I wrote a script that removes the Artist portion to the
track's artist tag and fixes what's left in the name tag.

The Code

This script acts on the selected tracks. If their Song Names contain a hyphen
flanked by a space on either side (-), the script splits the text on either side
of the those three characters, placing the first part in the artist tag and the
second part in the name tag:

```
property separator : " - "

tell application "iTunes"
  if selection is not {} then

    repeat with aTrack in selection

      tell aTrack
        if name contains separator then
          set {artist, name} to my text_to_list(name, separator)
        end if
      end tell

    end repeat
  end if
end tell

on text_to_list(txt, delim)
  set saveD to AppleScript's text item delimiters
  try
    set AppleScript's text item delimiters to {delim}
    set theList to every text item of txt
  on error errStr number errNum
    set AppleScript's text item delimiters to saveD
    error errStr number errNum
  end try
  set AppleScript's text item delimiters to saveD
  return (theList)
end text_to_list
```

This script works with a sequence of text that looks like this: "Artist - Song
Name". The first line defines three-character combination of space, hyphen,

---

space (" - ") as a *property* called `separator`, the piece between the two components we're after.

If any tracks are selected, a `repeat` block assigns each in turn to the `aTrack` variable. The script checks to see if the track is formatted as expected and, if so, passes the track's name to a special `text_to_list` handler (a *handler* is an AppleScript subroutine, a short routine that does a discrete processing task). The handler converts that text into a two-item list (Artist, Song Name) from the text string provided and returns it as a result of the handler.

The script then assigns the two values gleaned from the original song name to the track's `artist` and `name` properties, respectively.

Running the Hack

Enter the code into Script Editor **[Hack #72]** and save it to your iTunes *Scripts* folder as a compiled script (i.e., set the File Format in the Save As... dialog to Script) and name it *Artist - Song Name Corrector*.

Choose one or more iTunes tracks and run the script. The title of each selected track will be split at the hyphen, the first part set as the Artist and the second as the Song Name. Now isn't that a pretty simple way to get rid of a nagging problem?

Hacking the Hack

If you happen to encounter the reverse problem—songs titled "Song Name - Artist"—you can easily adapt this script to suit your needs by swapping the placement of the artist and name variables. Simply change this line:

```
set {artist, name} to my text_to_list(name, separator)
```

to this:

```
set {name, artist} to my text_to_list(name, separator)
```

—Doug Adams

HACK #75 Remove Unwanted Characters from Song Names ⓂⓍⓁ

Remove a specified number of text characters from the beginning of the selected track names.

Track numbers in your Song Names disquieting your chi? Here's an AppleScript that lets you delete a specified number of characters from the beginning of the name of each selected track; for example, you can delete the initial digits and the space from "01 First Track," "02 Second Track," and so on.

The Code

This script asks you for the number of text characters you want removed from the beginning of each of the selected track names and then removes that many:

```
tell application "iTunes"
  -- if no tracks are selected, exit
  set sel to selection
  if sel is {} then return

  -- get a number routine
  set this_offset to my get_a_number("")

  repeat with aTrack in sel
    tell aTrack
    -- use try block; skip this track if any errors
      try
        set name to text (this_offset + 1) thru -1 of (get name)
      end try
    end tell
  end repeat

  if frontmost is true then display dialog "Done!" buttons {"Thanks"} ¬
    default button 1 with icon 1

end tell

to get_a_number(addenda)
  -- ask for a number as text
  set myNumber to text returned of (display dialog "" & addenda & ¬
    "Enter number of initial characters to remove:" default answer ¬
    "" buttons {"Cancel", "OK"} default button 2)

  -- try to coerce the text string to a number
  try
    (myNumber as integer)
  on error
  -- if not, handler calls itself again
    tell me to get_a_number("Enter only numbers..." & return & return)
  end try

  -- are you sure? Include this if block if you think you need to
  if myNumber is greater than 7 then
    if button returned of (display dialog "" & myNumber & ¬
      " is rather large...use this number?" buttons {"Yes", "No"} ¬
      default button 2) is "No" then tell me to get_a_number("")
  end if

  return myNumber
end get_a_number
```

If you have selected some tracks, the script will proceed and set the variable sel to the selection. Otherwise, it will end.

Next, the script sets the variable this_offset to the number returned from the get_a_number( ) handler. The get_a_number( ) handler will ask you to enter a number. If the number you enter isn't recognized as an integer, the handler will call itself so you can try again.

Additionally, I've added a routine that checks to see if your number is larger than 7 and, if so, queries your choice. You can remove this from your script if you like; it just seems to me that more than a few characters might be excessive and warrant a double-check.

Back in the main routine, the repeat loop goes through each track reference in sel, assigning it to the variable aTrack on each loop. During the loop, the range of text characters of the track's name from the character after this_ offset through the last character is rewritten to the name.

Finally, if iTunes is the frontmost application, a dialog box will pop up to tell you that the script has finished.

Running the Hack

Enter the code into Script Editor [Hack #72]. Save this script in your iTunes *Scripts* folder as a compiled script (set the File Format in the Save As... dialog to Script) and name it *Remove n Characters from Front*.

The *target* of this script is one or more selected iTunes tracks. After selecting the tracks, run the script. You will be asked to enter a number, which will be the number of leftmost characters deleted from each selected track's Song Name.

Now you've got yourself a precision editing tool to use whenever any of your Song Names need some front-end work.

—*Doug Adams*

HACK
#76

Find a Track's File Path ⓂⓃⓁ

Display a track's file path without a lot of mouse-clicks and open windows.

Tracking down the location of a track's file can lead to having a lot of Finder windows open, especially if you're using the Show Song File command a lot. This hack adds a simple step: it displays the file path of the selected track or currently playing track in a dialog box. Then, going Get Info one better, you can choose to show the file in the Finder only, which saves a few mouse clicks.

The Code

This script will get the location property of a single selected file track or the currently playing file track and display it in a dialog box. Additionally, the dialog box buttons will allow the user to choose to reveal the file in the Finder:

```
tell application "iTunes"

    -- routine to select single selected or playing track
    if selection is not {} and ¬
        (kind of container of view of front window) is library then
        set sel to item 1 of selection
        set dd_message to "selected track"
    else
        if player state is not stopped then
            set sel to current track
            set dd_message to "playing track"
        else
            display dialog "Select a library track." buttons {"Cancel"} ¬
                default button 1 with icon 2 giving up after 15
        end if
    end if

    -- get the location property of the track
    if sel's class is file track and  ¬
        sel's location is not missing value then
        try
            set the_file_path to sel's location
        on error errText
            display dialog errText buttons {"Cancel"} with icon 0
        end try

        set name_of_track to sel's name

    else
        display dialog "Cannot discern the " & dd_message & ¬
            "'s file path." buttons {"Cancel"} default button 1 with icon 2

    end if
end tell

-- put CR after each ":" in file path for display purposes
set dd_filepath to  ¬
    replace_chars(the_file_path as string, ":", (":" & return))

-- show path, ask to show file in Finder
if button returned of (display dialog "The " & dd_message & " \"" & ¬
    name_of_track & "\"" & " is here..." & return & ¬
    dd_filepath buttons {"Show Song File", "Thanks"} ¬
    default button 2) is not "Thanks" then
```

```
     -- show file in Finder
     tell application "Finder"
        try
           reveal the_file_path
           activate
        on error errMs
           display dialog errMs
        end try
     end tell

   end if

   on replace_chars(txt, srch, repl)
     set AppleScript's text item delimiters to the srch
     set the item_list to every text item of txt
     set AppleScript's text item delimiters to the repl
     set txt to the item_list as string
     set AppleScript's text item delimiters to ""
     return txt
   end replace_chars
```

First, you need to determine what track the user is targeting—the selected track or the current track—and assign its reference to the variable sel. I use a variation of the first routine in several scripts (see "AMG EZ Search" [Hack #79], for example). I've also loaded the dd_message variable with a string for display dialog purposes later.

Once you have sel, the script will determine if its class is a *file track* and, if so, check if its location property doesn't contain the constant missing value. I've included the statement to get the location property in a try block, just in case there's any unforeseen problem. Next, I figured this was as good a place as any to store the name of the track in the variable name_of_track, which will be used in the final display dialog.

The track's file path is stored in the_file_path as a string, and it looks something like this:

```
Macintosh HD:Users:dougadams:Music:iTunes:iTunes Music:Faces:Ohh La La:06
Fly in the Ointment.m4p
```

The script then puts the file path through the replace_chars( ) handler, to add a carriage return after each colon (:) for the display dialog. The display dialog also includes a Thanks button to dismiss the script and a Show Song File button that activates the Finder routine to reveal the selected track's file.

Running the Hack

Enter the code into Script Editor [Hack #72]. Save this script in your iTunes *Scripts* folder as a compiled script (set the File Format in the Save As... dialog to Script) and name it *Where Is This?*.

The *target* of this script is a single selected track. If no track is selected, the currently playing track is the target. In either case, when you run *Where Is This?* from the iTunes Scripts menu, a dialog box pops up showing the path to the track's file and giving you an option to Show Song File, as shown in Figure 5-8.

Figure 5-8. *The "Where Is This?" final display*

Now when you want to know an audio file's location, all you have to do is ask "Where Is This?"

—Doug Adams

HACK #77   Get a Track's Running Time and File Size

Get the total time and total size of selected tracks.

It's easy to get the total running time and size of a playlist in iTunes; it appears right along the bottom of the main window, beneath the tracks. If you only want to know about a selection of tracks, though, you'd better break out the calculator—or use this simple script that will display the total time and combined size of just the selected or enabled (checkmarked) tracks.

The Code

This script sums the running time and size of either the selected tracks or the enabled tracks and displays the results in a dialog box:

```
tell application "iTunes"

    set lib to view of front window
    set total_size to 0
```

```
    set total_duration to 0
    set dd_buttons to {"Cancel", "Enabled", "Selected"}

    -- target selected or enabled tracks?
    if button returned of ¬
      (display dialog "Show total time and space of " & ¬
        "Selected or Enabled tracks in playlist \"" & (name of lib) & ¬
        "\":" buttons dd_buttons default button 2) is "Enabled" then
      set trackList to every track in lib whose enabled is true
    else
      set trackList to selection
    end if

    -- conglomerate each track's size and duration
    repeat with aTrack in trackList
      try
        set total_size to total_size + (get aTrack's size)
        set total_duration to total_duration + (get aTrack's duration)
      end try
    end repeat

    -- convert total bytes to megabytes
    set dd_size to (round total_size / 1024 / 1024 * 100 rounding up) / 100

    -- convert total seconds to hours, minutes, seconds
    set t_hour to ¬
      (round total_duration / 3600 rounding down)
    set t_min to ¬
      (round (total_duration / 60 - t_hour * 60) rounding down)
    set t_sec to ¬
      (round total_duration mod 60)
    set dd_time to t_hour & "h " & t_min & "m " & t_sec & "s"

    -- show totals
    display dialog "Total tracks: " & (count of trackList) & ¬
      return & return & "Total time: " & dd_time & ¬
      return & return & "Total size: " & dd_size & ¬
      "MB" buttons {"Thanks"} default button 1

  end tell
```

First, the script initializes a few variables, which include a list of strings used as button names in the upcoming display dialog and a reference to the selected playlist.

Next, the script puts up a dialog box asking whether you want to target the selected tracks or the enabled tracks (the ones that are checkmarked) in the selected playlist. If you select Enabled, the variable trackList will be set to a list of every checkmarked track (every track whose enabled property is set to true has its checkbox checked). Otherwise, trackList will be set to a list of references to each selected track.

A repeat block then sets the variable aTrack to each track reference in trackList on each loop. On each loop, the duration property (a track's time in seconds) and the size property (a track's size in bytes) of aTrack are successively added to the variables total_duration and total_size, respectively. When the repeat loop has finished, these two variables contain the total time in seconds and total size in bytes of all the tracks. Then the script converts the seconds to hours, minutes, and seconds and the bytes to megabytes.

Finally, the display dialog shows the results.

Running the Hack

Enter the code into Script Editor [Hack #72]. Save this script in your iTunes *Scripts* folder as a compiled script (set the File Format in the Save As... dialog to Script) and name it *time + space*.

This AppleScript examines each selected track (or, if you so choose, each enabled track) and totals each track's size and duration. As shown in Figure 5-9, the *time + space* script displays the total time and total size of the selected tracks.

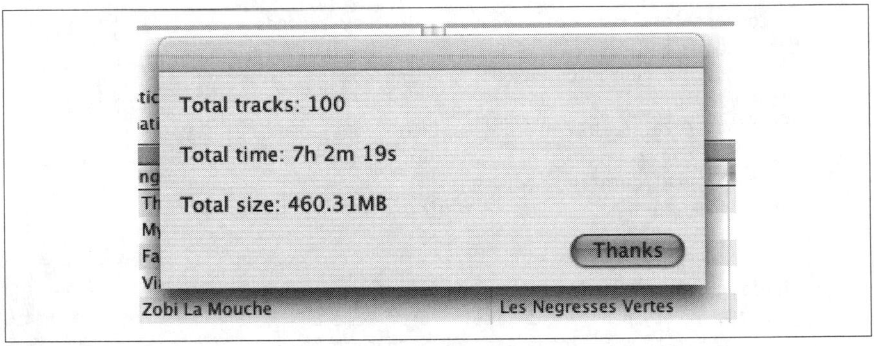

Figure 5-9. The total time and size of the selected tracks

I have found this to be one of the handiest scripts I've ever used, and I'm surprised that it is not a feature of iTunes itself already. Oh well. More joy from hacking!

—*Doug Adams*

Increase or Decrease the Play Count ⓜⓢⓔ

Automatically add to or decrease the play count of the selected tracks by a specific number.

Smart Playlists can be configured to regard play counts when assembling tracks. For even greater flexibility using this Smart Playlist criterion, here's an AppleScript that will uniformly increase or decrease the play counts of a batch of tracks or reset them to zero.

The Code

This script asks the user to first supply a number and then specify whether to add or subtract that number from the play counts of the selected tracks:

```
tell application "iTunes"

  -- if no tracks selected, exit
  if selection is {} then
    display dialog "No tracks selected." buttons {"Cancel"} ¬
      default button 1 with icon 0
  end if

  set sel to selection

  -- get the results from the handler
  set options to my get_a_number("")
  set thismany to text returned of options as integer

  repeat with aTrack in sel
    -- skip tracks without played count property
    if aTrack's class is file track then
      tell aTrack
        set curPlayCount to (get played count)

        -- add or subtract?
        if button returned of options is "+" then
          set played count to curPlayCount + thismany
        else
          if curPlayCount _ thismany then
            set played count to curPlayCount - thismany
          else
            set played count to 0
          end if
        end if
      end tell
    end if
  end repeat

  display dialog "Done!" buttons {"Thanks"} default button 1 ¬
    with icon 1 giving up after 15
```

```
end tell

to get_a_number(addenda)
  set myResult to ¬
    (display dialog (addenda & "Enter number to add or subtract" & ¬
      " from each selected track's \"Play Count\" and then " & ¬
      "click the appropriate button:") ¬
      default answer "" buttons {"Cancel", "-", "+"})

  -- try to coerce the text returned to a number
  try
    (text returned of myResult as integer)

    -- return text and button returned from dialog
    return myResult
  on error
    -- if not, handler calls itself again
    get_a_number("Please try again..." & return & return)
  end try
end get_a_number
```

This script starts with another variation on determining whether any tracks are selected. In this case, if no tracks are selected, the user is notified and the script exits. Otherwise, the variable sel is set to a list of references to the selected tracks.

Next, you'll set the variable options to the text (a number) and button (+ or –) returned from the result of the get_a_number( ) handler. This handler is similar to the one used in "Remove Unwanted Characters from Song Names" **[Hack #75]**, except that the button returned is included. The variable thismany is set to the text returned and coerced to a number.

A repeat loop targets each track reference in the variable sel. First, it checks to see if the track is a *file track*; file tracks are the only class of track with the played count property. Then it gets the current played count value.

The button returned property will contain + or –, which directs the script to add or subtract the number that was entered. The + branch of the if block is fairly straightforward: just add thismany to the track's played count property. The – branch makes sure that if the result of the subtraction is a negative number, 0 is used as a matter of course. Negative play counts do not compute!

Finally, when all the tracks in the selection have been processed, we throw up a Done dialog and exit the script.

Running the Hack

Enter the code into Script Editor [Hack #72]. Save this script in your iTunes *Scripts* folder as a compiled script (set the File Format in the Save As... dialog to Script) and name it *Add or Subtract Play Count*.

Select one or more tracks in iTunes and run the script. A dialog box will ask you to enter a number that will be used to increase or decrease the selected tracks' play counts. Then press the + or – button to tell the script to add or subtract the entered number to or from the play counts.

> To reset play counts to 0, select the tracks, fire up the script, enter an incredibly high number such as 10,000, and click the subtract (–) button.

—Doug Adams

HACK #79   AMG EZ Search   Ⓜ Ⓝ Ⓞ

Use info from the selected or playing track to search the All Music Guide web site.

You're tapping your toes to an iTunes song when suddenly you realize you need to know more information. This AppleScript hack puts artist and album information one click away by sending data on the song you are listening to the venerable music information site, All Music Guide (AMG) at *http://www.allmusic.com*, via Safari.

The Code

This script gets the `name`, `artist`, and `album` properties of the selected or playing iTunes track and then asks the user to select one of the properties to use as the basis of a search of the AMG. The script then creates a search URL, which it sends to the Safari browser to open:

```
-- determine selection
tell application "iTunes"
  if selection is not {} then
    set sel to item 1 of selection
  else
    if player state is not stopped then set sel to current track
  end if

  -- get artist, album and name properties
  try
    set myTags to ¬
      {get artist of sel, get album of sel, get name of sel}
```

```
      on error
        display dialog "No track selected or playing." ¬
          buttons {"Cancel"} default button 1 with icon 0 ¬
          giving up after 15
      end try

  end tell

  -- select a tag to search AMG
  set myOpt to ¬
    (choose from list myTags with prompt "Search AMG for..." ¬
      without multiple selections allowed) as string
  if myOpt is "false" then return

  repeat with prefix from 1 to 3
    if myOpt is item prefix of myTags then exit repeat
  end repeat

  -- replace in search string spaces with "+"
  set myOpt to replace_chars(myOpt, " ", "+")

  -- create the search URL
  set loc to ¬
    ("http://allmusic.com/cg/amg.dll?p=amg&sql=" & ¬
      prefix & ":" & myOpt)

  tell application "Safari"
    if name of front document contains "AMG " then
      set URL of front document to loc
    else
      open location loc
    end if
  end tell

  on replace_chars(txt, srch, repl)
    set AppleScript's text item delimiters to the srch
    set the item_list to every text item of txt
    set AppleScript's text item delimiters to the repl
    set txt to the item_list as string
    set AppleScript's text item delimiters to ""
    return txt
  end replace_chars
```

The script determines if there is a selected track and sets the variable sel to the first item in the *selection*. If no track is selected and iTunes is not stopped (that is, it is playing or paused), sel is set to a reference to the *current track*.

The artist, album, and name properties of the track reference in sel are stored as a list in the variable myTags.

I should pause to explain the reason why the properties must be in this order. The search engine at All Music Guide expects a URL containing a search string and an extra value—something that looks like this:

```
http://allmusic.com/cg/amg.dll?p=amg&sql=1:Big+Audio+Dynamite
```

Note that the sql value begins with a number and a colon followed by some text. The numbers 1, 2, and 3 correspond to an artist search, an album search, and a song name search, respectively, just as you might select in the search form at the AMG web site. (4 represents the label and 5 the genre, if that gives you any ideas.) We need to prefix our search string with the correct corresponding number.

A listbox lets the user select which tag to use in the search string, as shown in Figure 5-10. The result is stored in myOpt.

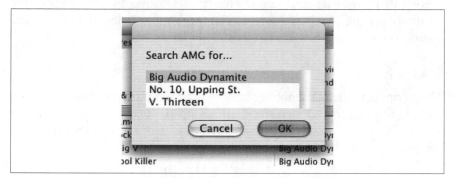

Figure 5-10. Choosing which tag to use when searching the AMG web site

To get the correct number (1, 2, or 3) corresponding to the user's choice, a repeat loop is used to figure the position of the chosen property myOpt in the myTags list. This number is stored in the variable prefix.

Next, any spaces in the selected text are replaced with +, and then the complete search URL is assembled as a string and stored in the variable loc.

Finally, the Safari tell block will open a new window in Safari using the URL string in loc, unless the front Safari window is already loaded with an AMG page, in which case it will open loc in that window.

Running the Hack

Enter the code into Script Editor [Hack #72]. Save this script in your iTunes *Scripts* folder as a compiled script (set the File Format in the Save dialog to Script) and name it *AMG EZ Search*.

The *target* of this script is a single selected track. If no track is selected, the currently playing track is the target. In either case, run *AMG EZ Search* from iTunes Scripts menu. From the listbox select the Song Name, Artist, or Album text to use to search the All Music Guide web site. The search results will appear in Safari.

The next time you want to know more about what's playing in iTunes, fire up *AMG EZ Search*, and start researching the easy way.

—*Doug Adams*

Search for Lyrics on Google ⓜⓢⓛ

#80   Use info from the current or selected track to search for lyrics pages via Google in Safari.

There are tons of lyrics sites on the Web that are ready to provide you with the words to your favorite songs. This hack Googles for the lyrics of the currently playing or selected song in iTunes. You'll be singing along by the second verse.

The Code

This script gets the name and artist of the currently playing track (or, if no track is playing, the selected track), tidies up the text, and incorporates it into a URL that is then used by Safari to search Google for sites containing the lyrics of that particular track:

```
-- base of the URL string, includes the term "lyrics"
property baseURL : "http://www.google.com/search?q=lyrics+"

tell application "iTunes"

    -- get a reference to playing or selected track
    if player state is not stopped then
      set theTrack to current track
    else if selection is not {} then
      set theTrack to (item 1 of selection)
    else
      display dialog "Nothing is playing or selected." buttons {"Cancel"} ¬
        default button 1 with icon 0
    end if

    -- get the name and artist and replace "bad" characters
    tell theTrack
      set nom to my fixChars(name)
      set art to my fixChars(artist)
    end tell

    -- assemble URL string, replace spaces with "+"
    set theURL to (baseURL & ¬
      (my replace_chars((art & "+" & nom), " ", "+"))) as text
```

```
     my open_location(theURL)

  end tell

on fixChars(a)
  set myDelims to {"!", "@", "#", "$", "%", "^", "&", "*",¬
    "(", ")", "-", "-", "+", "=", ":", ";", "'", ",", ".", "/", ¬
    "<", ">", "?", "{", "}", "[", "]"}
  repeat with curDelim in myDelims
    set AppleScript's text item delimiters to curDelim
    set s to every text item of a
    set AppleScript's text item delimiters to {""}
    set a to s as string
  end repeat
  return a
end fixChars

on replace_chars(txt, srch, repl)
  set AppleScript's text item delimiters to the srch
  set the item_list to every text item of txt
  set AppleScript's text item delimiters to the repl
  set txt to the item_list as string
  set AppleScript's text item delimiters to ""
  return txt
end replace_chars

to open_location(theURL)
  tell application "Safari"
    activate
    -- un-comment if you want to keep from opening windows:
    if name of window 1 does not start with "Google Search:" then
      make new document at end of documents
    end if
    set URL of document 1 to theURL
  end tell
end open_location
```

I've defined a script property (BaseURL) at the beginning of the script, setting it to the main portion of the Google search URL, along with the start of the query, the word lyrics. The script will add more to the base URL later.

First things first: the script determines whether there is a current track or a selected track and sets the variable sel to a reference to one or the other.

Next, the script gets the artist and name properties of the track referenced by sel. It will use these text strings in building the search URL. Additionally, it removes any undesirable characters that might lead to an incorrect search. The handler fixChars( ) removes a variety of *bad* characters from the text string sent to it and return the cleaned-up text.

Now, if the selected/playing song is "Third Uncle" by Brian Eno, the assembled theURL variable will contain a string that looks like this:

```
http://www.google.com/search?q=lyrics+Brian+Eno+Third+Uncle
```

All that's left to do is to send the theURL string to Safari, using the handler open_location( ). If the current front window in Safari doesn't already have a Google search result in it, a new window will be opened; otherwise, the same window is used to load the Google result.

The same effect is used in "AMG EZ Search" [Hack #79].

The Google search results page will (hopefully) contain a whole bunch of links to lyric pages for your song, as shown in Figure 5-11.

Running the Hack

Enter the code into Script Editor [Hack #72]. Save this script in your iTunes *Scripts* folder as a compiled script (set the File Format in the Save As... dialog to Script) and name it *Google Lyric Search*.

The script will target the currently playing track; if no track is playing, it will target a selected track. Using the Artist and the Song Name, a Google search URL will be constructed and sent to Safari.

If you want to emulate Google's I'm Feeling Lucky button, use the following as your baseURL at the start of the script:

```
http://www.google.com/search?btnI=I'm+Feeling+Lucky&q=lyrics+
```

Remember: results are not always fruitful...especially on instrumental tracks. (Da-*dum*!)

—Doug Adams

Remove Dead Tracks Ⓜ Ⓦ Ⓛ
#81
Automatically delete the tracks in iTunes whose files are no longer available.

Sometimes, you'll see tracks listed in iTunes with an exclamation point (!) next to their names. These are so-called *dead* tracks: tracks whose files iTunes cannot locate because the files either are missing or have been deleted. In any case, you can eliminate them all from your iTunes library and playlists with this AppleScript hack.

Figure 5-11. Wow, over 3,000 results!

The Code

This script examines each file track in the main library and checks if its location property is missing value. If it is, the track is removed from iTunes.

```
tell application "iTunes"

    -- initialize some variables
    set lib to library playlist 1
    set allUPNames to name of user playlists
    set prog to 500
    set delTracks to 0
    set checkedTracks to 0
    set ddMessage to ""
```

```
set fixed indexing to true

-- go through library tracks backwards
repeat with t from (count of file tracks of lib) to 1 by -1

  set aTrack to file track t of lib
  try
    if aTrack's location is missing value then
      delete aTrack
      set delTracks to delTracks + 1
    end if
  end try
  set checkedTracks to checkedTracks + 1

  if frontmost and ¬
    (prog is not 0) and ¬
    (checkedTracks mod prog) is 0 then

    if delTracks is not 0 then ¬
      set ddMessage to (delTracks & " dead tracks removed...")

    display dialog (checkedTracks as string) & ¬
      " tracks checked..." & return & ddMessage ¬
      buttons {""} giving up after 1
  end if

end repeat

set fixed indexing to false

repeat with aPlaylist in my allUPNames
  if (count of tracks of playlist aPlaylist) is 0 then ¬
    delete playlist aPlaylist
end repeat

if delTracks is 0 then
  display dialog "No tracks deleted." buttons {"Thanks"} ¬
    default button 1 with icon 1
else
  set ps to " was"
  if delTracks is not 1 then set ps to "s were"
  display dialog "Finished removing \"dead\" tracks." & return & ¬
    delTracks & " track" & ps & ¬
    " removed." buttons {"Thanks"} default button 1 with icon 1
end if
end tell
```

The script begins by initializing some variables it will use later. Included among these are variables used to keep track of how many tracks have been removed and to specify the number of tracks to wait before displaying a progress message.

Next, iTunes's fixed indexing property is set to true, to ensure that any changes made during AppleScript operations will not change the indexing (the sorting order) of the tracks in the targeted playlist. At the end of the script, fixed indexing will be reset to false.

Now the script will use a repeat loop that will target each track of the main library by index (its numerical play order position), from the last track to the first track, and check each one's location property. The loop has to proceed backward. If it were to go forward, the index of a track removed would point to the next track in the sequence, and since that index had already been checked, that next track would be skipped! But, by going backward, the script will always encounter a new as-yet unchecked index. If you are still a little confused as to why it is better to go backward than forward when surveying a playlist for dead tracks, see the sidebar "The Logic of Progressing Backward" for a more detailed explanation.

The variable aTrack is set to the track referenced by the repeat variable t. If aTrack's location property contains missing value, then its file, as far as iTunes is concerned, cannot be found. This track will be removed.

> When you delete a track from "library playlist 1," it automatically gets removed from any playlists it appears in. I love that.

When a track gets deleted, the script increases the delTracks variable. Also, the checkedTracks variable is incremented after a track's location has been evaluated.

Next, we will see if it's okay to put up the progress message. I included a progress message because sometimes I get antsy if I don't see anything happening. If you have thousands of tracks that need to be checked, a progress message can ease your anxiety. In this script, I have set the progress interval to 500 tracks, using the variable prog. Additionally, the progress message is

Lastly, a routine uses the delTracks variable to assemble and then display a final report, as shown in Figure 5-12.

Running the Hack

Enter the code into Script Editor [Hack #72]. Save this script in your iTunes *Scripts* folder as a compiled script (set the File Format in the Save As... dialog to Script) and name it *Super Remove Dead Tracks*.

Run the script from iTunes's Scripts menu. The script examines the file tracks in iTunes; if it cannot locate the file associated with the track, the

The Logic of Progressing Backward

Imagine you have a playlist of 10 tracks but instead of real song names, each of these tracks is named "Track 1," "Track 2," and so on through "Track 10." Additionally, each track is indexed sequentially, so that "Track 1" is 1, "Track 2" is 2, and so on. The index is the numerical position of the track in the play order of the playlist:

```
1 Track 1
2 Track 2
3 Track 3
...
10 Track 10
```

Suppose a repeat loop advances through each track starting with track index 1, which is our "Track 1." Let's say that the script traverses through three of the tracks and on the fourth track, "Track 4," it discovers that track index 4 has no location property and therefore no file, so the script deletes track index 4, our "Track 4." Here it gets tricky. There are now nine tracks in the playlist:

```
1 Track 1
2 Track 2
3 Track 3
4 Track 5
5 Track 6
6 Track 7
7 Track 8
8 Track 9
9 Track 10
```

Notice that "Track 5" has now assumed the track index 4 position, "Track 6" is in position 5, "Track 7" is moved up to position 6, and so on. The repeat loop wants to advance to track index 5 (since it is finished with track index 4, why would it check it again?), but when it does, it skips over "Track 5"! This is because "Track 6" is now in position 5. Indeed, for every track you delete, another will get skipped.

Now, look at it backward. The repeat loop starts with track index 10 and loops sequentially in reverse, such that the next track it checks is track index 9, then track index 8, and so on. When it comes to track index 4 it determines "Track 4" is a dead track and deletes the track from the playlist. As before, the playlist is reduced to nine tracks and each following track moves up in position. But since the script isn't interested in the tracks *after* track index 4 (it's going backward and already checked them), it loops next to track index 3, which will be "Track 3" and the correct track in sequence.

Figure 5-12. *The final report of how many tracks were removed*

script will remove the track from the library (which also removes it from all playlists in which it appears). Finally, any empty playlists are also deleted.

Hopefully, you'll only ever have to run this script a couple of times. But when you need it, you'll be very glad it's in your Scripts menu.

—Doug Adams

HACK #82 Build a Random Playlist Ⓜ❷❶
Shuffle several playlists together into a single random playlist.

Here's a hack a Smart Playlist or even Party Shuffle can't pull off: pick a bunch of playlists, combine all their songs into a single new playlist, shuffle 'em up, and play.

The Code

This script allows the user to select two or more playlists and then copy the tracks into a new user-named playlist. The new playlist will then be shuffled and played.

```
tell application "iTunes"

    -- variables used in choose from list
    set my_prompt to "Select playlists..."
    set my_ok_button to "Select..."
    set my_cancel_button to "Quit"

    -- default name of new playlist
    set defPName to "Random Bunch"

    -- list of all playlist names
    set allUPNames to name of user playlists

    -- select the playlist names to combine
    set selPlaylists to (choose from list allUPNames with prompt my_prompt ¬
        OK button name my_ok_button cancel button name my_cancel_button ¬
        with multiple selections allowed)
```

```
   if selPlaylists is false then error number -128

   -- get name for new playlist
   repeat
     set newPName to text returned of ¬
       (display dialog "Enter a new Playlist name:" default answer defPName ¬
         buttons {"Cancel", "OK"} default button 2)

     -- handle existing playlist
     if allUPNames does not contain newPName then
       exit repeat
     else if button returned of (display dialog (newPName & ¬
       " exists. Replace?") buttons {"No", "Yes"} ¬
       default button 1 with icon 2) is "Yes" then
       delete user playlist newPName
       exit repeat
     end if

   end repeat

   -- create the new empty playlist
   set newPlaylist to ¬
     (make new playlist with properties {name:newPName})

   -- copy tracks from selected playlists to new playlist
   repeat with thisPlaylist in selPlaylists
     try
       duplicate file tracks of playlist thisPlaylist to newPlaylist
     end try
   end repeat

   -- shuffle vigorously
   repeat 3 times
     set shuffle of newPlaylist to false
     set shuffle of newPlaylist to true
   end repeat

   -- select and play the new playlist
   set view of front browser window to newPlaylist
   play first track of newPlaylist
 end tell
```

Initially, I set some variables to be used later in the script. A choose from list
statement displays a list of the user playlists stored in the variable
allUPNames. The result is a list of the names of the selected playlists, which
will be stored in the variable selPlaylists.

Then, the user is asked for a name for the new playlist that will be created.
The default name I initialized at the beginning of the script as defPName will
be displayed, but the user can change this and enter something else in the
text box, as shown in Figure 5-13.

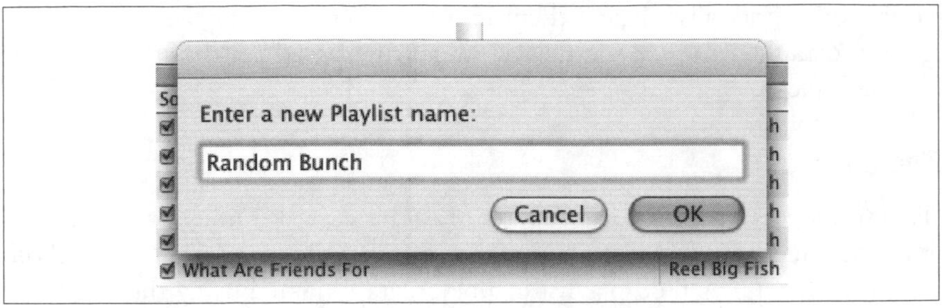

Figure 5-13. Entering a name for the playlist that will be created

The script checks to see if the name entered is already the name of a playlist and, if so, gives the user the option to replace the original playlist or go through the repeat loop and enter another new name. Then, the new playlist is created and a repeat block loops through the selected playlists and copies the tracks from each to the new playlist. Finally, the new playlist is shuffled (you can increase the repeat variable to get a more rigorous shuffle result) and selected in the source list, and it starts playing.

Running the Hack

Enter the code into Script Editor [Hack #72]. Save this script in your iTunes *Scripts* folder as a compiled script (set the File Format in the Save As... dialog to Script) and name it *Make a Bunch Random*.

Run the script from iTunes's Scripts menu, and select any number of playlists from the listbox it presents to you. The script will ask you for a name for the new playlist it will create, then copy all the tracks from your chosen playlists to the new playlist, shuffle the new playlist a few times, and start playing the new playlist.

Use this script liberally a few times a week, and you'll always have a fresh mega-playlist filled with a choice variety of songs.

—*Doug Adams*

HACK #83   Make a New iPod Playlist from Your Selections ◓◔◑

Send selected tracks in iTunes straight to your iPod, and optionally create a new playlist to put them in.

iTunes has a convenient New Playlist From Selection command (available from the File menu) to create a new playlist from a bunch of selected tracks. The only drawback is that it creates the playlist in the current source. This AppleScript hack lets you select some tracks in iTunes and send them to your iPod, optionally placing them in a newly created playlist. It even suggests a default name for the new iPod playlist based on the info from the selected tracks.

The Code

This script gets the `location` property of each selected iTunes track and uses it as the target of a `duplicate` command, copying the file to a mounted iPod. Additionally, a new iPod playlist can be created (named using the artist and album of the first selected iTunes track) to which the newly added iPod tracks can be copied.

```
tell application "iTunes"

  -- is iPod mounted?
  try
    set iPodSource to some source whose kind is iPod
  on error
    display dialog "Unable to detect iPod." buttons {"Cancel"} ¬
      default button 1 with icon 2 giving up after 15
    return
  end try

  -- selected tracks must be from library
  if selection is not {} and ¬
    (kind of container of view of front window) is library then

    set sel to get a reference to selection

    -- create a default name for new iPod playlist
    set suggestedPName to ""
    try
      tell item 1 of sel to set suggestedPName to ¬
        (((get artist) as string) & " - " & ((get album) as string))
    end try

    set myOptions to (display dialog ¬
      "Enter a name for the new iPod Playlist:" default answer ¬
      suggestedPName buttons {"Cancel", "No Playlist", "OK"} ¬
      default button 3)

    set new_iPod_tracks to {}
    repeat with thisTrack in sel

      -- if the track is able to be copied, copy it to iPod
      -- and add the reference to list of tracks
      try
        set end of new_iPod_tracks to ¬
          (duplicate thisTrack to library playlist 1 of iPodSource)
      end try
    end repeat
```

```
        -- if user wants new playlist, create it and
        -- copy tracks to it now
        if button returned of myOptions is "OK" then
            set new_Pnom to text returned of myOptions

            set new_iPod_playlist to ¬
                (make new user playlist at iPodSource ¬
                    with properties {name:new_Pnom})

            repeat with thisTrack in new_iPod_tracks
                duplicate thisTrack to new_iPod_playlist
            end repeat

        end if

        display dialog "Done." buttons {"Thanks"} default button 1 ¬
            with icon 1 giving up after 15

    else
        display dialog "Select some library tracks." buttons {"Cancel"} ¬
            default button 1 with icon 2 giving up after 15
    end if
end tell
```

The first thing the script does is make sure there's an iPod mounted and available to iTunes. If so, the iPodSource variable is set to its source.

Then the script determines if there are any selected tracks and if they are from a *library playlist*, rather than a *CD playlist* or *radio tuner playlist* (whose tracks can't be copied to an iPod). If the tracks pass muster, the sel variable is set to a list of references to the selected tracks. If they don't pass muster, the if block concludes with an else clause at the end of the script instructing the user to select some library tracks. When this dialog is dismissed, the script quits in order that the user can reselect the correct kind of tracks. The script must then be run again.

The script will use the artist and album of the first track among the selected tracks to create a default name for the potential new iPod playlist. It's fast and convenient to set the default here, even though in the following routine the user may decide not to create a new playlist.

The display dialog asks for a new name for the playlist using the default name we just created (stored in suggestedPName), as shown in Figure 5-14. However, the user can also decide not to copy the tracks to a new playlist by selecting the No Playlist button.

No matter what, the selected tracks will be copied to the iPod; copying them to a new iPod playlist is optional.

Figure 5-14. Entering a name for the new iPod playlist or deciding not to create a new playlist

The display dialog's result is a list that contains the text and button returned from the dialog. Those results are assigned to the myOptions variable, the items of which we will be using shortly.

Next is the routine that copies each track to the iPod. This is the last check for the correct kind of track. It will catch tracks whose files have gone missing (a.k.a. *dead tracks*), which can't be conveniently detected until this point in the script. It will also prevent errors from interrupting the script if a track, for some reason (if, for example, you have a few Ogg Vorbis files lying around your library), can't be copied to the iPod (the routine will skip over such tracks). Additionally, it creates a list of references to the new iPod tracks in the variable new_iPod_tracks.

If the button returned in myOptions is OK, the script creates a new playlist on the iPod and copies a reference to it to new_iPod_playlist, then uses the text returned from myOptions as its name. Finally, the repeat loop copies each track referenced in new_iPod_tracks from the iPod library to the new iPod playlist.

Running the Hack

Enter the code into Script Editor [Hack #72]. Save this script in your iTunes *Scripts* folder as an applet (set the File Format in the Save As... dialog to Application) and name it *New iPod Playlist from Selection*.

Remember that the continuation character (¬) is used to segment single lines of code so they look better in print; you can omit them in your code if you like.

Make sure your iPod Options are set to "Manually manage tracks and playlists" (if the iPod is set to auto-sync, files might be prevented from being moved) and that your iPod is connected. Select some library tracks in iTunes, and run the script. You will be asked to create a name for the new iPod playlist to which the selected tracks will be copied; optionally, you can skip making the playlist and just leave it at adding the tracks to your iPod library.

Now, fill up that iPod with playlists, and prosper!

—Doug Adams

#84 Change Your Encoder on the Fly ⓂⓈⒸ

Discover the freedom to convert or import selected tracks (whether in your library or on some sort of removable media—excluding your iPod—such as a CD/DVD) using an encoder selected on the fly, without changing your defaults.

I dislike having to visit iTunes Preferences whenever I want to change encoders. On the other hand, I like keeping the AAC encoder as my default encoder. Now I can have it both ways. This AppleScript converts or imports all or just the selected tracks in a playlist using your choice of encoders, restoring your Preferences-set encoder afterwards. You can also send all the new tracks to a new playlist if you like.

The Code

This script allows the user to select from a list of available iTunes encoders and then convert the selected tracks with that encoder. Additionally, the user can decide to copy the tracks to a new playlist, which will be created. When the script has finished, the default encoder will be reinstated.

```
tell application "iTunes"
  activate

  -- miscellaneous variables
  set addenda to "Put converted tracks into new Playlist named...?"
  set my_no_button to "No, Just Convert"
  set movem to false

  -- encoder information
  set myEncoders to name of every encoder
  set encoderBackup to name of current encoder

  set thisPlaylist to view of front window

  -- selected tracks or all tracks in selected playlist
  if selection is not {} then
    set selectedTracks to a reference to selection
  else if thisPlaylist is library playlist 1 then
    my alert_user_and_cancel("You should select some tracks first.")
  else
    set selectedTracks to a reference to ¬
```

```
            (every file track of thisPlaylist whose enabled is true)
        end if

    -- select an encoder to use
    set myNewEncoder to (choose from list myEncoders ¬
        with prompt "Select encoder..." default items ¬
        (encoderBackup as list)) as string
    if myNewEncoder is "false" then error number -128

    repeat
        -- make new playlist for newly encoded tracks?
        set make_new to (display dialog addenda default answer ¬
            "" buttons {"Cancel", my_no_button, "OK"} ¬
            default button 3)

        if button returned of make_new is my_no_button then exit repeat

        if text returned of make_new is not "" then
            set newPlaylistName to text returned of make_new
            set movem to true
            exit repeat
        else
            set addenda to "Enter name for new playlist..."
        end if
    end repeat

    set current encoder to encoder myNewEncoder

    with timeout of 300000 seconds
        repeat with thisTrack in selectedTracks
            try
                set newT to item 1 of (convert thisTrack)

                if movem then
                    if not (exists user playlist newPlaylistName) then
                        set newPlaylist to (make new playlist ¬
                            with properties {name:newPlaylistName})
                    else
                        set newPlaylist to user playlist newPlaylistName
                    end if
                    duplicate newT to newPlaylist
                end if

            on error m number n
                set current encoder to encoder encoderBackup
                if n is -1728 then
                    activate
                    my alert_user_and_cancel("User Canceled.")
                end if
                my alert_user_and_cancel((n as string) & " " & m)
            end try
        end repeat
    end timeout
```

```
    set current encoder to encoder encoderBackup

    if frontmost is true then
        if gave up of (display dialog "Done!" buttons {"Thanks"} ¬
            default button 1 with icon 1 giving up after 300) ¬
            is true then error number -128
    end if
end tell

to alert_user_and_cancel(message)
    tell application "iTunes"
        display dialog message buttons {"Cancel"} ¬
            default button 1 with icon 0
    end tell
end alert_user_and_cancel
```

First, since the applet becomes the frontmost application when it is run, the script tells iTunes to activate to bring it to the front.

Next, some variables that will be used later in the script are initialized. A list of available encoder names for the choose from list box that will appear later is stored in MyEncoders. The name of the current encoder is stored in the encoderBackup variable so that it can be restored when the script is finished. A reference to the selected playlist is also stored in the thisPlaylist variable.

The script determines if there is a selection of tracks and, if so, sets the variable selectedTracks to them. If not, it sets selectedTracks to all the enabled tracks in the selected playlist, unless it is the main library. You don't want to convert all the library tracks, do you? If the main library is selected, an error message will be displayed.

I should point out here that I am using the alert_user_and_cancel( ) handler to display a dialog with an error message and Cancel button, rather than writing a separate display dialog for each error-prone routine.

Next, the script sets the variable myNewEncoder to the result of a choose from list box. The choices in the listbox are the names of the encoders that were stored in myEncoders earlier in the script. The current encoder will be highlighted, as shown Figure 5-15. The result of the listbox will be a string with the name of the encoder we want to use.

Next, if the user wants the converted tracks copied to a new playlist, the variable movem, which was initialized to false at the beginning of the script, will be set to true and the newPlaylistName variable will contain the text the user enters into the text box, as shown in Figure 5-16. The movem variable is a flag that we'll use later. If there's a problem, we loop through the repeat block again.

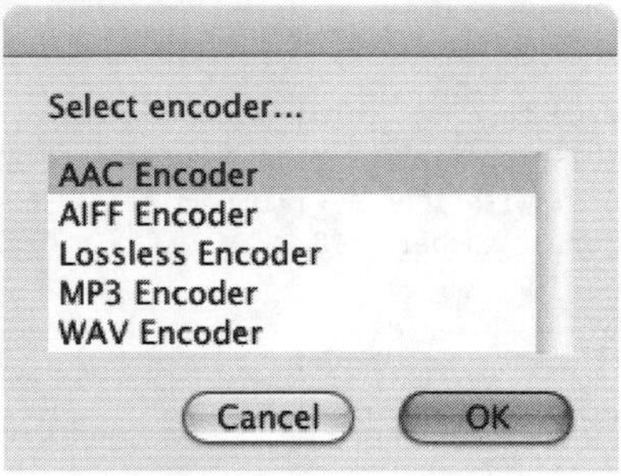

Select encoder...

AAC Encoder
AIFF Encoder
Lossless Encoder
MP3 Encoder
WAV Encoder

Cancel   OK

Figure 5-15. The listbox for choosing an encoder (the AAC Encoder is my current encoder)

Put converted tracks into new Playlist named...?

Cancel   No, Just Convert   OK

Figure 5-16. Entering a name for a new playlist or opting to just leave the tracks in the iPod's main library

Now we are ready to encode. The selected encoder is loaded as the current encoder, and a repeat block loops through each track referenced in selectedTracks.

> I put the repeat loop in a timeout block. This prevents the script from timing out if AppleScript has to wait for any reason.

If the movem variable is true, the converted track will be copied to a new playlist. This playlist is created on the first loop; on subsequent loops, since it already exists, the routine that creates it the first time is skipped.

I've enclosed this portion in a try block to intercept any errors—specifically, the error number -1728 that is generated if the user clicks the X button in the iTunes activity window. This will cancel the script.

Finally, the original encoder is restored and the script displays a Done! dialog.

Running the Hack

Enter the code into Script Editor [Hack #72]. Save this script in your iTunes *Scripts* folder as an applet (set the File Format in the Save As... dialog to Application) and name it *Quick Convert*.

This script targets the selected library tracks or CD tracks, or, if no tracks are selected, all the tracks in the selected playlist. Run the script from the iTunes Scripts menu. It is a script application whose icon will appear in the Dock. Select the encoder you want to use from the listbox, click OK, and the selected tracks will be converted or imported. Afterwards, your Preferences-set encoder will be restored.

Whew. There's a lot going on in this one, but I'd say this is one of my favorite scripts, if only because the alternative—setting and resetting Importing Preferences—is so awkward.

—Doug Adams

HACK #85 Whack the Current Track ⓜⓥⓛ

If you find the currently playing track is a real dud, quickly remove it from iTunes.

When that song you positively can't stand turns up in a Smart Playlist or Party Shuffle and plays, use this AppleScript hack to remove it completely from iTunes and move its file to the Trash.

The Code

This script checks for a current track and gets its database ID and location properties. The track is removed from iTunes' main library, thus removing it from all playlists, and the location property (its file path) is used to move its file to the Trash.

```
tell application "iTunes"
  if player state is not stopped then

    -- dialog is optional
    display dialog "Are you SURE you want to delete " & ¬
      "every copy of the currently playing track?" default button 1

    -- set some variables
    set lib to library playlist 1
    set curP to current playlist
    set theTrack to current track

    -- get some track properties
    set dbid to theTrack's database ID
```

```
      set trackClass to theTrack's class

      -- move to next track before deleting current
      if player state is playing then next track

  -- init theLoc variable
      set theLoc to missing value
      if trackClass is file track then
        set theLoc to theTrack's location
      end if

      -- delete from current playlist
      delete (some track of curP whose database ID is dbid)

      -- delete from iTunes
      try
        delete (some track of lib whose database ID is dbid)
      end try

      set dd_message to "Done. The track has been removed."

      -- if the file exists, move to Trash
      if theLoc is not missing value then
        try
          tell application "Finder" to delete theLoc
          set dd_message to dd_message & ¬
            " Its file has been moved to the Trash."
        on error
          set dd_message to dd_message & ¬
            " However, its file could not be moved to the Trash."
        end try
      end if

      display dialog dd_message buttons {"Thanks"} ¬
        default button 1 with icon 1

  end if
end tell
```

The initial display dialog, shown in Figure 5-17, is optional; it explains that a track is about to be removed and allows you to cancel the script if that isn't what you wanted to do.

If a track is playing or paused, the script sets some variables to references to the main library, the current playlist, and the current track. Otherwise, the script ends.

With references to the current track safely stored, the script will advance to the next track (if iTunes is indeed playing and not just paused) before deleting the current one.

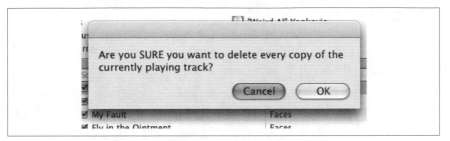

Figure 5-17. An optional warning dialog

Next, the script gets the database ID and class properties of the track. The database ID will identify the track in the main library; the class will determine whether the targeted track is a file track or a URL track. If the track is a file track, its file's file path is retrieved from the location property and assigned to the theLoc variable. Later, we won't try to delete a file if theLoc contains missing value, which it will if the track isn't a file track or if the track's location property itself contains missing value.

Now, the track can be deleted from iTunes. First, I will delete the referenced track from the current playlist, because if our current track is a URL track, it might not be in the main library playlist. Next, I will try to delete the track from the entire library. When a track is deleted from the library playlist, it is also removed from any other user playlists it is in. I'm using the try block because, as I mentioned earlier, it's possible a stream will not be in the library playlist. If my current track isn't in the library playlist, and thus can't be deleted, I don't want any errors.

Finally, if the file of the track exists, the script will move it to the Trash. The success or failure of the operation is reported in the final dialog box, as shown in Figure 5-18.

Figure 5-18. The script, reporting that it's finished

Running the Hack

Enter the code into Script Editor [Hack #72]. Save this script in your iTunes *Scripts* folder as a compiled script (set the File Format in the Save As... dialog to Script) and name it *Whack Current Track*.

While an undesirable track is either playing or paused, run the script. All copies of the track will be removed from iTunes, and its file will be moved to the Trash.

Now, the next time "I Think I Love You" by the Partridge Family comes around again in your Party Shuffle playlist, you'll know what to do.

—Doug Adams

HACK #86   Save Artwork to a Folder ⓂⓈⒷ

Copy the album artwork of a selected track as a JPEG or PNG file to a specified folder.

This hack shows how to export the artwork from an iTunes track as a graphic file and save it to a selected folder, so you can start stockpiling your artwork for safekeeping or for use in other applications.

The Code

This script exports the artwork of the single selected track as a graphic file to a user-specified folder:

```
tell application "iTunes"
  -- get a reference to selected track
  if selection is not {} and (count items of selection) is 1 then
    set theTrack to item 1 of selection
  else
    my alert_user_and_cancel("Please select one track.")
  end if

  -- does selected track have artwork?
  if class of theTrack is not file track or ¬
    artworks of theTrack is {} then
    my alert_user_and_cancel("Selected track has no Artwork.")
  end if

  -- choose folder to save file to
  set artFolder to (choose folder with prompt ¬
    "Where do you want to save Artwork?") as string

  -- get data and format of track's artwork
  try
    set artData to (data of artwork 1 of theTrack) as picture
    set artFormat to (format of artwork 1 of theTrack) as string
```

```
        if artFormat contains "JPEG" then
            set extension to ".jpg"
        else if artFormat contains "PNG" then
            set extension to ".png"
        end if

        -- create name for new file
        set theName to (artist of theTrack & " - " & album of theTrack)

        -- create paths for files
        set tempArtFile to (artFolder & "temp" & extension) as string
        set finalArtFile to (artFolder & theName & extension) as string

        -- make the temp file
        set fileRef to (open for access tempArtFile write permission 1)
        write artData starting at 0 to fileRef as picture
        close access fileRef

        -- shell script copies vitals from temp file to final file,
        -- removes temp file
        do shell script "cd " & ¬
            quoted form of (POSIX path of artFolder) & ¬
            ";tail -c+223 " & ¬
            quoted form of ("temp" & extension) & "> " & ¬
            quoted form of (theName & extension) & ";rm " & ¬
            quoted form of ("temp" & extension)

        -- finished
        if frontmost then
            if button returned of (display dialog ¬
                "Artwork exported" buttons {"Show File", "Thanks"} ¬
                default button 2) is not "Thanks" then
                tell application "Finder"
                    reveal file finalArtFile
                    activate
                end tell
            end if
        end if

    -- report any error and cancel
    on error errM
        close access fileRef
        my alert_user_and_cancel("Unable to export track's Artwork." & ¬
            return & return & errM)
    end try
end tell

to alert_user_and_cancel(message)
    tell application "iTunes" to display dialog message buttons {"Cancel"} ¬
        default button 1 with icon 0
end alert_user_and_cancel
```

First, the script gets a reference to a single selected track and makes sure it contains artwork.

Next, the user is asked to select a folder to which to copy the artwork. The path to the folder is stored in the artFolder variable.

The script determines the format of the artwork, JPEG or PNG (the only graphic formats iTunes supports), so it can establish a file extension. Then, it uses the artist and album names of the selected track to create a file name for the artwork. These elements are used to create a temporary file path and a final file path. The temporary file will be created and will contain all of the artwork's data. However, this file is not a graphic file. There is one more thing to do.

The shell script extracts the appropriate graphic data from the temporary file, copies it to the final file, then deletes the temporary file.

Finally, the script reports it is finished and offers the user the option to view the final file in the Finder.

Running the Hack

Enter the code into Script Editor **[Hack #72]**. Save this script in your iTunes *Scripts* folder as a compiled script (set the File Format in the Save As... dialog to Script) and name it *Save Artwork to Folder*.

Select a single track that contains artwork, and run the script. You will be asked to choose a folder into which the artwork will be exported as a graphic file. When the script has completed, you can select the file in the Finder or simply quit.

> A file in the chosen folder with the same name as the file being created will be overwritten without warning. In the interest of simplicity (and because I presumed that the user will be aware of what artwork has been and is being saved) I did not include a routine that checked for this.

This is a fairly basic hack and works fine as is. But it can also serve as the basis for more complex scripts that export more than one track's artwork or that export artwork to other applications.

I'd like to thank Olivier Hericord for assistance with this hack.

—Doug Adams

Send Current Track Info to iChat Ⓜ︎ⓥ︎Ⓐ

HACK
#87

Set your iChat status message to the name and artist of the currently playing track.

Want to let your iChat Buddies know what you're listening to? This simple hack updates your iChat status message with the Song Name and Artist of the currently playing iTunes track. The information will be visible beneath your name in your iChat correspondents' Buddy Lists.

This script is saved as a *stay-open application*, which, as you might imagine, stays open and running until you tell it to quit, or until some routine in its code executes a quit command.

The Code

This stay-open applet detects when the current track changes. When it does, it gets the name and artist of the current track and then sets the status message in iChat, replacing Available, Away, or Idle. Additionally, when the script is reactivated by clicking it in the Dock, it is reinitialized as if it had been restarted.

```
global curDBID, myIdleTime

-- initialize some variables
on run
  set curDBID to missing value
  set myIdleTime to 10

  if both_apps_are_running() then
    show(current_track_info())
  end if

  return myIdleTime
end run

-- check every 10 seconds
on idle
  if both_apps_are_running() then
    show(current_track_info())
  end if
  return myIdleTime
end idle

-- are iChat and iTunes active?
on both_apps_are_running()
  tell application "System Events"
    set allProcesses to name of every process
    if allProcesses contains "iTunes" or ¬
      allProcesses contains "iChat" then
```

```
            return true
        end if
    end tell
    return false
end both_apps_are_running

-- check for new current track,
-- format and return string for status message
on current_track_info()
    tell application "iTunes"
        if player state is stopped then return false
        if current track's database ID is curDBID then return false

        set curDBID to current track's database ID

        return (current track's name) & ¬
            " by " & (current track's artist)
    end tell
end current_track_info

-- set a new status message in iChat
to show(myStatusMessage)
    if myStatusMessage is false then return
    tell application "iChat" to set status message to myStatusMessage
end show

on quit
    tell application "iChat" to set status message to ""
    continue quit
end quit

on reopen
    run
end reopen
```

I first declare some *global* variables. This is necessary to make sure that these variables have scope throughout the script.

You'll notice the script is broken up into handlers. The run handler, which is executed when the script is first activated, initializes some variables and then executes the both_apps_are_running( ) handler. This handler returns true if both iTunes and iChat are running and permits the show( ) handler to run. The show( ) handler itself takes as a parameter the result of the current_ track_info( ) handler.

Next is the idle handler. This is a special AppleScript handler that runs during system idles—that is, when no activity vital to the operating system is happening. The idle handler also executes the both_apps_are_running( ) handler, which again will allow the show( ) handler to run. The last value returned in an idle handler will be the number of seconds that should pass before the `idle` handler is called again. I've set it to 10 seconds; thus, while the script is running, the `idle` handler will be called every 10 seconds.

The `current_track_info( )` handler determines if the current track has changed by comparing the current track's database ID property to the value of curDBID. If they are not equal, the current track is considered new. Its database ID is then copied to curDBID, and the handler returns a string comprised of the name and artist of the current track. If the current track's database ID and curDBID are the same, the handler is exited straight away. On first running the script, the value of curDBID is `missing value`, so comparing the current track's database ID to curDBID will always return the name and artist string the first time around.

The show( ) handler simply sets iChat's status message property to the string returned by current_track_info( ). My wife can now see what I'm listening to over the network or over the Internet, as shown in Figure 5-19.

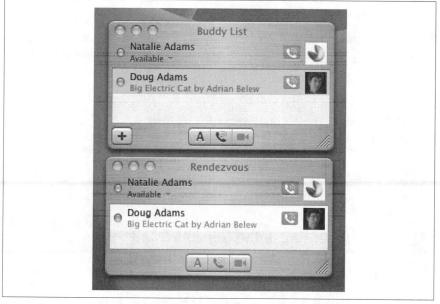

Figure 5-19. Displaying my current track info in iChat

The quit handler gets called when the script receives a message to quit (by clicking Quit in its File menu, Control-clicking/right-clicking on its Dock icon and selecting Quit, etc.). When quit is executed, it sets your iChat status to a blank message. iChat will restore the appropriate Available, Away, or Idle message of its own accord.

The reopen handler is called when the script is reactivated by clicking it in the Dock or double-clicking its icon in the Finder. When reopen is called, it just tells the script to run again, which will initialize the curDBID variable. This can be handy if you want to update your iChat status message immediately.

Running the Hack

Enter the code into Script Editor [Hack #72]. Save this script in your iTunes *Scripts* folder as an applet (set the File Format in the Save As... dialog to Application). Additionally, click on the checkbox next to Stay Open, but leave the other checkboxes unchecked. Name the script *Current Track to iChat Status*.

You can activate this applet from the iTunes Scripts menu or by double-clicking it in the Finder. It will stay running in the background (although its icon will appear in the Dock), periodically checking iTunes and updating iChat's status message with the new Song Name and Artist name whenever the song in iTunes changes.

To quit the applet, activate it and choose Quit from its File menu or press ⌘-Q. Alternatively, you can Control-click/right-click on its icon in the Dock and select Quit from the pop-up menu.

> As of this writing, iChat 2 allows only the first 42 characters of your status message to be displayed in others' Buddy Lists, regardless of the message's actual length. You might want to create a routine that truncates the myStatusMessage string to 42 characters.

—Doug Adams

Rewind or Pause the Current Track ⓜⓧⓛ
HACK #88
Rewind the currently playing track a specified number of seconds and then play, or pause the track.

If you use your iPod for recording and transcribing speeches, lectures, or meetings, you'll appreciate this hack. Import the recording into iTunes, and you can use this script to alternately rewind the current track a specified amount and pause it, making transcription a lot easier.

The Code

The script applet stays running until its reopen handler is called by clicking its icon in the Dock. When the reopen handler is called, it alternates between two actions: rewind the currently playing track seven seconds and then play it, and pause the currently playing track.

```
property secondsToRewind : 7
property iTunes_is_paused : false

on run
  rewindiTunes( )
  set iTunes_is_paused to false
end run

-- every other call to reopen performs one of two tasks
on reopen
  if iTunes_is_paused then
    rewindiTunes( )
    set iTunes_is_paused to false
  else
    tell application "iTunes" to pause
    set iTunes_is_paused to true
  end if
  -- tell application "Some Application" to activate
end reopen

-- handler to rewind the current track
to rewindiTunes( )
  tell application "iTunes"
    if player state is not stopped then
      set pos to player position
      if (pos is greater than secondsToRewind) and ¬
        (pos is less than finish of current track) then
        set player position to pos - secondsToRewind
        play
      end if
    end if
  end tell
end rewindiTunes
```

First, I've initialized some properties so they will have scope throughout the script. The first property, secondsToRewind, is initialized to the number of seconds you want to rewind the current track. The second property, iTunes_is_paused, is a flag that we will initialize to false; the script will reset it to true and then false every other time you activate the script via the reopen handler.

The run handler is executed when the script is first executed. It in turn executes the rewindiTunes( ) handler and then sets the iTunes_is_paused variable to false.

The rewindiTunes( ) handler is the routine that moves the player position of the currently playing track back the number of seconds specified in the secondsToRewind variable that was set earlier and then plays the track. This handler will be called within the reopen handler.

The reopen handler is called whenever you click the script's icon in the Dock. If the iTunes_is_paused property has been set to true (because, as you will see, iTunes will have been paused), the rewindiTunes( ) handler will be called.

If, on the other hand, iTunes_is_paused is false (because you just set it after running the rewindiTunes( ) handler), the script will branch to the else clause, pause iTunes, and reset the iTunes_is_paused property to true. In this way, the first click of the script's icon will rewind and play the track in iTunes, the next click will pause it, the following click will rewind, and so on.

If you know the name of the application you will be using to type your transcription, enter it in the commented-out line in the reopen handler and uncomment the line. This statement will bring your application to the front after you click the applet; you might say it returns focus back to your app. For example, if you are using TextEdit, the statement would need to look like this:

```
tell application "TextEdit" to activate
```

Running the Hack

Enter the code into Script Editor [Hack #72]. Save this script in your iTunes *Scripts* folder as an applet (set the File Format in the Save As... dialog to Application). Additionally, click on the checkbox next to Stay Open, but leave the other checkboxes unchecked. Name the script *Replay Last Bit*.

 The continuation character (¬) is used to segment single lines of code so they look better in print; you can omit them in your code if you like.

When you run this script, its icon appears in the Dock. When you next click on its icon in the Dock, the current track will rewind seven seconds and recommence playing. Click it again and the current track will pause. Click a third time and it will rewind seven seconds and recommence playing. You get the idea.

To quit the applet, activate it and either choose Quit from its File menu or press ⌘-Q. Alternatively, you can Control-click/right-click on its icon in the Dock and select Quit from the pop-up menu.

—Doug Adams

See What Other People Are Listening to ⓜⓧⓛ

Monitor which of your shared iTunes audio files are being played by other machines on your network.

Which of your shared songs are being listened to by other users on the network right now? Run this hack and get the lowdown.

The Code

This script locates your designated *Music* folder and uses the Unix command lsof to list and display the names of files in it that are open. Open files will be the ones that are being accessed by other machines.

```
-- locate Music folder
set xmlFile to "iTunes:iTunes Music Library.xml"
set musicFolder to ""
try
  set musicFolder to ¬
    parse_file((path to music folder as string) & ¬
      xmlFile) as string
end try
if musicFolder is "" then ¬
  set musicFolder to ¬
    parse_file((path to documents folder as string) & xmlFile)

-- get open files in Music folder
set song_list to paragraphs of ¬
  (do shell script "readout= lsof +D " & ¬
    (musicFolder as string) & ¬
    " | grep [mp3,m4p,m4a]; echo -n $readout;")

-- format list of shared files for display
try
  repeat with i from 1 to (count of song_list)
    set item i of song_list to ¬
      extract_data_from(item i of song_list)
  end repeat
on error m
  display dialog "No songs being shared right now." buttons ¬
    {"Cancel"} default button 1
end try

-- display shared songs
choose from list song_list with prompt ¬
  "Currently sharing:" with empty selection allowed

on extract_data_from(song_string)
  log song_string
  set AppleScript's text item delimiters to "/"
  set fnom to (text item -1 of song_string)
```

```
    set artist to (text item -3 of song_string)

    set AppleScript's text item delimiters to "."
    set fnom to (text item -2 of fnom)

    set song_string to ("•" & fnom & " by " & artist)

    set AppleScript's text item delimiters to ""
    if song_string's length is greater than 60 then
      set song_string to text 1 thru 60 of song_string & "..."
    end if
    return song_string
  end extract_data_from

  to parse_file(thePath)
    return (do shell script "grep '>Music Folder<' " & ¬
      (quoted form of POSIX path of thePath) & ¬
      " | cut -d/ -f5- | cut -d\\< -f1 | sed 's/%20/ /g'")
  end parse_file

  on replace_chars(txt, srch, repl)
    set saveD to AppleScript's text item delimiters
    set AppleScript's text item delimiters to the srch
    set the item_list to every text item of txt
    set AppleScript's text item delimiters to the repl
    set txt to the item_list as string
    set AppleScript's text item delimiters to saveD
    return txt
  end replace_chars

  on text_to_list(txt, delim)
    set saveD to AppleScript's text item delimiters
    try
      set AppleScript's text item delimiters to {delim}
      set theList to every text item of txt
    on error errStr number errNum
      set AppleScript's text item delimiters to saveD
      error errStr number errNum
    end try
    set AppleScript's text item delimiters to saveD
    try
      log ("theList: " & theList)
    end try
    return (theList)
  end text_to_list
```

The script needs to locate the user's designated *Music* folder. This is the folder set in iTunes's Advanced Preferences that presumably contains all the user's audio files. The file path to this folder can be discovered from the *iTunes Music Library.xml* file, so the script first needs to locate this file. Most often, it is available in the */Users/username/Music/iTunes* folder. However, some older installations of iTunes in OS X will have this file in the */Users/username/Documents/iTunes* folder. The script checks both of these locations.

Once the *iTunes Music Library.xml* file is located, the script parses it for the file path to the designated *Music* folder.

Next, knowing the file path to the *Music* folder, the script executes a Unix shell script that looks for any open MP3, M4A, or M4P files in the *Music* folder. The result of the do shell script statement will be returned as a list of file paths as strings delimited by carriage returns. The script then parses each file path for the artist name and the file's name (sans the extension) and then displays them in a choose from list box, as shown in Figure 5-20.

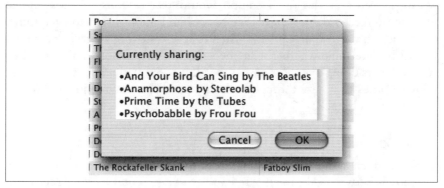

Figure 5-20. Currently open files, presented in a listbox

Note that choosing a song and clicking the OK button does nothing; the list-box is just convenient for display purposes.

Running the Hack

Enter the code into Script Editor [Hack #72]. Save this script in your iTunes *Scripts* folder as an applet (set the File Format in the Save As... dialog to Application). Name the script *What Are People Listening To?*.

 You don't have to put this script in your iTunes *Scripts* folder. Since it is an AppleScript application, you can run it by double-clicking on it wherever you place it. However, you might find it most convenient to run from your iTunes Scripts menu.

When you run the script, it will check to see which files in your *Music* folder are open and therefore which are being played by other networked users. Note, however, that this script might at times return slightly inaccurate results, because another user's iTunes on the network will have completed buffering the audio information from your file before the song actually finishes playing. In such cases, the file will no longer be open, and the script will not report that the file is being shared.

I'd like to thank Michael Hoffman for his assistance on this hack.

—Doug Adams

HACK #90   Play Snippets of Each Track in a Playlist

Sample a section of each track in a specified playlist.

Back in my early radio days (in the early 1980s, before CDs!) the DJs and Music Director at the radio station would receive tons of promotional albums from record companies. We never had time to listen to everything. So, typically, we'd sit around and listen to a few seconds of each track on a record to determine whether it fit the sound of the station. This would be referred to as doing a *needle drop* on the album. Similarly, here's a hack that allows iTunes to breeze through a playlist of tracks, playing just a few seconds from each track.

The Code

This stay-open applet gets a number from the user to be used as the number of seconds between calls to an idle handler that executes a next track command, thus playing each track in the selected playlist for the specified number of seconds:

```
global needle_drop_interval

on run
  -- get number of seconds
  set needle_drop_interval to get_a_number("")

  -- play first song in the playlist
  tell application "iTunes"
    play view of front window
  end tell
  return needle_drop_interval
end run

-- idle routine is called
on idle
  tell application "iTunes" to next track
  return needle_drop_interval
end idle

-- handler to get a number from user
to get_a_number(addenda)
```

```
    set myNumber to text returned of (display dialog "" & ¬
      addenda & "Play each track for how many seconds?" default answer ¬
      "" buttons {"Cancel", "OK"} default button 2)
    try
      return (myNumber as integer)
    on error
      get_a_number("Enter only numbers..." & return & return)
    end try
  end get_a_number

  on quit
    tell application "iTunes" to stop
    continue quit
  end quit
```

I've defined the needle_drop_interval variable as global to make its scope scriptwide.

The run handler sets the needle_drop_interval variable to the result of the get_a_number_handler( ) **[Hack #75]**. This number is used as the interval in seconds between calls to the idle handler. The script then starts playing the selected playlist in iTunes. When the idle handler is called, it simply executes a next track command.

The quit handler is called when the user quits the script. I've included the statement to stop iTunes playing in the quit handler. Otherwise, if you stop iTunes manually before quitting the applet, the applet will still continue playing the next track. This wouldn't be a bad thing, just messy.

Running the Hack

Enter the code into Script Editor **[Hack #72]**. Save this script in your iTunes *Scripts* folder as an applet (set the File Format in the Save As... dialog to Application). Check the Stay Open checkbox, but leave the other checkboxes unchecked. Name the script *Needle Drop*.

Run the script by selecting it in iTunes's Scripts menu or by double-clicking on it in the Finder. It will ask how many seconds of each track you want played, then will proceed to play each for that amount of time.

To quit the applet, activate it and either choose Quit from its File menu or press ⌘-Q. Alternatively, Control-click/right-click on its icon in the Dock and select Quit from the pop-up menu.

For extra points, add a routine that skips 30 seconds into each track, fades up on the track as it starts, and then fades down before the next track routine kicks in.

—Doug Adams

HACK
#91
Make Files Bookmarkable

Change the file type of your imported AAC files to make them bookmarkable.

If you make your AAC tracks bookmarkable, they will start playing right where you left off last. This simple hack makes any selected AAC files bookmarkable.

This hack works only on AAC files you have imported your-self. It does not work on protected AAC files purchased from the iTunes Music Store.

The Code

This script gets the location property of each selected track and, if the track is an AAC file, uses the location in a Finder routine that changes the file type of the file to M4B.

This is not the same as changing the extension of the file. The file type is an internal property of the file.

```
tell application "iTunes"
  if selection is {} then
    display dialog "No tracks selected." buttons {"Cancel"} ¬
      default button 1 with icon 2
  end if

  set sel to selection

  repeat with aTr in sel
    if kind of aTr is "AAC audio file" then
      my set_type(get location of aTr)
    end if
  end repeat

  display dialog "Done!" buttons {"Thanks"} default button 1
end tell

to set_type(loc)
  tell application "Finder"
    try
      set file type of loc to "M4B "
    end try
  end tell
end set_type
```

If there is a selection of tracks, the selection is stored in the sel variable. The repeat block loops through each track referenced in sel. On each loop, if the referenced track's kind is AAC audio file, it is passed to the set_type( ) handler. The set_type( ) handler executes a Finder routine that changes the file's file type to "M4B " (notice that M4B is followed by a space in the file type). This file type is recognized by iTunes as being *bookmarkable*. I used a try block just in case some problem with the file prevents its file type from being set, in which case that file will be skipped and no error will be reported.

Running the Hack

Enter the code into Script Editor [Hack #72]. Save this script in your iTunes *Scripts* folder as a compiled script (set the File Format in the Save As... dialog to Script) and name it *Make Bookmarkable*.

Select some AAC tracks in iTunes and run the script. Each track will be bookmark-enabled.

—Doug Adams

HACK #92 Search the iTunes Music Store for the Current Song

Search the iTunes Music Store using info from the currently playing track.

You can search the iTunes Music Store (iTMS) using the handy link arrows associated with each track in the library. But this AppleScript hack lets you search the iTMS for the currently playing song, even if it's playing from a stream.

The Code

The script gets tag info from the currently playing track and displays it in a listbox so the user can choose which tags to use as search criteria. The script then affixes the chosen data to a URL, which is sent to iTunes.

```
-- get info from current track
tell application "iTunes"
  if player state is not stopped then
    if class of current track is not URL track then
      tell current track to set {alb, art, nom, com} to ¬
        {album, artist, name, composer}
    else
      if current stream title is not "" then
        set {art, nom} to my text_to_list(current stream title, " - ")
        set {alb, com} to {"", ""}
      else
        display dialog "Can't get data from stream." buttons ¬
          {"Cancel"} default button 1 with icon 0 giving up after 30
      end if
```

```
        end if
    else
      display dialog "No track currently playing." buttons {"Cancel"} ¬
        default button 1 with icon 0 giving up after 30
    end if
end tell

-- build list to display in choose from list box
set theOptions to {"Song:" & tab & nom, "Artist:" & tab & art, ¬
  "Album:" & tab & alb, "Composer:" & tab & com}

-- display choose from list box
set searchOpts to (choose from list theOptions with prompt ¬
  "Select search terms:" OK button name ¬
  "Search iTMS" default items {} ¬
  with multiple selections allowed) as string
if searchOpts is "false" then error number -128

-- base search string
-- (remove the continuation characters!)
set searchStr to ¬
  "itms://phobos.apple.com/WebObjects/MZSearch.woa/¬
wa/advancedSearchResults?"

-- build search string URL
if searchOpts contains "Song:" then set searchStr to searchStr & ¬
  "songTerm=" & replace_chars(nom, " ", "%20") & "&"
if searchOpts contains "Artist:" then set searchStr to searchStr & ¬
  "artistTerm=" & replace_chars(art, " ", "%20") & "&"
if searchOpts contains "Album:" then set searchStr to searchStr & ¬
  "albumTerm=" & replace_chars(alb, " ", "%20") & "&"
if searchOpts contains "Composer:" then set searchStr to searchStr & ¬
  "composerTerm=" & replace_chars(com, " ", "%20") & "&"

-- send to iTunes
open location searchStr

on replace_chars(txt, srch, repl)
  set AppleScript's text item delimiters to the srch
  set the item_list to every text item of txt
  set AppleScript's text item delimiters to the repl
  set txt to the item_list as string
  set AppleScript's text item delimiters to ""
  return txt
end replace_chars

on text_to_list(txt, delim)
  set saveD to AppleScript's text item delimiters
  try
    set AppleScript's text item delimiters to {delim}
    set theList to every text item of txt
  on error errStr number errNum
    set AppleScript's text item delimiters to saveD
```

```
        error errStr number errNum
    end try
    set AppleScript's text item delimiters to saveD
    return (theList)
end text_to_list
```

If iTunes is not stopped (that is, if it is playing or paused), the script gets the name, artist, album, and composer info from the current track object. If the current track is a stream and the streamer is sending the info correctly, the script just gets the name and artist of the track. The info obtained is displayed in a listbox from which the user can select which tags to use in a search of the iTunes Music Store, as shown in Figure 5-21.

Figure 5-21. Selecting which of the current track's tags to use for a search of the iTunes Music Store

The result of the choose from list statement is stored in the searchOpts variable. It will contain a list of keywords and properties. The script checks for each keyword in searchOpts and adds the corresponding property to searchString. The script also converts any spaces to hexadecimal %20 using the replace_chars() handler.

Finally, the searchString is sent to the iTunes Music Store using the open location command. iTunes receives the result because the URL begins with the itms: protocol.

Running the Hack

Enter the code into Script Editor [Hack #72]. Save the script in your iTunes *Scripts* folder as a compiled script (set the File Format in the Save As... dialog to Script) and name it *Search iTMS for Current Song*.

While a song is playing in iTunes, run the script. It will present you with a listbox from which you can choose the current Song Name, Artist, Album, and Composer. If you are listening to a stream and the song data is available (at the discretion of the streamer), just the Song Name and Artist will be listed. Select which piece of track data you want to use as search criteria and click Search iTMS. Results will be displayed in the iTunes Music Store.

This hack is especially rewarding when you discover a really great song you've never heard before coming down from a stream, or when you want to check out the rest of an artist's catalog.

—*Doug Adams*

## CHAPTER SIX

Beyond iTunes
Hacks 93–100

iTunes is an awesome piece of software but, believe it or not, it doesn't do everything. For example, iTunes can't help you stream your music over the Web [Hack #95] or share your music with your friends via iDisk [Hack #97].

Or sometimes iTunes does too much, and you'd rather just play your music without any of its various whistles and bells. If you're a Unix-savvy Mac user, you might want to play music from the command line [Hack #93] or otherwise hack it from the Terminal [Hack #94].

Got some old records lying around that you want to digitize [Hack #99]? Care to create your own audiobook [Hack #100]? If you're looking to do more with your music than iTunes offers, then this chapter is for you.

At the very least, everyone needs to back up their music collection [Hack #98], which requires moving beyond iTunes.

HACK #93 Play MP3 and AAC Files from the Command Line ⓜⓦⓛ

With qtplay, you can play your music files from the Terminal, without opening iTunes.

There are times when you might want to listen to music without launching iTunes. If you prefer the minimal and fast interface of the Terminal, or if your system resources are being stretched too thin, you might want to consider qtplay. If you are a Unix power user, qtplay's command-line interface will appeal to your geeky side. qtplay is a Unix executable (sometimes referred to as a *binary*): a small program accessed via the Terminal. With qtplay, you can listen to any music file you can play via QuickTime, and that set includes every type of file iTunes can play.

To use qtplay you'll need to take a few steps away from the OS X interface (and a few strides into the land of the Terminal). Once the short journey is complete, you'll be listening to your CDs or music libraries via the resource-light Terminal. You'll also get some familiar functionality: you can play audio CDs, randomize tracks, control the volume, and listen to a playlist. Except for fast-forward and rewind (you have to listen to whole songs, even the boring parts), you'll get all the functionality you expect of any decent music player.

Here's what you'll need for this hack:

- Some music files (anything QuickTime can handle is fine, including the protected AAC file format)
- A willingness to poke about in the Terminal
- A copy of qtplay from rainbowflight software (*http://home.earthlink.net/ ~rainbowflight/*; free)

Before you can enjoy command-line control of your music, you need to install qtplay. This is no willy-nilly installation. The first thing you have to do is make a choice: do you want to allow systemwide access, meaning that all accounts can use qtplay, or do you want to restrict access to specific accounts? Let's take a close look at the systemwide install (the process is the same for specific users; only the destinations differ).

Once you've downloaded the software, open the qtplay folder to find the qtplay program icon.

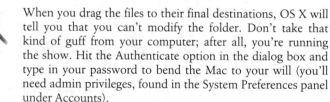

> When you drag the files to their final destinations, OS X will tell you that you can't modify the folder. Don't take that kind of guff from your computer; after all, you're running the show. Hit the Authenticate option in the dialog box and type in your password to bend the Mac to your will (you'll need admin privileges, found in the System Preferences panel under Accounts).

Now, drag the icon to the */bin* folder. The complete path is *<harddrive>/usr/ local/bin* (substitute the name of your hard drive for *<harddrive>*).

Once the qtplay application is safely ensconced, you'll want to put the manual (man) file where it needs to be. Once properly installed, this file will allow access to the qtplay manual from the Terminal (type qtplay man for all the qtplay info you'll ever need). Follow the same basic installation procedure as for the qtplay binary. The only difference is the final destination, which in this case is the */man1* folder. The complete path is as follows: *<harddrive>/usr/local/man/man1*.

If you desire single-user access, repeat these procedures, changing the destination to the intended user's home folder (you know, the one that looks like a house in the Finder window). Alternatively, you can do all the moving from the Terminal. If you're going to be playing music from the Terminal, using it to move a few files is great practice.

Open up a new Terminal shell, type mv (be sure to add a space after the v), and drag the qtplay binary to the %. This autocompletes the path. On my computer, the result looks like Figure 6-1.

```
Welcome to Darwin!
[Chris-Seibolds-Computer:~] chris% mv /Users/chris/Desktop/qtplay\ Folder/qtplay []
```

Figure 6-1. The Terminal autocompleting the path of a dragged folder

Now type the destination (in this case, /bin) for a command line that resembles Figure 6-2.

```
Welcome to Darwin!
[Chris-Seibolds-Computer:~] chris% mv /Users/chris/Desktop/qtplay\ Folder/qtplay ~/bin/[]
```

Figure 6-2. The destination path

Hit Return, and you're done.

Repeat the process for the man file (qtplay.1). The command line should look nearly identical, but when typing be sure to enter qtplay.1 (not just qtplay), and the destination should be ~/man/ instead of ~/bin/.

That's it as far as the hard and grungy work goes; the rest is system resource–light music-listening nirvana. Open a new Terminal shell (when you launch Terminal a new shell opens) and type qtplay. If you don't hear any music, it is most likely because qtplay looks for files only in the current directory. To remedy this, type cd ~/Music/ and hit Return. This changes the directory (cd) to your home folder (~) and tells the Terminal to look at your *Music* folder (remember, capitalization matters when using the Terminal) Type qtplay once again and hit Return. All the files in your music folder (likely, all your music files) will be played in order.

Of course, just playing one song after another lacks a little flexibility, so qtplay features several commands to adjust the order, play specific files, randomize the entire process, and so on. I won't list all of these commands here, but you can always type qtplay man in the Terminal to get the full scoop. To help get you started, Table 6-1 lists a few of the more commonly used commands. Remember that these commands are typed directly into the Terminal.

Table 6-1. Frequently used qtplay commands

Action	Command
Play files in current directory	Qtplay
Play all audio CDs	qtplay -cd
Play files (plays files in the order given)	qtplay /Volumes/Audio\ CD/ file.mp3 file2.mp3
Play files in randomized order (plays a random file, then another random file)	qtplay -Z file.mp3 file2.mp3
Play files shuffled and looped (plays each file once in a random order, then loops and plays each file once in a different random order)	qtplay -l -z file.mp3 file2.mp3
Play all of your music in random-ized order	qtplay -r -Z ~/Music/
Play one random song	qtplay -r -1 ~/Music/
Play files (playlist)	/bin/ls /Volumes/Audio\ CD/* > playlist.txt qtplay -f playlist.txt
Play files (playlist), alternate method	/bin/ls /Volumes/Audio\ CD/* | qtplay -
Play files (playlist) in shuffled order, keeping symphonies intact	/bin/ls /Volumes/Audio\ CD/Track\ 0[1-4].cdda > symphony1.txt /bin/ls /Volumes/Audio\ CD/Track\ 0[5-8].cdda > symphony2.txt qtplay -z symphony1.txt symphony2.txt

There's more to learn about qtplay, but there's plenty of information in this hack to get you started listening to your music without the desktop-cluttering iTunes interface. The added bonus is that while everyone can use iTunes, you'll be one of the few who can control the music coming out of your computer using just a few keystrokes.

—*Chris Seibold*

HACK #94 Manipulate Audio Using the Terminal ⓜⓢⓛ

iTunes isn't the only way to encode your CDs. With Mac OS X, you can get to the heart of Unix to rip in alternative encoders such as LAME.

One of the greatest advantages of Apple's OS X operating system is its Unix core. Unix is a flexible environment (once you learn how to use it) that lets you get your hands dirty and solve problems when other applications fall short. While I love iTunes' powerful "jukebox" environment, I wish it allowed more options when it comes to audio encoding. The LAME encoder (*http://lame.sourceforge.net*; free) is the Internet standard for quality MP3 encoding.

In the Usenet MP3 groups, you will find LAME in much wider use than any other codec, and your ears will hear the difference. Once I realized what I was missing by using the iTunes encoder, I set out to make using LAME easier.

Most command-line audio tools (such as the FLAC and LAME encoders) are designed to be used on only one file at a time, which makes batch processing tricky. A simple Unix shell script seemed the obvious solution to this problem. All big problems start small, however, and after I had written my batch LAME encoding script, I realized there were lots of little problems that I needed to solve in order to make CD archiving a more pleasant experience.

What began for me as a simple hack for batch encoding CDs and setting ID3 tags turned into a suite of programs aimed at streamlining the handling of MP3 and FLAC files from the command line. I chose the LAME (LAME Ain't an MP3 Encoder) and FLAC (Free Lossless Audio Codec: *http://flac.sourceforge.net/*; free) encoders, in part because they are both distributed under a version of the GNU General Public License (*http://www.gnu.org/licenses/licenses.html*), which keeps their development out in the open and ensures that end users are given rights to change the programs if they like. There are many advantages to both of these encoders, but audio quality and openness are chief among them.

Here, then, are eight scripts to make your audio life easier:

lameit
> Rips CDs to MP3 format using LAME

flacit
> Rips CDs to FLAC format

id3hack
> Uses the filename to set a track's name and number in its ID3 tag

vchack
> Creates a Vorbis comment for a FLAC file using the *id3hack* script

vctool
> Borrows the *id3tool* interface to set Vorbis comments in FLAC files

vcid3
> Converts Vorbis comments in FLAC files to ID3 tags in MP3 files

flacmp3
> Converts FLAC files to MP3 files

striptoc
> Reformats a cdrdao-generated table of contents file for use with FLAC files

There are, of course, some binaries that you need in order to make these scripts work. I recommend you install them using fink (*http://fink. sourceforge.net*) or darwinports (*http://darwinports.opendarwin.org/*), or compile them by hand and put them in your *$HOME/bin* directory:

- *cdrdao* (*http://cdrdao.sourceforge.net*; for *striptoc* only)
- *flac* (*http://flac.sourceforge.net*; for *flacit* and *flacmp3*):
- *id3tool* (*http://nekohako.xware.cx/id3tool*; for *id3hack* and *vcid3*)
- *lame* (*http://lame.sourceforge.net*; for *lameit* and *flacmp3*)
- *metaflac* (*http://flac.sourceforge.net*; for *flacmp3*, *vchack*, *vctool*, and *vcid3*)

To install each of these using fink, simply type:

```
% fink install <package-name>
```

Some packages might not be available under fink, or fink might use an out-dated version, and you might need to compile the executable yourself. Instructions for doing this can be found on each program's web site and in the *README* file included with the source archive. Compilation usually involves running a *configure* script, followed by the make command. I recommend placing the compiled binaries in either */usr/local/bin* (for system-wide use) or *$HOME/bin* (if you are not the system administrator or don't want to share the utilities with other users).

lameit

The first script uses LAME to rip a CD to the current directory. This process works best if you first set the CD metadata in iTunes. The easiest way to do this is to get the information from the Gracenote CDDB automatically by selecting Get CD Track Names from the Advanced menu in iTunes. If the CDDB information is incorrect, you can then edit it by hand within iTunes. Once you've done that (you might have to eject and reinsert the CD to make sure the info is updated), you're ready to start ripping.

The code. Type the following script and save it to a file called *lameit* in your *$HOME/bin* directory:

```
#!/bin/sh
#
# lameit - rip a cd to lame-encoded mp3s
#
if [ "$1" ]
then
  for file in "$1"/[1-9]\ *.aiff
  do
```

```
      if [ -e "$file" ]
      then
        lame -h -m s -b 192 "$file" "O$(basename "$file" .aiff).mp3"
      else
        echo >&2 "No appropriate files exist in directory: "$1""
        exit 1
      fi
  done
  for file in "$1"/[1-9][0-9]\ *.aiff
  do
    if [ -e "$file" ]
    then
      lame -h -m s -b 192 "$file" "$(basename "$file" .aiff).mp3"
    fi
  done
else
  echo >&2 "Usage: "$(basename "$0")" /path/to/cd"
  exit 1
fi
```

The script simply checks for appropriate *.aiff* files (with the track number followed by a space in the filename) and encodes each one using LAME. In this case, the encoding is with a 192k constant bitrate, stereo.

Running the hack. Make the script executable by opening the Terminal application (*/Applications/Utilities/Terminal*) and typing the following on the command line:

```
% chmod +x lameit
```

You can then run the script this way:

```
% lameit /path/to/cd
```

Replace */path/to/cd* with the path to the CD you're interested in, which can be found in the */Volumes* directory.

You can modify the LAME command line in the script to suit your needs. Type lame --help in the Terminal for some guidelines on encoding options.

flacit

The next script does the same thing, but with FLAC, a lossless encoder, instead of LAME.

The code. Type the following script and save it to a file called *flacit* in your *$HOME/bin* directory:

```
#!/bin/sh
#
# flacit - rip a cd to flac format
#
if [ "$1" ]
```

```
then
  for file in "$1"/[1-9]\ *.aiff
  do
    if [ -e "$file" ]
    then
      flac \
        --force-raw-format \
        --endian=little \
        --sign=signed \
        --channels=2 \
        --sample-rate=44100 \
        --bps=16 \
        --skip=20 \
        --output-name="0$(basename "$file" .aiff).flac" \
        "$file"
    else
      echo >&2 "No appropriate files exist in directory: "$1""
      exit 1
    fi
  done
  for file in "$1"/[1-9][0-9]\ *.aiff
  do
    if [ -e "$file" ]
    then
      flac \
        --force-raw-format \
        --endian=little \
        --sign=signed \
        --channels=2 \
        --sample-rate=44100 \
        --bps=16 \
        --skip=20 \
        --output-name="$(basename "$file" .aiff).flac" \
        "$file"
    fi
  done
else
  echo >&2 "Usage: "$(basename "$0")" /path/to/cd"
  exit 1
fi
```

Running the hack. Make the script executable by opening the Terminal application (*/Applications/Utilities/Terminal*) and typing the following on the command line:

```
% chmod +x flacit
```

You can then run the script this way:

```
% flacit /path/to/cd
```

Replace */path/to/cd* with the path to the CD you're interested in, which can be found in the */Volumes* directory.

You can modify the FLAC command line in the script to suit your needs. Type flac --help in the Terminal for some guidelines on encoding options.

id3hack

Next comes the question of labeling the files. I use *id3tool* (*http://nekohako. xware.cx/id3tool/*) to slap together ID3 tags before importing them into iTunes, because otherwise they get lost in my collection. *id3tool* works fine for labeling the artist, album, year, and genre, but setting the track number and song title can become tedious, so I whipped this little hack.

> This hack works only if the files are named with the two-digit track number followed by its name—for example, *04 And Here We Test Our Powers of Observation.mp3*, *01 Moondance.mp3*, or *05 500 Miles.mp3*. You can specify as many files as you want on the command line. I usually just use the *.mp3 wildcard.

The code. Type the following script and save it to a file called *id3hack* in your *$HOME/bin directory*:

```
#!/bin/sh
#
# id3hack - add track names and numbers to id3 tags
#
if [ "$1" ]
then
  for file
  do
    if [ -e "$file" ]
    then
      id3tool \
        --set-title="$(echo "$file" | sed 's/...\(.*\)\.mp3/\1/')" \
        --set-track="$(echo "$file" | sed 's/\(..\).*/\1/')" \
        "$file"
    else
      echo >&2 "No such file: "$1" -- skipping."
    fi
  done
else
  echo >&2 "Usage: "$(basename "$0")" INPUTFILE [...]"
  exit 1
fi
```

I used the Unix utility sed to extract the track name and number from the filename and set them as tags with *id3tool*. Of course, the script first checks to make sure that the files that you've given on the command line actually exist.

Running the hack. Make the script executable by opening the Terminal application (*/Applications/Utilities/Terminal*) and typing the following on the command line:

```
% chmod +x id3hack
```

You can then run the script by navigating to the directory containing the files you want to edit and typing:

```
% id3hack *.mp3
```

I used a wildcard here to apply to every MP3 file in the current directory, but I also could have supplied the filenames for each MP3 file. Either way, make sure the files exist in your current directory.

vchack

This is the same script as *id3hack*, except that it creates Vorbis comments for FLAC files instead of ID3 tags for MP3s.

 This script uses *metaflac*, a tool for editing FLAC metadata that is included with FLAC.

The code. Type the following script and save it to a file called *vchack* in your *$HOME/bin* directory:

```sh
#!/bin/sh
#
# vchack - add track names and numbers to flac files
#
if [ "$1" ]
then
  for file
  do
    if [ -e "$file" ]
    then
      metaflac \
        --set-vc-field=TITLE="$(echo "$file" |
          sed 's/...\(.*\)\.flac/\1/')" \
        --set-vc-field=TRACKNUMBER="$(echo "$file" |
          sed 's/\(..\).*/\1/' |
          sed 's/0\(.\)/\1/')" \
        "$file"
    else
      echo >&2 "No such file: "$1" -- skipping."
    fi
  done
else
  echo >&2 "Usage: "$(basename "$0")" INPUTFILE [...]"
  exit 1
fi
```

Again, this script is similar to *id3hack*. It uses sed and metaflac to pick apart the filename and assign pieces of it to metadata tags within the file.

Running the hack. Make the script executable by opening the Terminal (*/Applications/Utilities/Terminal*) and typing the following on the command line:

```
% chmod +x vchack
```

You can then run the script from the directory containing the files you want to edit by typing the following:

```
% vchack *.flac
```

I used a wildcard here to apply to every FLAC file in the current directory, but I also could have supplied the filenames for each FLAC file. Either way, make sure the files exist in your current directory.

vctool

Vorbis comments can be tricky to work with. Out of frustration, I wrote a script that brought the *id3tool* interface over to the world of Vorbis comments and FLAC. Type vctool -h at the command line to get usage information.

The code. Type the following script and save it to a file called *vctool* in your *$HOME/bin* directory:

```
#!/bin/sh
#
# vctool - set vorbis comments in flac files
#
if [ "$1" ]
then
  while getopts t:a:r:y:g:c:h option
  do
    case "$option" in
      t) TITLE="--set-vc-field=TITLE="$OPTARG"";;
      a) ALBUM="--set-vc-field=ALBUM="$OPTARG"";;
      r) ARTIST="--set-vc-field=ARTIST="$OPTARG"";;
      y) DATE="--set-vc-field=DATE="$OPTARG"";;
      g) GENRE="--set-vc-field=GENRE="$OPTARG"";;
      c) TRACKNUMBER="--set-vc-field=TRACKNUMBER="$OPTARG"";;
      h) echo ""$(basename "$0")" <options> <filename>"
         echo " -t WORD Sets the title to WORD"
         echo " -a WORD Sets the album to WORD"
         echo " -r WORD Sets the artist to WORD"
         echo " -y WORD Sets the date to WORD"
         echo " -g WORD Sets the genre to WORD"
         echo " -c WORD Sets the track number to WORD";;
    esac
  done
```

```
    shift $((OPTIND - 1))
    for file
    do
      if [ -e "$file" ]
      then
        for var in "$TITLE" "$ALBUM" "$ARTIST" "$DATE" "$GENRE" "$TRACKNUMBER"
        do
          if [ "$var" ]
          then
            metaflac "$var" "$file"
          fi
        done
      else
        echo >&2 "No such file: "$file" -- skipping."
      fi
    done
  else
    echo >&2 "Type "$(basename "$0")" -h for help."
    exit 1
  fi
```

In this script, each argument that you supply invokes a new instance of the program *metaflac*. I tried to make the script pass the arguments together to each file in one command but couldn't get it to work without *metaflac* assigning blank metadata tags. While the method used here is not ideal, it work's just fine; consider it a lazy hack.

Running the hack. Make the script executable by opening the Terminal application (*/Applications/Utilities/Terminal*) and typing the following on the command line:

```
% chmod +x vctool
```

Assigning metadata becomes much easier with *vctool*. Here is an example:

```
% vctool
Type vctool -h for help.
% vctool -h
vctool <options> <filename>
  -t WORD    Sets the title to WORD
  -a WORD    Sets the album to WORD
  -r WORD    Sets the artist to WORD
  -y WORD    Sets the date to WORD
  -g WORD    Sets the genre to WORD
  -c WORD    Sets the track number to WORD
% vctool -r "Archie Shepp" -a "Attica Blues" -y 1972 -g Jazz *.flac
```

Now, we've assigned artist, album, year, and genre metadata to every FLAC file in the current directory. That's a lot easier than typing this:

```
% metaflac --set-vc-field=ARTIST="Archie Shepp" *.flac
% metaflac --set-vc-field=ALBUM="Attica Blues" *.flac
% metaflac --set-vc-field=DATE=1972 *.flac
% metaflac --set-vc-field=GENRE=Jazz *.flac
```

vcid3

The *vcid3* script converts Vorbis comments to ID3 tags.

The code. Type the following script and save it to a file called *vcid3* in your
$HOME/bin directory:

```
#!/bin/sh
#
# vcid3 - convert vorbis comments to id3 tags
#
if [ -e "$1" ]
then
  if [ -e "$2" ]
  then
    TITLE="$(metaflac --show-vc-field=TITLE "$1" |
      sed 's/TITLE=\(.*\)/\1/')"
    ARTIST="$(metaflac --show-vc-field=ARTIST "$1" |
      sed 's/ARTIST=\(.*\)/\1/')"
    ALBUM="$(metaflac --show-vc-field=ALBUM "$1" |
      sed 's/ALBUM=\(.*\)/\1/')"
    TRACK="$(metaflac --show-vc-field=TRACKNUMBER "$1" |
      sed 's/TRACKNUMBER=\(.*\)/\1/')"
    YEAR="$(metaflac --show-vc-field=DATE "$1" |
      sed 's/DATE=\(.*\)/\1/')"
    GENRE="$(metaflac --show-vc-field=GENRE "$1" |
      sed 's/GENRE=\(.*\)/\1/')"
    if [ "$GENRE" ]
    then
      id3tool --set-genre-word="$GENRE" "$2"
    fi
    id3tool \
      --set-title="$TITLE" \
      --set-artist="$ARTIST" \
      --set-album="$ALBUM" \
      --set-track="$TRACK" \
      --set-year="$YEAR" \
      "$2"
  else
    echo >&2 "No such file: "$2""
    echo >&2 "Usage: "$(basename "$0")" FLACFILE MP3FILE"
    exit 1
  fi
else
  echo >&2 "No such file: "$1""
  echo >&2 "Usage: "$(basename "$0")" FLACFILE MP3FILE"
  exit 1
fi
```

This script avoids the resource fork issues of *vctool*, because *id3tool* does not
assign blank tags. Rather, it simply leaves off tags that contain the empty
string.

Running the hack. Make the script executable by opening the Terminal application (*/Applications/Utilities/Terminal*) and typing the following on the command line:

```
% chmod +x vcid3
```

To use the script, navigate to the directory containing the files you want to edit and simply supply the name of the FLAC file (containing the relevant metadata) and the name of the MP3 file (which will have the metadata assigned to it) on the command line:

```
% vcid3 "02 If You Want Me To Stay.flac" "02 If You Want Me To Stay.mp3"
```

flacmp3

Here's the way to get from FLAC to MP3 in one easy step. The script outputs the MP3 files to your current directory, but the FLAC files needn't be in your current directory.

 This script performs the metadata conversion (without *id3tool*) side by side with the format conversion, so you won't need to do that separately.

The code. Type the following script and save it to a file called *flacmp3* in your *$HOME/bin* directory:

```
#!/bin/sh
#
# flacmp3 - convert a flac file and its tag data to mp3/id3 format
#
if [ "$1" ]
then
  for file
  do
    if [ -e "$file" ]
    then
      flac -c -d "$file" |
      lame -h -m s -b 192 \
        --tt "$(metaflac --show-vc-field=TITLE "$file" |
          sed 's/^TITLE=\(.*\)/\1/')" \
        --ta "$(metaflac --show-vc-field=ARTIST "$file" |
          sed 's/^ARTIST=\(.*\)/\1/')" \
        --tl "$(metaflac --show-vc-field=ALBUM "$file" |
          sed 's/^ALBUM=\(.*\)/\1/')" \
        --ty "$(metaflac --show-vc-field=DATE "$file" |
          sed 's/^DATE=\(.*\)/\1/')" \
        --tn "$(metaflac --show-vc-field=TRACKNUMBER "$file" |
          sed 's/^TRACKNUMBER=\(.*\)/\1/')" \
        --tg "$(metaflac --show-vc-field=GENRE "$file" |
          sed 's/^GENRE=\(.*\)/\1/')" \
```

```
          - "$(basename "$file" .flac).mp3"
      else
        echo >&2 "No such file: "$file" -- skipping."
      fi
    done
  else
    echo >&2 "Usage: "$(basename "$0")" FLACFILE [...]"
    exit 1
  fi
```

I love this script. In one step, it performs a complete format conversion, including metadata, and it can do so on any number of files that you specify, even wildcards. Once again, sed to the rescue!

Running the hack. Make the script executable by opening the Terminal application (*/Applications/Utilities/Terminal*) and typing the following on the command line:

```
% chmod +x flacmp3
```

This script takes in FLAC files and spits out MP3 files. If you've assigned metadata to a FLAC file (using *vctool*, for example), it carries that information over to the MP3:

```
% flacmp3 *.flac
```

That's all it takes to do the job.

striptoc

Lastly, here's a script that takes a *cdrdao* table of contents (TOC) file and strips away all the unnecessary information in the file. *cdrdao* (*http://cdrdao. sourceforge.net*) is used for reading and writing raw CD data from the command line. Its most useful feature is its plain-text TOC files, which can be used to extract pregap information from source CDs. But the TOC files presume a single, huge data file, which is a really inconvenient way to archive a CD. This awk script takes a listing of FLAC files from the current directory and substitutes them for the track data file.

> You'll have to decompress your FLACs before burning, of course.

The code. Here's an example of the *striptoc* script in action, using a CD that contains only two tracks:

```
% ls
01 So Long Eric.flac  02 Praying With Eric.flac  Town Hall Concert.toc
% cat "Town Hall Concert.toc"
CD_DA
```

```
// Track 1
TRACK AUDIO
NO COPY
NO PRE_EMPHASIS
TWO_CHANNEL_AUDIO
FILE "data.wav" 0 17:48:03

// Track 2
TRACK AUDIO
NO COPY
NO PRE_EMPHASIS
TWO_CHANNEL_AUDIO
FILE "data.wav" 17:48:03 27:31:27
START 00:00:49

% striptoc "Town Hall Concert.toc" > "Town Hall Concert.toc.new"
% cat "Town Hall Concert.toc.new"
CD_DA

TRACK AUDIO
FILE "01 So Long Eric.wav" 0

TRACK AUDIO
PREGAP 00:00:49
FILE "02 Praying With Eric.wav" 0

% mv "Town Hall Concert.toc.new" "Town Hall Concert.toc"
%
```

As you can see, the file generated by *cdrdao* also explicitly states several
defaults for each file. This script throws that information out, as well as any
ISRC codes and catalog information (which this CD doesn't have). Here's
the script that does all the work:

```
#!/usr/bin/awk -f
#
# striptoc - Reformat cdrdao toc files for use with individual track files.
#
BEGIN { print "CD_DA\n" }
{ FS = "\n"; RS = ""
  if ($2 == "TRACK AUDIO") {
    print $2
    if ($NF ~ /^START/) {
      sub(/^START/, "PREGAP", $NF)
      print $NF
    }
    FS = " "; RS = "\n"
    "ls *.flac" | getline file
    sub(/flac$/, "wav", file)
    print "FILE \"" file "\" 0\n"
  }
}
```

awk can be harder to follow than a shell script, but basically, this script creates a new TOC file based on the pregap information given in the original file and the listing of *.flac* files in the current directory. It doesn't do any checks on the data beforehand, though, so make sure everything is in order before you run the script.

Running the hack. This AWK script sends its output to standard output, so you need to tell it where to put the newly generated file, and then (optionally) move that file back on top of the old file:

```
% striptoc Karma.toc > Karma.toc.new
mv Karma.toc.new Karma.toc
```

Final Thoughts

I hope you find these scripts useful. I think they really demonstrate the power and flexibility of Unix's programmer-friendly environment. Hopefully, they will inspire you to write scripts of your own to solve your little everyday problems.

—Chris Roose

HACK
#95 Stream Your Music Collection over the Web Ⓜ Ⓦ Ⓛ

Sure, an iPod can hold an awful lot of music, but can it hold your entire music collection? Probably not. Here's how to access your full iTunes library from any computer.

For the briefest period of time, Apple allowed iTunes users to stream their music over the Internet. Due to the bad intentions of a few, who took this as a chance to also share their music via P2P, Apple promptly plugged the Internet-sharing hole. Now iTunes users are limited to streaming music via Rendezvous, which works only within a local area network (LAN). .Mac members can still stream MP3 files to friends over the Internet using iDisk [Hack #97], but what about non–Mac users, or Mac users who don't have .Mac accounts?

This hack frees your music, allowing you to stream your tunes over the Internet and control them from any web browser. It won't let other people download your music (that would be illegal—tsk, tsk) but it will let others listen to your tunes. Of course, since this is all about you, the best use of this hack is to stream your music from home to work.

Turning Your Computer into a Music Server

Head on over to Slimp3.com and download the server software appropriate for your operating system (*http://www.slimp3.com/su_downloads.html*; free). The SlimServer software is available for Mac OS X, Linux, and Windows, and if you're feeling hackerific, you can even download the Perl source code.

Follow the included instructions for installing the SlimServer software. It's pretty straightforward.

To stream your songs over the Internet, you are going to need a broadband connection. Sorry, all you wacky modem users out there, but a telephone modem simply won't be able to stream the large amounts of data held within digital music files.

If you have a broadband connection, you need to open your machine to the outside world. Don't worry; this doesn't involve placing your computer on the front porch. If your computer is connected directly to a broadband modem, all you have to do is open the appropriate ports so that they're available to outside computers.

On a Mac, go to System Preferences → Sharing and click on the Firewall tab. If you have turned on Personal Web Sharing in the past to allow the outside world to view a web site you have designed and placed in your *Shared* home folder, this panel will look familiar to you. SlimServer operates out of port 9000. Since this isn't a preset port in OS X, you need to create a new setting. Click New and enter 9000 in the Port Number, Range or Series field. For Port Name, select Other from the pull-down menu and then enter Slim. Hit OK, and you're done! Your Mac's port 9000 is now open to the outside world.

If you are on a PC running Windows XP, navigate to your Control Panel and select Network Connections. Right-click on your connection and select Properties. Choose the Advanced tab. If your Internet Connection Firewall isn't enabled, go ahead and check the box now, and then click on Settings.... Under the Services tab, click Add..., give the SlimServer service a name under Description of service, enter your computer's name or IP address, and then enter 9000 in the two Port fields. After setting up this new service, make sure to activate it by checking its box.

If your machine's broadband connection is shared by a router such as Apple's AirPort or a Linksys router, follow the router's instructions for opening port 9000 on the router. Since a router includes a firewall, you have to open the port on it and on your computer.

The Mysterious IP Address

Every computer has a unique IP address. Unless you have paid extra, your IP address is dynamic (and it isn't possible to buy static IPs from many ISPs). From every few hours to every few days, your IP address will simply change. This isn't convenient, but fortunately there are many free services out there that allow you to assign your machine a proxy IP address.

One such service is DynDNS.org (*http://www.dyndns.org/services/dyndns/*). Follow the instructions on the site for signing up (which is a quick process). Make sure you select Dynamic DNS. You can choose from the following domain names:

blogdns.com	*game-server.cc*	*is-a-geek.com*
blogdns.net	*gotdns.com*	*is-a-geek.net*
blogdns.org	*gotdns.org*	*is-a-geek.org*
dnsalias.com	*homedns.org*	*isa-geek.com*
dnsalias.net	*homeftp.net*	*isa-geek.net*
dnsalias.org	*homeftp.net*	*isa-geek.org*
dynalias.com	*homeftp.org*	*kicks-ass.net*
dynalias.net	*homeip.net*	*kicks-ass.org*
dynalias.org	*homelinux.com*	*merseine.nu*
dyndns.biz	*homelinux.net*	*mine.nu*
dyndns.info	*homelinux.org*	*myphotos.cc*
dyndns.org	*homeunix.com*	*serveftp.net*
dyndns.tv	*homeunix.net*	*erveftp.org*
dyndns.ws	*homeunix.org*	*shacknet.nu*
game-host.org		

You get to pick a prefix that will be attached to the domain name. Let's say you want *mymusicrocks* with *homelinux.net*. Your URL (assuming it isn't taken yet) will be *mymusicrocks.homelinux.net*.

Now that you have signed up with DynDNS, you need to download a small client application that will automatically update DynDNS whenever your IP address changes. You can find clients for all operating systems at *http://www.dyndns.org/services/dyndns/clients.html*. Follow the specific instructions for your OS, and you'll be on your way.

Accessing Your Music

Now that you have a static IP address thanks to DynDNS.org, you can access your music from any web-enabled computer. To do so, simply go to a web browser, enter the URL you signed up with at DynDNS.org, and add the port number to the end of the colon. Your URL should look something like this: http://*whateveralias.net*: 9000. If everything is working, you should see a SlimDevices web page similar to Figure 6-3.

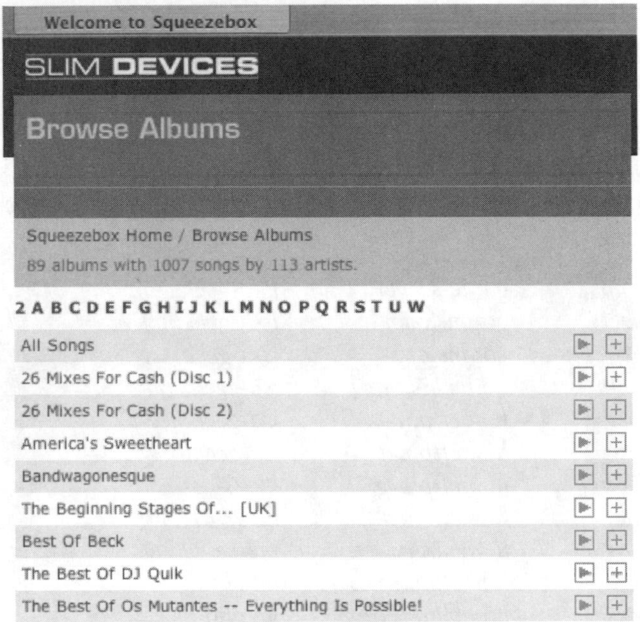

Figure 6-3. *Your music on the Web via Slim Devices*

This web page is being served by the computer on which you installed Slim-Server. You can now browse and play all your iTunes playlists and songs from a remote machine.

HACK #96   Make a Custom Mix CD

Digital tools allow you to do cool analog things too! With the right tools, you can make some fly mix CDs.

Back in the good old days, creating mix tapes was the popular thing to do. You've probably created a mix for your car or for the gym, or maybe you've made a mix tape for your girlfriend or boyfriend. When making the mix, you'd carefully choose each song, searching for the best transitions possible. Then, you would spend hours making the tape jacket (carefully crafted of cut-out pictures from magazines and transparent tape). With iTunes, you can create your very own musical masterpieces again, but this time you'll use a CD. Using iTunes's built-in print feature, you can print jewel case covers, but what if you want to take your package to the next level? Let's get mixing!

Creating the Playlist

You need to create a playlist if you want to burn a mix CD with iTunes. The following steps show how to set up a playlist so that it is ready to burn your mix CD.

Creating a new playlist. To create a new playlist in iTunes, select New Playlist in the File menu or type Control-N (⌘-N on a Mac). A file named Untitled Playlist will appear in the Source menu.

Naming your playlist. Once you create a new playlist, it will appear highlighted, allowing you to name it. At any time, you can rename this playlist by clicking the name in the Source folder. Make sure you name your playlist before burning your disc. The playlist name will become the name of your CD (see Figure 6-4), so if someone plays it on a computer, that is the name they will see.

Figure 6-4. A new playlist

Saving songs to your playlist. Filling your playlists is easy. First, select your library in the Source menu. All your encoded songs will be listed. Simply click and drag the songs from the library window over to your playlist, as shown in Figure 6-5. Voila! Your songs are now saved into your playlist.

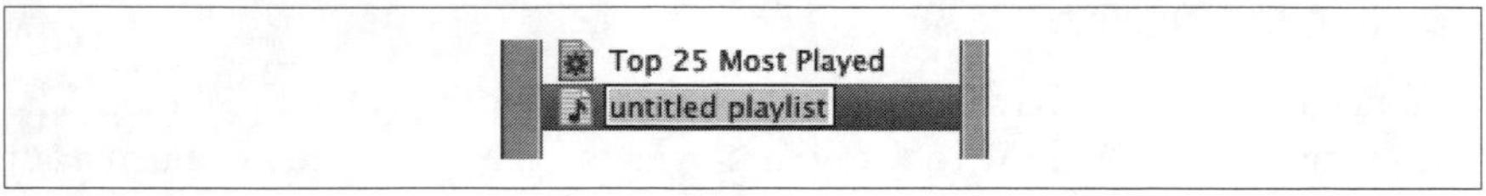

Figure 6-5. *Dragging and dropping your songs from your library onto the playlist*

Keep an eye on the bottom of the playlist window. iTunes displays the number of songs, total running time, and total disc usage here. Most CD-Rs have a capacity for 74 minutes of audio and approximately 650 MB of data. There are some that now offer 80 or 90 minutes of audio (or, in iTunes parlance, 1.2 or 1.3 hours). Your playlist must fall within both numbers (time and MB) in order to record in its entirety. If your playlist exceeds either, you will receive an alert message directing you to remove some songs.

Completing your playlist. After you have saved all your song choices to the playlist, it's time to put on the finishing touches before you burn the CD. Select your playlist in the Source menu, and you will see all of your song selections listed. To change the order, click on the Song Name column and click and drag the songs to your desired order. Now, you're ready to burn!

Songs that are listed in your playlist will still also remain in your library. This, however, does not mean that the song is duplicated. Songs listed in your playlist are merely aliases/ shortcuts that refer to the songs in your library. Any song deleted from your library will in turn not be available for your playlists, although deleting a song from your playlist will not erase the song from your library (unless you choose to do so).

Burning Your Mix to CD

Choosing the songs for your mix was the hard part. Burning the CD is the easy part. Let's first discuss CD-R media. CD-Rs (blank, recordable CDs) are now extremely affordable, especially when purchased in bulk. I prefer buying CD-Rs in spindles of 50 or 100 to truly maximize the bulk savings. In addition, I purchase unbranded, silver-coated CDs (unbranded because it eliminates the chance of the CD maker's logo showing through my CD label, and silver because the CDs I burn do not warrant the professional-quality sound that gold-coated CDs provide). Most office supply, computer, and electronic stores sell CD media. However, I have always found better savings and greater selection online. For one of the best places to buy CD media online, check out American Digital (*http://www.am-dig.com*).

Setting your preferences. iTunes offers a few options for burning CDs. select iTunes → Preferences to access iTunes's Preferences panel. Then, select the Burning option.

Preferred Speed

Your options will depend on your burner. Selecting Maximum Possible will ensure that your CD will burn in the least amount of time. Selecting this setting will not affect the sound quality.

Disc Format

For this hack, we will select Audio CD. The final product will be playable in most audio CD players.

 iTunes also gives you the option of burning an MP3 CD. These CDs will play in MP3 CD players and most computers. When burning MP3 CDs, all ID3 tags are preserved and you are bound only by the disc space limitation. This means that depending on the length of your songs, you could possibly fit eight full albums' worth of music on one disc. But be warned, if your playlist for an MP3 CD is over the disc space limit, iTunes will not alert you.

Gap Between Songs

This setting is a matter of preference. The selected time will determine how much blank space will be inserted between songs. I prefer two seconds. If you are producing a mix CD that you want to play like a nonstop DJ performance, select "none." You can also choose to activate cross-fading between songs.

Use Sound Check

With this setting turned on, iTunes will make sure every song in your playlist will be the same volume. This is a useful option for mixes that contain audio from a diverse number of sources (e.g., songs, interviews, movie clips, sound effects, etc.).

Burning. Click the Burn Disc button in the top-right corner of the iTunes window. You'll see a message that says "Please insert a blank disc." Insert a blank disc and click the Burn Disc button.

Creating CD Labels

So, you've burned your mix. Now what? Well, with the help of precut adhesive CD labels, you can design, print, and affix professional-looking labels for your CD.

With Neato's DiscLabel Neato Edition CD/DVD Labeling System (*http://www.neato.com*; $39.95; free trial available), you have everything you need: software, adhesive CD label sheets for your printer, and a label applicator.

 It is extremely important that the CD label is affixed perfectly centered. A label just a tad off-center can cause the CD to wobble when spinning in a CD player, thus making a pulsating racket or even damaging the CD player. In addition to Neato's applicator, the CD Stomper is a great option.

To create your very own personalized full-color CD labels with your iTunes playlist, follow these steps:

1. Press the Template function button.

2. Select "disclabel Templates" from the Category menu and click on the design to preview it. If you would like to create your own design, click the cross button.

3. Select a template you like and press New Design from Template.

4. Enter a name for your new design in the Design List.

5. Press the iTunes Import button and select your playlist, as shown in Figure 6-6.

6. Press "Assign to Selected Design," and your playlist will be flowed into your template.

Figure 6-6. Importing the track names from your iTunes playlist

Here are a few things to consider when designing your CD label:

• If you plan on including a CD jacket with your CD, you should consider using imagery that relates to each other. This will ensure continuity in the complete package. For instance, if you are making a mix CD about your dog, Spike, you might put a picture of Spike wagging his tail on the CD label and then a picture of Spike chewing a rawhide on the CD jacket.

• If you do not plan on a CD jacket, it's important to list all song names on the CD label.

- When making a mix that contains more than one disc (a two-disc set, perhaps) you should clearly mark one disc 1 and the other disc 2 (and so on). This will ensure that the right CD is put in the CD player.

Finally, use the Neato CD Label Applicator to make sure your label is perfectly centered on your CD. Simply peel off the CD label from the sheet, place it adhesive side up on the applicator, put your CD face down onto the label, and push down.

The Final Touch: CD Covers and Tray Liners

Now that you have designed, printed, and applied a label to your mix CD, it's time to talk about the packaging. If you are designing for a jewel case, Neato's DiscLabel software makes it easy again. Simply select the CD cover icon in the Edit section, as shown in Figure 6-7, or the CD trayliner icon, as shown in Figure 6-8.

Figure 6-7. Neato's cover design tool

All the song information imported from your iTunes playlist is available to set into the template. If you want a more custom solution, use a design program such as Adobe Photoshop, Adobe Illustrator, or QuarkXPress.

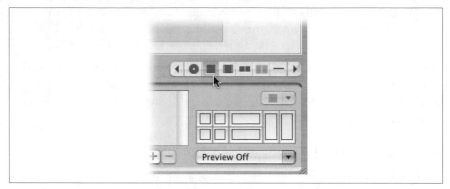

Figure 6-8. Neato's trayliner tool

Plastic jewel cases are the standard when it comes to CD packaging. But this is *your* mix. You have the freedom to create whatever you like. Jewel cases have the advantages of fitting in all CD racks and being inexpensive, but they are also very brittle and traditional. Other options include slimline cases, clamshell cases, and trigger CD cases. Check out Uline (*http://www.uline.com*) for a good selection.

Listening to digital music is good and all, but sometimes you want to give someone an old-school mix CD. It's kind of like getting a letter in the mail. With this hack, you have the tools you need to make mix CDs to your heart's content.

—Gregory Ng

Stream Your Music via iDisk ◍◍◍

If you want to share a favorite song quickly and easily with a friend, this hack is for you. Using .Mac's iDisk, you can make your tunes available to anyone over the Internet.

Using iDisk, you can stream MP3 files (but not AAC files) over the Internet. Friends won't be able to download songs from your iDisk, but they will be able to listen to them. Want to share a mix of your favorite tunes or your latest GarageBand creation with friends? Don't bother burning a CD (although, if you do, make sure to check out "Make a Custom Mix CD" **[Hack #96]**). Instead, all you have to do is copy them over to your iDisk and email your friends a URL.

For this hack, you need to be a .Mac member. Apple no longer gives out free iDisk access. Mount your iDisk in the Finder either by clicking on the iDisk icon in your Finder window or by going to Go → iDisk → My iDisk. Your iDisk will now mount in the Finder. Alternately, if you are on Windows XP, you can download the iDisk Utility (*http://www.mac.com/1/idiskutility_download.html*) and use it to load your iDisk into Windows Explorer, so that you can navigate to it like any other Windows folder.

Copy any songs you want to include into your iDisk's *Site* folder. Your iDisk comes with 100 MB of storage (which you can upgrade to up to 1 GB). Depending on what you already have stored on the disk (and the bit rate at which your MP3s will rip), you will be able to copy over a maximum of approximately two hours of music.

Once you've copied over the files, other people can access the music by entering the following URL in their browsers:

```
daap://homepage.mac.com/your.mac username/mp3 filename
```

When they click Enter, iTunes will open up and your song will start streaming. Just like that, your friend is listening to your MP3!

The key to this hack is the Digital Audio Access Protocol (DAAP), which Apple developed specifically for sharing iTunes music over a network. If you have ever used Rendezvous sharing over a network, DAAP is what makes it tick. To use this streaming protocol, you enter daap instead of http as the Internet protocol.

As long as your files are on your iDisk, they can be accessed over the Internet. If you want to share more than an album or two or want to stream your entire digital collection from your home computer to your work machine, check out "Stream Your Music Collection over the Web" **[Hack #95]**.

Back Up Your Digital Music Collection Ⓜ Ⓦ Ⓛ

HACK #98

Hard drives don't last forever, so it's best to start thinking now how you can safely back up your digital tunes.

So, you've got your 1,000-CD collection ripped to your computer, as well as the 100 or so songs you've purchased from the iTunes Music Store. Your CDs have now all been given away or sold for a buck a piece (if you're lucky) to a secondhand CD store. You are all digital, all the time! Good for you—until your hard drive decides to bite the dust. All that work converting your CDs and all those songs purchased are as good as gone. This hack will help you prepare for the inevitable. Hard drives do crash, and when they do, you want to make sure you have your music backed up somewhere safe.

The first decision you need to make is what media to use. Backing up to CD-Rs, DVDs, and a hard drive each has its advantages and disadvantages. Blank CDs are great because they are very cheap; however, they hold only approximately 650 MB of data. DVDs hold more data (up to 4.5 GB) but are more expensive and burn at a much slower rate than CDs. A typical CD burner can burn at 10–50X, whereas a DVD burner maxes out at 2X. An external hard drive is super-fast but is more costly. The best way to make your decision is to look at the size of the music collection you are backing up. Only have 20 GB on your computer? Then either blank CDs or DVDs are probably the way to go. If your collection is 100 GB or more, you might want to consider purchasing an external FireWire, IEEE1394, or USB 2.0 hard drive. The time you save will more than make up for the cost of the hard drive.

Regardless of the media you choose, you have to figure out a way to get all of your music transferred. If you purchase a hard drive, this is easy; simply plug it in and drag and drop your music folder onto the new hard drive. Wait for the files to copy over, and you are done! You might want to consider keeping the hard drive at a different location than your computer, such as at the office, just in case something physical happens to your computer (fire, flood, a child pouring juice over it, etc.).

If you choose to back up to CDs or DVDs, it helps to use some kind of backup software that will do the job automatically. Yes, you can back up to CDs using iTunes, but the process is arduous at best. You have to create a playlist, drag the songs to that playlist, and then hit Burn. It might not sound difficult, but what if you want to back up a serious amount of music? This is where some third-party software comes to the rescue.

Good backup software will do something called *disk spanning*. This means that if you have 10 GB of music to back up and you want to burn it to CDs, the software will automatically figure out how many CDs are needed and will prompt you to insert each CD throughout the burning process. Both PC and Mac users have many options available, including shareware applications. Check VersionTracker (*http://www.versiontracker.com*) for any number of options. For the PC, you can use Handy Backup (*http://www. handybackup.com*; $30; 30-day trial). Macintosh users might want to use Apple's Backup application, which is included with a .Mac membership (*http://www.mac.com/1/iTour/tour_backup.html*). Dantz also makes a great cross-platform product, Restrospect (*http://www.dantz.com*; $129.99), that you might want to consider, particularly if you also want to back up your hard drive documents on a regular basis.

On the Mac

When you launch Dantz Retrospect, the main window pops up, as shown in Figure 6-9. You have four main options: Backup, Restore, Duplicate, and Archive. To back up to a series of CDs or DVDs select Backup.

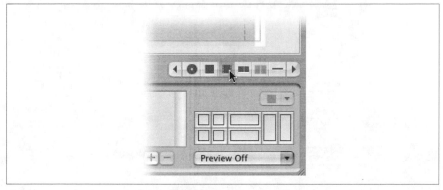

Figure 6-9. The Main window in Retrospect

Here, you name your backup project and select a type. Since in this case we are doing a straightforward backup, click the Backup button. The Backup Set Creation dialog pops up, as shown in Figure 6-10. Choose to back up to a hard drive or CD/DVD. If you select CD/DVD, Retrospect figures out the number of CDs or DVDs you need, based on the amount of data (in this case, music) you have to back up.

Retrospect then prompts you to select a *source folder* (the folder from which it should copy files). By default, iTunes keeps its music in an *iTunes Music* folder within the *Music* folder in your home directory. Even though you are backing up to CDs or DVDs, Retrospect needs to create a document in which to keep data about your backup, not your backup itself. Hit Save to let it save this *backup set*.

Click the Start button to get things rolling. Retrospect prompts you to insert a disc, spends a few minutes burning and verifying the disc, and then ejects the disc and asks for another. Shampoo, rinse, and repeat until all your music is backed up.

While feeding Backup or Retrospect CD after CD or DVD after DVD (you should be cursed with so much music!) might seem rather tedious, at least the program takes care of all the rest for you.

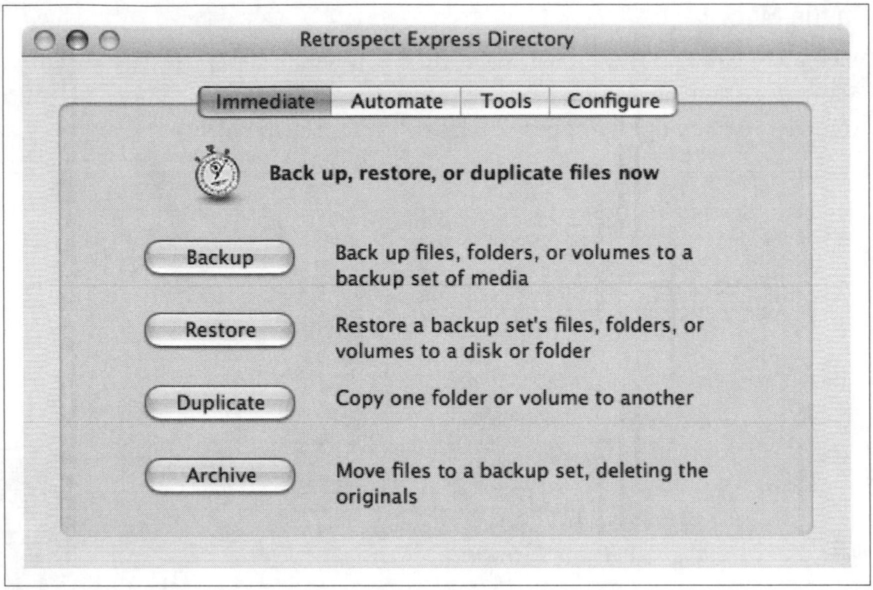

Figure 6-10. The Backup Set Creation dialog

On Windows

Let's take a look at backing up with Handy Backup on the PC, which conveniently comes with a 30-day demo period. When you launch the application, a New Item Wizard window pops up, as shown in Figure 6-11.

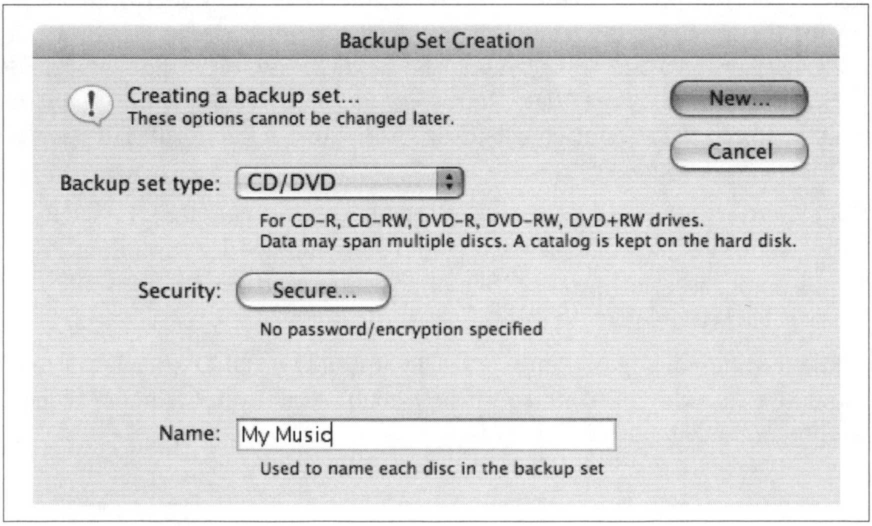

Figure 6-11. Naming the backup project and selecting the item type (in this case, we are doing a backup)

You'll need to tell Handy Backup which folder to back up, as shown in Figure 6-12. Navigate to your topmost folder and select the *iTunes Music* folder. If you aren't sure where your music is kept on your hard drive, you can find out by going to iTunes Preferences → Advanced. Handy Backup will automatically include all subfolders.

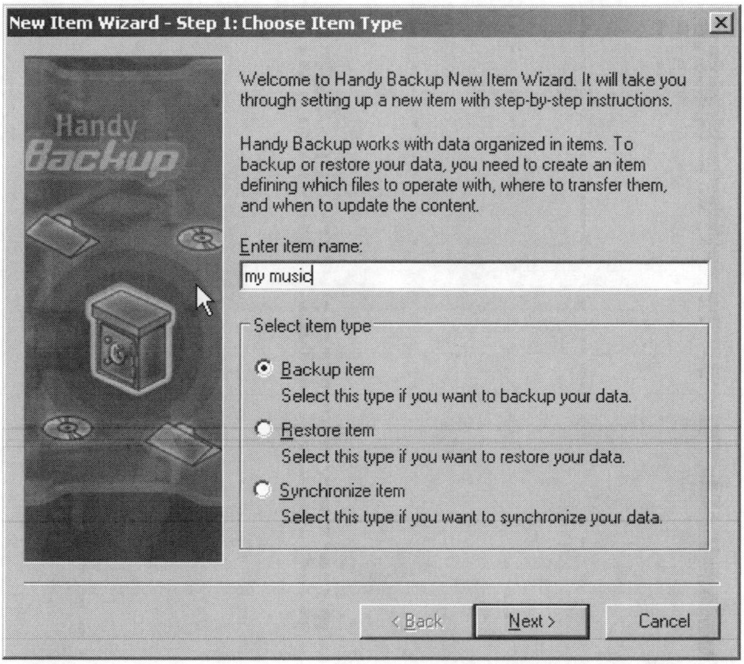

Figure 6-12. Selecting the folders you want to back up

In the next window, you can select where you want to back up to, as shown in Figure 6-13. If you want to back up to another hard drive or another machine on your network, select Local/LAN. Although you probably don't want to, you can also back up to an FTP server. For this backup, we are going to back up to CDs. We are now finished with setting up a project in Handy Backup.

All we need to do to execute the backup is select our project in the main Handy Backup window, as shown in Figure 6-14, and click the Execute button (the blue arrow). Handy Backup will prompt you to insert the CDs one by one.

Doing your backup this way will save a ton of time. Instead of having to manually figure out how much can fit on each CD, you are letting the software do the work for you.

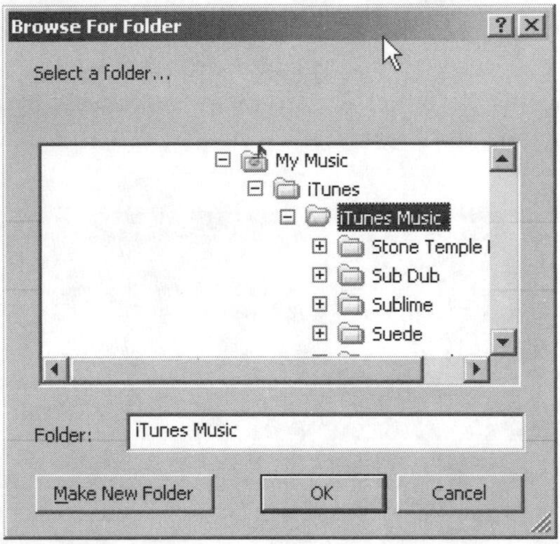

Figure 6-13. Selecting where to back up your music

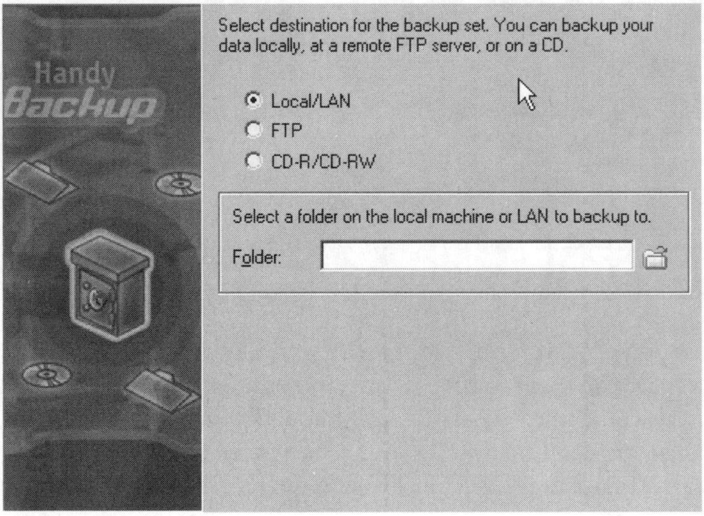

Figure 6-14. The primary interface window for Handy Backup

Whether you back up to CDs, DVDs, or another hard drive, make sure you back up! If you don't, those iTunes music purchases will be literally worthless if your hard drive crashes.

Get Your Record Collection into iTunes ⓂⓌⓁ

HACK #99

Are your old records collecting dust, now that you've gone digital? You can digitize your old records (remember those?) for playback in iTunes and on your iPod.

So, you've already digitized your CD collection [Hack #55], but what if you have old records that you'd like to play on your computer or your iPod? Many of music's greatest albums have been resampled, digitized as CDs, and eventually ripped as AACs for purchase from the iTunes Music Store (iTMS). But what about that favorite album that hasn't caught up to the digital age? Some of my favorite jazz albums are not available on CD, let alone on the iTMS. If only there were a way to import that vinyl into iTunes....

And indeed there is, thanks to the combination of a dongle called the Power-Wave USB Audio Interface and Desktop Amplifier with a piece of software called FinalVinyl.

Connecting

First, connect your old turntable to your computer. I use the PowerWave USB Audio Interface *http://www.griffintechnology.com/products/powerwave/*; $99.99). This little beauty is more than an integrated desktop amplifier that lets you connect a set of home speakers to your computer. It lets you archive records and tapes to MP3/MP4, enables you to record instruments or voice into your computer, and can act as a standalone amplifier for your iPod.

Turntables require preamplification and a special equalization curve. You will need to run your turntable through a receiver/amplifier before connecting to the PowerWave. Any old amplifier will do, including the receiver that powers your current stereo. If you don't have a receiver, just go to RadioShack and pick up a cheap one; nothing fancy is needed for this hack. I recommend RadioShack's RCA® SA-155 Mini Stereo Amplifier ($59.95).

Connect your turntable to your receiver/amplifier, and connect that in turn to the PowerWave by plugging in an RCA cable from the receiver/amplifier's audio out port to the PowerWave's RCA in port. Connect the PowerWave to your computer using the supplied USB cable. Power-on the PowerWave by plugging in the supplied AC power adapter, and you're goin' vinyl.

There are other ways to record your LPs to iTunes. One option is to run an RCA cable from the audio out port of your stereo amplifier to the audio in port of your computer and use the audio recording software listed in the following section. You can also record your records using a consumer-audio CD burner hooked up to your stereo system and then rip the newly created CDs in iTunes [Hack #55].

Recording

Now that all the hardware is good to go, it's time to get the software up and running so you can begin to create some MP3s/AACs. A number of audio recording programs are available for PCs, the best being PolderbitS Sound Recorder and Editor 3.0 (*http://www.polderbits.com*). In this hack, we'll focus on a tool for the Mac, FinalVinyl. The procedures are similar whether you're using a different tool for the Mac or one for the PC.

FinalVinyl for Mac OS X. FinalVinyl (*http://www.griffintechnology.com/software/software_imic.html*) is a Mac application that comes right along with the PowerWave on the accompanying CD. It is an audio recording and editing program that is specifically designed to work with the PowerWave. FinalVinyl can record any analog source, including records. It also includes a handy-dandy 10-band equalizer and waveform-based editing.

With FinalVinyl, you can actually skip the intermediary preamplifier and connect your turntable directly to the Power-Wave unit.

Install and launch FinalVinyl, as shown in Figure 6-15. Start your turntable playing and click FinalVinyl's Preview button to hear the music being played through your computer's speakers. Adjust the Input slider in the FinalVinyl control panel up or down until you are satisfied with the volume for your recording.

Once you are satisfied with the input level, cue up your record (i.e., put the needle at the right place on the record) and click the Record button. The program will begin recording the audio as one long track. To create separate tracks for each song, click the Cue+ button at the end of each track. This will place a marker on the file that will tell the program to save the marked segments as separate tracks. You can use the Cue+ button as the audio is being recorded or after the recording is complete, using the horizontal slider to navigate through the track, as shown in Figure 6-16.

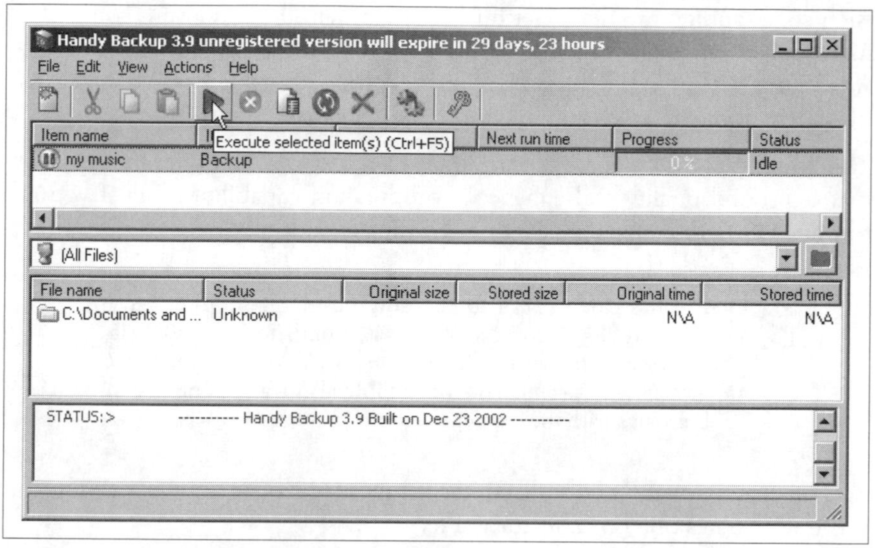

Figure 6-15. The FinalVinyl interface

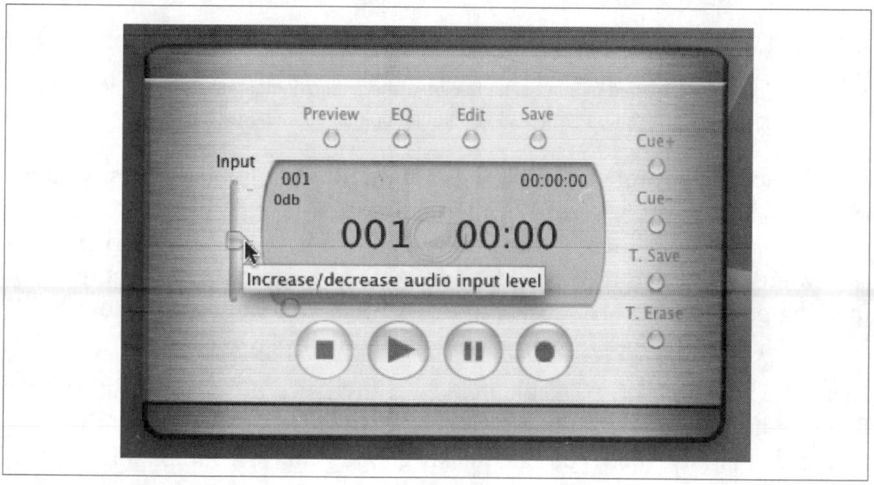

Figure 6-16. Splitting audio into its proper component tracks

With all your song cues placed, select File → Save, indicate where to save your files, and all your tracks will be saved to your hard drive. The default format is AIFF.

Converting to MP3/AAC. So, now you have a bunch of AIFF files saved to your computer. How do you get them into your iPod? iPods recognize AIFF files, but the file size makes them impractical. First, use iTunes to convert the files to MP3 or AAC format. Add your AIFF files into your iTunes library, select each song, and go to File → Get Info (⌘-I). Enter all the relevant song information. To convert your songs to MP3 or AAC files, select them and go to Advanced → Convert. Your AIFF files will now be ripped to MP3 or AAC files, depending on what you selected in iTunes Preferences → Importing.

The PowerWave is compatible with Mac OS 9 and OS X. I prefer the AAC format for sound quality and enhanced compression capabilities, but if you are running OS 9, you must use iTunes 3.0, which cannot play AAC files.

 If you decide to burn your freshly ripped album to CD, you can find album cover art **[Hack #56]** from sites such as Amazon.com (*http://www.amazon.com*) or AllMusic.com (*http://www.allmusic.com*). You'll probably also want to update all the songs with the correct track information **[Hack #52]**.

You can now walk about listening to your favorite vinyl without the unsightly bulges or a portable turntable.

—Gregory Ng

HACK 100   Create Your Own Free Audiobook

There are a myriad of interesting books in the public domain on the Web, and each of which can be turned into an audiobook for listening on the go.

The iTunes Music Store currently lists about 5,000 audiobook titles. While a reasonable selection, it's not exactly a massive library. What if you want to listen to a book out there in the public domain or, if you are a writer yourself, want to listen to the latest draft of your own words? Got an important meeting presentation or speech coming up that you want to hear out loud? Need to memorize lines for that community center play you are in?

Using Apple's built-in speakable items, a nifty piece of software called Text Reader (*http://www.codepoetry.net/projects/textreader*; donationware), iTunes, and (optionally) an iPod, you can quickly create your own audiobooks.

Before we start with the technical stuff, though, let's talk content. Apart from your own words, there is a great amount of content out there in the public domain (their respective copyrights having lapsed or expired). Public-domain content might not be the most current, but some pretty good stuff was written before the 20th century.

One fantastic source for public-domain books is Project Gutenberg (*http://www.gutenberg.net*). Named after the inventor of movable type (which spawned the printing revolution), Project Gutenberg is "a volunteer effort to digitize, archive, and distribute cultural works." More than 10,000 books have already been digitized, with approximately 400 titles added every month. The books are all in a readily accessible text format, usually either as plain text (*.txt*) or web pages (*.html*). You are free to use them as long as you don't do something silly like resell them.

For the purposes of this hack, we are going to use O. Henry's classic short story, "The Gift of the Magi," a fable about the ironies of gift-giving. Pick up a copy by pointing your browser at *http://www.gutenberg.net* and searching for "Gift of the Magi." This particular piece is available as HTML. Go ahead and select it and copy it. Now switch to Text Reader, and paste the text into the Untitled window that appears when you launch the application.

To convert the text to audio and import it into iTunes as an MP3 or AAC file, select File → Export to iTunes. Text Reader will chug away, as shown in Figure 6-17.

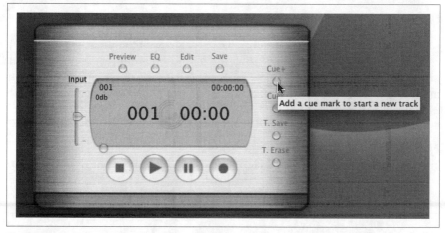

Figure 6-17. Turning text into spoken words

Text Reader will use whatever default voice you have specified in your Speech Preferences panel. If you'd prefer to hear your book in a different voice or at a faster clip, visit System Preferences → Speech, as shown in Figure 6-18. Click on the Default Voice tab to see all your choices. Apart from a variety of male and female voices, there are some silly ones too. If you want *War of the Worlds* (also found on Project Gutenberg) read to you by a robot (not available to you on Project Gutenberg ;-), select Trinoids the robot. While you're there, you can also adjust the speed of the voice. After making any desired changes, go back to Text Reader and export the text again as audio.

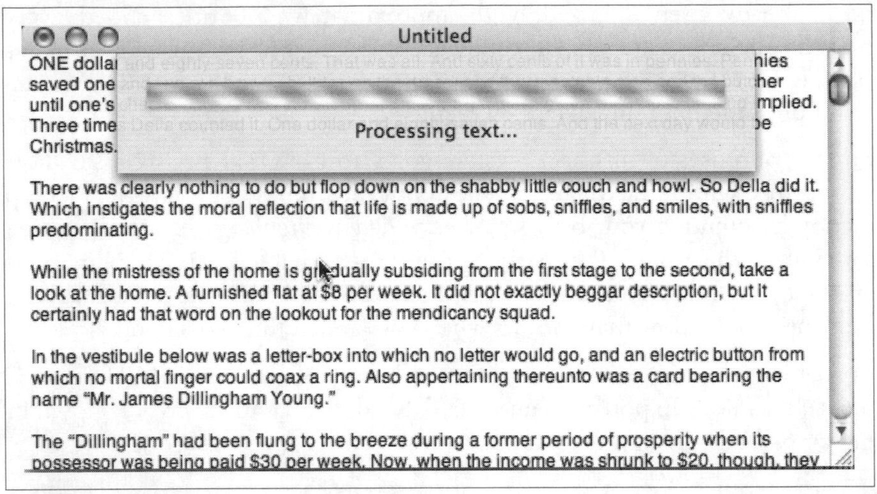

ONE dolla[r] and eighty-seven cents. That was all. And even [most of it was in pennies.] [Pennies] saved one [...] [...] her until one's [...] [...] [...] [...]mplied. Three time[s] [Della counted it. One do]llar [...] [...]. And the next day would [b]e Christmas.

Processing text...

There was clearly nothing to do but flop down on the shabby little couch and howl. So Della did it. Which instigates the moral reflection that life is made up of sobs, sniffles, and smiles, with sniffles predominating.

While the mistress of the home is gradually subsiding from the first stage to the second, take a look at the home. A furnished flat at $8 per week. It did not exactly beggar description, but it certainly had that word on the lookout for the mendicancy squad.

In the vestibule below was a letter-box into which no letter would go, and an electric button from which no mortal finger could coax a ring. Also appertaining thereunto was a card bearing the name "Mr. James Dillingham Young."

The "Dillingham" had been flung to the breeze during a former period of prosperity when its possessor was being paid $30 per week. Now, when the income was shrunk to $20, though, they

Figure 6-18. The Speech System Preferences pane

In addition to these speech settings, Text Reader's Preferences (Text Reader → Preferences) lets you adjust the pitch and the number of words per minute, as shown in Figure 6-19. To save yourself an unnecessary wait, you might prefer to experiment with a smaller chunk of text before exporting the full text of a book.

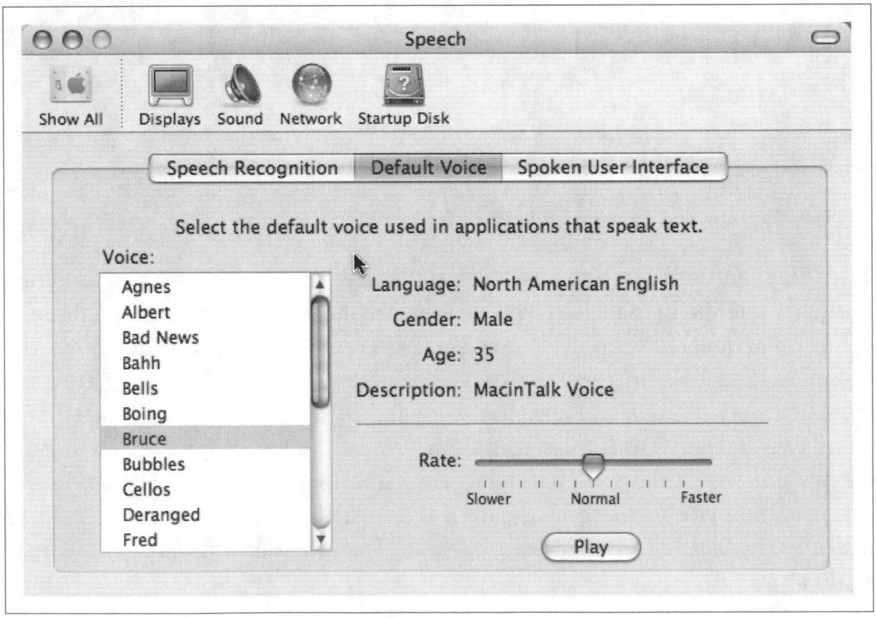

Figure 6-19. Text Reader's preferences

You can also control the tags that the application will add to your AIFF file. Before exporting O. Henry's story, for example, you can adjust the artist name, playlist title, and genre to your liking. Simply go to Preferences and enter the appropriate information in the relevant fields. Whatever you enter here will carry over into iTunes. You can also designate an Export folder. Finally, select Encode after Export, and your AIFF file will be coded according to iTunes's encoding preferences.

Sure, it's a computer-generated voice rather than that of the silk-tongued James Earl Jones. Yes, there are odd fits and starts and mispronunciations, some of which are laughable, others of which are simply painful. But converting text to speech is a good enough solution and will save you having to record the audio in your own voice or shell out cash (better spent on iPod accessories) for books on tape.

Index

We'd like to hear your suggestions for improving our indexes. Send email to *index@oreilly.com*.

Colophon

Our look is the result of reader comments, our own experimentation, and feedback from distribution channels. Distinctive covers complement our distinctive approach to technical topics, breathing personality and life into potentially dry subjects.

The illustration on the cover of *iPod and iTunes Hacks* is a set of spoons. The spoon is commonly known as an eating and cooking utensil, but has also known more colorful usage in music, combat, and even courtship. In an old Welsh tradition, a hopeful suitor would carve a spoon from a durable local wood such as sycamore, decorate it with carved symbols of his romantic intent, and then present it to the object of his affection; if she accepted the spoon, a courtship ensued. The oldest known existing "love spoon" dates to 1667.

Jamie Peppard was the production editor and the proofreader for *iPod and iTunes Hacks*. Rachel Wheeler was the copyeditor. Marlowe Shaeffer and Claire Cloutier provided quality control, and Julie Hawks wrote the index.

Emma Colby designed the cover of this book, based on a series design by Edie Freedman. The cover image is an original photograph. Clay Fernald produced the cover layout with QuarkXPress 4.1 using Adobe's Helvetica Neue and ITC Garamond fonts.

David Futato designed the interior layout. This book was converted by Julie Hawks to FrameMaker 5.5.6 with a format conversion tool created by Erik Ray, Jason McIntosh, Neil Walls, and Mike Sierra that uses Perl and XML technologies. The text font is Linotype Birka; the heading font is Adobe Helvetica Neue Condensed; and the code font is LucasFont's TheSans Mono Condensed. The illustrations that appear in the book were produced by Robert Romano and Jessamyn Read using Macromedia FreeHand 9 and Adobe Photoshop 6. This colophon was written by Jamie Peppard.

Better than
e-books

Search

inside electronic versions
of thousands of books

Browse

books by category.
With Safari researching
any topic is a snap

Find

answers in an instant

Read books from cover
to cover. Or, simply click
to the page you need.

**Search Safari! The premier electronic reference
library for programmers and IT professionals**

Related Titles Available from O'Reilly

Digital Media

Adobe InDesign CS One-on-One

Adobe Encore DVD: In the Studio

Adobe Photoshop CS One-on-One

Creating Photomontages with Photoshop: A Designer's Notebook

Digital Photography: Expert Techniques

Digital Photography Hacks

Digital Photography Pocket Guide, *2nd Edition*

Digital Video Pocket Guide

Illustrations with Photoshop: A Designer's Notebook

In the Loop with Soundtrack

iPod & iTunes: The Missing Manual, *2nd Edition*

Photo Retouching with Photoshop: A Designer's Notebook

Windows Media Hacks

O'REILLY®

Our books are available at most retail and online bookstores.
To order direct: 1-800-998-9938 • *order@oreilly.com* • *www.oreilly.com*
Online editions of most O'Reilly titles are available by subscription at *safari.oreilly.com*

Keep in touch with O'Reilly

1. Download examples from our books

To find example files for a book, go to:
www.oreilly.com/catalog
select the book, and follow the "Examples" link.

2. Register your O'Reilly books

Register your book at *register.oreilly.com*

Why register your books? Once you've registered your O'Reilly books you can:

- Win O'Reilly books, T-shirts or discount coupons in our monthly drawing.
- Get special offers available only to registered O'Reilly customers.
- Get catalogs announcing new books (US and UK only).
- Get email notification of new editions of the O'Reilly books you own.

3. Join our email lists

Sign up to get topic-specific email announcements of new books and conferences, special offers, and O'Reilly Network technology newsletters at:

elists.oreilly.com

It's easy to customize your free elists subscription so you'll get exactly the O'Reilly news you want.

4. Get the latest news, tips, and tools

http://www.oreilly.com
- "Top 100 Sites on the Web"—PC Magazine
- CIO Magazine's Web Business 50 Awards

Our web site contains a library of comprehensive product information (including book excerpts and tables of contents), downloadable software, background articles, interviews with technology leaders, links to relevant sites, book cover art, and more.

5. Work for O'Reilly

Check out our web site for current employment opportunities:

jobs.oreilly.com

6. Contact us

O'Reilly & Associates
1005 Gravenstein Hwy North
Sebastopol, CA 95472 USA

TEL: 707-827-7000 or 800-998-9938
         (6am to 5pm PST)

FAX: 707-829-0104

order@oreilly.com
For answers to problems regarding your order or our products.
To place a book order online, visit:
www.oreilly.com/order_new

catalog@oreilly.com
To request a copy of our latest catalog.

booktech@oreilly.com
For book content technical questions or corrections.

corporate@oreilly.com
For educational, library, government, and corporate sales.

proposals@oreilly.com
To submit new book proposals to our editors and product managers.

international@oreilly.com
For information about our international distributors or translation queries. For a list of our distributors outside of North America check out:
international.oreilly.com/distributors.html

adoption@oreilly.com
For information about academic use of O'Reilly books, visit:
academic.oreilly.com

O'REILLY®

Our books are available at most retail and online bookstores.
To order direct: 1-800-998-9938 • *order@oreilly.com* • *www.oreilly.com*
Online editions of most O'Reilly titles are available by subscription at *safari.oreilly.com*